Hollywood in Havana

Hollywood in Havana

US Cinema and Revolutionary Nationalism in Cuba before 1959

MEGAN FEENEY

The University of Chicago Press
Chicago and London

The University of Chicago Press, Chicago 60637
The University of Chicago Press, Ltd., London

Published 2019
Printed in the United States of America

28 27 26 25 24 23 22 21 20 19   1 2 3 4 5

ISBN-13: 978-0-226-59355-5 (cloth)
ISBN-13: 978-0-226-59369-2 (paper)
ISBN-13: 978-0-226-59372-2 (e-book)
DOI: https://doi.org/10.7208/chicago/9780226593722.001.0001

Library of Congress Cataloging-in-Publication Data

Names: Feeney, Megan, author.
Title: Hollywood in Havana : US cinema and revolutionary nationalism in Cuba before 1959 / Megan Feeney.
Description: Chicago : The University of Chicago Press, 2018. | Includes bibliographical references and index.
Identifiers: LCCN 2018020252 | ISBN 9780226593555 (cloth : alk. paper) | ISBN 9780226593692 (pbk. : alk. paper) | ISBN 9780226593722 (e-book)
Subjects: LCSH: Motion pictures, American—Cuba—History—20th century. | Motion pictures, American—Cuba—Influence. | National liberation movements—Cuba.
Classification: LCC PN1993.5.C8 F44 2018 | DDC 791.4307291—dc23
LC record available at https://lccn.loc.gov/2018020252

♾ This paper meets the requirements of ANSI/NISO Z39.48–1992 (Permanence of Paper).

Contents

Acknowledgments

I have first to thank the many Cubans living on the island who made this project possible *and* deeply rewarding. Filmmaker Consuelo Elba Álvarez made her home mine and became a second mother to me. Beyond feeding me and nursing me through a few bouts of heat exhaustion, she happily hoofed it through Havana with me, searching for old cines and office buildings. Her husband, Alejandro, who loves to ponder the universe from the eye of his telescope, was also brilliant at navigating me through the channels of Cuban bureaucracy back on earth. The men and women at the Instituto cubano de artes y industrias cinematográficas's Cinemateca—including Vice Director Dolores Calviño and, especially, Mario Naito—treated me like a colleague and made my research possible.

I am also grateful to the many Cubans who kindly submitted to interviews. Walfredo Piñera, a pre-1959 film critic, opened his home to me along with three bulging scrapbooks of publicity for Hollywood films that came to Havana during his youth, when he lovingly put the scrapbooks together. Subsequent interviews proved equally inspiring and fruitful, especially those with José Massip, Nelson Rodríguez, and Enrique Pineda Barnet, who each spent hours recalling for me their film-related activities in the 1940s and 1950s. I am also grateful to the reference librarians at Havana's Biblioteca Nacional José Martí and the Instituto de Literatura y Lingüística, who brought me edition after edition of crumbling Cuban fanzines and trade journals.

Back in the United States, I owe thanks to the University of Minnesota's Graduate School for a Harold Leonard Film Studies Fellowship and to the University of Minnesota's Humanities Institute for a second fellowship. This support allowed me to conduct research in Cuba as well as in the United States, particularly at the United Artists Collection at the Wisconsin Historical

Society; in the Cuban Heritage Collection at the University of Miami; at the Academy of Motion Picture Arts and Sciences' Margaret Herrick Library; and in the Warner Brothers Archives at the University of Southern California. A grant from the Rockefeller Archive Center allowed me to dig into their files on the Office of the Coordinator of Inter-American Affairs' Motion Picture Division. I am grateful to the committed and knowledgeable archivists at all these collections, and especially to a few that went above and beyond: Barbara Hall and Kristine Krueger at the Margaret Herrick Library and Rosa María Ortíz at the Cuban Heritage Collection.

Over many years, I have incurred intellectual and personal debts to many colleagues, including those who read and constructively commented on drafts in early stages: Matt Becker, Jennifer Beckham, Jenny Gowen, John Kinder, Dave Monteyne, and especially David Gray. Lary May, Elaine Tyler May, and Haidee Wasson have been invaluable advocates and uncompromising critics. I also owe thanks to Louis A. Pérez Jr., who opened up his incomparable mental catalog of Cuba studies to advise me to research the Machado era as an important precursor to what would come in subsequent decades. At St. Olaf College, where I taught for years, I am thankful to members of the History Department who generously read a chapter draft. I am especially grateful to Jim Farrell, Eric Fure-Slocum, and Bill Sonnega. And, for helping me to imagine this project in new and exciting ways, I have to thank filmmaker Gaspar González. More recently, I have come to owe a debt of gratitude to my editors at the University of Chicago Press—Douglas Mitchell, Kyle Adam Wagner, and Jo Ann Kiser—for their faith in this book and their work polishing it into its present form.

I have been working on this book for more than a decade and could not have finished it without the support of my family, which has grown over that period. My father's influence pervades every page; from him, I learned a passion for history and the cinema. The unswerving faith of my mother can be perceived particularly on the final page; she always knew I could get this done even when I did not. Such faith and encouragement might be expected of a mother, but I also received equal amounts from my sister, my in-laws, and my most constant friend, Dina Drits. And then there are my two wonderful children, whose mother's mind has been "elsewhere" in many moments throughout their young lives. I thank them for their love and patience. Finally, this book would not be possible without the loving support of my husband, John Geelan. For all this, and much more, I am grateful.

FIG. I.1. Korda (Alberto Díaz Gutiérrez), "Fidel Castro at the Lincoln Memorial in Washington, DC" (also called "David and Goliath"), 1959. © 2017 Artists Rights Society (ARS), New York / ADAGP, Paris (Courtesy of Art Resource, Inc.)

FIG. I.2. James Stewart as Jefferson Smith gazes up reverentially at the Lincoln Memorial in a still from Frank Capra's *Mr. Smith Goes to Washington* (1939).

INTRODUCTION

Looking Up: Hollywood and Revolutionary Cuban Nationalism

> Have you ever thought of the American motion picture in another light—as a powerful, even a revolutionary, instrument to increase human desires? . . . It keeps alive or recreates the desire for freedom where freedom and democracy have been snuffed out or flicker feebly. It keeps alive faith and hope in democracy.
>
> ERIC JOHNSTON, President, Motion Picture Association of America, 1949

> [Cubans] admire this nation, the greatest ever built by liberty, but they dislike the evil conditions that, like worms in the blood, have begun their work of destruction in this mighty republic. [Cubans] have made the heroes of this country their own heroes, . . . but they cannot honestly believe that excessive individualism, reverence for wealth, and the protracted exultation over a terrible victory [in the Mexican-American War] are preparing the United States to be the typical nation of liberty. . . . We love the country of Lincoln as much as we fear the country of Cutting.
>
> JOSÉ MARTÍ, the "Apostle" of Cuban Independence, 1889

In April 1959, Fidel Castro's official photographer captured an image of Cuba's new leader gazing up at Abraham Lincoln's larger-than-life likeness. As Castro and his photographer were likely aware, the image echoes a famous sequence from Frank Capra's 1939 *Mr. Smith Goes to Washington*. Early in that film, the newly elected senator Jefferson Smith (James Stewart) visits Washington's most inspiring sites—the White House, the Capitol, the Washington Monument, Arlington Cemetery—in a heavy-handed montage that asks the viewer to admire the progressive arc of US democracy. Sacred words carved in marble—Equality, Justice, Liberty, and the Pursuit of Happiness—are double-exposed over the junior senator's dewy-eyed, upturned visage. At the Lincoln Memorial, where the montage ends, Smith overhears a young boy reading the final lines of the Gettysburg Address, emphasizing the words *freedom* and *resolve*. Smith thus gathers the inspiration he will need later in the film when he witnesses the corruption of democracy by greed for wealth and power, personified in the film by a land-grabbing capitalist, Jim Taylor, and his lackey senator. To redeem the democratic ideal, Smith will have to become, as one character puts it, "a David without even a slingshot [who] rises to do battle against the mighty Goliath."[1]

While more than a half-century of rule subsequently proved Fidel Castro no Jefferson Smith, the analogy would have made sense to US and Cuban citizens alike in early 1959. In Washington, the US press and public treated Castro to a hero's welcome, as he conducted a tour of the US capital that seemed an intentional mimic of Smith's.[2] Swarmed by fans seeking his autograph at the Jefferson Memorial, Castro asserted that the US Declaration of Independence "supported the ideals of the Cuban revolution," according to the *Washington Post*. At the Lincoln Memorial, like the young boy in *Mr. Smith*, Castro reverentially read the Gettysburg Address, according to the *New York Times*. Here and elsewhere, the US press presented the Cuban Revolution as the latest advance in the progressive arc traced in *Mr. Smith's* montage: a Cuban hero had redeemed the *Pan*-American ideal of sovereign democracy from the powerful agents who sought to subvert it, in this case, Cuban dictator Fulgencio Batista and the now discredited US policymakers who had supported his regime. Seemingly convinced of Castro's genealogy, one female fan in New York City, where Castro traveled next, gushed to *Time* magazine, "Doesn't he remind you of a younger Jimmy Stewart?"[3]

Indeed, analogies between Hollywood heroes and Castro had abounded during the years of insurrection against Batista. One US journalist deemed Castro "a combination Robin Hood, George Washington and Gregory Peck," invoking and conflating masculine ideals from populist lore, US political history, and Hollywood cinema.[4] Describing the effects of reading such press reports, a US citizen recalled, "I had been raised on Errol Flynn's Robin Hood and the endless hero-actors fighting against injustice and leading the people to victory over the tyrants. The Cuban thing seemed a case of classic Hollywood proportions."[5] As if to corroborate these associations, Errol Flynn himself traveled to Cuba in 1958 to report on the insurrection for the Hearst press, attempting to recuperate his fading celebrity by associating it with Castro's rising star. On the authority of his famous screen persona and many previous visits to Havana (the first of which was in 1938 to promote *The Adventures of Robin Hood*), Flynn proclaimed Castro "a Robin Hood" and "a man, a *real* man."[6] Or perhaps he meant a *reel* man, a strapping hero recognizable for his conformity to a Hollywood type.

As steeped in US movie culture as their US counterparts, most Cubans living in Havana also received Castro and his fellow rebels as heroes, at least through early 1959, when Cuban opinion about Castro and the Cuban Revolution famously split. In the early weeks after Batista's ouster, Havana crowds thronged parades of victorious guerrillas; women kissed their bearded faces and children begged for autographs. "These were, after all, our young liberators and they looked the part," one Havana resident later recalled.[7] For Cubans in Havana, as much as for their US counterparts, that "part" was shaped by decades of exposure to Hollywood "good guys"—righteous men of action who defied impossible odds to triumph over the "bad guys." For some forty years, Havana's movie theaters had been dominated by the US film industry, an important component of US cultural and economic hegemony that bound Cuba to the United States in "ties of singular intimacy" during the first half of the twentieth century.[8] Even the young Cuban men who participated in the insurrection tended to see themselves through a Hollywood lens: marveling that their experiences were "like something out of a movie," and cognizant, to varying degrees, that their "revolutionary self-image" was Hollywood-informed.[9] They "wanted to be like James Dean," one Cuban rebel remembered.[10] Castro himself identified with Marlon Brando, the star he hoped would play him in the film that Hollywood producer Jerry Wald, that same spring of 1959, planned to make about the insurrection and its leader.[11]

In Havana, analogies between Hollywood heroes and Cuban rebels were especially resonant not only because of the US film industry's powerful presence in that city. It was also because Cubans had long sutured Hollywood's preoccupation with heroic, virile (and often armed) men fighting for democratic ideals onto what one scholar calls "Cuban nationalist masculinity," a version of manhood honor-bound to defend to the death Cuba's sovereignty and democracy that was reiterated *ad infinitum* in national political discourse and popular culture since the island's founding rebels (the *mambises*) fought Spanish colonialism in the late nineteenth century.[12] In that century's three-decades-long anticolonial movement, Cubans had made US political heroes "their own heroes," Cuba's founding father José Martí wrote in 1889; in fact, Martí made such appropriations a condition of belonging to the Cuban national community just then being imagined into existence (see second epigraph above).[13] By the mid-twentieth century, Cubans had also come to make US *film* heroes their own, like Jimmy Stewart's Jefferson Smith and, in the 1940s and 1950s, a steady procession of strapping citizen-soldiers fighting fascism, who were explicitly likened to revolutionary Cuban heroes. Thus, the Cuban audience for whom photographer Alberto Díaz Gutíerrez (aka Korda) snapped the April 1959 photograph captioned "*Rinde homenaje a Lincoln* [Paying Homage to Lincoln]," for a Havana newspaper, would have recognized not only the reference to *Mr. Smith Goes to Washington*, but also the moral equivalences it implied.[14]

At the same time, it is telling that Korda himself called the 1959 photograph "David and Goliath," inviting an alternative interpretation, and one that would have been equally decipherable to its Cuban audience. In this interpretation, the oversized Lincoln becomes "the Colossus of the North," capable of bullying little Cuba and undermining its sovereignty and democracy in the name of US interests; the United States becomes less the source and more the target of Cuban underdogs' freedom fighting, personified by the bearded and uniformed Castro here sizing up his formidable foe.[15] Korda was surely aware that his title "David and Goliath" quotes Martí's oft-cited summary of living in the United States in exile at the end of the nineteenth century and not only observing closely that which was to be admired about US democratic ideals and its productive industrial energies, but also diagnosing the corruption and declension of democracy in the United States (which Martí calls "worms in the blood" in the epigraph above) and its extraterritorial expansionism, which was Latin American republics' greatest threat: "I lived in the monster, and I know its entrails—and my only weapon is the sling of David," Martí wrote famously.[16] "*Our* América," he wrote—meaning the Latin American republics just then struggling to overcome Spanish colonialism and its legacies (i.e., dependent economies, racial hierarchies, and the concentration of land, wealth, and power among the elite)—would be wise to study and emulate the best of *North* America, but also to have a "clear-eyed" knowledge of its failings, including its greed for Latin American territory, resources, and markets. Latin Americans' best weapon against subjugation to the United States, then, was to know "the truth about the United States," particularly its "crude, unequal, and decadent character, and the continual existence within it of all the violence, discord, immorality, and disorder of which the Hispanoamerican peoples are accused," Martí concluded.[17] Thus, Korda's alternate title for the 1959 photo, "David and Goliath," references another founding pillar (along with freedom-fighting masculinity and democratic idealism) of revolutionary Cuban nationalism: *independentismo*, a deep and abiding commitment to national sovereignty, and an accompanying resistance to the emergent US imperialism against which Martí warned.

These two interpretations of the April 1959 photo, in fact, could coexist easily in the Cuban imagination, which had long learned to see the United States as a model of sovereign democracy (in its ideal form) *and* a looming threat to Cuba's own sovereign democracy (in its real practices). Moreover, this ambivalence about the United States was fomented by decades of Hollywood films seen by Cubans, opening so many windows into their Goliath's soul, with many Hollywood films (even whole genres) extolling US democracy and its heroes (i.e., World War II antifascist films) while others dramatized the United States' democratic degradation (i.e., postwar noirs). Sometimes evidence supporting Cuban ambivalence about the United States could be found in the space of a single film. *Mr. Smith Goes to Washington*, for instance, toggles between two poles: between Smith's rousing idealism at the film's beginning and his profound disillusionment midfilm.

Havana film critics encouraged Cuban audiences to interpret such films as so many windows into their Goliath's soul; to identify with Hollywood's democratic idealism *and* its social criticisms; and to make particular connections between film content and the Cuban national condition. One Cuban review of *Mr. Smith* serves as a useful first illustration of this practice. Writing in *El Mundo* in 1939, Cuba's preeminent film critic, José Manuel Valdés-Rodríguez, admires Capra's early montage and Smith's first visit to the Lincoln Memorial, which captured, the Cuban critic writes, the "pure spirit of the country's [the US's] best traditions and its most enlightened, humane, and honest men." Describing the very shot included above of Smith framed between two large columns (see fig. I.2 above), Valdés-Rodríguez writes prescriptively that Smith's "palpable devotion prevails upon the spectator despite the distance of the shot." But the critic immediately contrasts that early montage to Smith's second visit to the memorial midfilm, in which Smith cries in the dark shadows of those columns, now "with eyes open," no longer deluded by "his simplistic naiveté." As Valdés-Rodríguez synopsizes, Smith—and with him the Cuban spectator—has witnessed "*that which we all know*. . . : that there is corruption in the legislative bodies of the United States, that there are political cliques subservient to the interests of rapacious and unscrupulous financial interests." After prescribing that common knowledge, Valdés-Rodríguez proceeds to translate *Mr. Smith* into a lesson about the "monster's entrails" and their effects on Cuba. He writes,

> For *our* country, in which the same scourge on [Pan-]American democracy exists, but is excessively enlarged by the tropical environment, by the colonial precedents, the survival of [*caudillismo* and *latifundia*] within our democratic-liberal politics, and by the imposition of foreign elements rooted in the presence of [US] financial interests precisely [like those depicted in the film], Capra's brave film has an exemplariness and unique relevance. . . . There are few Cubans so uninformed or so inattentive that they cannot signal by name the Taylors and other cheats of his sort that move within *our* "honorable" legislative bodies.[18]

In other words, to be Cuban—to belong to the "we" and "our" constantly invoked by Cuban writers—is to admire and identify with US heroes, but also to recognize and reject Yankee villains such as Francis Cutting (a leading proponent of US annexation of Cuba in the late nineteenth century, to whom Martí refers in the second epigraph) and the US businessmen corrupting

Cuban politics, which *Mr. Smith* exposed so realistically, according to Valdés-Rodríguez. As this excerpt begins to demonstrate, Havana film critics worked to construct a national community around *Cuban* ways of seeing Hollywood films, and, through them, the so-called American Way and Cuba's relationship to it, ultimately toward the condemnation of, and mobilization against, US imperial hegemony on the island.

This phenomenon of Cuban engagement with the US film industry is what *Hollywood in Havana* sets out to explore, not only in critical (and popular) film reception but also in local film business practices. In short, it is a study of Cubans' intimate relationship with US cinema throughout the republican period of Cuban history (1902–58), and of how that relationship shaped—and was shaped by—the ongoing construction of revolutionary Cuban nationalism. The US film industry exercised considerable economic and cultural power in Havana, but Cubans engaged actively with its influence in complex ways, even bending it to their own ends. *Hollywood in Havana* argues that Havana's movie theaters—and the local film business community and print culture that revolved around them—were what historians have called "contact zones" of US empire: sites of foreign-local interaction where US power is wielded strongly but unstably; is subject to negotiation and adaptation; and has unpredictable, even counterhegemonic effects.[19] *Hollywood in Havana*, thus, challenges us to rethink some long-held truisms about the sort of "Americanization" that Hollywood affects abroad. As the case of Cuba demonstrates, Hollywood's "Americanization" of foreign audiences—and the ways those foreign audiences localize Hollywood's meanings—can subvert US global hegemony, paradoxically enough, by "keeping alive" not just desires for consumer goods but also for the "democracy and freedom" that US foreign policy sometimes "snuffed out," an outcome that ardent cold warrior and US film industry leader Eric Johnston would not have advocated even as he cheered Hollywood's "revolutionary" potential, in the first epigraph above.[20]

Seeking to better understand pre-1959 US-Cuban relations via the register of everyday cultural encounters, *Hollywood in Havana* turns our attention away from Fidel Castro, despite opening with his image. For too long, a fascination with Castro has undermined the ability of US policymakers and scholars alike to think clearly about the roots of the Cuban Revolution, which run far deeper than this one man.[21] It shifts our lens not only from Castro and "great man" theories of history but also from other traditional concerns of US foreign relations scholarship, that is, State Department diplomacy, economic policy, and armed combat, though all of these come into focus inasmuch as they intersect with film business and moviegoing practices. Traditional approaches to the Cuban Revolution, and their focus on the years immediately before and after 1959 (and the question of who was a communist and when), have only partially answered the perplexing question of why the most "Americanized" country in the world launched one of the (if not *the*) most infamous *anti*-American revolutions of the twentieth century.[22] In many ways, in fact, *Hollywood in Havana* rejects that formulation altogether, finding that the Cuban Revolution, at least in its early days, was not as much an expression of anti-Americanism (or of any Marxist program) as it was an expression of a highly idealistic version of (Pan-)Americanism, one that had been as consistently ballyhooed by progressive US filmmakers as it was contradicted by US foreign policymakers.[23]

Hollywood in Havana also shifts away from traditional approaches to film studies. For one thing, it is more interested in broad sociopolitical trends and film business practices—in the US film industry and in Havana—than in individual films. Close readings of film texts are offered only inasmuch as they elucidate those sociopolitical trends and, especially, the interpretive choices available to, and made by, Cuban critics and audiences. Rather than focus on meanings made at the point of production, *Hollywood in Havana* focuses on the meanings Cubans made of Hollywood at the stages of promotion, exhibition, and consumption in Havana, where national community building is as much in evidence as is "Americanization." Moreover, *Hollywood in Havana* refuses to understand film *content* in isolation from the US film industry's monopolistic and imperialistic *business practices*, not least of all because Cuban film critics and trade journalists worked hard to connect them in the Cuban public's consciousness. Studying these phenomena helps recover the more complex role that pre-1959 Hollywood played in shaping Cuban film culture (and Cuban culture more broadly), a role largely ignored (or dismissed as wholly repressive) by previous US and Cuban film scholarship's focus on Cuban film *production*, anemic before the revolution and flourishing under its tenure, thanks to the state's creation of the Cuban Institute of Cinematographic Art and Industry (ICAIC) in 1959.[24] Though Hollywood did stifle national film production before 1959, Cubans engaged with it in ways that developed their critical skills as spectators and as citizens, skills which were understood as preconditions to national belonging.[25] Finally, *Hollywood in Havana* also shifts our attention to Hollywood representations of masculinity and their reception from film scholars' previous emphases on Hollywood representations of femininity and *their* effects, perhaps a by-product of long-held associations between (media) consumption, passivity, and women.[26]

Which brings us back to the 1959 Korda photo. Rather than intended to focus the reader's attention on Castro, *Hollywood in Havana* opens with it to offer the reader a sort of shorthand visual for the assertive and ultimately anti-imperialist act of "looking up" that is this book's object of study. Neither prostrate adulation nor unambiguous defiance, it captures an ambivalent posture toward the so-called American Way that shaped revolutionary Cuban nationalism. In Havana, "looking up" at the United States through its own cinematic self-representations and film business practices meant aspiring to and mobilizing around (Pan-)American democratic ideals and identifying with the heroes that fought for them. But, it also meant looking northward to evaluate and excoriate US failures to realize those ideals, and to connect those failures to the degradation of Cuban sovereignty, democracy, and economic opportunity. Relatedly, when Cubans "looked up" through Hollywood they also saw US citizens' propensity for "looking down," in the double sense of casting their eyes greedily southward on Latin America's resources and markets *and* in adjudging Latin Americans inferior, in what amounted to a derogatory and emasculating "imperial gaze." In response, Cubans engaged in what postcolonial cultural theorists have identified as a sort of "reversal" of "relations of looking."[27] Like Castro in the photo, Cuban film writers and moviegoers paid homage to US ideals and their heroes but also asserted themselves as agents of an adjudicating gaze rather than its passive objects.

Entangled in the Entrails: The Historical Context of Pre-1959 Cuban Film Reception

Knowing "the truth about the United States" became all the more urgent in 1898 when US imperialism replaced Spanish colonialism as revolutionary Cuban nationalism's foil. After decades of Cuban insurgency against Spain, the US Army bounded in to "rescue" Cuba, erasing Cuban agency from their own independence in the tellingly misnamed "Spanish-American War," a "symbolic emasculation" against which revolutionary Cuban nationalism would strain henceforth.[28] After just six weeks of fighting, the defeated Spaniards transferred Cuba to US military occupation (1899–1902), during which US military authorities opened wide channels for US investment and trade, installed a handpicked president, and, before departing, forced the insertion of the Platt Amendment into the constitution of the First Cuban Republic. Widely decried in Cuba as a national humiliation, the Platt Amendment granted the United States "the right to intervene for the preservation of Cuban independence," paradoxically enough.[29] Over the next three decades, under the pretext of protecting Cubans from their own government's mismanagement of fiscal and political affairs, the United States invoked the Platt Amendment to intervene militarily in order to protect *US* interests five times. Moreover, under constant threat of US intervention, Cuban administrations took little significant action without consulting the US embassy. Though it was abrogated in 1934, by then the Platt Amendment had entrenched Cuba's condition of "semi-sovereignty," which distorted and destabilized the Cuban economy and politics throughout the republican period.[30]

Beginning in 1903, US-Cuban trade agreements also facilitated US imperial hegemony on the island. They drastically reduced tariffs for many categories of US goods—including for US films—in exchange for Cuba's preferred status as sugar exporter to the United States, thus ensuring Cuban dependency on the island's sugar crop and on US purchase of it. Cuba became a one-crop export economy, with ravaging boom and bust cycles and a chronic high cost of living. Because US manufactured goods flowed so easily onto the island, industrial development in Cuba was greatly stunted.[31] One example of this underdevelopment was, indeed, the way that the flood of Hollywood films (uninhibited by the protectionist barriers erected in other countries) made it all but impossible for an ever-inchoate Cuban film industry to compete.

Cuba's status as a semi-sovereign state with a dependent economy had profound effects on republican Cuban society, effects that fueled both Cuban admiration of and resentment toward the United States. As US companies came to dominate most important sectors of the Cuban economy, working-class Cubans struggled as those US companies worked to keep wages low, by importing cheap foreign labor, obstructing unionization efforts, and repressing strikes. Some (generally lighter-skinned) Cubans fared better. Seeking the upward mobility that US culture promised, straining to become "self-made men" (a phrase given in English in Havana periodicals), aspirants to "success" (also often given in English) wedged themselves into the new US-dominated order as white-collar workers and professionals.[32] Some even became local managers for US companies, as would be the case in a number of the Hollywood studios' distribution offices in Havana. A middle class developed in Havana, characterized by a deep ambivalence about US hegemony given the opportunities it offered but also circumscribed, a phenomenon evident in the Havana film business community.

At the same time, for many Cubans the only sure route to financial security was through political office, allowing them the opportunity to trap some of the capital flowing northward. The Cuban political class did so through extensive corruption: embezzling from the state treasury, rewarding themselves with public lands, speculating on real estate, and securing kickbacks from US companies in exchange for public works contracts and favorable legislation. Political scandals were a staple of the Cuban press. No wonder then to find that Havana film critics made analogies between *Mr. Smith Goes to Washington* and the corruption of Cuban politics by US financial interests. Generally speaking, US imperial hegemony incentivized Cuban government officials to prioritize the demands of US policymakers and investors over the will of the Cuban electorate: United States intervention could unseat them whereas Cuban votes could be bought or coerced through incumbent politicians' access to the treasury and state power. Cuban administrations proliferated *botellas* (civil service posts with little work but substantial pay and power), tinkered with electoral codes, placed soldiers at the polls, and/or tampered with results. And US policymakers condoned such practices. After all, an entrenched party—or even an extra-constitutional strongman—generally meant stability and a mutually beneficial alliance based on US capital's imperatives and a Cuban political class's ability to siphon a portion of its profits.[33]

However, this environment also all but guaranteed sporadic crises because opposition parties were left with little option but to mobilize armed insurrection. This was the case in 1906, in 1912, in 1917, and in 1921, each of which saw US military interventions. This political violence and these US interventions, and the egregious insult that was the Platt Amendment generally, fueled revolutionary Cuban nationalism and its association with righteously armed men of action. The most astute Cuban politicians learned to agitate this spirit, presenting themselves as revolutionary nationalists while pledging behind closed doors to protect US interests, a strategy of double-dealing used by both of republican Cuba's notorious dictators, Gerardo Machado (who ruled from 1925 to 1933) and Fulgencio Batista (who ruled from 1934 to 1944 and again from 1952 to 1958). Their despotic reigns, and the insurrections they provoked, further elevated the virtue of revolutionary violence. In short, US imperial hegemony in Cuba fomented economic dependency as well as political corruption and strongmen, which in turn further agitated the freedom-fighting masculinity and *independentismo* at the heart of revolutionary Cuban nationalism.

Rethinking Hollywood and "Americanization"

At the end of the nineteenth century, US cinema arrived in Cuba almost simultaneously with US imperialism, with the former often serving to promote the latter. Some of the first moving pictures ever made celebrated the United States' intervention in Cuba in 1898; they trumpeted US soldiers' selfless heroism in liberating Cuba and the paternal benevolence of the United States' self-declared "Empire of Liberty." And as the US film industry grew into a global behemoth in the twentieth century, US motion pictures continued to romanticize US imperialism as a series of epic adventures.[34] Particularly, the so-called Spanish-American War (aka the War of 1898) proved lasting fodder; movies like *A Message to Garcia* (1916 and 1936) and *Santiago* (1956) recounted the thrill of virile freedom fighting for US audiences, while reminding Cuban audiences of the "debt of gratitude" they owed their US liberators, a premise with significant currency in both countries throughout the republican period.[35] More generally, film scholars have long argued that even Hollywood films without content explicitly celebrating US imperialism do so implicitly, promoting the globalization of US power and the American Way through the allure of Hollywood's expensive production values, the glamor of its stars, and the evidence of abundance in the US products crowding its films' *mise-en-scène*.[36] Certainly, US policymakers became convinced of Hollywood's incomparable capacity to promote US-made products and US interests abroad more generally; both the US Commerce and State Departments lent considerable aid to secure the US film industry's global dominance.[37]

Seen in Havana, Hollywood films surely did impress some Cubans in these ways. Broadly surveying Hollywood's presence in Cuba before 1959, as part of his exhaustive cataloging of the United States' cultural influence in republican Cuba, preeminent Cuba historian Louis A. Pérez, Jr., concludes that Hollywood's overall effect was plain: Cubans bought (into) the specific US-made products and US-centric capitalist modernity the stars and their films endorsed. Hollywood narratives informed Cuban expectations of individual (and national) upward mobility under US imperial hegemony, and their optimism that success was ensured by emulating the American Way of Life, with its emphases on individual initiative and material self-fulfillment. Pérez concludes, then, that the aspirations for affluence and consumer goods instilled by US *cultural* hegemony (via Hollywood and other sources) were frustrated by the underdevelopment of the Cuban economy resulting from US *economic* hegemony, which ultimately provoked a collective revolt.[38]

This is certainly part of the story. However, as the brief excerpt above of Valdés-Rodríguez's review of *Mr. Smith Goes to Washington* begins to suggest, Hollywood films are more ideologically ambiguous, and Cuban appropriations more active, and at times more *counter*hegemonic, than Pérez allows or than predominant presumptions about "cultural imperialism" acknowledge.[39] In pre-1959 Havana, Hollywood films and film culture stoked Cubans' convictions that democracy and sovereignty—not just US-made consumer goods and material well-being—were their birthright to defend at all costs. Cubans did not only identify with Hollywood's rags-to-riches narratives, which then engendered frustration and resentment; they also identified with Hollywood's democratic idealism and its freedom-fighting heroism, which they mobilized against US-supported dictators and US imperial hegemony in Cuba.

In fact, even before we consider Hollywood's reception in Havana, a closer look at the US film industry itself demands a rethinking of its propensity to "Americanize." To begin, Hollywood is a famously cosmopolitan industry, attracting talent from around the world (including from Cuba). Most of the studio's founding moguls were immigrants themselves, as were many of classical Hollywood's most iconic artists, whose films often capture a critical outsider's perspective on US society, not unlike Martí's. Frank Capra, as just one example, was Italian-born. Moreover, the men that the studios sent to manage their foreign distribution offices, including in Havana, also tended to be immigrants who were born and/or spent most of their lives outside the United States, which complicates our understanding of these US businessmen as agents of "Americanization." Nor does replacing the term "to Americanize" with "to spread consumer capitalist ideology" return us to an uncomplicated paradigm for Hollywood's global effects. Classical Hollywood films were no more simple advertisements for consumer capitalism than they were for US global hegemony, despite the hopes of some US government propagandists and film industry boosters and contrary to outdated schools of cultural theory.[40] Due in part to the personal convictions of various filmmakers, and in other part to the dramatic imperative of conflict and resolution, Hollywood films taken as a whole offer a mixed message about US society and capitalist modernity.[41]

Again, the case of *Mr. Smith Goes to Washington* is illustrative, reminding us of the profound influence of politically left-leaning film artists on Hollywood's midcentury Golden Age. Many of them were highly idealistic about US popular democracy and deeply committed to pointing out when their ideal was degraded in practice. As such, they set out to dramatize US social problems like economic inequality, labor exploitation, racial discrimination, organized crime, and political corruption. Their influence was especially felt during the 1930s and during World War II, when a loose coalition of New Deal left-liberals and radicals working in the US film industry—since given the name the "Hollywood Left"—came together to collaborate as political activists and as filmmakers, making some of the era's biggest commercial and critical hits, including *Mr. Smith*.[42] Though he would later disown them, Capra traveled in Hollywood Left circles during the 1930s and relied heavily on leftist screenwriters, such as *Mr. Smith's* scenarist Sidney Buchman, himself a second-generation Russian immigrant and member of the US Communist Party. And though most Hollywood films, including *Mr. Smith*, strive to resolve tensions and assuage cultural anxieties in their signature "happy endings," the expression of these tensions and anxieties open the possibility of "negotiated readings," and of some audiences making the most of their "latent oppositional potential."[43] Witness again Valdés-Rodríguez's review of *Mr. Smith*.

In other words, films mean (and can be actively interpreted to mean) different things to different people. Capra himself claimed *Mr. Smith* to be "a ringing statement of America's democratic ideals" for "the people of the world." Conversely, US congressmen found it irreverent, even subversive; and US State Department officials worried it might do harm to the United States' reputation abroad.[44] Nor can US film scholars agree on *Mr. Smith*'s meaning. Some have interpreted it as a patriotic paean to conservative national myths threatened by the Great Depression, that is, the self-made man and US exceptionalism.[45] Others interpret it as a progressive condemnation of unregulated capitalism, media manipulation, and corrupt government.[46] Still others argue that *Mr. Smith*, and indeed Capra's entire oeuvre, is politically confused.[47]

But *Hollywood in Havana* is less interested in the ways that North Americans have interpreted *Mr. Smith* than in the ways that Cubans interpreted that film and other classical Hollywood films, especially those made by artists of the Hollywood Left. As scholars in the growing field of film reception studies have been arguing for some years now, moviegoers interpret films within the context of local moviegoing practices and fan cultures, the broader circumstances of their lives, and their (always intersecting) social identities, especially in terms of gender, race, sexuality, class, and nationality.[48] Their studies have found that moviegoers, especially marginalized ones (i.e., women, African Americans, gay men and women, working-class immigrants, and colonial subjects) are not so readily interpolated into the dominant ideological positions once believed to be *coded* unambiguously into Hollywood cinema (i.e., what scholars have analyzed as the camera's male, white, heterosexual, bourgeois, and imperial gaze).[49] In fact, real communities of viewers have *decoded* films and consumed film culture in ways that subverted (or at least negotiated) patriarchy, racism, hetero-normativity, embourgeoisement, and imperialism; and have even forged alternative public spheres through shared interpretive practices.[50]

In colonial and imperial contexts in particular, researchers have found that local audiences "indigenize" Hollywood films' meanings, as the natural result of a different context of reception and/or through intentional acts of interpretation.[51] From colonial India to colonial Africa, "unruly" audiences have used film projections as occasions to talk back at, ridicule, denounce, and reject the colonizer and colonization.[52] Hollywood films have been used as proof of the moral depravity and social ills of the West, including its denigration of peoples of color. And Hollywood films *and* Hollywood's monopolistic business practices have been used as strategic sites from which to decry and organize against the colonizer's cultural derogations and economic exploitation.[53] Of course, a "national audience" is no more homogeneous than a female, black, working-class, or gay one, but it is a useful category of analysis and one that is further justified in the Cuban context by the constant invocation of it by Cubans, including exhibitors, trade journalists, film critics, and fans.[54] In Havana, as in other parts of the world, Cubans actively engaged with Hollywood in ways that strengthened their sense of belonging to a national community with shared grievances against a foreign power.

"Cubanizing" Hollywood in Havana: A Brief Overview

None of the above is meant to suggest that Hollywood was not (or is not) powerful. And nowhere was Hollywood's substantial economic and cultural power more evident than in pre-1959 Havana. In Havana, the US studios translated the imbalance in US-Cuban trade relations, together with their advantages in the global film market generally, into a virtual monopoly from the 1920s through the 1950s. Enjoying up to 98 percent market share in Havana, Hollywood sent hundreds of films a year to that city's movie theaters (*cines*), of which there were some 138 by the 1950s, giving Havana one of the highest seat-to-citizen ratios in the world.[55] Given Hollywood's pervasive presence and the avidity of Cubans' moviegoing habits, it is no surprise that Hollywood had profound effects on the ways that Cubans ate, dressed, assessed attractiveness, kissed, recreated, and even spoke.[56] English-language words and phrases—like "gangster," "cowboy," and "happy ending"—migrated into the Cuban vernacular via Hollywood movies. Moreover, the Hollywood stars that Cubans adored did not just appear on Havana's screens; they came in person. Among the many US tourists visiting sunny Havana were the hottest of Hollywood stars, including its most famous masculine icons, for example, Marlon Brando, Gary Cooper, Errol Flynn, and John Wayne, to name a very few. Cubans could thus worship their matinee idols in the flesh, as well as in the myriad of popular film magazines that proliferated in Havana.[57] Cubans proved willing to pay for these fanzines even though they could easily learn the latest about Hollywood from Havana's most important newspapers and magazines, most of which had a film page and a film critic on staff.

Not surprisingly, then, Hollywood was king in the city's film business community (often referred to as the film *giro*, pronounced "hero"), made up of distributors, exhibitors, publishers of fanzines and trade journals, theater supply stores, and other related businesses. Physically and financially, this film giro revolved around the US studios' distribution offices, in a section of Central Havana that came to be called the "*barrio peliculero*." In this bustling movie barrio, Cuban exhibitors contracted—and Cuban film writers (including critics and trade journalists) screened and publicized—the latest Hollywood films that their patrons (and readers) demanded. Working in the giro, and especially working in one of the US studios' branch offices, Cubans acclimated to US business methods and corporate culture, not least of all ideals of white-collar masculinity. They not only perfected their English-language skills but also learned US workplace discipline and hierarchical management systems. In the giro, Cubans came to admire US "know-how," industriousness, efficiency, and professionalism; to varying degrees, they were acculturated into twentieth-century US society's emphasis on "success"—and the covetable material accoutrements that went with it—through individual initiative and self-discipline within the corporate hierarchy.[58] Though the top spot of manager was usually reserved for a US citizen, the Hollywood branch offices employed hundreds of Cubans—and ensured the daily bread of many others, including exhibitors, publishers, and journalists—who became part of what historians have called a "dependent client class," a group of Cubans "willing to serve as an instrument of [US] hegemony" in exchange for personal advancement.[59]

Yet the interests of Cubans in the film giro were *not* always in perfect alignment with those of the US studios, and there were limits to Cubans' willingness to subordinate and/or "Americanize" themselves. The language of "family" used to describe film giro relations often shifted to the language of "warfare." The denial of wage increases, benefits, and promotions to Cuban office employees and the forcing of unfavorable rental terms on Cuban exhibitors, for instance, stirred frustration and resentment and, often enough, the invocation of anti-imperialist nationalism. In trade publications and even in the film columns of the mainstream press, US-Cuban tensions in the film giro became occasions to lament the emasculation of Cuban men by the foreign film companies and to call on local business leaders and the Cuban state to protect native over foreign interests through, for example, boycotts, labor laws, state subsidies of domestic film production, film quotas, and censorship. And the experiences of Cubans in the giro of sharing grievances and collectively organizing fostered their sense of being *Cuban*, of needing to act together to resist US exploitation, to build nationalist solidarity between the middle and working classes, and to prioritize the national community's well-being, even over individual enrichment. Indeed, in the film giro, Cubans who put personal gain through cooperation with the US companies ahead of their commitments to the nation and their compatriots were accused of not being Cuban enough, or even of *vende-patria* (selling out the country).[60] In other words, the US-Cuban encounter in the film giro simultaneously exerted "Cubanizing" and "Americanizing" pressures on its constituents.

Moreover, to succeed in Cuba, the US companies had to "Cubanize" their operations to an extent. Cubans working in the film giro fully expected the US film companies to adapt to local customs: to the Latin workday (with its midday break); to summer hours (in concession to the tropical heat); to the Catholic liturgical calendar (closing offices on saints' days and during Carnival); and to a variety of national holidays celebrating Cuban independence and its Cuban heroes, much to the US companies' chagrin. Many Cuban giro employees and Cuban exhibitors rejected the "white collars" of US-style business suits (too hot for the local climate) and wore *guayaberas*, the ubiquitous linen dress shirts allegedly popularized by revolutionary hero Máximo Gómez.[61] This conscious symbol of Cuban nationalism suggests the currency that *Cubanidad* (Cuban-ness) had in the film giro precisely because it was so dominated by foreign companies. Indeed, the most successful US managers of the Hollywood Havana offices were those who learned to trade in that currency. A number of them stayed in Havana for decades, learned to speak Spanish fluently (and even to joke in Cuban slang and to gesticulate animatedly in the Cuban way), paid public homage to revolutionary Cuban nationalism, donned *guayaberas*, befriended their Cuban colleagues (making them "family," it was often said), integrated themselves fully into the local community, married Cuban women, raised Cuban children, and even became Cuban citizens. This is all to say that the Havana film giro was a site where US citizens and Cubans alternately collaborated and competed with one another; where Cubans might advance professionally but also feel personally the sting of subordination to, and discrimination within, Cuban economic dependence on the United States; where vague discontentment with US imperial hegemony became specific; where US corporate culture was only selectively incorporated; and where Cuban nationalism was tested and reiterated.

Like Cubans working in the giro, Havana moviegoers also Cubanized Hollywood, weaving its films and stars into the local context, in daily acts of cultural syncretism. One habanero with whom I spoke laughingly remembered that his mother's *santero* (Santería priest) received a vision that the spirit of Bette Davis, her favorite star, watched over her as an *Orisha*, a sort of personal saint.[62] Famed Cuban novelist Guillermo Cabrera Infante, who grew up in Havana, recalls Havana residents' common "habit of Cubanizing all the names of [their] favorite American actors. Robert Taylor became Roberto Tilo. Gregory Peck was Gregorio Peca and Clark Gable, of more difficult domestication, became Clarco Gabla." He also recalls that there was "little urge to be silent at the movies. . . . Havana spectators not only spoke among themselves but often embarked on monologues which seemed like dialogues with the apparition on the screen."[63] By all accounts, Havana's cines throughout the republican period were unruly, loud spaces, where audiences were *not* passive.

Havana audiences heartily cheered that which they approved, and they hissed (or whistled) at that which they did not, including in newsreels depicting national and global current events and even their own governments.[64] Paramount's Havana office reported with dismay that Cubans sometimes laughed "at" instead of "with" their films, and generally lamented "the idiosyncrasies of our [Cuban] audience, which can be disappointingly perverse."[65] Cuban audiences were especially vocal in criticizing Hollywood films that touched on anything having to do with Latin America generally or, especially, with Cuba specifically. Protests and boycotts were waged against films that belittled Cubans' own role in their independence (i.e., the aforementioned *A Message to García* and *Santiago*) or denigrated contemporary Havana as a city of sin and vice.

During these decades, Havana film critics and trade journalists became key barometers and influential directors of Cubans' "idiosyncratic" interpretive practices, consciously invoking a national audience—"our way of seeing," "our market," "our tastes," "Cuban sensibilities," "a Cuban point of view"—in ways that were shaped by, and helped to further shape, revolutionary Cuban nationalism.[66] Following Martí and other Latin American intellectuals (*pensadores*) who have played crucial roles in political movements (not least of all as mediators of foreign influence), most of the film critics considered in *Hollywood in Havana* were among Cuba's most influential and well-known intellectuals. They were politically active writers in other capacities who wrote film criticism because they recognized Hollywood's considerable sway on the *clases populares*.[67] Others devoted their careers to film criticism and, in it, to extrapolating progressive politics from Hollywood films to serve revolutionary Cuban nationalism, as Valdés-Rodríguez's *Mr. Smith* review begins to suggest. From reviews in Havana's most important periodicals, from editorials in fanzines, and eventually from lectures in university classrooms and cine clubs, they directed Cubans toward particular films to see and particularly *Cuban* ways of seeing them. And Cuban film writers did not limit themselves to writing about film content. Bent on demystifying Hollywood's "Dream Factory," they delineated the US film industry's hypercommercial mode of production (i.e., its assembly line production method; its profit motive above Art or social consciousness) and monopolistic trade practices. Moreover, they presented them as concrete examples of what was wrong with the American Way and its negative consequences for Cubans. Cuban film writers were quick to champion publicly the cause of their film giro compatriots whenever conflicts arose between them and the US film companies, often interpreting those conflicts through the lens of aggrieved nationalism.

Hollywood in Havana explores these phenomena in chronological order.

Chapter 1 examines their roots during the cinema's silent era, which coincided roughly with the Plattist (aka First) Republic (1902–33). In this period, rudimentary exhibition spaces gave way to purpose-built cines, which multiplied prodigiously. While European cinema dominated at first, the new Hollywood studios, which established their Havana branch offices during and immediately after World War I, usurped the market by the early 1920s. In that generally prosperous decade, Cuban and US exhibitors erected picture palaces and held glamorous premieres for Hollywood films, building associations in the public mind between the United States, capitalist modernity, and national progress. And yet, this "Americanization," of which Hollywood was part and parcel, agitated revolutionary Cuban nationalism, a phenomenon also evident in Havana's early exhibition venues and film print culture. Chapter 2 examines the advent of Cuban film criticism in a pivotal moment in Cuban history: during the revolutionary movement against Machado and the Platt Amendment at the end of the 1920s and beginning of the 1930s. In new film columns in the Havana press, Cuban intellectuals began to point to Hollywood business practices as concrete examples of Yankee treachery and to appropriate the critiques of US society articulated by Hollywood's most progressive film artists. It was during this period that Charlie Chaplin became something of a mascot in Havana intellectuals' ongoing project to bend Cuban film reception toward revolutionary ends.

Chapter 3 covers a period in which both US imperial hegemony and Cuban strongman politics recrudesced after the 1933 Cuban revolution. It traces Cuban reception of Hollywood's Good Neighbor films and its "good neighborly" business practices, as the economy rebounded and as Hollywood worked hard to prove that it did not "look down" at its southern neighbors and that its market hegemony represented opportunity rather than exploitation for Latin Americans. It also explores the ways that US-Cuban rapprochement was negotiated complexly within the film giro. In it, US managers were accepted as "goodwill ambassadors" to the extent that they respected, and even assimilated to, *Cubanidad* and to the extent that Hollywood profits trickled down, even as its Cuban benefactors struggled with the paradox of being "self-made men" within a dependent economy. Chapter 4 turns its focus to Cuban reception of Hollywood antifascism during World War II, which elevated the Hollywood Left's democratic idealism and its promotion of Pan-American freedom-fighting masculinity to fever pitch, which was encouraged by US government propaganda agencies. In Havana, during this high-point of US-Cuban bonds, Hollywood's liberty-loving soldier-heroes were avidly embraced by moviegoers and members of the film giro, and Cuban film writers adopted them as advocates for armed revolt not only against the Axis powers, but also against

Latin American dictators, past, present, and future. Chapter 5 is about the disillusionment that followed the righteous crusade of World War II, both within the Hollywood Left and in postwar Havana, where political corruption was rampant. In Hollywood, leftist artists continued to articulate progressive social critiques, and even heightened them in the famous cycle of postwar film noirs, despite the repressive Red Scare. These dark films—with their gritty depictions of nonconforming (anti)heroes struggling with US society's homicidal greed, ruthless criminality, and emasculating inequity—spoke to Cubans' own disillusionment and were interpreted as true indices of US society's depravity. In fact, it is in the critical reception of noirs and their (anti)heroes that the Cuban practice of appropriating Hollywood films to spotlight the "monster's entrails" and to mobilize a certain spirit of resistance is most starkly evident. Chapter 6 is about Cuban film reception and film business relations during Batista's dictatorship (1952–58), in which the Cuban appropriation of pre-1959 Hollywood toward revolutionary ends reached its culmination. (A brief Epilogue traces film business and critical reception practices into the first years of the revolutionary government, as indices of rapidly deteriorating US-Cuban relations that nonetheless point to historical continuity rather than a complete break from the past.)

By the 1950s, Hollywood had profoundly shaped the Cuban cultural imagination; and Cubans' particular ways of "looking up"—identifying with Hollywood's freedom-fighting heroes and appropriating its critiques of the American Way into the Cuban context—had been broadly disseminated. Thus, it made sense for the Cuban public to judge rebel leaders, and to make celebrities of them, to the extent that they conformed to Hollywood ideals of the "good guy." It made sense for rebel youth in Havana to see themselves through the same lens, attending John Wayne and Burt Lancaster movies by day and participating in anti-Batista marches and/or underground activities by night.[68] And it made sense for Ernesto "Che" Guevara to rally the Cuban rebels under his command in the Sierra Maestra mountains with speeches he described as "straight out of the movies."[69] Nor is it surprising that Havana cines became sites for fervent speeches against Batista's dictatorship. Nor that film columns were sites for arguing not only against Batista's dictatorship but also against US imperialism. Nor that Havana's new cine clubs were used as recruiting grounds for the movement and then as covers for small cells of its armed activists, a climactic materialization of pre-1959 Cuban film reception's counterhegemonic potential.

In other words, whether revolutionaries organized within the interior of a cine or not, the cinema tended to organize their—and other Cubans'—ways of thinking about their rebellion. Those who later rejected the Revolution's post-1959 directions remembered disdainfully that it had been fought by "kids who saw far too many war movies, and too many Westerns." In a memoir about his Havana childhood, Carlos Eire remembers that he and his friends wanted to be like the Hollywood heroes they saw in countless movies about World War II, "shooting dead all those evil Nazis." And, as Eire puts it in another passage, "I wanted to be Jimmy Stewart. . . . He reminded me of my grandfather. I'm sure Jimmy would have brushed lizards off his shoulders with the same aplomb as Abuelo [Grandpa] Amador."[70]

To better understand how Hollywood's influence as refracted through the Cuban context—how wanting to be a Cubanized version of Stewart or how posing like him before the Lincoln Memorial—relates to the 1959 Cuban Revolution, we must now go back to the turn of the nineteenth century, when the cinema and US imperial hegemony arrived together in Havana.

1

The Film Business That Unites: Early US Cinema in Havana, 1897–1928

April 1922. In the flickering shadows of a packed auditorium, the young assistant manager of the Teatro Fausto, owned and operated by Paramount, watches his compatriots watch a movie. This night's feature is D. W. Griffith's *Way Down East*, one of the first films to be distributed by United Artists' new branch office in Havana. Up onscreen a pale, young woman lurches through a blinding snowstorm and collapses on an ice floe, while the theater's fans hum loudly, battling the tropical heat. Shots of the unconscious damsel-in-distress rushing downriver alternate with shots of her handsome hero, bravely giving chase, finally snatching her up just inches before a precipitous waterfall. Caught up in Griffith's fast-paced editing, the Cuban moviegoers at the Fausto grab their seats and hold their breaths.[1]

As the young assistant manager, José Manuel Valdés-Rodríguez, would later recall, his compatriots "were experiencing one of the first works of cinematic art." They "left the projection hall that night with eyes clouded over by a new type of emotion, a direct, discombobulating, physical feeling" caused by "the stimulus of a new medium of expression that would direct the spirit and intelligence of man through his most alert and direct sense, his vision."[2] When Valdés-Rodríguez wrote these lines in 1939, he was well on his way to becoming Cuba's most influential film critic, leading a movement not only to explain but also to *re*direct the cinema's effects upon "the spirit and intelligence" of Cubans, not least of all through its representations of the colder land to the North. But in 1922, he was just another Havana spectator cum film giro employee caught up in Hollywood's emerging power.

This chapter traces the rise of cinema in Havana in the first two decades of the twentieth century, and then the rise of Hollywood in that city in the 1920s, covering the period of silent cinema and Cuba's First Republic, which

FIG. 1.1. The Teatro Fausto, from *Cuba en 1925*. (Courtesy of the Cuban Heritage Collection, University of Miami Libraries, Coral Gables, Florida)

roughly overlapped. Citizens of a new nation increasingly tied to the United States, Cubans forged their national identity in a process that involved complex negotiations with US power. In this process, early moving picture halls in Havana were not just sites for the conveyance of US influence but also for the continued promotion of revolutionary Cuban nationalism. In many ways, habaneros' earliest experiences of the cinema were less about being incorporated into North American ways and more about fomenting local social belonging. In part, this was due to the nature of early film production (before the more absorbing and transporting narrative techniques that Griffith helped to develop) and the nature of early exhibition practices (which tended to "localize" the moviegoing experience).[3] Moreover, at first, local entrepreneurs dominated in the businesses of film distribution and exhibition, and European films were preferred.

Around the time of World War I, however, conditions shifted. Films' lengths grew from minutes to hours, and cinematic storytelling grew more engrossing. The new Hollywood studios began their global expansion and made Havana one of their first stops in establishing foreign distribution offices. From these, the Hollywood studios muscled out Cuban distributors; displaced European films with Hollywood product; built, purchased, or leased new picture palaces; and spread US star culture pervasively. It was in the 1920s, then, that Hollywood became an important tie that bound Cuba to the United States on US terms. And yet, Hollywood's overwhelming influence provoked forms of resistance with nationalist underpinnings. For instance, Cuban exhibitors organized collectively in the face of the US studios' power, and Cuban intellectuals began to develop a print culture to shape local reception practices. Thus, the conditions were set for a revolt against Hollywood in the late 1920s and early 1930s, in which film critics like Valdés-Rodríguez made *Cuban* ways of seeing Hollywood and Cuban resistance to its business practices part of the 1933 revolution, to be covered in chapter 2.

The Arrival of the Cinema and US Imperialism in Havana, 1897–1902

The cinema arrived in colonial Havana in January 1897 at the tail end of a thirty-years-long revolt against Spanish colonial rule that had cost hundreds of thousands of Cuban lives and devastated much of the island. The Cuban Liberation Army and its *mambí* fighters were finally within sight of Havana, itself filled with rebel conspirators. By then, even the once loyalist Cuban elites had come to reject Spanish rule as despotic, beyond reform, and counter to their economic self-interest, especially as Madrid punitively blocked Cuban trade with the United States.[4] Separation from Spain was all but inevitable, even as US intervention was fifteen months away.

It was then that Gabriel Veyre, sales representative for the French cinema inventors, the Lumière Brothers, steamed into Havana Harbor with his *cinématographe*, a hand-cranked projector that doubled as a camera. On January 23, 1897, in a small public hall next to the grand Teatro Tacón (see fig. 1.2), on colonial Havana's central boulevard, the Paseo del Prado, Veyre projected short scenes onto a wetted bed sheet for an invited group of journalists. To the audience's amazement, pictures moved on screen: cavalry charged, a train pulled into a station, Czar Nicholas II arrived in Paris.[5]

The reports in the following week's newspapers were adulatory, brimming with optimism about *fin de siècle* modernity. According to Havana's theater critics, the cinématographe was "the marvel of century's end," far surpassing the single-user moving picture viewers, like Edison's Kinetoscope, that were now passé in the nearby Salón de Ilusiones Ópticas. The cinématographe seemed conjured from the "miraculous imagination of ancient magicians" or even God himself; or, less supernaturally, it was "the final expression of science, the greatest advance in inventive genius." Havana's dailies sought to outdo each other in hyperbole. The cinema proffered "life copied in plain palpitating action." It was sure to "transform the face of modern life" and to

FIG. 1.2. "View of Tacón Theater in Havana, Cuba," taken by Juan Francisco Chaple y del Corral, circa 1897. The exhibition hall in which moving pictures were first seen in Havana was located under the sign that reads "Havana Museum Co.," *to the left* of the Tacón's grand entrance. (Courtesy of the Cuban Heritage Collection, University of Miami Libraries, Coral Gables, Florida)

"circle the world winning the applause of all peoples and enriching the businesses entrusted with exhibiting it." Havana's journalists beamed with pride that their own city merited an early stop on this global conquest, just thirteen months after the cinema's debut in Paris, less than a year after New York City, and only a few months after Buenos Aires and Mexico City. Above all else, they exhorted habaneros to experience it for themselves. Havana's premier theater critic, Francisco Hermida, wrote, "Go, go and see it. I assure you that whoever goes will leave amazed at this very new invention."[6]

Go they did and amazed they were. When Veyre opened screenings to the public on every subsequent evening for the following two months, hundreds of habaneros streamed in and out of the cramped hundred-seat hall, paying fifty centavos each for ten two-minute scenes. Hermida reported that audiences responded "with frenetic applause, exclamations and screams of enthusiasm." Another theater critic, Ancieto Valdivia, enthused that by the end of the month "all of Havana has been to appreciate this invention of the Lumière Brothers and has been left, like me, astounded."[7] Thus, from the start, Havana critics worked to construct a collective local audience whose reception matched their own.

But astonishment was not the only response reported or prescribed. Hermida, for one, also saw the new medium's potential to promote revolutionary Cuban nationalism. This despite the Spanish authorities' best efforts to make it a tool of colonial rule, by insisting that Veyre project spectacles of Spanish military might, showing titles like *Charge of the Spanish Lancers* and *The Spanish Artillery in Combat*.[8] Refusing to be cowed, Hermida imagined how the cinema might similarly capture the heroics of "our soldiers" in Cuba's ongoing insurrection, to be watched by Cuban audiences once the colony became its own nation. "Our successors will be able TO SEE MATERIALLY the facts of our days, they will see history instead of reading it as we do today. . . . A Cinematógraph . . . will present exactly to us the generals marching ahead of the battalions under their command. . . . We will see flags wave, weapons gleam and, sadly but gloriously, blood spilled for one's country."[9] This is not simply a diatribe on the cinema's utility for historical preservation; it is a call to arms. It invokes a national community (of "our," "us," and "we") just then being imagined into existence around dramatic narratives of heroic freedom-fighting masculinity, even in this very article.

Though the French were the first to bring the cinema to Havana, the North Americans were quick to follow. On the morning of Valentine's Day, February 14, 1897—an appropriate beginning to Cubans' romance with US cinema—the Havana press announced that an Edison Vitascope was projecting short "actualities" in the Salón de Ilusiones Ópticas. For twenty centavos less than what Veyre charged up the block, Cubans could enjoy marvelous scenes of US commerce and industry, of bustling city streets, and the comings and goings of fire trucks, trains, and steamships. Undersold, Veyre was forced to lower his admissions at about the same time that he suffered Havana's first (quickly squelched) film fire, a perpetual menace given the combustible mix of nitrate film and tropical heat.[10]

Neither small blazes nor grand conflagrations seemed to deter the public's interest, or Cuban impresarios' eagerness to satisfy it. A number of Havana's smaller variety halls began to complement or even replace live forms of entertainment with cinema projections. Cuban playwright Federico Villoch warned of "an alarming cinematographic epidemic," with moving picture shows popping up "on every corner."[11] Also noting this trend were the savvy impresarios of the magnificent 2,500-seat Teatro Irijoa, a block off the southernmost point of the Prado. In April 1897, they unveiled a Biograph projector, and the US films compatible with it that they had procured in New York City. This made the Irijoa the first of Havana's grand stage theaters to offer the moving pictures (first as a novelty between other acts) that would largely displace live theater by the 1920s.[12] The Teatros Payret, Tacón, Alhambra, and Albisu quickly followed suit throughout 1897. Cubans sat in Havana's colonial theaters, surrounded by their Spanish past, looking ahead at a more US-centric future projected onscreen.

That future came nearer in February 1898, when the *U.S.S. Maine* exploded in Havana Harbor. Hastily attributed to Spanish treachery, the deaths of 266 American sailors gave jingoistic US expansionists the pretext for the war they sought. Within days of the explosion, Edison and his competitors had cameramen in Havana to capture this mortal insult that demanded retribution. They made films like *Wreck of the Battleship Maine* and *Divers at Work on the Maine,* thus furnishing the (moving) pictures that would furnish the war, to borrow the famous line of William Randolph Hearst, who helped to transport a number of these cameramen to Cuba.[13]

Once the United States declared war against Spain in late April 1898, the so-called Spanish-American War revived the US public's waning interest in the novelty of moving pictures. Dramatic war films satisfied US spectators' desire for action and national purpose. They were voraciously consumed in US theaters plastered with American flags, where fallen soldiers were mourned with the playing of "Taps" and living soldiers were regaled with patriotic songs. Often strung together, shorts like *Cuban Refugees Waiting for Rations*, *Spanish Infantry Attacking American Soldiers in Camp*, and *Fighting with Our Boys in Cuba* traced a narrative arc from Spanish villainy and Cuban helplessness to US heroism, the United States' men of action proceeding through a hail of bullets to bring liberty to Cubans. In the United States, these films served to assure Americans about the righteousness of their venture into imperialism.[14]

Victorious in battle, the United States signed a treaty with Spain that transferred Cuba (as well as Puerto Rico, Guam, and the Philippines) to US control. During the US military occupation of Cuba that followed—from January 1899 through May 1902—US occupation authorities laid the seeds of US imperial hegemony. They disbanded and disarmed the *mambises*; rejected calls for land redistribution; restricted suffrage; and used the assignment of government posts to purchase allegiance, all toward empowering a minority elite amenable to US interests while disempowering the racially mixed majority. But even this elite landowner class struggled as US authorities denied its members public loans and debt forgiveness. Their insolvency and depressed land prices enticed thousands of Americans (including individual speculators and corporations like the United Fruit Company) to buy up as much as one-third of Cuban land.[15] United States' occupation authorities enticed still more Americans with public works contracts for reconstruction and sanitation improvements, projects designed to increase Cuba's commercial capacities (for trade with the

United States) with the added benefit of impressing Cubans with the United States' paternal benevolence, industrial might, technological progress, and civilizing virtues.[16] United States' laborers, white-collar professionals, and import-export merchants followed, as did US goods, the import of which tripled during the occupation.[17]

United States' cultural practices and values spread, too, especially in Havana. Buildings, transportation, fashion, and business practices were modernized "in the American style." The use of English spread rapidly.[18] Much of this resulted from the influx of Americans and US goods, but some of it was the result of official US policy that sought to achieve "annexation by acclimation."[19] Occupation authorities decreed the recognition of US holidays like Thanksgiving and George Washington's birthday while refusing to sanction proposed Cuban holidays on October 10 and February 24, to commemorate the outbreak of wars of independence in 1868 and 1895 respectively. In Cuban public schools, occupation authorities mandated the teaching of English and adopted particular textbooks, such as *The Rescue of Cuba*, to teach Cuban schoolchildren the debt of gratitude they owed US heroes.[20]

Already in these first years, US films shown in Cuba also promoted US hegemony. Sanctioned by occupation authorities, US cameramen made films celebrating parades of US servicemen in Havana and the raising of the US flag in the city's famous Morro Castle. It is likely that such films were supplied to the increasing number of US-made projectors and moving picture halls opened by Americans in Havana. For instance, in July 1900, US entrepreneurs bought the little hall where Veyre had first shown moving pictures, and renamed it La Estrella (The Star) to capitalize on national feelings for the new one-starred Cuban flag.[21] Just up the street, in January 1901, a US company leased the Teatro Payret and adapted a corner of the building for cinema exhibitions. Christened the Cine Niza, its front door faced the Parque Central, into which a barker announced that day's film offerings, likely in Spanish and English. His shouts might have been heard by the men removing the park's statue of Spanish queen Isabel II, replacing it with a replica of the Statue of Liberty. After US occupiers left in 1902, that statue was replaced with the statue of José Martí that stands there today.[22]

Yet, as the naming of La Estrella hints and the story of the statues clarifies, sights and sounds of revolutionary Cuban nationalism competed with the sights and sounds of Americanization during this first US occupation. *Independentismo*—the continuing fervor for national sovereignty at the heart of Cubans' emergent national identity—intensified in reaction to US occupation. Throughout Havana, Cuban revolutionary heroes were commemorated in stone monuments and street names; national symbols were forged; and the impositions of a new foreign power were denounced. The Teatro Irijoa was renamed the Teatro Martí in February 1899 in a grand ceremony attended by the martyred hero's family. And the Tacón was being readied for its rechristening as the Teatro Nacional on May 20, 1902, on which day US occupation was scheduled to end and the Cuban Republic to begin.[23]

Such expressions of revolutionary nationalism in theaters during the occupation were not limited to official events. Havana theaters were draped in Cuban flags and portraits of Cuban revolutionary heroes; and US occupation authorities grew concerned about raucous audiences who broke out into "eruptions" of the new national anthem, "La Bayamesa," rising together to sing, "To live in chains is to live / In dishonor and ignominy."[24] It is easy to imagine that this was true during projections of US-made films about the Spanish-American War, no matter how US-centric they skewed. And if such films aroused patriotic sentiments among US audiences, imagine how charged were the national feelings of *Cuban* audiences. In Havana theaters, such films must have stoked Cubans' fervent commitment to independence for which so many Cubans had died instead of accepting the "semi-sovereignty" offered by their northern neighbor.

It was in this context that the proposed Platt Amendment—which the US Congress insisted on as a condition of US withdrawal—was met with vehement protest in Havana. The Cuban delegates to the Constitutional Assembly denounced the Platt Amendment ferociously but, in the end, had no choice but to append it to the Cuban constitution of 1901, which would serve as the nation's governing document from 1902 to 1934. Moreover, desperate for economic recovery, Cuban officials had little choice but to accept US trade terms: the United States would guarantee US purchase of Cuban agricultural products in exchange for Cuba's drastically reducing tariffs on imported US manufactured goods. Over the next three decades, the continually renewed US-Cuban Reciprocity Treaty of 1903 ensured Cuban dependency on sugar production and ensured the underdevelopment of Cuban industry and enterprise, dampened as they were by the competitive advantages enjoyed by US goods and investors. By the 1920s, North Americans would control major sectors of the Cuban economy: mining, shipping, transportation, utilities, and banking.[25]

By the 1920s, too, North Americans would dominate the film business in Cuba. However, during the first decade and a half of Cuba's Plattist Republic, European films outsold US films and Cuban exhibitors and distributors made the most of the opportunities presented by the new medium and its popularity in Havana.

"Moving Picture Theatres Are Everywhere": Early Cines in Havana, 1902–1914

After the end of the first US occupation, the "Americanization" of Havana continued apace as its inhabitants adjusted to the new order. Over the next two decades, the city's population nearly doubled to half a million, as upended rural Cubans and immigrants from Spain and surrounding Caribbean islands poured in, the most ambitious of them anxious to learn US-style business practices and English, hoping to find opportunity in the country's rapidly growing economy. Americans continued to arrive as well, along with the US goods that clogged Havana's port. The city's streets were crowded with new businesses with English-language names like the American Grocery and the Greater New York Café.[26] Along the southernmost end of the Prado, construction of Havana's Capitolio—which bore a more than accidental, and more than slight, resemblance to the US Capitol—began in 1912.[27]

By then, there were dozens of exhibition venues showing moving pictures within blocks of the capitol grounds, most of them operated by *Cuban* impresarios. While they continued to adapt existing stage theaters, they also began to build theaters expressly for the projection of cinema. The first of these purpose-built cines, the Actualidades, was opened in 1906, a few months before the start of the second US military occupation, which would last more than two years.[28] Over the next eight years, Cuban impresarios launched Havana's first cine construction boom. Moving picture halls multiplied in the theater district, on and around the Prado, which ran from the capitol grounds northward to the famous Malecón sea wall, the first section of which had been completed during the first US occupation. There was the Alaska (perhaps thus named to suggest a cool interior rare in the city's steamy, poorly ventilated theaters), the Manhattan, the Monte Carlo, and the Norma, to list a very few. Though these early cines had seating capacities in the low hundreds only, impresarios could accommodate plenty of patrons by offering as many as four "continuous" showings a day, on an *entre y salga cuando quiera* (come and go as you please) basis. Thus profiting, Cuban impresarios had opened some forty moving picture halls in Havana by June of 1914, on the eve of World War I. That same year, one US tourism guidebook for Havana simply advised that "Moving Picture theatres are everywhere," in lieu of offering a list with addresses.[29]

In fact, moving pictures weren't only available in theaters. As early as 1899, one Cuban entrepreneur, José Casusús, strapped a Lumière projector and two electric generators to a mule cart and held traveling cinema shows, stringing up electric lightbulbs (the first many Cubans had seen) in the colors of Cuba's (and the United States') flag: red, white, and blue. Into the early twentieth century, there were cinema exhibitions in traveling tent shows in Havana and at the city's new amusement park, the Parque Palatino (built by a US company on the model of Coney Island).[30] At the end of 1913, there was even a "Hale's Tours" attraction, a US-invented exhibition venue made to look like a passenger train car. Situated a half block off the Prado on Calle Animas, the Metropolitan Cinematour's façade looked like the platform of a train station, with a board announcing arrivals and departures. Employees in railway uniforms sold tickets for first, second, or third class, which were collected by the "conductor" inside the "train" before the "trip" began. Straw seats faced a screen upon which appeared moving pictures that had been captured by cameras mounted on trains around the world. The illusion of industrial age travel was perpetuated by ingenious engineering: a lug-laden belt that moved under the car to mimic the satisfying clickety-clack of the rails, a fan that blew gusts of air, and a lever that rocked the car back and forth. Habaneros thrilled about the chance to "visit" destinations in the United States and around the globe.[31]

Meanwhile, some habaneros really did travel internationally because of the cinema, namely Cuban entrepreneurs entering into the business of film distribution. They traveled to New York City and European capitals to purchase copies of films to show in their own cines and, later, to rent to others. Havana's first film distributors were partners Pablo Santos and Jesús Artigas, the city's most successful impresarios, who also began to distribute for French and (later) Italian film companies. To promote their films and their theaters, starting in 1912, Santos and Artigas also introduced Cuba's first publication devoted to the cinema, *Cuba Cinematográfica*, with a print run as high as five thousand.[32] These pioneers in the Cuban film business also ventured into film production, making a number of films about Cuban revolutionary heroes that did well in Havana, capitalizing on Cubans' patriotic sentiments as well as Santos and Artigas' (temporary) dominance in distribution, promotion, and exhibition.[33]

As Havana cines continued to multiply and to grow in seating capacity, Cuban exhibitors sought to outdo one another. They dreamed up novelties, publicity stunts, and tie-ins. There were cigar coupons on movie tickets and movie tickets in cigar boxes. The Cine Máxim lured male patrons with the novelty of an all-girl orchestra, while the Cine Salas tempted female patrons with "women only" programs, reduced ticket prices, complimentary bars of perfumed soap, and even a beauty contest, with a ride home in an automobile as its prize. More and more cines, however, sought to promote the heterosocial nature of their spaces, guaranteeing their patrons' safety, moral as much as physical. One impresario boasted that his was the only cine to leave the aisle lights on to discourage lovers' exploitation of the dark. Everywhere, fireproof equipment, emergency exits, and improved ventilation were selling points. So was comfort. Cines began to boast fixed (even upholstered) seats and sloped floors for better sightlines.[34]

In many ways, cinema exhibition in Havana before World War I was like cinema exhibition in US cities. Havana's moving picture halls were relatively small, sparsely decorated within, and decorated on the exterior with a small box office and various degrees of electric ornamentation. Hand-painted posters and barkers announced the film programs that changed on a daily basis. Inside, the audience faced a screen tacked to the wall above a raised platform, used as a stage for live acts between reels. In the back, a projectionist hand-cranked film through a projector, whose ether-oxygen burning light heated the cramped hall and filled it with noxious smells (until the end of this period when projectors were increasingly powered with electricity and contained within projection rooms). Most early Havana moving picture halls were equipped with a piano or with space for a small orchestra. Exhibitors combined the era's relatively short "story films" (most lasting less than twenty minutes) and live acts to create a "balanced program" shown multiple times a day, with spectators popping in and out as they liked, jostling each other, rearranging chairs, and generally disrupting the show.[35]

Yet there were important differences. Whereas US-made films dominated US screens by 1909, European films dominated in Havana until World War I.[36] When US films did play in Havana, they were often in terrible condition, either poorly pirated or horribly scratched from previous runs in the United States or Mexico. Not surprisingly, then, Cubans expressed an overwhelming preference for European films: first Italian, then French, then Danish. In a 1914 poll of habaneros' favorite film companies, only one US producer (Vitagraph) registered at all, with a mere 2 percent of votes. In 1915, the new Cine Prado nearly went bankrupt offering a season of US films.[37]

For another thing, in Havana the cinema was not understood primarily to be a "lowbrow" amusement confined to immigrant neighborhoods as it was in US cities.[38] The earliest cinema exhibitions—taking place in the posh residential and theater district on and around the Prado—attracted members of Havana's elite, sometimes even listed by name in turn-of-the-century press reports.[39] Thereafter, the multiple cines that opened in the vicinity continued to pride themselves in attracting the "best publics." And, as Havana's elites and an emerging middle-class moved out of the city's center and into the new neighborhood of Vedado, "*cines de elegancia*" appeared there to cater to them. For instance, the Cine Vedado charged the princely sum of one peseta for the box seats that neighborhood families liked to claim.[40]

Even as "high-class" movie halls were constructed in the city center and affluent districts, Cuban entrepreneurs began erecting simpler *cines de barrio*, sometimes called *baratos* (cheapies), in working-class neighborhoods. Some of these were famously rowdy. So much so that the Cuban Congress of Mothers, like their counterparts among US progressives, declared them "a school of corruption and perversity," especially for the impressionable young boys who frequented them.[41] At the Cine Palacio Gris, in the Cayo Hueso neighborhood, hooligans in the gallery were known to piss on the hats of ladies below.[42] Just a block away, respectable women stayed away altogether from the Cine Oriente, whose audience—of pimps, prostitutes, drug addicts, and toughs—so frequently devolved into epic brawls that its orchestra's musicians sat behind a metal screen to protect them from flying rocks and bottles. In the Puentes Grandes neighborhood, the Cine París was the site of at least one raucous fight, which pitted Cuban-born workers against their Spanish immigrant counterparts when a film about the Spanish-American War roused the national feelings of both groups.[43]

But these more violent disruptions were not the only things that might have distracted spectators from being transported by the cinema out of their lived context. The silent images onscreen had to compete with all the sounds and sensations of the tropics: oppressive heat in indoor theaters; sudden rain showers and pesky cockroaches in open-air ones. Moreover, early exhibition practices continued to distract. Especially in cines de barrio, Havana exhibitors resisted foreign producers' longer, multireel features; they insisted that they knew their compatriots well enough to know Cuban audiences would not sit still for them (which allowed exhibitors to put off the expense of the second projector needed to show such features without interruption). While projectionists changed reels between short films, Havana's most revered singers continued to belt out *boleros* and *sones*, or to recite Spanish poetry or Spanish plays with Catholic morals.[44]

Even while the films rolled, local sounds vied with the imported images for the spectators' attentions. The cinema's silence of this era meant the bodies onscreen had to compete with live bodies in orchestras (with whom female spectators were said to flirt) and their music, which could be quite overwhelming indeed. By the end of the silent era, a fifty-piece orchestra and thirty-piece choir accompanied at least one film at the Teatro Payret.[45] But even with more modest musical offerings, the local live talent likely outshone foreign screen talent. The pianos at the Cines Orión and Monte Carlo boasted teenage prodigies who would later become internationally renowned composers, Ernesto Lecuona and Gonzalo Roig respectively.[46] And, especially in this early era of silent cinema before studios even provided suggested scores, musicians and/or conductors were free to improvise accompaniments as they saw fit. Along with the internationally standard repertoire of marches, waltzes, and ballads, Cuban *charanga* bands accompanying films in Havana cines often played the *danzón*, a style of music derived from Afro-Cuban origins then considered synonymous with *Cubanidad*.[47]

As these music choices suggest, films and their meanings were more subject to modification at the point of exhibition during this early era. Projectionists slashed films they considered overly long in order to fit the cine's balanced program, or they increased the speed at which the films cranked. Havana audiences were said to applaud projectionists who sped or slowed scenes for dramatic effect, making action heroes superhuman and/or drawing out romantic moments.[48] And Cuban *parlantes* (talkers) and *ruidistas* (noise makers) also modified films' meanings. *Ruidistas* used rudimentary tools—such as chains, metal sheets, wooden blocks, cap guns, police whistles—to create sound effects, sometimes so overzealously that spectators complained of pounding headaches. Beginning around 1905, *parlantes* improvised dialogue loosely synchronized with onscreen lips, with only brief afternoon rehearsals before evening showings. Teams of *parlantes* (typically two men, two women, and a child) were common in Havana cines until 1914, when the US film companies (just beginning to court the Latin American market) began to provide Spanish-language intertitles, obviating the need for *parlantes*. But until then, Havana's best *parlantes* were local celebrities, more revered than the foreign actors onscreen, who remained mostly anonymous before the advent of the Hollywood star system.[49]

Like their musician colleagues in the orchestra pits, the *parlantes* contributed to the "Cubanization" of foreign cinema. In a rather literal example, one *parlante* took license to reset a film scene from England to Cuba; he inserted the names of Havana *calles* in place of the London street names that the protagonist called out earnestly to his chauffeur. The resulting senselessness of the directions prompted one spectator to shout out jokingly that the protagonist was a fraud. One Cuban commentator fondly recalled the "inventive wit" of the *parlantes* whose "wisecracks" and "funny phrases . . . provoked the public's laughter."[50] According to a number of such anecdotes, Havana audiences especially appreciated *parlantes* who made light of foreign films, voicing brawny gallants with high-pitched squeaks, deflating the films' drama and giving Cuban audiences a chance to bond over a shared laugh at the foreigners' expense. Such anecdotes are evidence that Havana cines were not just sites for the conveyance of foreign influence but also for the construction of a national identity collectively resistant to such influence.

Finally, Havana cines occasionally featured *Cuban* films, often financed and/or ballyhooed by Cuban exhibitors like Santos and Artigas, invariably focused on the Cuban wars of independence and their heroes, promoted with great fanfare, and lavished with praise in the Havana press. Such was the case with *Manuel García*, a Santos and Artigas–produced biopic about that late nineteenth-century revolutionary guerrilla leader, which premiered in August 1913 at two Santos and Artigas–operated theaters. Attending this premiere as a teenager, José Manuel Valdés-Rodríguez later claimed the film had powerful spectator effects: the film's action, he remembered, "infected the hypnotized spectators, who were converted into participants in the heroic and tremendous events."[51] Over the next few years, a handful of Cuban films about independence war heroes followed "In Honor of Those That Were and For the Encouragement of Those That Will Be," as one film poster put it.[52] Like the marble statues, new parks, museums, *mambí* autobiographies, history books, and parades on national holidays (now enacted by the Cuban legislature), such films fully converted Havana's early cines into sites for the promotion of revolutionary Cuban nationalism and the freedom-fighting masculinity at its core.[53]

But during World War I and in the 1920s, conditions would change in the film business in Havana. A flood of US productions displaced European films and made it all but impossible for Cuban films to compete. From 1916 through most of the 1920s, the new phenomenon known as "Hollywood" came to dominate in Havana and began to make its mark on Cuban society.

"Our Cuban Colony": Hollywood Expansionism in Havana, 1915–1929

The Great War brought great changes to the international balance of cinema power. As Europeans put filmmaking on hold for war making, US filmmakers were poised to fill the vacuum. Newly centered in Southern California and just beginning to consolidate their power through the vertical integration of production, distribution, and exhibition nationally, a number of emerging "Hollywood" film companies reaped the rewards of the world's most lucrative domestic market and their cost-effective studio system, reinvesting their profits in grandiose productions that then allowed them to dominate in international markets.[54] This was especially true in what the US trade journal *Moving Picture World* gleefully called the "successful invasion of the Latin-American film market," where US film exports more than quadrupled during World War I.[55] Recognizing opportunity in that market, *Moving Picture World*'s publishers started a new Spanish-language publication, *Cine-Mundial*, naming a Cuban, Francisco Ortega, as its director.[56] After all, if Latin America—"right here on our own hemisphere"—was one of Hollywood expansionists' favored targets, then Cuba—or "our Cuban colony"—was their bull's-eye.[57]

That Cuba, and especially its capital city, should become a focus of Hollywood's global expansionism can be explained partially by geographic proximity. The studios' new export offices in New York City could send films to Havana by ship in just seventy-two hours and, after 1920, even more quickly by air.[58] It can also be explained by Havana's relative, if uneven, prosperity. During World War I, high sugar prices sent the Cuban economy soaring. Because of this, and because of the US-Cuban Reciprocity Treaty, US imports in Cuba skyrocketed by six times above their prewar levels.[59] When sugar prices collapsed after the war, the Cuban economy plunged into crisis in 1920 and 1921, precipitating yet another US military intervention, a $50 million, strings-attached US loan, and another wave of US investments, up to $1.3 billion in 1924, more than in any other Latin American country.[60] Also fueling Cuba's economic recovery was a boom in US tourism to the island; when the Great War cut off vacation destinations in Europe and then Prohibition cut off booze, Americans flocked to Cuba for sun and rum. As a result, after recovering from the brief postwar crisis, Cuba, and especially Havana, experienced enough economic growth during the early half of the Roaring '20s for both US interests and the emergent Cuban middle class to prosper.[61] As the "ties of singular intimacy" were thus knotted tighter, Hollywood's focus on Cuba also had a cultural logic, a presumption of familiarity and, with it, the sense of entitlement that characterized US trade with Cuba generally. As *Moving Picture World* pitched it in 1917, Cubans "know and understand American customs and methods better than any other Ibero-American people."[62]

Thus, as the emerging Hollywood studios began their invasion of Latin America, Havana was often their first stop. Late in 1915, just as it was opening its massive 235-acre studio in California, the Universal Motion Picture Manufacturing Company was the first US studio to open a distribution office in Havana. *Moving Picture World* commended Universal for "render[ing] yeoman service to the whole industry by hewing a path . . . through the rocky trenches of the enemy," to facilitate greater volume and cut out local distributors.[63] Universal also endeavored to cut out local *exhibitors* by operating its own Havana theater. Beginning in September 1916, Universal leased the Teatro Campoamor, a 1,200-seat new theater on the southeast corner of Parque Central.[64] The Campoamor's gimmick of handing out tin sheriff badges during showings of Universal's serial westerns generated much buzz.[65] The real attraction, though, at the Campoamor, and at a number of other Havana cines, were the new US serial films, which drew growing numbers of Cubans to their action-packed weekly episodes.

To little avail, local distributors of European films waged what *Cine-Mundial* referred to as "a war to the death" against Hollywood's first encroachments.[66]

In the October 1916 issue of their *Cuba Cinematográfica*, Santos and Artigas attempted to galvanize Cuban nationalist resistance. "Our people, understanding Mr. Entertainment-Peddler well, reject all that is grotesque, lacking good taste and art," they wrote. "To swindle them [the Cuban public] is impossible. Its intellectual level is superior to that of many of its so-called *civilizers*. . . . The *hurry-scurry* movies and interminable serials, with their boxers, *cowboys*, Indians and detectives, will continue to incur the disdain of publics nourished by fine wines."[67] Here, Santos and Artigas appeal to *Arielismo*, after Uruguayan José Enrique Rodó's 1900 poem "Ariel." Influential around the continent at this time, *Arielismo* contended that the spiritual depth and cultural refinement of Latin Americans proved them superior to North Americans, who were materialistic, shallow, and brutish; it thus reversed US imperialism's racial and national hierarchies. Like Rodó, Santos and Artigas assert the cultivation of "taste" as an anti-imperialist act (against "our so-called *civilizers*"), constructing an "our people" characterized by their recognition that US mass culture—pushed on them by US businessmen ("Mr. Entertainment-Peddler")—is beneath them.

But Santos and Artigas' prescriptive (and self-interested) prophecy proved wrong. Habaneros kept showing up for those "interminable" US serials, the vogue of which paved the way for US features. By 1918, the *Film Daily* cheered that "American pictures are coming into their own in Cuba."[68] Into Havana that year, the US companies released as many feature-length films—now provided with dual English- and Spanish-language inter-titles—as all the European film companies put together. Under this onslaught, Hollywood's displacement of European cinema was abrupt. By the end of World War I, recalled one Cuban commentator, European films "had already passed so out of fashion that they seemed to belong to the prior century."[69]

While US serials paved the way, it was Hollywood's new movie stars that threw open the doors to Cubans' affections (see fig. 1.3). As early as 1918, *Cine-Mundial's* correspondent in Havana, Eduardo Quiñones, reported that US stars were as familiar to habaneros as their own family members, and that stars' photos adorned the rooms of love-struck young men and women. As Quiñones explained, mature European actresses had been "dethroned" by so many young and spirited American starlets.[70] Women in Havana began to copy Pearl White's fashions and girls began to copy Mary Pickford's ringlets. Those two plucky starlets were among habaneros' favorite stars, along with Charlie Chaplin and male action heroes George Walsh, William S. Hart, Tom Mix, and Douglas Fairbanks.[71]

Given this favorable environment, the other emerging US studios followed Universal's lead to open distribution offices in Havana after World War I.

EL CINE OLIMPIC

¿Quien es él? ¿Quien es el guapo que nos sostiene lo contrario? ¿Quien no le debe a la dulce intimidad del cine algunos minutos deliciosos? ¿Quien no recuerda en la poética penumbra de un salón de proyecciones alguna charla que culminó con una afirmación temblorosa, entrecortada? ¿Quien no ha llorado un poquito ante la desesperación de María Jacobini? ¿Quien no ha sentido honda emoción ante la trágica máscara de Hart? ¿Quien no ha reventado de risa ante el célebre Max? Por esa afición grande y justificada que hay por el de arte de Fairbank y de Farnum, la empresa Linares y Cª, ha abierto en el Vedado el alegre, confortable y ventilado *Olimpic*, en la Avenida Wilson (antes Línea) en su cruzamiento con la calle B. Solo las mejores películas, de los mejores actores de las mejores casas productoras, serán exhibidas en este cine, uno de los mejores de la Habana.

FIG. 1.3. A popular monthly magazine in Havana promotes the opening of the Cine Olimpic in Vedado. Note the association of moviegoing pleasure with Charlie Chaplin, as well as the reiteration of national belonging via exhibition practices, per the proudly flown Cuban flags. *Social*, July 1920. (Courtesy of the Cuban Heritage Collection, University of Miami Libraries, Coral Gables, Florida)

United Artists opened its Havana office in 1921; the Fox Film Corporation in 1922; Metro-Goldwyn-Mayer in 1923; First National Pictures (soon to be Warner Bros.) in 1925; and Paramount in 1926.[72] Located within blocks of each other, the US studios' offices clustered on and around Calle Consulado in Central Havana, a residential and commercial district just west of the Prado and north of the Capitolio.[73] This "*barrio peliculero* [movie neighborhood]" was also where the young upstarts Columbia and RKO Radio opened offices in 1931 and 1937 respectively.[74]

Instead of hiring locals, the studios sent US citizens to manage their Havana offices. More often than not, these early branch managers were first- or second-generation immigrants to the United States, often Jewish. Universal's first Havana manager was Bernard Lichtig, followed in that post in the 1920s by Nat Liebeskind and Charles Brookheim, all three of them American Jews of Eastern European descent.[75] MGM's first Havana manager was Louis Goldstein, a US-naturalized Russian Jew.[76] And United Artists' was Max Ehrenreich, the son of Austrian Jews. Ehrenreich lasted just three months, replaced in August 1921 by his assistant, Henry Weiner, a US-naturalized Jew born in Eastern Europe.[77] For many of these managers, adjusting to their Cuban posts was made easier by their incorporation into a local community of American Jews that had been successfully assimilating into Havana society since the first US occupation.[78]

Still, these "pioneers" of Hollywood's global expansion encountered manifold challenges, including their own lack of Spanish-speaking skills; Cuba's unstable economy; the acrimony of local distributors; exhibitor resistance to rental fee hikes; widespread film piracy; unauthorized use of US stars in local advertising; outdated projectors that chewed up their films; and fires in their film vaults.[79] United Artists' Ehrenreich lost twenty pounds due to stress in his short tenure; he was convinced that his hired translator intentionally mistranslated terms to favor his exhibitor compatriots and that the Cuban distributors despised him "like a poison."[80] In fact, the job could be a killer: one Havana manager for Universal during the 1920s died of typhoid fever.[81] Those who survived did so by acclimating to local conditions and winning over Cuban exhibitors; it was said of MGM's Goldstein, for instance, that "he knows a theatreman's troubles and doesn't mind lending a hand. . . . [He] can take tickets when a jam occurs, run a projection machine, and put out fires when the occasion comes up."[82] Some even earned Cuban citizenship, real or honorary, and stayed in their posts for decades, like the aforementioned Weiner, who served as United Artists' Havana manager from 1921 to 1952.

On the other hand, the US studios' success in the Cuban market also rested on the exercise of considerable US muscle, including some provided by the US government. Convinced of the diplomatic utility of "the film business that unites Cuba with the United States," as *Cine-Mundial's* Havana correspondent put it in 1920, the US State and Commerce Departments supported the Hollywood studios' growing presence in Cuba; they exerted pressure on the Cuban government to reduce tariffs and taxes, to crack down on film piracy, and to minimize censorship.[83] Further, the US Commerce Department, working with Hollywood's new collective trade organization, the Motion Picture Producers and Distributors of America (MPPDA), encouraged the US managers in Havana to organize themselves locally into the Cuban Film Board in 1925. Renamed the Havana Film Board two years later, this board allowed the US studios to present a "united front" in their relations with Cuban exhibitors throughout the republican period.[84] Together, they demanded high rental fees (and, later, percentages of box office receipts), charged the lion's share of advertising costs to exhibitors, and forced them to accept "block-booking" and "blind-booking" (the new practices of contracting for a large number of a studio's films sight unseen).[85]

Again following Universal's lead, the US studios also sought to circumvent Cuban exhibitors altogether by operating their own cines in Havana. In 1918, Paramount leased the new 1,660-seat Teatro Fausto, the scene of this chapter's opening (see fig. 1.1). With an enviable location halfway down the Prado, the Fausto became known as "the Temple of Paramount" (at least until 1931 when Warner Bros. took control of its lease).[86] In 1925, Warner Bros. signed an exclusive contract with, and modernized the film exhibiting capacities within, the grand Teatro Nacional (the old Tacón), which had been substantially reconstructed.[87] Some habaneros grumbled that a national treasure was being degraded into a moving picture hall, but the Teatro Nacional's impresario had little choice if he wanted to compete with the Payret and the Martí, both of which had increased their film showings.[88] United States' entrepreneurs and investors also opened a number of new cines, outfitting them with the latest US film equipment (which US cinema supply companies also began to sell directly from offices in the movie barrio).[89] The manager of Universal's Havana office, Nat Liebeskind, opened the Cine Esmeralda while the ex-manager of Universal's Teatro Campoamor, Alexander W. Kent, came to operate ten Havana movie theaters.[90] Dismayed about the US companies' "siege" of Havana's exhibition business, Cuban exhibitors banded together in 1926 to lobby (unsuccessfully) for a municipal ordinance prohibiting the construction of any new cine within one thousand meters of an existing one.[91]

By the end of the 1920s, Hollywood had conquered Havana. The US studios enjoyed as much as 95 percent of Havana's market share, which helped make Cuba (with a population of just 3 million) Hollywood's ninth most important foreign market by volume sold.[92] By then, Havana was fast becoming a popular attraction for the US film business world. Everyone in the industry—from studio presidents to cast and crew members—seemed to join the annual migration of US tourists to Cuba, combining business with pleasure, according to the Hollywood trades, which would chronicle a continual flow of industry executives and stars traveling to Havana over the next three-plus decades. In 1931, the *Film Daily* noted that Havana's movie barrio "more and more resembles the region around 729 Seventh Ave, NY [where most US studios had their export offices]. You literally fall over [US] film people."[93] Hollywood, it seems, had successfully Americanized the film business in Havana and, through it, was working towards further Americanizing the city's inhabitants.

Seeing Stars in Picture Palaces: 1920s Movie Culture in Havana

In many ways, Hollywood and the film culture that developed around it in Havana during the 1920s promoted the idea that Cuba's Americanization would lead to a material and existential "happy ending" (a phrase written in English in Havana) for individuals and the nation. Not even the devastating economic crash of 1920 and 1921, nor the subsequent US military intervention, seemed to temper habaneros' new Hollywood mania and their related optimism about the American Way. In 1920, Havana exhibitors christened two neighborhood cinemas with the names of US presidents, the Teatro Wilson and the Teatro Roosevelt, the latter name selected from patrons' submissions. In 1921, a cine de barrio was inaugurated the Teatro Edison.[94]

And habaneros' adoration of Hollywood's matinee idols only increased as those idols visited Havana in the flesh. In the 1920s, the Cuban press and public gushed over celebrity visitors like the stars of the aforementioned *Way Down East*, Richard Barthelmess and Lillian Gish, and many others, including Harold Lloyd and William Powell.[95] Years before the US government sponsored actors' Good Neighbor goodwill tours, star travelers to Havana served a diplomatic purpose, sometimes even meeting with heads of state. In 1924, Gloria Swanson shared cocktails with Cuban president Alfredo Zayas at the grand opening of the Biltmore Roof Garden. In 1928, Will Rogers tagged along with US president Calvin Coolidge, who traveled to Havana to address the Sixth Pan-American Conference. And in 1930, the wildly popular cowboy star Tom Mix was a special guest of President Gerardo Machado in Havana. There, Mix was heralded for his legendary (and exaggerated) heroism as a Rough Rider during the Spanish-American War, making his visit a special occasion on which to commemorate (and for Hollywood to endorse) Cuba's "debt of gratitude" to the United States.[96]

But US film stars did not have to appear in person to be made objects of worship or ties of singular intimacy. As in the United States, Hollywood stars filled the pages of the movie fanzines that proliferated in Havana. While Santos and Artigas' *Cuba Cinematográfica*, which had mostly focused on European cinema, ceased publication in 1919, Hollywood-centric Cuban fanzines multiplied during the 1920s. Among the first was *Arte Mudo* in 1920, followed over the next two years by *Diario del Cine*, *La Pantalla*, and *Cintas y Estrellas*.[97] In addition, two Spanish-language fanzines published in the United States were available in Havana: the aforementioned *Cine-Mundial* (which repositioned itself around 1920 to appeal to fans as well as industry insiders) and *Cinelandia*.[98]

Compiled largely from material provided to the Havana branch offices from the US studios' growing foreign departments in New York, Cuban fanzines synopsized Hollywood films, chronicled US stars' astronomical ascents to fame and fortune, and gushed over stars' glamorous style, not least of all the new bobbed hair that Hollywood helped to make ubiquitous in Havana. Articles on how the stars ate, exercised, and dressed encouraged Cuban women to achieve the "glamour" and "sex appeal" of the "flapper look" (all in English) and, to these ends, suggested the purchase of US products advertised on adjacent pages. Cuban fanzines also published the addresses of Hollywood studios, inviting Cubans to write to their favorite stars. And even if Cubans' love letters went unrequited, fanzines offered the next best thing to intimacy: the illusion of it. Fanzines brought Cubans onto sets and into stars' homes, their closets, their marriages, and their minds (or at least publicists' versions of them). Over the next decades, fan culture wove Hollywood more deeply into Cubans' everyday lives, enhancing Cubans' identification with US film actors and the characters they played.[99]

At the same time, Havana's mainstream newspapers and magazines began to show more interest in the film business, seeking to capitalize on Hollywood's popularity. Before World War I, writing about the cinema was largely the province of *cronistas*: writers who chronicled all aspects of Havana social life. But toward war's end, columns specifically devoted to the cinema began to appear. A number of these early film columns were written by women or by men who adopted (female) pseudonyms, suggesting that writing about film was not yet considered a serious endeavor worthy of male intellects.[100] Imitating the *cronistas*, these early film columnists focused on the social practices of moviegoing, especially on which cines were currently fashionable. They wrote very little about individual films; after all, reviews were largely moot since films were rarely held over for more than one night. For the most part, a more critical engagement with the cinema in the Havana press would have to wait until the late 1920s. Through most of the 1920s, the mainstream Havana press's treatment of Hollywood was largely indistinguishable from that of the new fanzines, not least in their adulation for Hollywood stars. As just one example, Tom Mix, surrounded by wife and child, smiled from the September 1925 cover of *Carteles*, a popular weekly magazine. Inside, the magazine's editors explained that "our cover has a family air," gesturing not only to Mix's literal familial unit but also to the US-Cuban brotherhood of 1898 and a transnational family of fans, intimately familiar with Mix's Rough Rider reputation and his cowboy character type.[101] The inside pages of Havana weeklies were also peppered with Hollywood stars. Again, one example will have to suffice: in May 1928, the popular magazine *Social* printed a photo of Adolphe Menjou in the *Evening Clothes* (a tuxedo) of his recent film of that title. Marking up Menjou's photo, *Social* offered a head-to-toe breakdown of "how to wear tails impeccably."[102]

Cubans could practice their tuxedo-donning skills at glamorous premieres of Hollywood films held at Havana's new picture palaces, designed to rival the United States' own. The first of these Havana palaces was the Teatro Capitolio, opened by Santos and Artigas in 1921, with President Zayas in attendance. Four stories tall and curving elegantly around a corner facing the capitol grounds, the Capitolio was billed by Santos and Artigas as "the only theater in Cuba in the American style, with all the modern advancements of Broadway."[103] Its spacious lobby was decorated in ivory and gold, and its auditorium featured lighted emergency exits, a large main floor, and two levels of box seats for a total seating capacity of two thousand.[104] Needing to fill these seats, Santos and Artigas now conceded to Hollywood's drawing power, premiering some of the US film industry's biggest features of the early 1920s: Rudolph Valentino's films *The Four Horsemen of the Apocalypse*, *Camille*, and *The Sheik* (all 1921); Charlie Chaplin's *The Kid* (1921); and Harold Lloyd's *Safety First* (1923) and *Hot Water* (1924).[105] For such premieres, tickets sold for as much as $1.50.[106] In 1925, the name of the Teatro Capitolio was changed to Teatro Campoamor, taking the name of the aforementioned theater, which was demolished that year (see fig. 1.4). (The words "Teatro Capitolio" could still be seen engraved on the theater's exterior until the theater collapsed in 2011.) In 1926, Loews (MGM's parent company) leased the Campoamor for a year, added a $30,000 organ to the thirteen-piece orchestra, and introduced the practice of weeklong runs in Havana.[107]

Indeed, the Hollywood studios continued their invasion into Havana exhibition, bringing with them US practices and standards. In 1928, Universal leased and renovated the Cine Rialto, just off the Prado on Calle Neptuno.[108] Also on Neptuno, that same year, Paramount signed a thirty-year lease for its second theater (after the Fausto) in the movie barrio: the Teatro Encanto, recently built by the owners of the famous Havana department store of the same name (see fig. 1.5). With seating for 1,500, the Encanto's interior was made to look like a Spanish colonial courtyard at night, following the atmospheric style then popular in US picture palaces. While the Encanto's interior was designed

FIG. 1.4. The Teatro Campoamor, from *Cuba en 1925*. (Courtesy of the Cuban Heritage Collection, University of Miami Libraries, Coral Gables, Florida)

to evoke Old World romanticism, its equipment offered New World technological progress, all of "standard American make," like the majority of films the Encanto showed. The theater was also outfitted with a Carrier cooling system, making it the first air-conditioned cinema in Latin America, according to its proprietors, and a very popular spot to escape Havana's heat.[109]

After all, Havana's most exacting moviegoers expected the grandeur of their cine's interiors to match the grandeur of Hollywood's productions. As Gerardo del Valle put it in Havana's most widely circulating weekly magazine, *Bohemia*, in April 1928, the moviegoing *señora* of Havana demanded:

> a temple brimming over with luminous surprises, of well combined colors, of magic curtains and dazzling thresholds of luxury. . . . She needs the personnel to have the distinguished look of castle guards and to wear uniforms that harmonize with the whole of the theater. The personnel have to be discreet, mute, pleasant and smiling. The music and performers have to be of sublime qualities, under the direction of a true master that is able to interpret the soul of the scene in all its essence, so that such harmony produces only one united emotion. The "*cine de moda*" [fashionable cine] has to enjoy more and more virtues, so that each day . . . its hall will be without a single empty seat.
>
> . . . .
>
> As Havana advances at vertiginous paces toward the pinnacle of progress and is transformed in all ways, many new "*cines de moda*" are rising in the most

FIG. 1.5. Interior of the Teatro Encanto. *Exhibitors Herald and Moving Picture World*, August 4, 1928.

> strategic places . . . and try to surpass those that already exist. The exhibitor has to resort to all the resources of Art and intelligence to be able to score "points" in this difficult joust. . . . If the "*cine de moda*" is not in a state of constant renovation, like everything of this era, the elegant public will turn their backs on it with a disdainful smile.

The bar was high, Del Valle concluded, but if the *cine de moda* did everything right, then spectators "lose their sense of place: they are imaginatively transformed into the love scene's protagonists." And since the protagonists in the Hollywood films that predominated in Havana's fashionable cines tended to be Americans, it follows that Cuban spectators were "imaginatively transformed" into Americans.[110]

This description of Havana's picture palaces reveals much about how 1920s Hollywood culture encouraged habaneros' expectations of a US-centric modernity in which the "Americanized" Cuban citizen-consumer would rule a world of sensual pleasure, harmonious labor-capital relations, material comfort, novelty, and leisure. With one of Latin America's fastest growing economies, Cuba's US-dependent prosperity (uneven as it was) made all these picture palaces, and all this optimism, possible.[111] Del Valle's final line also suggests how much more engrossing the cinema had become. With the arrival of longer multireel features and with the US studios managing Havana's most popular trend-setting cines, the practice of continuous showings, with moviegoers coming and going as they pleased, was replaced by programs with fixed schedules. Both the greater length of films and the less interrupted screenings of them—as well as improved projection—meant viewers could be more absorbed by a single compelling narrative, more transported out of their own lived *Cuban* context.

Yet, Del Valle's description of Havana's cinemas is laced with sarcasm: about "elegant" Cubans' pretensions, their deferential love of all things foreign, and their fickle and fleeting allegiances. Through this sarcasm, Del Valle critiques habaneros' mindless rush toward a questionable "progress," in which the pursuit of novelty trumps all, human relations are superficial, art is commodified, and capitalist competition is fierce. Del Valle's critical intent is also suggested by his assignment of female gender to this sort of superficial spectator-consumer. (Elsewhere in the article, Del Valle disdains the *cronistas* who list the names of the "ladies that grace [the *cines de moda*] with their presence.") Conversely, Del Valle genders true film connoisseurs as male: "For *he* that simply loves the cinema for the film, whatever movie house is the same to *him*."[112] In fact, Del Valle belonged to a generation of Cuban intellectuals, predominately male and self-professed cinephiles, who were just beginning to articulate a more assertive and critical stance in relation to Hollywood and the Americanization it engendered.

"Their Sense of Place": Cuban Nationalism in 1920s Havana Cines

In other words, there is plenty of evidence for Hollywood's hegemonic effects in Havana in the 1920s. However, under the surface, nationalist resistance to Americanization is also evident. Havana's film columns, and even its fanzines, asserted the idea that there were particular *Cuban* ways of seeing Hollywood films and Hollywood culture. For instance, take another *Bohemia* film writer's commentary on Havana's first picture palace. In 1921, "Gypsy" insisted that the new Teatro Capitolio should impress habaneros about *local* enterprise rather than *foreign* models, writing, "But if all its comfort and elegance made me dream myself transported to Broadway, on the other hand, the distinguished audience that overfilled the theater was Cuban, very Cuban, the orchestra that caused the resounding applause was certainly Cuban, and above all, the firm [Santos and Artigas'] that had achieved with perseverance, effort and tenacity the construction of our most modern theater was Cuban."[113] Here, rather than succumb to what some Cubans diagnosed as a national "inferiority complex," Gypsy asks Havana moviegoers to maintain their sense of place, their national identity, and their pride in it.

In this regard, exhibition practices continued to help. Exhibitors still featured live Cuban acts between reels, and Cuban musicians continued to enjoy latitude in their accompaniments to silent films since Hollywood studios provided full scores for only a handful of prestige pictures, and musical cue sheets for others.[114] According to anecdotes, Cuban musicians continued to favor upbeat Cuban dance music even during films' tragic moments, prompting at least one observer to gripe that Havana's cine conductors "unwittingly or deliberately destroy the effect of that which they have been paid to maintain," turning "a catastrophe into a comedy."[115] Undoubtedly deliberate at least some of the time, these discordant musical interpretations continued to serve as opportunities for Cuban audiences to mock Hollywood collectively and thus to assert a certain cultural superiority over it.

Setting out more consciously to check Hollywood's power, in 1921 Cuban exhibitors organized themselves as the Asociación Nacional de Exhibidores (ANE) to lobby the Cuban government for their collective interests and to present their own "united front" before the powerful US distributors. Threatening boycotts and cine closings, even engaging in a full-scale "Exhibitor-Distributor War in Cuba" according to one US film trade journal, ANE members resisted (with varied success) the US studios' attempts to force US business practices disadvantageous to exhibitors in Cuba, that is, advance payments, blind- and block-booking, weeklong runs, and single features.[116] For instance, whereas exhibitors in big US cities were moving toward single features, Havana exhibitors insisted that Cuban audiences preferred the "balanced program," including *two* features, a newsreel, and at least one short, often a comedy. Aiming as high as four programs a day, Havana exhibitors squeezed all this content—plus live acts—into two to three hours, sometimes cutting features regardless of story coherence. The endurance of the balanced program in Havana complicates the picture of the absorbed and transported spectator painted above by Del Valle.

But the thing that most disrupted US cinema's claim on Cubans' hearts and minds was its blatant offenses against *Cubanidad*, including US filmmakers' continued use of the "Spanish-American War" to celebrate the United States' "Empire of Liberty" and Cuba's "debt of gratitude."[117] Such had been the case with the Edison Company's 1916 version of *A Message to Garcia*, the story—by then legendary in the United States—of a fearless US hero, Lieutenant Andrew Rowan, who sneaks into Cuba to deliver a message to the *mambí* leader, General Calixto García, namely that US troops were on the way to save the day. Premiered in Havana at the Teatros Campoamor and Fausto in 1917, the film was met with protest. Santos and Artigas' *Cuba Cinematográfica* lambasted it as a "piece of nonsense historically" in which "great pages of our redemptive war have been stained" by the inflation of US heroes at the expense of Cuban ones; at the premiere, they wrote, it had rightly provoked "anger among audience members deeply familiar with this episode of our emancipatory epic."[118] Indeed, after the premiere, public outrage forced Cuban councilmen to rescind a commendation for the film that the Campoamor's exhibitor had obtained from them for publicity purposes.[119] In other words, instead of promoting US imperial hegemony, *A Message to Garcia* in Havana provoked revolutionary Cuban nationalism and its anti-imperialist *independentismo*.

In the 1920s, Cuban nationalism was also provoked by a number of Hollywood films that represented Prohibition-era Havana as a place that corrupted Americans' souls (or, put another way, liberated them from Puritan restraints in titillating ways that sold movie tickets). As just one example, *Cytherea* (1924) set its protagonist's adulterous affair in a notably seedy Havana.[120] Cubans chafed that Cuba was being made synonymous with sin and sex, and *Cuba libre* with the freedom to lose one's inhibitions. They protested *Cytherea* for denigrating them and their country, and the Cuban government prohibited its exhibition as well as the exhibition (temporarily) of all films by *Cytherea's* distributor, First National Pictures (later Warner Bros.).[121]

By the end of 1926, Hollywood's offensive representations of Cuba had provoked enough protest that the Cuban government formed the Comisión Revisora Nacional de Películas (National Film Censor Board). Comprised of Cuba's secretary of the interior and five additional Cuban citizens, the Comisión Revisora's stated objective was to censor films for their moral content and for their capacity to "injure" Cuban "national feelings." However, whereas the Mexican government's film boycotts did effect changes in Hollywood's representations of Mexico and Mexicans, Cuban censorship was largely ineffectual. Just as the *Film Daily* predicted, the US studios' Havana Film Board exercised their considerable sway with the Cuban government—including with President Gerardo Machado himself, who assured the US companies that he was "averse" to such censorship—to ensure that "the [Cuban] board [would] show a liberal disposition and that censorship [would] be exercised with as little pressure and expense on the picture business as possible."[122]

Conclusion

In the thirty years since its arrival in 1897, the cinema had spread wildly in Havana. By the 1920s, Hollywood films enjoyed a virtual monopoly in the city's movie theaters, as many as fifty by decade's end.[123] Many of the biggest of these were owned, leased, financed, and/or managed by North Americans, and even more of them played Hollywood films the majority of the time. Signs of Hollywood's influence could be seen all over the city, on marquees and posters, in newspapers and magazines, in hairstyles and fashion. It is little wonder, then, that anti-imperialist Cuban intellectuals—like that Teatro Fausto manager-turned-film-critic José Manuel Valdés-Rodríguez—felt compelled to address it as part of their revolutionary movement of the late 1920s and early 1930s, as the following chapter explores.

2

Teaching Eyes to See: The Advent of Cuban Film Criticism, 1928–1934

June 1931. In the dark, the curtain rises but the man that everyone has come to see remains momentarily obscured. Onscreen, a large sheet covers a marble monument to "Peace and Prosperity"—"*Paz y Prosperidad*," according to the inter-title. The statue is about to be unveiled by a gaggle of pompous officials, whose speeches are represented as ridiculous kazoo vibrations on the film's soundtrack. As the crowd gazes up expectantly, the sheet lifts to reveal Charlie Chaplin's homeless Little Tramp dozing in the outstretched hand of Prosperity. Rubbing sleep out of his eyes, he attempts to compose himself, tipping his hat to all. He ties his tattered shoes, then catches his ragged pants on the sword of Peace, struggling off balance as a band plays "The Star-Spangled Banner."[1] The Cuban audience gathered here for the much-anticipated Havana premiere of *City Lights* enjoys a collective laugh over Chaplin's send-up of smug North Americans and their empty rhetoric. Swept into Chaplin's tragicomic tale for the next eighty minutes—in which the Little Tramp is persecuted by butlers, bosses, and burglars and in which he is accused of stealing from the rich to provide for the poor—these Havana moviegoers briefly escaped not only the sweltering heat but also the political unrest just outside the cine.

Or did they? If some Havana film critics had their way, the Cuban moviegoers filing out onto the street that night would have been applying *City Light's* sociopolitical critique to the Cuban sociopolitical context. By 1931, a group of Havana intellectuals were taking Chaplin seriously indeed, and they urged Cuban moviegoers to do the same. In Chaplin's films, they saw reflected back to them their own ideas: about art made to mobilize the masses, about the ways the powerful trampled the powerless, and about the challenges of living at the margins of a deeply unjust capitalist modernity. They made teaching

Cubans to see Chaplin's films—indeed, all Hollywood films—from the correct aesthetic and political perspectives an important part of their cultural politics and, ultimately, the revolutionary movement of the early 1930s that would dethrone a US-supported dictator and force the abrogation of the Platt Amendment.

Like their hero José Martí, these Havana intellectuals considered it of grave importance that Cubans "know the truth about the United States," especially the expansionist greed that had shaped its Big Stick and Dollar Diplomacy policies, policies that were now provoking a wave of anti-Yankee movements throughout Latin America. Adopting film criticism as a political modality, Havana intellectuals used Hollywood films as evidence of US culture's soul-deadening materialism, its anti-Hispanic racism, and its ideological stupefactions, even as they began to identify allies in progressive Hollywood filmmakers like Chaplin who made US "entrails" visible to Cuban audiences. At the same time, they pointed to Hollywood business practices as concrete evidence that US imperial hegemony in Cuba amounted to exploitation rather than opportunity and to underdevelopment rather than progress. In other words, it was in the late 1920s and early 1930s that Cuban film criticism began to model engagement with Hollywood characterized by the simultaneous denunciation of its general practices and appropriation of its most critical films toward the construction and mobilization of revolutionary Cuban nationalism.

Sound and Fury: The Arrival of the "Talkies," Dictatorship, and Depression

At the end of the 1920s, a number of seismic changes—cultural, economic, and political—converged to shift Cuban public opinion about the United States and its films. For one thing, the US film industry converted to sound, creating new challenges in its foreign-language markets. At first, Cubans in Havana seemed excited about the novelty of synchronized sound. The Teatro Campoamor's premiere of Warner Bros.' *The Jazz Singer*—with recorded music and effects but only a few lines of speech—in February 1928 was celebrated as a cultural event of the highest order.[2] Quickly on the heels of *The Jazz Singer*, the US studios extended sound synchronization to spoken dialogue and fully committed to the new technology, wiring their studios and theaters for sound, first in the United States and then in the rest of the world. At the end of 1928, Paramount fully wired the Teatro Fausto for sound, making it the first in Latin America; this was vaunted as proof that Havana was Latin America's most modern city. It was in the Fausto, in January 1929, that Cubans saw their first true "talkie": Ernest Lubitsch's *The Patriot*.[3] Paramount followed up on its

FIG. 2.1. The Teatro Rivoli. *Exhibitors Herald and Moving Picture World*, October 11, 1930.

success at the Fausto by installing the same equipment at the Teatro Encanto. To remain competitive, Cuban exhibitors had little choice but to follow suit. By that summer, the eight leading cines in Havana had "gone talkie." And by 1930, even Havana's cines de barrio were wiring for sound, with a number of exhibitors grumbling they would be bankrupted by the costs (mostly paid to US film equipment companies, for whom Cuba was then the third largest foreign market) (see fig 2.1). Cuban musicians working in cines also found cause to complain; through their newly organized union, they argued that "the synchronized movie has robbed us of our livelihoods"[4]

But it wasn't just exhibitors and cine musicians that were troubled by the advent of sound cinema. Many Cubans worried that English-language talkies represented a more threatening "Yankee-izing invasion" than Hollywood's silent films had.[5] Concerns about English were not new in Havana. For decades, Havana intellectuals had been warning that its increasing use among Cubans was tantamount to cultural extinction.[6] But the threat to *Cubanidad* seemed even more acute now that English would be spoken by Cubans' beloved Hollywood stars. In a mainstream Havana newspaper in May 1929, Jorge Mañach wrote about the talkies playing at the Fausto:

> So it is that, in one of Havana's most important cines, which has already passed into foreign hands, it is taken as something natural and not at all an aggression

> to make a thousand people listen to a language that the greater part of them don't understand.
>
> What right is there—I asked, and with me, surely, many other spectators—to force onto a Spanish-speaking Cuban public film dialogue in a foreign language? . . .
>
> [. . .] Isn't this reason to be scandalized and alarmed? [. . .]
>
> To presume that any other language—English primarily—has in Cuba equal validity as our own, is to force us to accept in the cultural order [the same that we have accepted in] the humiliating fiduciary system that makes the dollar the national coin in Cuba.[7]

Working to denaturalize US economic and cultural power, Mañach argues that wiring for sound is proof of Havana's degradation rather than of its progress. He explicitly imagines into being a community of Cubans who see (and hear) things his way ("with me, surely, many other spectators"). Note, too, the gendered rhetoric: the repositioning of the movies from the feminine realms of consumption and leisure to the more masculine realms of conquest, aggression, penetration, and force. Here, Hollywood offends Cuban honor; Hollywood emasculates. The response of Cubans, especially its men, should be outrage and resistance.

As Mañach's final line hints, this nationalist reaction against Hollywood's talkies must be understood within a larger context of local and global developments that were raising grave doubts about US imperial hegemony in Cuba. First of all, President Gerardo Machado was making a mockery of the Cuban constitution and *independentismo*, even though he had campaigned in 1925 promising to reform political corruption and revise the Platt Amendment. Once in office, having received large campaign donations from US companies, Machado worked to enhance their profitability in Cuba; for instance, for General Electric's subsidiary, the monopolistic Cuban Electric Company (which became a major target of anti-Yankee ire), Machado reduced tariffs, vetoed rate reductions, and broke consumer boycotts.[8] He also worked to keep labor cheap and weak, including through his outlawing of the Cuban Communist Party (PCC), founded in 1925. In 1928, Machado revised the constitution to extend his presidential term through 1935. As opposition mounted, he censored the press, forbade demonstrations, created a brutal secret police force (La Porra), and closed the University of Havana, from where students and faculty organized against him. Despite Machado's troubling despotism, US policymakers continued to support his presidency.[9]

The situation deteriorated further when the US stock market crashed in October 1929. As US policymakers sought to protect struggling *domestic* sugar producers, the Hawley-Smoot Act of 1930 greatly reduced the United States' purchase of Cuban sugar. The Cuban economy buckled and unemployment soared, while US banks kept granting loans to Machado's corrupt government to stave off the island's total economic collapse.[10] Anti-Machado and anti-Yankee sentiment grew together, as the dream of Cuban democracy and prosperity seemed to be turning into a nightmare. Conditions were in place for a revolutionary movement against political corruption, economic inequity, and US imperialism.

"Enseñándolos a ver": The Minoristas and the Advent of Cuban Film Criticism

In the late 1920s, a new revolutionary cohort, known as the "Generation of '30," emerged in Havana. An important subsection of this cohort, the Grupo Minorista was a loose coalition of young intellectuals and artists who opposed Machado and US imperial hegemony. They wrote scathing essays about the national condition and developed nationalistic art that celebrated *Cubanidad*. Conversant with international intellectual developments of the interwar years, and with growing anti-imperialism throughout Latin America, minoristas subscribed to a variety of progressive ideas from humanism to communism; some of them cited Marx, most invoked Martí. In May 1927, they declared their objectives in a "Manifesto" published in *Carteles*. The manifesto called for the transformation of Cuban consciousness—for "the revision of false and wasteful values"—toward ending "*imperialismo yanqui*" and "political dictatorships" and toward achieving cultural nationalism, economic independence, and popular democracy.[11] Signatories included the Generation of '30's most important intellectuals, including Alejo Carpentier, Jorge Mañach, Juan Marinello, and Francisco Ichaso. Announcing themselves as dissidents, many minoristas served time in jail and/or in exile over the next five years.[12]

The minoristas endeavored consciously to construct a critical, civic-minded Cuban public roused out of what they considered to be its apathetic acquiescence to the status quo. Thus, they availed themselves of space on the pages and editorial boards of popular periodicals like *Carteles* and *Social*, both of which shifted toward more intellectual rigor and anti-imperialist pronouncements during this period. Beginning in 1927, the minoristas also published *Revista de Avance*, considered the most important Cuban cultural journal of its era along with *Social*.[13] Inclined themselves toward European and Latin American vanguard art, *Revista de Avance*'s editors recognized that for "a political or social crusade" to be realized through cultural criticism, it would have to engage with "the mediums most in consonance with the masses that it intends to affect."[14] In Cuba, this meant having to engage with

Cubans' beloved Hollywood, and so began serious-minded film criticism in the Havana press.

Launching his film column in *Revista de Avance* in June 1928 (notably with a review of Chaplin's *The Circus*), Francisco Ichaso explained that writing about the movies was not "an extravagance, but rather, in a certain way, a necessity." The movies, he wrote, were "eminent parts of modern life," and thus it was necessary "to redeem the cinema from the gossipy and womanly little film sections" in other Havana periodicals.[15] The cinema, in other words, was now deemed worthy of *male* intellectual engagement. Another minorista proclaimed the arrival of "the high critic of cinema" in Havana and contemptuously denounced his inferior antecedent: "*el gacetillero* [the gossip columnist]," who merely reprinted "ready-made" content provided by Hollywood studios.[16] These intellectuals' interest in film criticism arose out of minorista cultural politics but also out of changing exhibition practices. As Hollywood films came to have weeklong runs in Havana's first-run cines and then moved on to subsequent runs in other cines, there was enough time for critics to publish their assessment before the film disappeared from the city. Now, instead of simply frequenting their favorite cine, discriminating moviegoers might choose a cine according to the film being shown, and whether or not a critic recommended it.

But the minoristas also seemed to value film criticism as a way to fly under the radar of Machado's censorship. One especially striking example is offered in *Social's* film section, "Notas del Celuloide," regularly written under the byline "Cinefan" (thought to be a pseudonym for minorista and communist Juan Marinello).[17] In April 1932, Cinefan's first subsection was titled "Continúa la revolución [Carry on the revolution]," just as Cuban workers and lower-rank soldiers were joining more radical elements in widespread protests against Machado. For a first, long paragraph, Cinefan feigned apologetic for broaching the topic of revolution in *Social*'s film section. "Regarding the very interesting process of revolution," he facetiously assured the reader that he would limit himself to discussing film fiction and not political reality: "In this section, we can only talk of tyrants, assassins, thieves, gunmen, criminals, political operators, and villains *of the screen*. Our heroes, our martyrs, our men of courage and our idealists appear before the camera and the microphone to bring to life—falsely, intensely, splendidly!—heroic deeds of high rank and epic poems of liberation." Despite such (disingenuous) demurring, Cinefan did *not* abide by a limited role for the film critic, as he demonstrated in his coded call to arms against tyrannical despots that followed: "In the beautiful lie of the cinema, the blood of heroes is fertile and they defeat the despot in a sudden and fatal flash. . . . The cinema . . . links together the black pearl of an overthrown tyrant [with] the miraculous ruby of a people that knows that to regain their liberty will cost blood." Here the critic deftly appropriates Hollywood's freedom-fighting masculinity to advocate (slyly) for violent struggle to overthrow Machado. And while he warned revolutionaries not to expect the sort of quick "happy ending" seen in the movies, he concluded the column by assuring them of their revolution's "inevitable success."[18] Tellingly, Cinefan was disdainful of Hollywood's facile oversimplifications (sarcastic and dismissive on the surface) but was not above deploying them to inspire real-life heroism on behalf of revolutionary Cuban nationalism (earnest at heart).

In other days' film sections, Cinefan did stay focused on the cinema and on his stated objective to convert "bourgeois spectators" into "intelligent spectators" by making them see the inhumanity of Hollywood's business practices, as well as the ideological underpinnings of its mediocre products.[19] He wrote that Hollywood's profit-driven executives treated their stars inhumanely, working them like dogs and making their private lives the subject of studio publicity, thus demonstrating the "elastic conception of human dignity that sustains North American businessmen as a general rule." Worse yet, Hollywood magnates were sacrificing the cinema's potential as Art on the altar of their "commercial criteria" and were turning their studios "into agents for the diffusion and penetration of imperialist Yankee politics." Cinefan made no apologies for the Marxism and anti-imperialist nationalism informing his analyses. He deemed the US government's use of trade policy to help Hollywood push its "made in U.S.A." film products around the world to be "among the most dangerous manifestations of capitalist Yankee imperialism." Goodness knows, he wrote, the great people of Lenin's Russian revolution would never stand for it. Nor should Cubans, went the implication. Thus Cinefan denounced the Cuban exhibitors who showed Hollywood films exclusively as *vende-patrias* (traitors; literally "homeland sellers"), motivated by "*patriotería del dinero* [allegiance to the dollar]" over allegiance to country.[20]

Occasionally, Cinefan did get around to discussing a specific Hollywood film, precious few of which he recommended. He considered D. W. Griffith's *Abraham Lincoln* (1930) to be a "very poor version of this great man's life," stripped of its revolutionary implications, obviously scripted so as "not to stir up old resentments."[21] Many a Hollywood film was branded "typically mediocre," its actors nothing more than "soulless marionettes." But Cinefan did identify some exceptions. For instance, he admired the work of the Austro-Hungarian Jewish émigré director Joseph Von Sternberg, not least of all for his "rebellious attitude" toward Paramount's "industrial management," from which the director demanded autonomy.[22] Cinefan recommended Von Sternberg's *Morocco* (1930) as a socially critical film from which he could extract a usable lesson: that Americans are spiritually starved materialists, chasing after "the false pleasures that money buys," driven by "ambition, egoism, hypocrisy, vice, and malice."[23]

Cinefan's minorista colleague, the aforementioned Jorge Mañach—a Harvard graduate, Martí scholar, *Revista de Avance* editor, and cofounder in 1931 of the ABC Revolutionary Society (an underground organization that mounted violent attacks against the Machado regime)—also dabbled in film criticism.[24] Like Cinefan, Mañach found usable material in Von Sternberg's work. In *Revista de Avance* in July 1928, he wrote a review of Von Sternberg's *Underworld*, often cited as the first gangster film. Echoing Martí's "entrails," Mañach wrote that the film, set in New York City, "admirably exposed the underside of the modern world." Then, the critic went on to contrast *Underworld*'s mobster-protagonist Bull Weed (George Bancroft) to Robin Hood-esque figures from Spanish and revolutionary Cuban folklore. Bull Weed was *not* to be held up as an outlaw hero like "the Seven Children of Ecijia" (Spanish patriot-guerrillas who stole from the rich to fight Napoleon's invasion in the early nineteenth century) or like Cuba's own martyred Manuel García (who stole from the Spanish colonial elite to fund the poor *mambises* in the late nineteenth century). Unlike these unimpeachable Hispanic bandit-heroes who sought "social equality" and answered to the higher call of the nation, *Underworld's* Bull Weed is just a mob boss seeking personal gain, Mañach explained.[25] In other words, Mañach's film review did a lot: reclaimed a usable Hispanic past, celebrated a Cuban national hero, implied the righteousness of raising arms against tyranny and foreign domination, *and* highlighted brutish greed as a defining characteristic of US life.

As noted briefly above, Cinefan and Mañach's fellow minorista (and fellow cofounder of the ABC Revolutionary Society), Francisco Ichaso also began to write film reviews.[26] His review of King Vidor's *The Crowd* (1928) in *Revista de Avance* in August 1928 further illustrates the contours of minorista film criticism. Before turning laudatory attention to *The Crowd*'s exposé of US working-class woes, Ichaso emphasizes to his reader that it is a step above the usual "ostentation and absurdity of . . . all these [Hollywood] productions [that constitute] the '*sopa boba*' [foolish stew] that the Sunday public gobbles up with avidity and perverse pleasure." In contrast, *The Crowd* is an exceptional Hollywood film that makes art from "the daily life" of a "common man." Ichaso goes on to highlight a famous early scene that draws the viewer's eye to the looming verticality of skyscrapers and, as Ichaso puts it, the dwarfed "anthill of men on New York's streets." Ichaso admires the technical ingenuity that allows the camera to travel up one towering building, in through a window, into an enormous room and then along its infinite rows of desks occupied by anonymous accountants, emphasizing their lack of individuality and freedom. The accountants are "numbers" tallying numbers, "insignificant squires of this standardized multitude," Ichaso notes.[27] The scene, if not the entire film, is a diatribe against the emasculating effects of US capitalist modernity, or at least according to Ichaso's interpretation.

One of the scene's accountants is the protagonist John Sims (John Murray), who still operates under the delusion (which Ichaso calls "tragic Bovarism") that he will "be something big someday," that his "ship will come in," according to the film's inter-titles. The film, and Ichaso's review of it, constantly undermines Sims's romanticism about the American Way of upward mobility available to all. The film moves from the grand expectations pronounced at Sims's birth (a "man the world's going to hear from alright!") and his hopeful arrival in New York City, to his life in a cramped apartment, his downward spiral into poverty, and finally his suicide attempt.[28] Especially in Ichaso's interpretation, *The Crowd* debunks Horatio Algeresque individualism. The omnipresent crowd, which Ichaso declares "the true protagonist of the work," is ever pressing upon Sims. It threatens to overcome him with the "sensation of being a number that is accentuated . . . in the great cities [which are] prisons in their way." Applying the film's social determinism to his Cuban readers' lives, Ichaso employs the first-person plural, "*We* are numbers."[29] In their futile race to get ahead, Cubans should expect precisely what Sims finds: fleeting pleasures and inevitable sorrow.

While Ichaso continued to write for *Revista de Avance* until a wave of censorship and arrests closed its doors in September 1930, his fellow minorista Alejo Carpentier was forced into exile early in 1928, shortly after he helped to found that magazine. From Paris, though, Carpentier continued to contribute to *Social* and *Carteles*.[30] Remembered today as a world-class novelist, Carpentier was also known by contemporaries as an astute and prolific cultural critic. Perhaps least remembered today, his writings about the cinema were part of the minoristas' efforts to teach Cubans proper ways to see not only films but also the national condition and the imperative to change it.

In articles appearing in *Carteles* in 1928, Carpentier complained that the profit-motivated US studios had dumped on the world's moviegoers "some thousands of completely idiotic movies, without any artistic valor, that only serve to show off the agreeable figure of this or that highly coiffed boy or of some *girl* [in English]." Like Cinefan, he chafed that Hollywood "studios are in the hands of men with commercial interests, devoid of culture, who are only interested in making films with the greatest possible speed. The concept of the '*business-man*' [in English] has prevailed tyrannically over the artistic ideal."[31] Indeed, Carpentier explained, these exploitative moguls dehumanized the very stars that Cubans so adored and aspired to emulate. In a 1932 *Carteles* article, Carpentier worked to disillusion Havana youth who dreamed of making it big in Hollywood themselves. "If they only knew the truth," he writes, followed up by an exposé of that truth: about actors' fourteen-hour days; their eyes ruined by high-powered lighting; their skin destroyed by cosmetics; their heads throbbing from directors' bullhorns; and their nerves frayed and morals compromised by the demands of stardom—only to be discarded readily because of advancing age or public disinterest. And the end product of this inhumane, assembly-line Hollywood production: only one good film for every mediocre one hundred.[32]

But Carpentier was also an emphatic defender of the cinema as a new art form with unrealized potentials. Late in 1928, Carpentier wrote that, despite being in its "tender infancy," the international cinema had offered to "those that love the cinema—as he who writes this article," some twenty masterpieces in just a quarter-century, which included just a handful of US-made movies, that is, Griffith's *Broken Blossoms* (1919) and *Way Down East* (1920); and Chaplin's *The Kid* (1921), *The Gold Rush* (1925), and *The Circus* (1928).[33] Along with a number of German films, he especially admired Soviet films like Sergei Eisenstein's *Battleship Potemkin* (1925), about a popular uprising against the Russian tsarist regime in 1905, which Carpentier called a "revelation."[34] The previous spring, in May 1928, *Potemkin* had shown at the Teatro Nacional after a protracted struggle between its exhibitor and the Comisión Revisora, which deemed the film to be communist propaganda that might incite Cubans' "always dangerous passions."[35]

The films that made Machado's censors worry, those were the ones Carpentier recommended. In *Carteles* in July 1932, Carpentier explained that he liked films that showed that the world was a "spectacle of imbalance." "War, revolts, threats of war, demonstrations broken up by gunshots, dictatorships, hunger, misery . . . the sadistic tortures that are applied in certain police headquarters [and] millions of unemployed workers. . . . [Such films show] that the moment in which we live would be intolerable, if we weren't sustained by the hope of a great general sweeping, that will end the vices of this old barbaric world." As further examples, he offered a number of German films, like G. W. Pabst's *Comradeship* (1931), that had a "revolutionary character, for the reflection they offer us of the great inconformity of the masses, of their anger, of their grievances."[36] To any Cuban reader, it would have been clear that Carpentier was thinking not only of these films' Soviet and German settings. He was thinking of his own Cuba, its dictator, its sadistic secret police, its hunger and misery, its ongoing revolt, and Cubans' hopes for sweeping changes.

So, too, should Cubans keep that local context in mind when at the cine, with such films helping them to see it more clearly. The best films, Carpentier wrote in *Social*, "are capable of educating our eyes anew, teaching them to see [*enseñandolos a ver*], revealing to them the things that surround us, and over which we pass every day, insensible."[37] Unfortunately, "very few people know how to see a film," Carpentier wrote, scolding those spectators who gleam from a film only its "frivolous anecdote." "Learn to see a movie," Carpentier intoned in direct address, and one would achieve aesthetic and political enlightenment.[38]

"Drag[ging] the Public Out of Its Somnolence": Valdés-Rodríguez in the Machado Era

In teaching Cubans how to see movies in these ways, no one was more important than José Manuel Valdés-Rodríguez. He was at the center of this generation of film writers and revolutionary activists, just as he would be a major influence on the revolutionary generation of the 1950s. Interestingly enough, Valdés-Rodríguez began his career in the cinema working for Paramount. In 1921, at the age of twenty-five, he was hired as an assistant manager at that US company's Teatro Fausto, where he spent the next eight years watching Cubans watch movies, collecting insights like the ones with which the previous chapter opened. But he grew disenchanted with Hollywood's growing monopoly over Havana's screens. Beginning in 1927, Valdés-Rodríguez began to hold screenings at his home in Vedado, showing films that were otherwise hard to see in Havana. Onto his neighbor's garage wall, he projected German and Soviet films like Eisenstein's *Battleship Potemkin* and *October* and Vsevolod Pudovkin's revolutionary trilogy (*Mother*, *The End of St. Petersburg*, and *Storm over Asia*). These screenings gathered an impressive array of intellectuals and activists. Alongside such Cuban luminaries as Fernando Ortíz and Pablo de la Torriente Brau, minoristas in attendance included Marinello, Raúl Roa, and José Zacarías Tallet.[39] Given the films shown and the audience assembled, it is likely that post-screening discussions were rife with anti-Machado and anti-imperialist pronouncements.

Valdés-Rodríguez quit his job at the Fausto in May 1929 (the same month that Mañach launched his criticism of the talkies therein). Having dabbled in film criticism for a few Havana periodicals using the pseudonym Don Q., Valdés-Rodríguez was hired to write the film column for the Sunday supplement in *El Mundo*, one of Havana's most widely circulated newspapers, with a largely middle-class readership.[40] From 1929 to 1933, he also wrote reviews and articles for minorista publications including *Revista de Avance* and *Social*. In the latter, he promoted Soviet cinema and derided Hollywood, whose "banality and stupidity" should "drag . . . the public out of its somnolence, to violent protests."[41] Like many of his compatriots, Valdés-Rodríguez was radicalized during these years: he read Marx and Lenin, joined the Cuban chapter of the Communist International's Anti-Imperialist League, sheltered anti-Machado insurgents, and held clandestine meetings in his home.[42]

In 1932, Valdés-Rodríguez served as an editor and correspondent for the Marxist journal *Experimental Cinema*, published in the United States from 1930 through 1934. For the journal, he also contributed an essay entitled "Hollywood: Sales Agent of American Imperialism." In it, Valdés-Rodríguez rails against the history of US meddling in Cuban affairs—such that Cuba remained a "colony disguised as a Republic!"—and especially Hollywood's "pernicious" role in perpetuating Cubans' colonization. "What a weapon the bourgeoisie and American imperialism have in cinema!" he seethes.[43] He then offers a condensed version of the minoristas' cultural politics vis-à-vis Hollywood business practices and film content. He explains that "a moving picture trust has been formed in Cuba by the American picture companies, which fixes the prices of the tickets, the size of advertisements in the newspapers, and which obstructs European and Soviet films." Hollywood's role in the United States' "imperialistic scheme" was not only economic but also cultural, he continues: "By means of its pictures, Hollywood infects all other countries with the philistine, hypocritical, rotten American life-conception. At the same time, to the American masses, Hollywood presents the Latin American people as the lowest, most repulsive scoundrels on earth." For the latter charge, he offers the evidence of films like MGM's *The Cuban Love Song* (1931) and lists the Hispanic stereotypes naturalized in them: Latins are treacherous, sinful, slothful, and "of low mentality."[44] Like Martí, Valdés-Rodríguez warns that such representations had real effects, making US citizens receptive to their government's imperialist endeavors, based on the ideological construction that Latin Americans are incapable of self-rule.

For the most part, though, it was not the US citizen but the Cuban with whom Valdés-Rodríguez was most concerned. He writes, "The whole population of Cuba suffers drastically from the influence of Hollywood pictures." The Cuban bourgeoisie were hypnotized by the false promises of upward mobility within Hollywood films, which "glorify the world in which they, snobs that they are, wish to live." He explains,

> To the boys and girls of the Cuban bourgeoisie, there is nothing so worthy of imitation as the boys and girls they see in the American films, and they want

> to shape their lives in conformity to the lives of motion picture heroes and heroines. From all this there arises . . . a narrow, American, utilitarian life-conception, an ardent paean to those who *win*, no matter how.
>
> . . . .
>
> Hollywood pictures are furiously individualistic. They exalt what the North Americans call "self-made men," the men who have always accomplished great success by themselves, as if in society (especially in a society so highly interrelated as modern capitalist society) things were like that.[45]

According to Valdés-Rodríguez, Hollywood had Cuba's middle-class aspirants duped into imagining that they, with enough individual effort and singular self-interestedness, would come out on top. Here the critic works to expose and disarticulate that illusion.

Worse still was how Hollywood prevented Cuba's working class from achieving "class consciousness," through its films' obfuscations of capitalism's structural inequities. In this, Valdés-Rodríguez is not even willing to make an exception of Chaplin, who expresses his "social preoccupation" too timidly: "Both Charles Chaplin and the average American director do the same thing: evade the social problem," he writes.

> In the American film there is always a perfect understanding between Capital and Labor, between master and wage-slave, the former (Capital) as well as the State [are] like a tender, comprehending father. No mistake in this: if you are obedient and laborious, they (the bosses) will recognize it some day and "raise" you with a gracious gesture. If there is some cruelty or injustice . . . then, at the end of the picture, with God's will, everything is fixed and the good get their recompense.
>
> And the Cuban worker, who lives in very different conditions, with a low salary and high living costs, without liberty or the right to express his own class convictions, [and] poisoned with the slogans and lies of the American films is supposed to hope that someday his country, under the capitalistic system, will be as "*civilized*" as the great North American Republic. And even more: the Cuban worker is supposed to feel gratitude to that Anglo-Saxon race, so "pure," "strong" and "clean," helping this ill-disciplined and sometimes revolutionary little nation to acquire honest political institutions, good finances, etc., etc.[46]

Hollywood disingenuously offered dazzling promises to Cubans: the happy ending of personal success and national progress granted for submission to foreign bosses. With biting sarcasm, Valdés-Rodríguez sought to disarticulate these discourses of upward mobility and gratitude, crucial to capitalist and imperialist ideologies operating in Havana respectively. A footnote in the essay leaves no doubt that he was writing not only to make Cubans rethink their abeyance to US imperialism but also to "the brutal Machado," who was a puppet to the latter, just like all the Cuban presidents that had preceded him since 1902.[47]

"A Dagger Blow": Chaplin, Minoristas, and the Enlightened Cuban Audience

While Valdés-Rodríguez was unwilling to make an exception of Chaplin's films, most minoristas were. In fact, in their project to direct Cubans to the right sort of films and the right way to see them, they found no greater ally than Chaplin. The British comic had been a top star in Havana since at least 1918, when the capital's major theaters had shown *A Dog's Life*. In December 1921, the Teatro Capitolio broke box office records with *The Kid*, in which the Little Tramp raises an abandoned orphan, and Chaplin raises the level of pathos and social criticism in his films.[48] By the time *The Gold Rush* and *The Circus* premiered in Havana in 1925 and 1928 respectively, Chaplin was a staple of Havana film columns and fanzines, which reported on his films, his rags-to-riches biography, and his global success.[49] And when *City Lights* premiered in Havana in June 1931, a great deal of advance publicity had assured Cubans that the long-awaited film confirmed Chaplin's status as the cinema's greatest artist.[50]

For some years, in fact, the minoristas had been proclaiming Chaplin a great artist who offered profound criticisms of capitalist modernity. As noted above, Ichaso had inaugurated his foray into film criticism in *Revista de Avance* in 1928 with a glowing review of *The Circus*. In it, Ichaso announced that, in future columns too, he would "gab incessantly in recognition of Chaplin's genius."[51] Carpentier also wrote continually of Chaplin's artistry in the highest terms: "There are passages of his movies that I love intimately, like I can love some movements of Bach or Stravinsky, or certain verses of Rimbaud." *The Kid* was a "poem," *The Gold Rush* was a "marvel," and *City Lights* was a "masterpiece."[52] *Social*'s Cinefan also fawned over Chaplin, "the most stupendous tragedian that has ever graced the silver screen"; *City Lights* was "the most perfect movie of our times," a "masterwork" that proved conclusively the failure of the talkies, which were patently incapable of achieving Chaplin's universal humanism comprehensible across all languages.[53]

As minoristas made an exception (and a mascot and a mirror) of Chaplin, they also sought to Hispanicize him, to make him their own. Along with using his French moniker "Charlot," Cubans (and other Latin Americans) affectionately referred to the Little Tramp as "Canillitas" (little newsboy), granting him what one film scholar calls "honorary *latinidad*."[54] Relatedly, they traced Chaplin's artistic genealogy back to seventeenth-century Spanish picaresque novels (most famously Miguel de Cervantes' *Don Quixote*), with their accidental commoner-heroes taking on institutionalized power (i.e., the Catholic Church, nobility); their satirical critiques of corruption and hypocrisy; their sympathies for the poor; and their episodic form and tragicomic tone. In *Revista de Avance*, Mañach explained that "the pathos—and the philosophical resonance—of Chaplin's humor" was derived from the clash between the Little Tramp's incorruptible innocence—just like the "moving ineptitude of Don Quixote"—and the world's "maliciousness."[55] Carpentier likewise proclaimed the Little Tramp to be "a Quixote in a minor key," filled "with idealism but tormented by the ambushes of an implacable reality."[56] Like Quixote, the Little Tramp demonstrates that romantic individualism is laughably (if tragically) delusional in a world in which fates are predetermined by an inflexible social system.

Thus, the minoristas instructed Cuban spectators that Chaplin should be understood *not* as a common clown but as a great poet, expressing both misery and the assertion of human dignity in its face. To "laugh uproariously" at the Little Tramp's antics put one in the low category of spectators who "have the sensibility of crude artillery, incapable of perceiving the most delicate shades of poetry," wrote Carpentier. "In the ten vanguard cinemas of Paris today, where Chaplin's productions are projected, his works provoke scarce hilarity. The learned public knows to see them as poetic creations," Carpentier noted.[57] Learned Cubans should do the same, if they wanted to consider themselves cultured. Back in Havana, Cinefan joined the minorista chorus, writing, "We have always believed that while some millions of inhabitants of this planet adore Chaplin, only a few 'understand' him." But that didn't make him any less revolutionary, Cinefan explained: Chaplin's Little Tramp "lives as a dagger blow in the side of a hypocritical, exploitative, immoral and unjust civilization."[58]

Thus, according to the minoristas, the correct response to Chaplin's films was aesthetic and political enlightenment: appreciate his artistry and become outraged by the social ills he revealed. Properly understood, Chaplin would arouse Cubans from what the minoristas had diagnosed as their chronic resignation and would mobilize them to action. In his *Revista de Avance* review of *The Circus*, Ichaso offered a literal invocation of a more active spectatorship. He wrote prescriptively that "in some moments . . . the adventures of the film startle us to the point that we feel the desire to straighten up in our seats and scream at the projectionist: 'enough, enough!'"[59] For his part, Carpentier wrote that the Little Tramp teaches that there is heroism in fighting for ideals; the proper response is not despair or surrender. "Life is hard," wrote Carpentier, "and Chaplin fights fiercely."[60] So too, went the implication, should Cubans.

From Silence to Sound, From Words to Action: The Revolution of 1933

If minoristas loved Chaplin's silent films for all they (could be made to) say, they despised Hollywood's new sound films. Recall Mañach's fulmination against the advent of English-language talkies at the Fausto in May 1929. That July, Mañach's minorista colleague Raúl Roa (contributor to *Revista de Avance*, member of the radical Student Left Wing and the Anti-Imperialist League) responded to Mañach in a public letter in *Orto*, another magazine associated with the minoristas.[61] The young Roa wrote that the talkies represented "cinematic imperialism residing in Hollywood just as economic imperialism resides in Wall Street." He decried Vitaphone and Movietone as "new Golden Calves," false idols of an errant people.

> But fortunately some—you [Mañach] in the first place—have valiantly raised their voices in objection. I raise mine now. . . . The deplorable thing is precisely this: the sheep-like attitude of our public. Its incredible meekness in resisting the foreign invasion—intuitively presumed mortal to *cubanidad*—makes one wonder if we are a people without any sense of history. Vitaphone and Movietone represent something more than aesthetically worthless talking air: they represent one more—extremely powerful—vehicle of Yankee penetration in our country. . . . They have no right to insult the public with dialogues in a strange tongue. . . . North American imperialism today has two central stations in Cuba: the naval—and repugnant—one at Guantánamo and the cinematic one—also repugnant—at the Fausto and its branch cine the Encanto. . . . To the definitive disappearance of these our best efforts must be mobilized.[62]

Here Roa adopts the same tactic of gendered rhetoric Mañach did: the submissive Cuban body politic has been penetrated by the Yankees; the proper response of true men is not to genuflect before US technological ingenuity but to mobilize collectively in valiant defense of the nation's insulted honor. Roa's public letter to Mañach underscores again the consciousness—and militancy—with which minoristas approached their intervention in Hollywood's influence, and the priority they placed on it in the forging of anti-imperialist revolutionary nationalism.

Despite the minoristas' concerns about the Cuban masses' sheep-like abeyance, Cubans did seem to become less enamored of Hollywood, not least of all thanks to the dissemination of the minoristas' critical practices. In 1932, in an essay entitled "Cinemanía," popular Cuban writer Wenceslao Gálvez y del Monte described his conversion to more critical spectatorship, which he attributed to his reading of minorista publications. He began by poking fun at his adolescent Hollywood fandom, describing himself as "more submissive than a slave." His bedroom walls were adorned with photos of US stars, and he was as eager to know about their lives as his sister was to know about the lives of the saints. He recalls his childhood idolatry: "That which I admire most is the American hero. Such a haughty way of dodging the greatest dangers! He always triumphs in his endeavors." But Gálvez quickly clarifies that he has been disillusioned of his awe. He continues, "A cavalcade of Americans mounting hills, fording rivers, leaping barriers, is intimidating. But are they, indeed, as grand as they seem? One night I was determined to decipher the mystery and I went to see closely a roll of film. How very little they are! They only seem grand because we see them through an augmenting lens reflected on the screen."[63] Like the minoristas, though with more humor, Gálvez disparages noncritical spectatorship. Literally disarticulating the power of the cinematic apparatus, he argues for a mode of "looking up" at the United States that eschews genuflection.

In the late 1920s and early 1930s, the Cuban public also expressed its disenchantment at the box office. The US studios' revenues and their market share in Havana were down annually from 1929 through 1933.[64] "Economic conditions coupled with the current revolution, are seriously handicapping the film industry," reported the manager of Warner Bros.' Havana office in 1931.[65] Indeed, as if in answer to Roa's call to arms, anti-Machado insurgents exploded bombs in the Encanto, Nacional, and Wilson theaters in the winter of 1930, resulting in panics and injuries.[66] But minorista agitation, the faltering Cuban economy, and isolated explosions could not account for all of Hollywood's declining popularity. As Cinefan explained to "alarmed exhibitors" in February 1931, while Havana cines might be half-empty at curtain time due to the "terror of bombs, political distress, [and] economic crisis," they were "4/5th empty" at show's end due to the public's disgust at Hollywood's sound films, often presented with little to no translation, sometimes simply presented as silents, with or without a few explanatory Spanish-language inter-titles appended to the film's beginning.[67]

United States' observers came to a similar conclusion about Cubans' negative reaction to Hollywood's sound films. Reporting from Havana in the fall of 1930, a *Motion Picture News* correspondent surmised that Cubans did not like "the Gringo talkies" at all: "until all prints shown in Cuba are [dubbed or titled in] Spanish, those people are just not going to go to the pictures," he lamented.[68] But when the Hollywood studios did start dubbing in Spanish, Cubans were not impressed. Cubans found American artists speaking Spanish to be unbelievable, which broke the cinema's spell; "the illusion is not complete," reported the US Commerce Department.[69] Worse yet were Hollywood's ghastly Spanish-language-version films (some seventy made between 1929 and 1931): meagerly financed Spanish-language versions of English-language talkies, sometimes reset in some vaguely Latin land with US actors mangling Spanish. As minorista critics liked to point out, these version films were filled with denigrating stereotypes and treated Hispanic dialects and cultures as interchangeable.[70] Thus, Hollywood's ill-handled conversion to sound helped to reveal Hollywood's profit motives and superficiality, as well as its Anglo-centrism and anti-Hispanic racism, just as minoristas were working to do the same.

As the Cuban press and public soured on Hollywood, Cuban politicians responded. Citing "patriotic motives," Cuban congressmen introduced bills to ban English-language talkies and to give preferential tariffs to films from Spanish-speaking countries. Though these bills were defeated by the combined lobbying efforts of the US studios' Havana Film Board and Hollywood-dependent Havana exhibitors, they were evidence of rising sentiment against Hollywood. Taxes on US distributors were raised and loopholes they had exploited for years were closed. The municipality of Havana established significant tax deductions for cines that maintained their orchestras, responding to the grievances of the Cuban musicians' union against Hollywood sound cinema.[71] Indeed, organized labor was on the rise during the movement against Machado and immediately thereafter. These years also saw the formation of a projectionists' union and another—the Unión de Empleados de Espectáculos Cinematográficos de Cuba (UEECC)—for all other cine employees (i.e., box office attendants, ushers, janitors), whose members demanded higher wages and an eight-hour workday, and who joined waves of striking workers as part of the anti-Machado movement.[72]

Moreover, Cubans became even less tolerant of insults to *Cubanidad* or to Latin America more generally.[73] In the fall of 1930, the Cuban embassy in Washington protested the "distorted and disparaging" version of Havana presented in American Pathé's *Her Man* and successfully lobbied the MPPDA to demand cuts of specific references to the city. But the changes were superficial; anyone watching the film can recognize Havana through its distinctive architecture and the film's compendium of pre–Production Code representations of that city: a Caribbean port where Americans gather in dive bars full of drunken US sailors, prostitutes, and local conmen.[74] In fact, the unresolved insult of *Her Man* helps explain Cubans' adamant reaction against MGM's *The Cuban Love Song* (1931). Rumblings about the film began even before its US release. In November 1931, Cuban composer Ernesto Lecuona returned from its set disgusted. He told *Bohemia*'s new film critic, Germinal Barral (aka Don Galaor), that Cuban male characters were played for laughs and were represented as weak and easily subjugated to the US Marines, including the film's US protagonist, Terry (Lawrence Tibbett). Further, Lecuona reported, Terry's

Cuban love interest, "Nenita," was played by Lupe Vélez, a Mexican whose accent made her unbelievable as a "*cubana*," and the film's sets were recycled from MGM Spanish-language-version films about Spain, as if all Hispanic cultures were one brown-skinned, tile-roofed blur. In sum, Lecuona deemed the movie "a disaster, *from a Cuban point of view*" and predicted that it would invite protest.[75] He was right. After screening the film in New York, a number of Cubans protested to the Comisión Revisora that it "depicts the island as an uncivilized country where the natives are half-clothed and bare-footed."[76] The Havana press erupted in outrage; and the Cuban exhibitors' union, the ANE, banned the film and then boycotted all MGM films until the studio withdrew *The Cuban Love Song* from circulation in January 1932.[77]

Back in Hollywood, the head of the MPPDA's Foreign Department, Frederick Herron, was caught off-guard, reporting that he was "having a Hell of a time" with "the conflagration that this picture has caused." "Every paper in Havana and in all the cities in Cuba are burning us alive," he fumed. Herron blamed the fracas on what he diagnosed to be Cubans' "super-sensitiveness"; they were overreacting to a handful of cultural inaccuracies (insignificant, to him) and the film's favorable representation of the US Marines, who Cubans considered "the symbol of *so-called* American despotism," Herron complained. Finally, Herron especially blamed the irrational anti-Hollywood bent of Cuban periodicals: "There is one thing that Latin-American newspapers love and that is to pick up something that is an attack on American pictures, and God knows our receipts from that part of the world are shot to Hell as it is." In view of this box office decline, he concluded, "I do think we have to tighten up on these Latin-American things."[78] Though patronizing and dismissive of Latin Americans' grievances, Herron was right about the US film industry's problems in Latin America, about growing disenchantment with US imperialism and Hollywood's role in it, and about the local press's role in fueling those trends.

A little over a year after *The Cuban Love Song* controversy, popular protests against Machado and the Platt Amendment swelled to their high mark. By July of 1933, the US State Department was convinced that Machado had to go so that order could be restored. The US embassy initiated talks between the regime and the opposition, seeking to ease Machado out and manage a transition to the opposition's most moderate figures. But Machado balked as did the more emphatically anti-imperialist elements of the opposition—the PCC, trade unions, and radical students—who rejected US mediation as just one more example of "Yankee meddling." As the talks unraveled, a Havana bus driver strike ballooned into a general strike. The city—and the rest of the island—virtually shut down. Encouraged by the US embassy and citing the imminence of a US intervention, a group of Cuban military officers successfully demanded Machado's resignation on August 12, 1933.[79]

But the provisional president they named, Carlos Céspedes, was decried as a US puppet, and violent protests continued. Early in September, a group of anti-Machado junior officers revolted against their superior officers. Among those revolting was a light-skinned Afro-Cuban of humble origins named Sergeant Fulgencio Batista. Supported by the leading student organization, Batista and his fellow junior officers—including one who had just spent time in Hollywood playing bit parts in Westerns—grew their "Sergeants' Revolt" into a bloodless coup on September 4, 1933.[80] They named as provisional president Ramón Grau San Martín, a University of Havana professor with strong anti-Machado credentials; and they named Batista "Revolutionary Leader" of the Cuban military. Over the next four months, with the motto "Cuba for the Cubans," Grau set out to actualize the objectives of the revolution. He officially disavowed the Platt Amendment; instituted land and prolabor reforms (e.g., a minimum wage, maximum hours, and the "Law of 50 Percent," which required that companies operating in Cuba employ 50 percent native-born workers); decreed the reduction of electricity rates; and granted autonomy to the University of Havana.[81]

For their part, the minoristas were split about Grau's "100 Days Government." They joined the growing schisms into which the revolutionary movement devolved, schisms that would fuel political violence for decades to come. Carpentier remained in Paris while Marinello returned from exile but criticized Grau's administration as insufficiently revolutionary. Mañach defended the recent developments in Cuba as "the first phase of a genuine revolution"; Cubans were becoming "the masters of their own destiny," having achieved a "profound mobilization of the national will against the historic causes which had alienated it." But, Mañach warned, the revolution would not be complete until the eradication of those historic causes: a corrupt political system that encouraged despotism, economic dependency on the United States, and the Platt Amendment.[82]

Throughout the fall of 1933, various revolutionary factions formed new underground societies and "action groups," and they clashed in the streets. Taking advantage of this disarray, and green-lighted by the US embassy (which had refused to recognize Grau's presidency), Batista—now self-identifying as the revolution's one true defender—forced Grau's resignation in January 1934. Grau went into exile in Miami, and Batista installed a puppet in the presidency. Assured that its interests would be protected, the United States immediately recognized this new government and restored diplomatic relations.[83] Thus, the 1933 revolution's most radical potentials were effectively circumscribed, and

FIG. 2.2. A Havana cine is closed during a period of revolutionary protests against Machado. Walker Evans (American, St. Louis, Missouri, 1903–1975), *Havana Cinema*, 1933, Gelatin silver print; 14.8 × 23.5 cm (5 13/16 × 9 1/4 in.). (Courtesy of the J. Paul Getty Museum, Los Angeles © Walker Evans Archive, the Metropolitan Museum of Art)

Batista began his six-year behind-the-scenes rule through a series of puppet presidents. Henceforth, Cubans came to call the early 1930s movement "the Frustrated Revolution," connoting disappointment but also the worthiness of aspirations left unfulfilled, just as they had been unfulfilled after 1898.

During this tumultuous year from the spring of 1933 through the spring of 1934, Hollywood's falling stock in Cuba plummeted further. Radical students continued to place bombs in cines while the general chaos—and anti-Yankee fervor—closed many others. At the beginning of this period, Walker Evans (later of *Let Us Now Praise Famous Men* renown) arrived in Havana, on assignment to provide photographs to accompany journalist Carleton Beals's *The Crime of Cuba*, an exposé that very much implicated US imperialism in the island's contemporary predicament. To capture a sense of the city's Americanization as well as Cubans' deflated optimism about it, Evans turned his lens to at least two Havana cines, plastered with Hollywood advertisements but closed due to the unrest.[84] (See fig. 2.2.) In August 1933, just days after Machado's resignation, *Variety* reported that "a tightening of the ill-feeling [toward Americans] among the revolutionary faction" was keeping more and more cines closed. A few days later, the *Film Daily* reported that an angry mob had attacked two Paramount News cameramen who just barely escaped as shots were fired at their car. During Grau's provisional presidency, *Variety* reported that revolutionary ferment continued, characterized by "high anti-[US] intervention feelings here," which negatively affected the box office.[85] Disturbances in cines forced another round of closings again in November 1933. One day after Grau's resignation in January 1934, *Variety* announced the reinstatement of martial law: "Theatres may open if they wish to but there are no patrons brave enough to risk attending them." Indeed, Cuban cines remained closed for some time. At the end of 1934, the *Film Daily Yearbook* noted that of the island's four hundred movie theaters, less than half were operating, and even those only opened their doors sporadically "due to the very abnormal conditions prevailing in Cuba."[86]

Conclusion

Conditions did slowly improve, and Cuban cines reopened in the mid-1930s. By the late 1930s and early 1940s, Hollywood had recovered the market share it lost during the 1933 revolution. But to do this in Havana, as elsewhere in Latin America, Hollywood would have to reexamine the mechanisms of its hegemony at the same time that US government policymakers were forced to reexamine the mechanisms of their own. In Cuba specifically, the Platt Amendment had caused such deep resentment, and provoked such a strong nationalist backlash, that its abrogation—which finally came in May 1934—became a key test of the United States' new Good Neighbor Policy and its commitment to non-intervention in Latin America. Though not as universally loathed as the Platt Amendment, Hollywood too had been used to stoke anti-imperialist Cuban nationalism during the revolt against Machado. The minoristas had worked hard to weave more critical spectatorship into revolutionary Cuban nationalism, teaching Cuban eyes to see Hollywood's monopolistic business practices, its denigration of Hispanics, the falseness of its promises of upward mobility, and, at the same time, its critical depictions of US capitalist modernity produced by progressive artists like Chaplin. Such were the conditions that precipitated the Good Neighbor Policy and Hollywood's enthusiastic participation in it, as well as Cubans' reception of both, to be covered in chapter 3.

3

Our Men in Havana: Hollywood and Good Neighborly Bonds, 1934–1941

September 1941. A large map of the Americas covers the lobby floor of the new Teatro América, Havana's most luxurious movie house. Inlaid in terrazzo, the western hemisphere is represented as a golden unity, with the United States centered and on top, with Cuba small but highlighted in a darker hue. Inside the new theater's 1,700-seat auditorium, under a planetarium ceiling, a grand screen sits within five successively larger Art Deco arches, everything streamline moderne, with intentional echoes of New York's Radio City Music Hall (see fig. 3.1). The content playing onscreen likewise suggests progress, prosperity, and inter-American harmony. Preceding a Hollywood feature (the only kind then shown at the América), a Cuban newsreel opens the night's program with scenes from a banquet at the new Tropicana Club, thrown by Havana exhibitors and film critics to celebrate Henry Weiner's twentieth anniversary as United Artists' Havana manager.[1]

These scenes, and the space in which they were exhibited, capture Cubans' renewed optimism about their island's Americanization, particularly during this era of the United States' new Good Neighbor Policy. They also suggest that Hollywood played a role in successfully selling the ideal of a US-centric Pan-American Good Neighborhood, of a hemisphere united under US leadership and by shared commitments to democracy and social progress. In Cuba, this was no small achievement given the island's recent history. Yet, the United States' good neighborly pledges of non-intervention, mutual respect, and shared prosperity did convert (at least partially) some of Cuba's most adamant anti-imperialists. As evidence of this trend, it was none other than José Manuel Valdés-Rodríguez that gave the toast at Weiner's anniversary banquet (see fig. 3.2), the onetime author of "Hollywood: Sales Agent of American Imperialism" now extolling one of Hollywood's salesmen in Havana. With

FIG. 3.1. Interior of the Teatro América, circa 1941. Cinematreasures.org.

obvious affection and some gentle ribbing (about Weiner's widening girth and thinning hair), Valdés-Rodríguez lauded Weiner as a skilled merchant but, more importantly, as a "good man."[2]

What made Weiner a good man—and a Good Neighbor—in Valdés-Rodríguez's estimation is telling. Weiner was a veteran of the War of 1898, the critic emphasized in his toast. Weiner "took up arms for the liberation and independence of Cuba . . . compelled by the noble qualities that throbbed in his selfless core, as it did in many other North American lads." ("There were others that were compelled by ulterior motives and mercenary intentions and we don't have to discuss these here," the critic added, not quite able to repress his anti-imperialist impulse or to overestimate Cuba's "debt of gratitude.") After the war, Valdés-Rodríguez continued, Weiner returned to Havana and "fused with us through his identification with *lo cubano* [all things Cuban], a true gone-native."[3] In this toast and throughout a season of accolades, Weiner's anniversary at United Artists was made an occasion to reiterate revolutionary Cuban nationalism (including its freedom-fighting masculinity) and to suggest that the admirable success of US businesses and their representatives locally was contingent upon the respect they paid to *Cubanidad*.

This chapter explores US-Cuban rapprochement from the aftermath of the 1933 revolution to the eve of World War II, a period in which US-Cuban bonds were reforged even as strongman rule and US imperial hegemony recru-

FIG. 3.2. At the head table at the banquet to celebrate Henry Weiner's twentieth anniversary at United Artists' Havana office are seated (*left to right*) Cuban exhibitor, Ernesto P. Smith; Mrs. Henry Weiner; Henry Weiner; Miliza Korjus (Polish-born Hollywood actress); and film critic, Jose Manuel Valdés-Rodríguez. *Around the World* 9, no. 3. (Courtesy of Wisconsin Center for Film and Theater Research)

desced, in slightly revised forms. Its title gestures to Graham Greene's famous 1958 novel *Our Man in Havana* (and the 1959 British film version, distributed by Columbia). But mostly the titular "men" refers to different (and intersecting) groups of men involved in renegotiating the relationship between US power and Cuban nationalism. First, it refers to Batista, who became Cuba's US-backed military strongman in this period; this chapter's title thus also gestures toward that famous phrase "He may be a son-of-a-bitch, but he's *our* son-of-a-bitch," reportedly first used by Roosevelt to rationalize US support of Nicaraguan dictator Anastasio Somoza during this same period.[4] Second, "our men" refers to the Anglo-American male stars in Hollywood's 1930s "Good Neighbor films" who woo Latin American women onscreen, acting as surrogates in Hollywood's attempt to win (back) the hearts of Latin American audiences. With some reservations, habaneros allowed themselves to be wooed.

This chapter's first two sections, then, offer the broader historical context of US-Cuban relations and the US film industry in the 1930s that affected the business and reception of Hollywood in Havana covered in subsequent sections. The third section covers the era's Good Neighbor relations as they developed in Havana's film business community (giro), spotlighting the US managers of Hollywood's branch offices, like Weiner, who worked as "goodwill ambassadors" in their daily interactions with Cubans.[5] The fourth section covers yet another group of "our men" in Havana: the hundreds of Cubans employed in the film giro. These included a handful of Cuban managers of Hollywood's Havana offices, as well as Cuban exhibitors, who depended on Hollywood for their livelihoods and whose personal successes testified to the mutual prosperity of US-Cuban relations. Yet, as hinted in Valdés-Rodríguez's toast, anti-imperialist *independentismo* was not completely suppressed by shared profits and close personal relationships; and when tensions did arise, revolutionary Cuban nationalism flared. In other words, the film giro was a place where Cubans continually assessed whether their northern neighbors were, indeed, good, and what to do about it when they weren't.

So were Havana's film columns and trade journals. Cuban critics used Hollywood films to evaluate, and pontificate upon, US-led Pan-Americanism as well as to continue to gird Cuban nationalist masculinity. In the final sections of this chapter, then, it is through Cuban critics' eyes that we see the last category of "our men" in Havana: Hollywood's male heroes of the later 1930s, in films reflecting not only the US film industry's support of Roosevelt's Good Neighbor Policy—namely *A Message to García* (1936)—but also reflecting the rise of the Hollywood Left—namely Chaplin's *Modern Times* (1936) and Capra's *Mr. Smith Goes to Washington* (1939).

"Our Son-of-a-Bitch" in Havana: The Good Neighbor Policy and Colonel Batista

In March 1933, the new US president Franklin Roosevelt pledged that the United States would recover from the Great Depression and would reform the excessive inequities of finance capitalism and imperialism that had caused it. Wall Street bankers had hoarded the nation's wealth, leaving the common man penniless, without the purchasing power that economists argued was key to the nation's economic health. In the global economy, and according to the same logic, unbalanced trade relations had stymied the healthy circulation of money, deepening the Depression in the United States and the world. Guided by this recognition of "interdependence" and a recommitment to American "social values more noble than mere monetary profit," Roosevelt pledged that US capitalism would be more socially responsible at home and that the United States would act as a "good neighbor" abroad.[6]

Thereafter, Roosevelt's vague pledge to respect the sovereign rights of other nations was elaborated into the Good Neighbor Policy in Latin America, which sought to ameliorate the anti-Yankee backlash caused by decades of the Big Stick Policy and Dollar Diplomacy. Along with abrogating the Platt Amendment, the Roosevelt administration pulled the Marines out of Nicaragua and Haiti, allowed the nationalization of oil companies in Mexico and Bolivia, and negotiated non-intervention treaties and new trade agreements with its "sister republics." That gendered phrase nicely connotes the continued subordination of Latin America that US policymakers presumed as well as the cultural construction of "Pan-America" as a geographic entity defined by a shared history of overthrowing Old World colonialism to establish sovereign democracies, a construction which allowed the United States to claim moral superiority in relation to emerging expansionist fascist dictators in Europe and Asia.[7] In other words, the Good Neighbor Policy did not represent the abnegation of US imperialism but a shift in its exercise—from using coercion to building consensus—in order to preserve and even strengthen it.[8]

The case of Cuba illustrates much about the Good Neighbor Policy. After all, the first trial of its non-intervention pledge was the island's 1933 revolution. As protests reached a fevered peak in mid-1933, Roosevelt resisted the temptation to send in the US Marines to save Machado or the Platt Amendment. But non-intervention was not the same as non-interference. Roosevelt's State Department put its finger on the scale by denying recognition to Grau and by green-lighting Batista's 1934 coup. Thereafter, Colonel Batista—who ascended to de facto ruler of Cuba—became "our" man in Havana, the only person deemed capable of restoring the order that US interests required. To shore up Batista's consolidation of power, the United States granted recognition to his six puppet presidents from 1934 to 1940, suspended Cuba's debt obligations, gave financial assistance, enhanced trade, and discouraged Batista's civilian opponents.[9]

Batista was "our son-of-a-bitch" in Cuba, a military strongman—like Anastasio Somoza in Nicaragua and Rafael Trujillo in the Dominican Republic—that embarrassed the very Good Neighbor policymakers who *claimed* to want to advance democracy in the Americas. To rationalize their hypocrisy, Roosevelt's State Department argued that such strongmen were regrettable offspring of Latin America's colonial past, residual *caudillos* temporarily needed to maintain stability until its young and unruly democracies matured. Publicly, State Department officials argued that Batista was a champion of Cuba's evolution toward democracy.[10] Privately, though, they expressed doubts about that progress narrative. In 1938, the US ambassador to Cuba deemed it ironic that the revolt against Machado's dictatorship had led to Batista's "military dominance—more or less benevolent at the time, but nevertheless fairly complete and in a position to be arbitrary. This situation," Ambassador Butler explained to his boss, the US Secretary of State, "is psychologically repugnant to the mass of Cubans."[11]

Lest repugnance evolve into another revolt, both the Roosevelt administration and Batista had to exercise their power with greater sensitivity to the revolutionary Cuban nationalism that had been aroused by the 1933 revolution. Blatant US interference and/or direct military dictatorship were likely to fuel that still-smoldering fire. Thus, the US ambassador kept a low profile in Havana, counseling Batista behind closed doors. And Batista himself was rarely found at the Presidential Palace or the Capitolio, instead pulling strings from army headquarters at Camp Columbia, just outside of Havana.[12] Still, since everyone knew who pulled the strings, Batista's touch had to be dexterous. On the one hand, his power was predicated on his self-promotion as a revolutionary standard-bearer. He promised that, once order was fully restored, elections for delegates to a constitutional assembly would be held and a new constitution penned. Meanwhile, Batista burnished his revolutionary populist image by championing legislation to promote national industry and to protect the rights of Cuban labor in the face of foreign capital (while privately promising US officials and business leaders he would not go too far). And his growth of the Cuban military's budget included making it the source of many progressive social programs modeled on the New Deal.[13]

On the other hand, Batista's power was predicated on his control of the army and national police, which he used to quell residual revolutionary activism. Sporadic strikes—which cine projectionists joined in October 1934—continued to paralyze the country.[14] This unrest culminated in March 1935, when workers and students organized the largest general strike in Cuban history. Batista brutally quashed it and, thereafter, outlawed labor organizations and the PCC. His regime also used censorship, imprisonment, torture, and assassination to silence dissident journalists and political adversaries. Shut out of the political process, action groups formed and reformed continually, using bombs and assassinations to assert their opposition. More seasoned revolutionaries, like Raúl Roa, denounced these reckless upstarts for their lack of strategy, for acting like "*cowboys* in western movies who come into town with guns blazing."[15] Indeed, such political violence might have been counterproductive. Unable to stomach more revolutionary instability, Cuba's middle and upper classes proved willing to live with Batista's undemocratic power, especially as restored order led to economic recovery.[16]

That economic recovery also made the reinstitution of US power more palatable. While the United States abdicated the "Big Stick" of the Platt Amendment, it still wielded powerful financial "carrots," including loans, US tourism dollars (which doubled in this period), and sugar consumption.[17] Replacing the Reciprocity Treaty of 1903, the 1934 US-Cuban Reciprocity Treaty reduced US tariffs on Cuban sugar in exchange for reduced Cuban tariffs on a variety of US goods even wider than previously. As a result, the value of US imports to Cuba quadrupled from 1933 to 1940; the Cuban economy's diversification continued to be stifled; and US policymakers henceforth used the threatened cancelation of this treaty to control developments on the island.[18] In other words, Cubans traded the revolutionary goal of long-term political and economic independence for desperately needed short-term economic recovery. The recently exiled Grau complained that the 1934 Reciprocity Treaty emasculated Cuba once again, making it more "submissive, dependent and enslaved" than it had been under the Platt Amendment.[19]

But Grau could do little but grumble, at least until the end of the decade, when conditions shifted and Batista was forced to allow the promised Constitutional Assembly and a legitimate presidential election in 1940. In the meantime, in various ways, most Cubans accommodated themselves to the restoration of strongman rule and US imperial hegemony, which, after all, seemed to bring peace and prosperity, for now.

Looking Up at Good(-Looking) Neighbors: Hollywood Pan-Americanism in Havana

The Roosevelt administration believed that helping the US film industry in Latin American markets would help the Good Neighbor Policy, because Hollywood promoted US-made goods and engendered "goodwill and understanding."[20] In a number of Good Neighbor trade agreements, the US Commerce and State Departments pushed for "preferred status" for Hollywood films. As the first of these, the 1934 US–Cuban Reciprocity Treaty guaranteed US films 20 percent lower duties than those imposed on other countries' films.[21] In 1939 and again in 1941, when this treaty was renegotiated, Hollywood's "unconditional most-favored-nation treatment" was elaborated, limiting the Cuban government's ability to raise not only duties but also taxes and municipal fees, or to give preferential treatment in any way to Spanish-language or even Cuban-made films.[22] In short, the US government agreed with the US studios' sense of entitlement to the Cuban market. Without a hint of irony, the Commerce Department's Motion Picture Division reported in 1935 that "every foreign film exhibited in Cuba"—and by "foreign" they meant non-US—"may be said to displace an American picture, since American producers have more than sufficient material with which to supply this market."[23]

In exchange for helping Hollywood in Latin America, the US government expected Hollywood to advance its Good Neighbor Policy, or at the very least not to subvert it by offending Latin Americans. Fortunately toward this end, by the early 1930s, the US's studios were doing more to self-police against such offenses. In 1930, the MPPDA introduced its "Production Code," and gave it enforcement teeth in 1934 with the formation of the Production Code Administration (PCA). And while the code focused on sex and crime, it also insisted that "the just rights, history and feelings of any nation are entitled to most careful consideration and respectful treatment."[24] Regarding Latin America, the PCA admonished that Hispanic characters were not to be made villains or played for comedic effect. The PCA's powerful chief, Joseph Breen, also advised the studios to beef up their research departments and to hire Latin American "experts."[25] Of course, Hollywood had its own reasons to revise its representations of Latin America and its peoples. The negative effects of the early Depression years on studios' bottom lines made foreign markets all the more important to profitability, especially in Latin America since European and Asian markets were increasingly closed by national protectionism. Hollywood's derogatory representations of Hispanics—as lazy bandits or lusty gigolos, speaking laughably broken English—not only undermined US foreign policy but also hurt the studios at the Latin American box office. This was a lesson that studio executives had learned from a number of costly boycotts, including the aforementioned Cuban boycott against *The Cuban Love Song*, and more recently a Cuban boycott against the Warner Bros. picture *Havana Widows* (1933) for "ridiculing and degenerating the good name of Cuba."[26]

But Hollywood's good neighborly revisions went well beyond trying not to offend. Starting in 1933 with RKO's production of *Flying Down to Rio*, Hollywood made a number of films, especially musicals, that presented Pan-America as a fun-filled transnational community, even family. When US protagonists traveled to Latin America, they respected, economically benefited, and even fell in love with the natives. The latter were played by Hispanic stars whose top billing and ascent to Hollywood royalty further evidenced the United States' esteem for its "sister republics." In *Flying Down to Rio*, Mexican beauty Dolores Del Rio's Brazilian character, Belinha, falls in love with a US bandleader, Roger Bond (Gene Raymond), whose surname hints at the inter-American union he will achieve by saving Belinha's father's business from craven European capitalists and thus winning Belinha's heart.

As film scholars note, pre–World War II Good Neighbor films tend to figure Pan-American relations as heterosexual romance in which Latin Americans desire, and become available to, North Americans; the former are usually represented by female characters and the latter by males. The union of the Pan-American couple, and the sexual politics between them, communicate an imperialistic model for the US–Latin American relationship: hierarchical, sure, but consensual and mutually beneficial.[27] The United States is made "good looking" in a double sense in these films. Not only because of its actors' handsomeness, the United States is an attractive partner because it has transformed the way it looks upon its southern neighbors, now with respect, even adulation. Hollywood seemed to understand that Latin Americans wouldn't look up again to the United States until they were satisfied that they weren't being looked down upon.

In Havana, there is evidence that Hollywood's Good Neighbor films had the desired effect, to some extent. In fact, the promotion therein of *Flying*

Down to Rio literally made the city's inhabitants look up. In May 1934, in the month of the Platt Amendment's abrogation, RKO's representative in Havana, Charles Garrett, and the Teatro Nacional's exhibitor, Heliodorio García, sent a plane aloft over Havana to drop handbills and free movie passes, linking their own aerial stunts to those famously featured in the film. *Variety* noted that this promotional gimmick also exploited Cubans' anxiety about residual revolutionary violence, which made them especially apt to crane their necks upward at the roar of a plane engine and items falling from the sky. In any case, such showmanship helped *Flying Down to Rio* do record box office in Havana, despite Cubans' aforementioned trepidation about returning to their cines.[28]

Conversely, films that fell short of "good neighborliness" still provoked Cubans' so-called "super-sensitiveness," as was the case with Paramount's *Rumba* (1935), set in Havana. Though Paramount consulted with Cuban advisers, followed their advice to delete references to Cubans' love of gambling, hired Cuban choreographers, and even worked directly with Batista himself to procure real Cuban police badges and military uniforms in the name of respectful authenticity, *Rumba* stirred up a firestorm of protest in Cuba.[29] In the film, Havana is still full of seedy cabarets packed with criminals, and Cuba's rural interior full of libidinous natives dancing a highly sexualized rumba. The Cuban Tourist Commission protested to the US embassy that the film was "an affront to [Cuba's] national dignity"; and Havana's mayor threatened to ban it, along with all other Paramount films. In response, Paramount cut the film's most offensive material and screened the revised film at the Teatro Nacional for Cuban officials, who were satisfied enough to relent on the ban.[30] But the controversy didn't end there. In response to *Rumba*, the Cuban government planned to establish a second censorship board in New York, one more effective than the lax Comisión Revisora in Havana. However, the US studios' Havana Film Board, the MPPDA, and the State Department protested strenuously and forced the Cubans to "retrea[t] on the censorship front" and ditch the idea of the new board, *Variety* reported.[31]

The US studios learned a lesson from the controversy over *Rumba*: the 1933 revolution made Cuban settings too hot to handle. However, this did not stop them from continuing to use Cuban *music*—then wildly popular in the United States—to signify all things "Latin" in its Good Neighbor musicals, a sort of rhythmic shorthand for Pan-American fun and intimacy. For example, "La Carioca," the centerpiece song and dance number in *Flying Down to Rio* (and Fred Astaire and Ginger Rogers' first cinematic pairing), is, in fact, a Cuban rumba rather than a Brazilian samba. Likewise, the title song in *Down Argentine Way* (1940) is a Cuban rumba rather than an Argentine tango.[32] And, though wary of Hollywood's use of their island as setting, Cubans mostly seemed flattered by Hollywood's use of their music and interpreted it, as well as Hollywood's new *hispanofilia* generally, as evidence of US good neighborliness. *Bohemia* cheered that Cuban musicians and choreographers—who taught A-list stars like Joan Crawford how to rumba—were "Cubanizing Hollywood."[33] Cuban fanzines and other periodicals happily noted the Latin craze in Hollywood soundtracks, wardrobes, and even A-list actors. They especially cheered the Hollywood stardoms of their own native sons, such as Desi Arnaz, Pedro de Cordoba, and Cesar Romero, who were "loved and respected by all" in Hollywood.[34] Further suggesting that Hollywood loved and respected Cuba and its people, Cuban fanzines and other periodicals printed publicity photos that Hollywood stars had signed with personal salutations to the island and/or its inhabitants.[35]

Still, Havana film writers in the film giro were not naïve about Hollywood's motives. Their wariness is evident in the pages of *Cinema*, Havana's newest (and ultimately longest-lasting and most widely circulated) fanzine, which was actually a hybrid "trade-fan magazine" that catered to the general public as well as to exhibitors and others working in the film giro.[36] In his tellingly named weekly column, "*Son cosas nuestras*" (roughly, Things Pertaining to Us), *Cinema*'s editor, Enrique Perdices, wrote this about the US studios: "They think that rapprochement with Spanish-speaking countries depends on their making films that flatter us, and in this they are not ill-founded." However, "by *our way of seeing*," he continued, "if the intent is as cordial as they say, it would be preferable for [US] producers to install studios in [our] countries . . . , such that, our artists and technicians" could find the success the US film companies claimed to want for them.[37] In other words, Hollywood's hiring of Latin American artists did not indicate respect as much as it did talent poaching; rather than progress it contributed to underdevelopment. And while Perdices lauded Hollywood for improved representations of Latinos and Latin America, he noted some failures in execution, including films that continued to trade in denigrating stereotypes, willingly played by Hispanic actors who too "quickly forget their origins," which was tantamount to *vende-patria*.[38]

The most famous Cuban in Hollywood at this time, of course, was Desi Arnaz. Born to a wealthy family in Santiago de Cuba, Arnaz attended the same Jesuit high school, *Colegio de Dolores*, later attended by Fidel Castro. In 1933, Arnaz's family moved to Miami, where the talented teenage Desi landed a gig with the orchestra of Cuban bandleader Xavier Cugat (himself to become a staple of Hollywood's wartime Pan-American films). From there, Arnaz captured the attention of Broadway, where he appeared in a musical entitled *Too Many Girls*. This, in turn, won Arnaz a role in RKO's 1940 film version of the same, in which he plays a Latin American exchange student whose conga drumming stirs the passions of American college girls in a New Mexican (Pan-American-esque) town. While filming, Arnaz fell in love with his fellow cast member and future wife, Lucille Ball, their famous pairing nicely symbolizing midcentury US-Cuban ties of singular intimacy and Hollywood's role in tying them.[39]

In the Havana press, Arnaz's success was interpreted as evidence of the United States' good neighborliness. Not only had Desi won Lucy's heart, he "had conquered Hollywood" and the US public, according to one enthusiastic Cuban trade journal.[40] Best of all, to do so, Arnaz emphasized his Cuban identity rather than sublimated it. In *Cinema*, seasoned film writer María Garrett hyperbolized: As "the first person to write a truly Cuban page in Hollywood's history," Arnaz did great honor to *Cubanidad*, which served as "the brilliant torch he wore close to his heart to light his path of glory."[41]

"A Great Big Family": Ties of Singular Intimacy in Havana's Film Giro

Not just on studio sets in Southern California, the US film industry also brought US citizens and Cubans together in "ties of singular intimacy" in Havana's own film business community. In July 1934, María Garrett's son, Charles Garrett (the aforementioned RKO representative and a US citizen), took a Cuban wife. Regarding his wedding day, Garrett reported to the *Film Daily* how amused he was to hear "La Carioca" from *Flying Down to Rio* playing repeatedly from a neighboring Cuban's phonograph as Garrett said his vows in a Cuban courthouse, the soundtrack from that onscreen Pan-American love story seeming to affirm his own union off-screen.[42]

Not that he needed such affirmation. After all, Garrett was himself a product of US-Cuban diplomatic, business, and marital relations. His father, Edward B. Garrett, had been a member of the US consular corps in Havana when he married Charles's Cuban mother, María, in 1907. "Carlos" was born in Havana the following year. A few years later, the Garretts moved to New York for Edward's new job as an executive of the Universal Film Manufacturing Company.[43] When Edward died in 1915, María brought Charles and his toddler sister, Marion, back to Havana, where Universal gave the young widow a job as stenographer in its new office there. María used this post to launch a long, varied, and transnational career in film publicity and journalism. In 1925, María returned to New York with her children to serve as a correspondent for *Cine-Mundial*; later, she also wrote for *El País*, *Bohemia*, and *Cinema*. In 1929, she moved to Hollywood to work on Columbia's Spanish-language-version films; and in 1935, she moved back to New York to serve as the Warner Bros. Foreign Department's publicity chief.[44] By the late 1920s, the young Charles was also in the film business. He worked in New York as Pathé's foreign publicity chief before moving back to Havana to build a résumé as long as his mother's, working in both distribution and trade journalism.[45] In the mid-1930s, his sister Marion briefly joined him in Havana as a translator for a British film distributor, but she found her way back to New York. There, she met and married an exiled Cuban, who had participated in revolutionary plots against Batista in the mid-1930s and would earn renown for doing so again in the 1950s, this time with Marion by his side.[46] In the 1930s, however, the Garretts were best known as "quite a film family," according to the *Film Daily*.[47]

Charles Garrett's wedding-day anecdote, his family history, and its members' transnational résumés—as well as this chapter's opening anecdote about Henry Weiner's banquet (at which Weiner was accompanied by *his* Cuban wife)—reveal much about "our men" who worked in the Havana film giro and about the good neighborly Pan-American relations engendered therein during this period. In the film giro, Americans, Cubans, and Cuban-Americans—as heads of Hollywood's Havana offices, exhibitors, office employees, publicists, and journalists—formed bonds that did, indeed, seem intimate. While not everyone in the giro formed literal families like the Garretts did, some Cubans said the giro itself formed a figurative one: "a great big family composed by those from abroad and those who are here."[48]

As elsewhere in this era of US-Cuban rapprochement, reconciliation in the film giro depended on economic recovery, which came slowly after the 1933 revolution and its aftershocks. While 1935 saw cines reopening, Weiner reported to his bosses in United Artists' Foreign Department in New York that "the political situation" continued to keep spectators away, "especially when different factions are fighting each other with bombs and other acts of terrorism," including inside cines still.[49] With box office receipts more than halved, Cuban exhibitors fought harder with US distributors for a greater portion of the shrunken pie. To strengthen their bargaining position vis-à-vis Hollywood, Havana's first-run exhibitors split from the ANE to form the Unión Nacional de Exhibidores (UNE). Its members collectively refused to pay more than 35 percent of ticket sales to the US distributors, whereas they had previously agreed to as much as 60 percent.[50] As another strategy to strengthen their bargaining position, a handful of Cuban exhibitors consolidated their cines into chains. Most notably, at the end of 1934, Ernesto P. Smith began to build his "Smith circuit"; by 1938, it would be comprised of nine cines, including the Campoamor, Encanto, and Fausto. His closest rival, Edelberto de Carrerá, had a chain of five.[51]

As order was restored and the economy began to recover, the film business in Havana improved dramatically; box office receipts tripled in 1936. This expanding pie satisfied both US distributors and UNE exhibitors, who reported record-breaking annual grosses and had less cause to squabble about percentages. The expanding pie also precipitated another cine construction boom. By 1939, Havana had some ninety cines—forty more than during the silent-era peak of fifty in the late 1920s.[52] New deluxe cines continued to cluster in the movie barrio, whose western edge now expanded to Avenida Galiano, a bustling commercial artery. Among these was the three-thousand-seat Radio Cine, Cuba's largest movie theater to date, which was opened in November 1936 by exhibitor José Valcarce. A few blocks away, in July 1938, Valcarce also opened Cuba's first "newsreel" theater. Hoping to replicate a successful trend in London and New York City, this six-hundred-seat Cine Rex projected short films exclusively, especially newsreels (Cuban- and US-made), which were increasingly popular as the world marched toward war.[53]

Cine construction was matched by cine renovation. Most notably, Smith demolished the old Fausto to make room for the new Cine-Teatro Fausto (see fig. 3.3), which opened in April 1938, a celebrated example of Art Deco architecture whose streamlined pastel façade still towers over the Prado, though its marquee no longer puts on its once-famous displays of multicolored neon lights. Like its exterior, the new Fausto's interior also represented the height of Art Deco style and modern technology, from acoustics-enhancing building materials to the latest US-made projectors.[54] And the US studios were happy to have another Havana cine worthy of their prestige pictures.[55] In September 1940, MGM debuted *Gone with the Wind* at the Fausto in what Charles Garrett described as "the greatest event in the history of premieres in Cuba." In attendance were President Federico Laredo Brú, US embassy officials, and "the very swankiest families of Havana society," according to Garrett. In reference to this and other well-publicized premieres, *Variety* cheered: "The meaning of the word 'exploitation' is at last being interpreted in the correct showmanship sense here."[56] Without meaning to, this statement captures the US film industry's awareness of Cuban anti-imperialist nationalism, and the ways they thought Hollywood razzle-dazzle could overcome it.

The Cuban economy boomed further with the run-up to World War II, as the United States increased its sugar purchase. Benefiting from this prosperity, the film business continued its upward trend in 1940 and 1941. Cine construction and renovation continued apace, and by the end of 1941, Havana had 110 cines, more than some of Europe's most "civilized" countries, one Cuban film trade journal boasted.[57] The high mark came in March 1941, when Valcarce opened the Teatro América on the ground floor of a new twelve-story skyscraper, the América building on Galiano. Adjacent to Valcarce's own Radio Cine, the Teatro América was built on an even grander scale. And, as noted

FIG. 3.3. The façade of the rebuilt Cine-Teatro Fausto dressed up to promote Walt Disney's *Pinocchio* in January 1941. *Motion Picture Herald*, January 18, 1941.

above, from the lobby's floor to the Hollywood features announced on the marquee to the financial success of its Cuban exhibitor, everything about the Teatro América bespoke Cuban optimism about US-led Pan-Americanism.[58]

Indeed, the movie barrio exuded such optimism during these years. In the late 1930s, the US studios upgraded their offices on and near Calle Consulado, where oversized movie posters lined the streets and exhibitors popped in and out to contract films and conduct other business, that is, in the adjacent offices of publicists, theater supply companies, Cuban newsreel companies, non-US film distributors, and fanzines and trade publications.[59] Among the latter, two of Cuba's most important were new in this era: the aforementioned *Cinema* and the *Anuario Cinematográfico y Radial Cubano* (*ACRC*). Published weekly from 1935 to 1962, *Cinema* was a fanzine–trade journal hybrid full of Hollywood-provided publicity and advertising, but also commentary on the film business (local and global) and film reviews explicitly addressed toward both exhibitors and moviegoers. Published annually from 1940 through 1960, the *ACRC* was a trade journal that contained directories of cines, distributors' offices, lists of films to be released, information about tariffs and taxes, as well as advertisements and biographical blurbs about individuals working in the giro. Both publications are invaluable resources not only for exploring critical and popular film reception in Havana, but also for reconstructing the social and cultural life of the movie barrio and the "film family" residing in it. During this period, *Cinema* and the *ACRC* suggest that the movie barrio was a model Good Neighborhood: a happy and profitable place, where Cubans and Americans worked together amicably, traded endearing nicknames and pranks, played dominoes and dice, partnered for golf and tennis, and formed social clubs where their camaraderie was fueled with liberal quantities of rum. Bar Los Peliculeros, a watering hole on Consulado frequented by Cuban and US giro members, advertised, "Here is practiced the politics of 'good neighbor' and 'the client is always right,'" indicating the absorption of both Pan-Americanism and US business culture with one's collegial drinks.[60]

If the Hollywood offices constituted the good neighborly film giro's center, the managers of those offices were at the center of the center. For the most part, these top posts were still reserved for US citizens, though with enough exceptions—e.g., Ramón García at Fox—to mitigate the anti-Yankee resentment that such glass ceilings provoked in other US-dominated industries in Cuba.[61] While material incentives for Cubans working in the film giro (i.e., relatively high pay, stable employment, and the possibility of advancement) explain some of the goodwill enjoyed by the US managers, their personal backgrounds and their willingness to respect local customs and to assimilate to *Cubanidad* also played a role.[62] As a (hyphenated) Cuban-American,

RKO's Charles "Carlos" Garrett had a particular leg-up at this assimilation, but most of the other US managers were also non-Anglos with fluid, transnational identities that facilitated their "Cubanization." Many of them blended into the melting pot that was pre-1959 Havana, an ethnically heterogeneous city of immigrants, including a sizable community of US- and European-born Jews.[63]

In fact, the only *Anglo*-Americans among the Hollywood managers in this period were Edward O'Connor and Arthur Pratchett, neither of whom spent much of their lives in the United States prior to arriving in Havana. O'Connor had spent sixteen years opening US studio distribution offices in various Asian cities, before MGM made him its Havana manager in 1936.[64] In Havana, according to *Cinema*, O'Connor "w[on] the friendship of all Cubans"; treated his Cuban employees like "a great big family"; and learned to speak "the language of Cervantes" fluently, peppering it with plenty of Cuban slang. On the occasion of his fifth anniversary in Cuba in 1941, *Cinema* reported that O'Connor's banquet bore the "unmistakable stamp of sincere Pan-Americanism."[65] Even more acculturated and feted was the England-born, US-naturalized "Arturo" Pratchett, who served as Paramount's Havana manager for eighteen years (1917–1934), and became "something of a national institution," according to *Cinema*. After 1934, when Pratchett was promoted to regional manager in Mexico City, his return trips to Havana were met with ceremonies befitting a high statesman. After all, as the *ACRC* put it in 1944, Pratchett had practiced "the politics of good neighborliness . . . long before Roosevelt instituted it in the diplomatic relations of this Hemisphere."[66]

However, as Anglo-Americans, O'Connor and Pratchett were exceptions to the rule. In the 1930s, as in the 1920s, the Hollywood studios still tended to send first- and second-generation US immigrants, often Jewish, to man their Havana offices. For instance, to replace Pratchett, Paramount sent Jacob Rapoport, a second-generation Russian Jew who served in that post for seven years until 1942, by which point he too had married a Cuban woman.[67] Over at the Warner Bros. office, Prieto (aka "Pedro" or "Peter") Colli, an Italian-born Jewish immigrant to the United States, arrived in 1932 to become that office's longest-serving manager, holding the post for almost three decades. During that time, Colli likewise took a Cuban wife. He also joined Havana's Beth Israel Temple, became a Cuban citizen, and came to call Havana "home," according to the *ACRC*.[68]

And then there was Henry Weiner, the man of honor in this chapter's opening anecdote. He served as manager of United Artists' Havana office for thirty-one years, from 1921 to 1952. Though he never naturalized as a Cuban citizen as Colli did, by the time he retired, Weiner considered himself "more Cuban than many Cubans:" "150% Cuban," in fact. And Cubans in the film giro endorsed Weiner's self-assessment. Along with Valdés-Rodríguez's compliment that Weiner had "gone native," *Cinema* enthused in 1940 that Weiner's "nationality did not impede him from feeling Cuban at heart."[69] The *ACRC* explained that he was "one of the most popular figures on *Consulado*, because in him are found notable civic virtues, and he is rarely referred to by his name only, without the addition of a term of endearment, such as 'old Henry,' 'dear Weiner,' 'veteran Manager,' etc." In other words, the film giro regarded Weiner as a sort of benevolent patriarch, not least of all because he acted like a good (Cuban) citizen.

Weiner's "Cubanization" was facilitated by his own early history. He was born an Ashkenazi Jew in 1876 in Bohemia (now a part of the Czech Republic), which was then struggling to achieve independence from the Austro-Hungarian Empire. In 1890, Weiner immigrated to New York. Eight years later, in 1898, "memories of his native land" compelled Weiner to enlist in the American Expeditionary Forces to help liberate Cuba, according to Valdés-Rodríguez's toast. Interestingly enough, however, Weiner seems to have embellished his war service, or at least not corrected others' embellishments. In truth, Weiner had been too busy battling malaria in an army hospital in Kentucky to have battled any Spaniards in Cuba. By the time Weiner returned to active duty in September 1898, the "splendid little war" was over.[70]

After mustering out, Weiner became a citizen of the United States for the express purpose of leaving it. In May 1900, one day after naturalizing, Weiner applied for a US passport, likely to travel on behalf of the Jewish cigar maker who vouched for his naturalization application.[71] Shortly thereafter, Weiner finally landed in tobacco-rich Cuba, which he made his permanent residence by 1907.[72] As such, Weiner belonged to a wave of Jewish American entrepreneurs who came to Havana during and after the first US occupation, worked for US import-export firms, prospered, and eventually gained a degree of social prominence.[73] According to the *Almanaque Hebrea Vida Habanara* (Hebrew Almanac of Havana Life) in 1944, Weiner was an important member of Havana's "Hebrew Colony" and a "famous patriot," meaning a *Cuban* patriot.[74] He belonged to the United Hebrew Congregation of Havana, and he buried his first wife in its Ashkenazi cemetery in 1927. Thereafter, he married a Cuban woman and helped to raise her Cuban son from a previous marriage.[75]

By the early 1940s, Weiner's "150%" Cuban-ness was central to his identity as well as to the many celebrations of his twentieth anniversary at United Artists. Kicking it off in October 1940, President Laredo Brú decorated Weiner "for taking part in our country's liberation."[76] To this event, *Cinema* devoted a full page, headlined with Martí's famous phrase, "*Honor a quien honor merece*" (Honor to Whom Honor Is Due); it praised Weiner for joining the US Army "that so efficiently contributed to our independence." But *Cinema* also reasserted that it was *Cuban* men that merited the *most* honor, noting that the US Army *supported* rather than led "our *mambises*, in liberating Cuba from the Spanish yoke." In August 1941, Cuban film critics presented a medal to Weiner in the great hall of a Havana veterans' association, "to which Weiner belongs, since he fought in our lands for Cuba's liberty," noted *Cinema*. In September 1941, Cuban exhibitors and critics threw the aforementioned Tropicana banquet. There, Valdés-Rodríguez toasted Weiner's revolutionary *Cubanidad*—his inextricable attachment "to the struggle of our country." It was this, he explained, that made Cubans "feel themselves so united to Henry Weiner, to esteem him and love him and to offer him this sincere tribute."[77]

Back in New York, United Artists' Foreign Department was thrilled that Weiner's "Cubanization" enhanced the company's profits, making Cuba one of United Artists' top-grossing markets by 1938.[78] The department's mimeographed newsletter, *Around the World*, held up Weiner as the sort of goodwill ambassador the company expected its "foreign legionnaires in the field" to be.[79] (See fig. 3.4.) His success and longevity inspired *Around the World* to pontificate wittily that "a company is known by the men it keeps."[80] *Around the World* cheered Weiner's adoption of Havana as "home" and the resulting devotion of his Cuban staff.[81] In his adopted country, Weiner was "revered by all who know him—from the President to the lowliest laborer."[82] His "promoting and strengthening [of] friendly relations with exhibitors, picture-goers, communities and even governments" was precisely what the company advocated as just plain "good business."[83]

United Artists benefited not only from Weiner's personal relationships but also from his intimate knowledge of Cuban life, which he imparted in monthly reports in the late 1930s. Weiner helped the company adjust its strategies (and expectations) to what he called "political convulsions" as well as to local customs, legislation, and even weather.[84] He explained, for instance, Cubans' reactions to the Spanish Civil War (concerned about relatives; tending to side with the anti-Franco, leftist Republicans) and their seemingly excessive number of national holidays to commemorate Cuban revolutionary heroes (on which cines had to close and employees had to be paid double). Weiner explained that unrest could be expected each year around the anniversary of Batista's September 1933 coup and that political scandals negatively affected receipts.[85] And with some sympathy, he explained post-1933 Cuban labor laws: a minimum wage, an eight-hour workday split by the midday siesta, the "Law of 50 Percent," and the requirement for government arbitration in any Cuban employee's dismissal.[86] But Weiner's reports also reveal that his

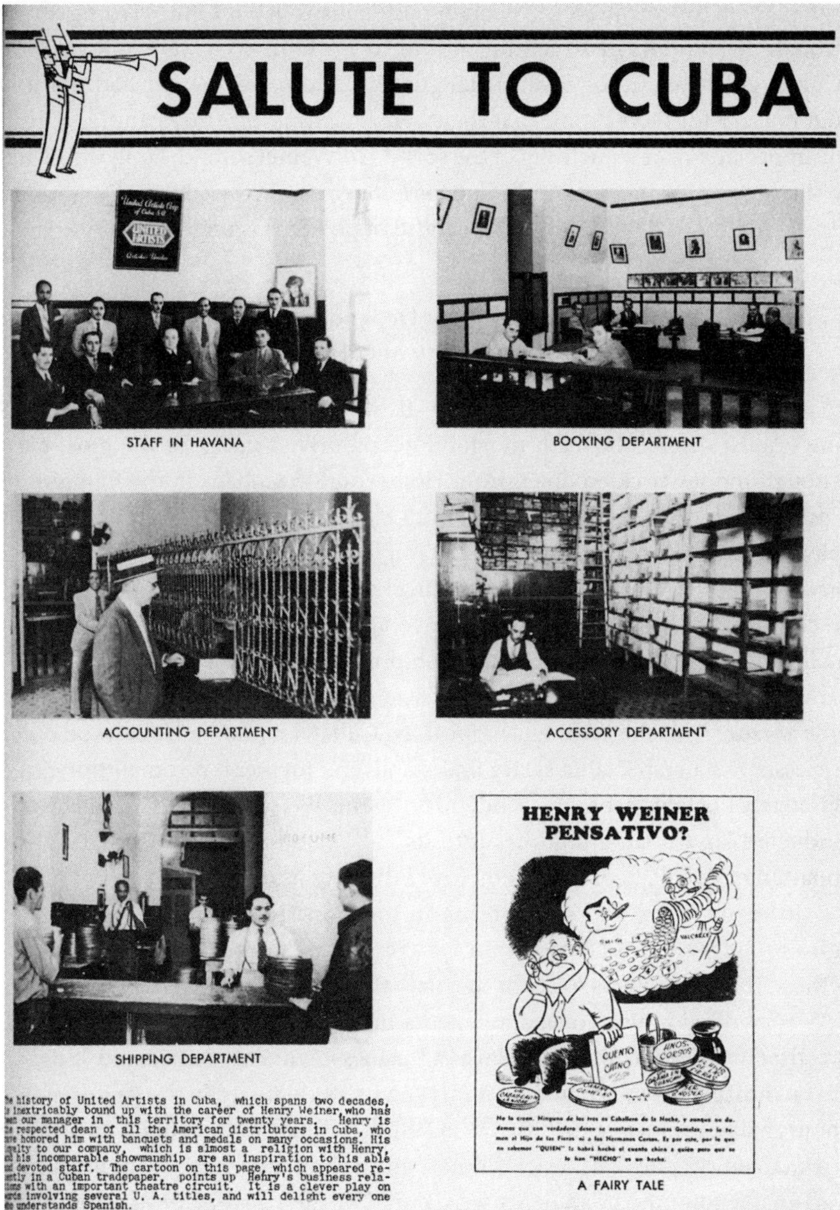
SALUTE TO CUBA

STAFF IN HAVANA

BOOKING DEPARTMENT

ACCOUNTING DEPARTMENT

ACCESSORY DEPARTMENT

SHIPPING DEPARTMENT

history of United Artists in Cuba, which spans two decades, inextricably bound up with the career of Henry Weiner, who has our manager in this territory for twenty years. Henry is respected dean of all the American distributors in Cuba, who honored him with banquets and medals on many occasions. His alty to our company, which is almost a religion with Henry, his incomparable showmanship are an inspiration to his able devoted staff. The cartoon on this page, which appeared re-tly in a Cuban tradepaper, points up Henry's business rela-with an important theatre circuit. It is a clever play on involving several U. A. titles, and will delight every one understands Spanish.

HENRY WEINER PENSATIVO?

A FAIRY TALE

FIG. 3.4. United Artists' Foreign Department celebrates the professionalism and camaraderie in their Havana branch office. The caption especially notes that its US manager, Henry Weiner, is an "inspiration to his able and devoted staff." *Around the World* 10, no. 3. (Courtesy of Wisconsin Center for Film and Theater Research)

sympathies for revolutionary Cuban nationalism had a limit. Writing about Cuban distributors of Argentine and Mexican films who were lobbying the Cuban government for Spanish-language film quotas, Weiner had nothing but disdain for their claims that they were "'victims' of American Capitalism or Imperialism, or something of the sort."[87] To Weiner's mind, Hollywood had built the very business to which Cubans in the film giro owed their livelihoods. To accuse the U.S. film industry of abuse of power was ungrateful, indeed.

"Self-Made Men" in a Dependent Economy: The Conditionality of Giro "Success"

While Weiner's report about Cuban distributors' grievances hints at anti-imperialist discord beneath the good neighborly surface, for the most part, enough money trickled down from Hollywood to Cubans in the film giro to contain that discord during this period. By the 1930s, each Hollywood office payrolled up to twenty Cubans, for example, as assistant managers, salesmen, accountants, secretaries, and film checkers (who examined and repaired reels). Most of these jobs paid above average in Havana. Even the offices' unskilled laborers, such as porters and shipping clerks, were paid above Cuba's $1-a-day minimum wage, while an assistant manager could make as much as $67 a week.[88] For skilled, English-speaking Cubans, a job in a Hollywood office represented a respectable salary and stable employment, no small thing in a famously unstable economy. Underscoring this job security, MGM in Havana inducted six Cuban employees into its "10 Years Club," and United Artists boasted of two Cubans it had employed for over fifteen years.[89]

In many ways, Cubans working in the US studios' offices and the film giro broadly were socialized into US corporate culture and its aspirational ethos. To help Cubans excel in the giro, the "Havana Business Academy" (a US-accredited junior college) opened a branch in the movie barrio and advertised in *Cinema*. Since the Havana Business Academy considered "English to be indispensable" to success, it insisted its students study the language two hours a day, promising to make them "think in English" by course's end. Using "American systems," "American 'tests,'" and a simulated office space filled with US-made equipment, students were cured of their bad habit of thinking in Spanish and other "deficiencies." And they learned to value individual initiative, discipline, and verve; each student's "ambition to advance" allowed him to progress "at his own speed. If he is on the ball and works with enthusiasm," the Academy advertised, he could shorten his road to "a better job" and a "good salary"; he would be well "prepare[d] *to fight* in the field of business."[90] As this last line suggests, the Havana Business Academy worked to esteem the "business-man" as properly masculine and Cuban, in contrast to the minoristas' denunciation of that figure as emasculated and foreign.

Havana's film trade journals offered their own sort of continuing education on how to achieve "success" (a word often given in English). In them, the Havana visits of US studio executives, for instance, became opportunities to demystify the essential characteristics of successful corporate masculinity, or "the elemental factors of commercial *triumph*," as *Cinema* put it using the manly language of combat.[91] David O. Selznick, for instance, was "a man of power" who had "conquered Hollywood and the whole world" through hard work, confidence, and youthful enthusiasm; and Fox president Spyro Skouras, who possessed an "irrepressible dynamism," was "the prototype . . . of the 'self-made man.'"[92] They also used US managers working in Havana to highlight the key attributes of success: ambition, charisma, resourcefulness, "indefatigable labor," a "fighting spirit," and the "optimism of winners."[93]

Cubans who wanted to succeed did well to learn from US models, the Cuban film trades also insinuated when describing successful Cubans in the film giro. For instance, Ramón García—who served as Twentieth Century-Fox's Havana manager from 1928 through 1939—started humbly, working as an assistant copy editor in Fox's Foreign Department in New York. Through dogged hard work, he was singled out for promotion to foreign publicity chief—the basis of what *Cinema* deemed his "great experience gained in North America"—before being given charge of Fox's Havana office.[94] Likewise, Pedro Sáenz knew how to make the most of his great experience working as Charles Garrett's assistant manager at RKO's Havana office since 1932, setting himself up to succeed Garrett in the top post in 1939, which Sáenz held for fifteen years.[95] Cubans also did well to reciprocate "the spirit of the good neighbor" that the US companies now ballyhooed. When RKO executives visited Havana for that studio's Caribbean sales conference, *Cinema* praised Sáenz for just that. In exchange for his RKO bosses' commitment to "camaraderie, democracy [and] better collective understanding," Sáenz helped them to better understand "all the multifaceted characteristics of *el cubano* [that which is Cuban], especially its seemingly incomprehensible 'idiosyncrasies.'"[96]

The success stories of Cubans like Ramón García and Pedro Sáenz encouraged the aspirations of other Cubans in the film giro. So did all the material accoutrements of success advertised in the Cuban film trades, not least of all US goods generally associated in Havana with middle-class status.[97] The *ACRC* advertised air travel on Pan-American Airways for "real men of business," as well as US-made pianos and furniture for the well-appointed home and US-made suits for the well-dressed man.[98] In ads proclaiming Studebakers to be "the automobile preferred by distributors' managers and exhibitors," a Havana car dealership started listing successful Cuban giro members' enviable makes and models; Ernesto P. Smith (not just chain cine exhibitor but also Columbia's Havana manager from 1931 through 1959) and a dozen other exhibitors drove shiny new Champions, Commanders, and Presidents.[99]

Indeed, as the Cuban film trades cheered, Havana's chain exhibitors were doing especially well for themselves. According to the *ACRC*, Smith's "favorite sport" was counting ticket stubs at his overflowing box offices, while José Valcarce was "a man of few words and much money" whose "marvelous kind of modern abracadabra" was best represented as a crescendo of dollar signs.[100] In ads targeted at exhibitors, Hollywood's Havana offices used other metaphors to argue that their films were the source of all this largesse. In *Exhibidor* (the ANE's official organ, started in 1937), Fox represented its titles as so many raindrops pouring down on Valcarce and the Radio Cine box office (a literal trickle-down effect); and United Artists represented its titles as gold coins pouring forth from a horn of plenty held aloft by Smith and Valcarce, both chomping cigars, the latter equipped with a sword (see fig. 3.4). In *Cinema*, Paramount represented its titles as hefty moneybags that Popeye piled high on a truck labeled "success."[101]

However, behind all this enthusiasm for material success—and behind the manly metaphors of rugged self-reliance (of Cuban exhibitors as sportsmen, swordsmen and muscle-bound sailors)—lie a pervasive cultural anxiety: that Cuba's economic dependency on the United States emasculated Cuban men, that they were not the masters of their own destinies. Their vulnerability to the whims of foreign companies was especially highlighted in May 1939, when Fox unexpectedly fired Ramón García, who had served as Havana manager for eleven years, to replace him with an Anglo-American, Herbert A. White (a surname that might have highlighted the racial implications of the insult). And though García was quickly hired as manager at Universal's Havana office (where he served for the next sixteen years), this blatant offense to *Cubanidad* inflamed Cuban nationalism in the giro. The UNE boycotted Fox, fuming that its exhibitors had no choice but to act "in defense of the native against the arbitrary and arrogant aggression of those that try to put foreigners in the film giro's most important posts, an unspeakable aggression against the inalienable right of those born in this land."[102] When other giro unions and the Havana press joined the fight, Fox capitulated, sort of. In September 1939, Fox hired a Cuban giro veteran, Enrique López Porta, as "manager," but he reported to White, who was given the title of "president."[103]

Cubans worried that this subjugation of Cuban men undermined not only their individual self-determination but also the nation's. By working for foreign companies, they were failing to lend their talents to Cuban ones. Describing the republican era, historian Robert Whitney explains that "working for a large and modern American business could be seen as either seizing a rare opportunity for personal and professional advancement, or as turning one's back on building Cuban-owned and -run businesses."[104] This ambivalence about Cuban success within US companies and US-dominated industries is amply evident in the giro trades. For instance, even as they congratulated first-run exhibitors for their personal fortunes, they also shamed them for being too closely aligned with the Hollywood distributors (i.e., joining them in lobbying against Spanish-language film quotas and against government mandates for live Cuban performances in their cines) and accused them of *vende-patria* for not doing more to promote national film production. In *Cinema*, trade journalist Pedro Pablo Chávez seethed that "the [Cuban] capitalists that move their money in the business of distribution and exhibition—in which they earn good profits—don't worry at all to invest a single cent in making films." Instead, he complained, they spend their "abundant profits to buy the latest automobile" for themselves and more Hollywood films for their cines. "With all and for all" was Martí's rallying call, *Cinema* editor Enrique Perdices wrote, but too often in the film giro it had been replaced with the phrase "me, me . . . and always me."[105] In other words, Cuban admiration of material success had limits: it should *not* come through subordination to foreign interests and certainly not at the expense of the national community.

Havana first-run exhibitors' dependency on the US studios, and their prostration before them, was highlighted especially in the summer of 1940, when the long-simmering conflict over blind- and block-booking came to a boil. In May, Cuban exhibitors of the ANE and UNE successfully lobbied for Cuban legislation—Decree 1396—prohibiting those practices.[106] The US studios' Havana Film Board responded with outrage; they argued that Decree 1396 violated the film clauses in the US-Cuban Reciprocity Treaty and refused to sign any new contracts with exhibitors.[107] The UNE's first-run exhibitors quickly folded, arguing that the decree was "all a mistake" that had "damaged the pleasant relations that must exist" in the film giro.[108] For this flip-flopping, the ANE's subsequent-run exhibitors (less dependent on Hollywood and less able to survive its disadvantageous terms) denounced UNE members as *vende-patrias*. Not that it did much good. The combined lobbying of the Havana Film Board and the UNE persuaded the Cuban government to modify Decree 1396 in March 1941 to allow blind- and block-booking again. As if to assuage *Cubanidad*, however, a clause was added requiring Havana's largest cines to put on a number of live stage acts per month, thus providing work for Cuban artists and musicians who had long fought for such provisions. (Legislated quotas of live acts would continue throughout the rest of the republican period.)[109]

Despite such sporadic conflicts, revolutionary Cuban nationalism was largely sublimated in the film giro during this period. The film giro was a "contact zone" where (mostly) amicable if hierarchical US-Cuban relations were renegotiated, where US hegemony—and Hollywood's power—was reconstituted on the conditions that profits were shared (if unevenly) and that adequate respect was shown to *Cubanidad*. The following sections return to critical film reception for further insight into the complex dynamics of US-Cuban rapprochement during this period.

"The Applause Should Be Directed": *A Message to Garcia* in Havana

Late in 1935, Twentieth-Century Fox began production on a remake of *A Message to Garcia*, this time with greater care not to inflame revolutionary Cuban nationalism into anti-Yankee ire. After all, the 1916 version had caused an uproar in Havana by overstating the heroism of US Lt. Rowan while belittling Cuba's *mambises*' heroism in their own wars of independence. The recent 1933 Revolution had rendered Cubans more "super-sensitive" about their national heroes, not less, and had rendered good neighborly Hollywood wary of Cuban settings, as noted above. To avoid giving offense to Cubans this time, Fox hired a Cuban consultant to advise on the script and delayed production for weeks to ensure they got it right.[110]

This attention to Cuban sensitivities is apparent in the finished film. While opening with a clear focus on US heroism—with "Stars and Stripes Forever" playing over the opening credits, followed by images of US soldiers joining up, and then President McKinley assigning Rowan (John Boles) his dangerous mission—the film quickly introduces a US citizen living in Havana, Dory (Wallace Beery), who is anything but heroic. In fact, Dory embodies contemporary Latin American critiques of US soldiers, businessmen, and tourists rolled into one. He is a drunk who deserted the US Marines and has spent the last ten years profiting through duplicity: by selling munitions to the Spanish military and information to the Cuban rebels. Nonetheless, Rowan decides to use Dory as a guide into the Cuban interior, convinced that Dory is not "rotten to the core" as others warn. Shortly thereafter, the film introduces its third protagonist, a Cuban woman named Lita (Barbara Stanwyck), first seen crying over the dead body of her father, a fictitious *mambí* leader executed by the Spanish. She agrees to help Rowan get his message of imminent US aid to General Calixto García. "My father died for his country. Can I do less?" she reasons.[111]

Predictably enough, romance ensues between the US gallant and the Latin American damsel. Rowan and Lita fall in love, their professed willingness to die for their respective countries a powerful aphrodisiac. Dory, too, is wooed by Lita's patriotic selflessness. When she is shot and implores Rowan to forge ahead without her, Dory is deeply impressed. He tells Lita, "I learned a lot being around you." In other words, a US character expresses a debt of gratitude to a Cuban one for saving his rudderless soul.[112]

The rest of the film unfolds to show us Cuban heroism as well as Dory's conversion from self-interested cynicism to selfless idealism and, by proxy, US foreign policy's conversion from Big Stick and Dollar Diplomacy to Good Neighbor. Leaving Lita behind per her pleas, Dory guides Rowan to what Dory *thinks* are General García's headquarters, which have been recently over taken by the Spanish unbeknownst to Dory. A short time later, Dory learns from García himself that he unintentionally delivered Rowan to the Spaniards and their torture chamber. Horrified that Rowan will now think Dory betrayed him for money, Dory endeavors to redeem himself. He joins a massive *Cuban* operation to save Rowan, with scores of *mambises* riding in like the US cavalrymen of so many Hollywood westerns. They rout the Spaniards, but not before Dory is fatally wounded. In his dying words, Dory expresses his redemption through this ultimate sacrifice: "Can you imagine *me* dying for my country and not getting a dime for it?" Rowan and Lita then deliver President McKinley's message to García, who proclaims, "This message means the liberation of our people."[113] While this final line suggests Cuban deliverance by US hands, the film has been at pains to emphasize that Cubans devised their own liberation: Lita's patriotic heroism is even more romanticized than Rowan's; García is treated with due reverence; and the *mambí* army is represented as disciplined and able. Finally, within the film's time frame (which ends long before US troops land), it is Cubans who ride in to save the American rather than the other way around.

In Havana, Cubans in the film giro transferred even more agency back to Cuban heroes at the point of distribution and exhibition. While promotion of the film in the United States promised a film about Rowan's "unselfish heroism [and] high adventure," promotion of the film in Havana emphasized General García and the *Cuban* freedom fighters. For instance, Fox's Ramón García placed ads in Havana newspapers that cheer, "The Redeeming Machete Opens the Way/A Nation Oppressed by Ignominy and Slavery Fights/Desperately for the Right to Liberty."[114] Here, Cuba ("a nation oppressed") is the subject of the thrilling action not its object. Further emphasizing the film's homage to Cuban heroism, Ramón García and exhibitor Ernesto P. Smith pledged to donate 10 percent of all box office receipts from its three-day debut at the Encanto to a monument to General García then being planned by city officials. This great show of revolutionary nationalism was well-received in the Havana press.

Diario de la marina's film page pronounced it a "beautiful gesture," making "señores Smith and García and the public that attends these three days at the Encanto the first to contribute" to the García monument.[115] In other words, in Havana, watching *A Message to Garcia* was made an occasion to honor *la patria*, an opportunity to commemorate a revolutionary *Cuban* hero rather than a US one.

In his review, Francisco Ichaso (then serving as resident film critic at *Diario de la marina*, Havana's most widely circulating daily newspaper) further appropriates *A Message to Garcia* to fortify revolutionary Cuban nationalism. He opens with a pointed history lesson, more Cuba-centric than the film's. Ichaso explains that the Americans sought to collaborate with García not because of his weakness (his desperation for US aid), but because of his strengths: his knowledge of the terrain, the size of his army, his brilliance as a strategist, and his "battle-hardened" courage. Not happy to elevate García alone, Ichaso also reminds his reader of another Cuban hero, the leader of the Cuban Republic-in-Arms in exile and (later) Cuba's first president, Tomás Estrada Palma, whose sage counseling made Rowan's success possible. Ichaso then uses the character of Lita to commemorate female *mambises*.[116]

Having elevated Cubans' heroism, Ichaso then downgrades Americans'. Sounding like an anthropologist, he makes US popular culture the subject of Cuban dissection. He explains Americans' fascination with the Rowan Myth as "this propensity to legend that all peoples have." "Metamorphosi[zed]" by hyperpatriotism ever since 1898, Rowan had been made "not only a good soldier, fulfilling his duty, but rather a mythological hero that defeats all the furies of Averno to fulfill his destiny." And, finally, Ichaso concludes his review by linking the film, again, to the planned García monument. Describing the ovation the film received at its Havana premiere, Ichaso prescribes its object: "The applause should be directed at the owner of the Encanto and at Fox for ceding 10% of the admissions to General Calixto Garcia's monument."[117] Explicitly, then, Ichaso intervened in Cuban spectatorship, appropriating *A Message to Garcia* to celebrate Cuban heroes rather than an US imperial one dressed up as a Good Neighbor.

"Not Just a Big Laugh": The Hollywood Left and Chaplin's *Modern Times* in Havana

Along with the "Good Neighbor," President Roosevelt coined another term in his bid to redefine America in the 1930s. Running for president in 1932, he speechified via radio about "*the forgotten man* at the bottom of the economic pyramid."[118] Economic inequality was not only unjust but also disastrous for the national (and global) economy, which depended upon the financial health, and purchasing power, of "the forgotten man," aka "the Common Man." Thus, the New Deal set out to put the common man back to work while also reforming capitalism's excessive structural inequities, by regulating Wall Street and Big Business while granting Labor more power and protections. In promoting this New Deal, the Roosevelt administration famously relied on the support of US artists, for example, painters, poets, playwrights, photographers, who, in turn, relied to some degree on the support of New Deal programs. Generally, in fact, the deprivations of the Great Depression pulled US artists, US popular culture, and US politics notably leftward. And while most left-leaning US artists did not join the Communist Party (CPUSA), some did, swayed by its prediction of capitalism's inevitable self-destruction and, in the meanwhile, the CPUSA's proven ability to organize effectively for progressive causes. However naïve it seems in retrospect (given what is now known of Stalinism and so many totalitarian communist governments), US artists joined the CPUSA as democratic idealists; they believed the party's 1936 campaign slogan: "Communism is Twentieth-Century Americanism." They did not seek to overthrow the US government, but to deepen and strengthen US popular democracy. And they were not fringe radicals. During the Depression, CPUSA members collaborated closely with left-liberals on progressive causes and cultural production. Some of the era's most famous artists belonged to this loose coalition: for example, Orson Welles, John Steinbeck, Clifford Odets, and Woody Guthrie. Not incidentally, their work evidences a preoccupation with the Forgotten Man, and a "masculinist rhetoric" pervades the era's art and popular culture.[119]

By the mid-1930s, Hollywood, too, had its own highly influential network of left-liberals and radicals, energized by the arrival of leftist New York theater artists and European emigrés escaping right-wing fascism. As in other culture industries, a minority of this Hollywood Left joined the CPUSA even as they worked closely with their left-liberal colleagues on progressive causes: their own unionization; socialist Upton Sinclair's End Poverty in California gubernatorial campaign; and for the rights of migrant agricultural workers (and against international fascism, to be covered in chapter 4). Top-billed male movie stars active in this Hollywood Left included Humphrey Bogart, James Cagney, John Garfield, and Paul Muni. But the Hollywood Left's most active members were some of the era's most popular screenwriters; leading figures among these included CPUSA members, such as Sidney Buchman, John Howard Lawson, Robert Rossen, Budd Schulberg, Donald Ogden Stewart, and Dalton Trumbo, as well as noncommunist left-liberals such as Philip Dunne, Dudley Nichols, and Robert Riskin.[120]

Golden Age Hollywood's most famous leftist, though, was Charlie Chaplin. After the release of *City Lights* in 1931, Chaplin toured the globe, enjoying his enormous celebrity while witnessing the devastation wrought by the global depression. He met with world leaders and became more vocal about his left-leaning politics. While advocating progressive *reform*, he also defended popular *revolution*. Without substantial reform of capitalism, he argued, revolution was likely since "there's every evidence that the world needs a drastic change."[121] Upon returning to Hollywood, Chaplin publicly praised Roosevelt's New Deal and became a fixture at Hollywood Left social gatherings. By 1935, according to the *New York Times*, he had a reputation as a "parlor pink."[122] Not that this reputed flirtation with radical ideas did anything to undermine his popularity. When Chaplin released *Modern Times* in 1936, he was at the height of his stardom, with much of the world eager for him to weigh in on contemporary events.

And weigh in he did. Though Chaplin publicly demurred that *Modern Times* should be understood simply as entertainment, it is hard *not* to see the film as an indictment of US industrial capitalism and its effects on the "forgotten" Common Man. It is full of alienated, striking, unemployed, homeless and/or overworked laborers, of desperate "Have Nots" contrasted with powerful and inhumane "Haves." *Modern Times* opens with its most famous sequence, set in an US factory. Borrowing from Soviet cinema's "intellectual montage," Chaplin compares its workers to herded sheep. He then focuses on one among these men: the Little Tramp, tightening bolts on an assembly line. The Little Tramp's boss booms orders to increase the speed of production and even appears on a screen in the bathroom to bark at the Little Tramp to return to work. Toward maximizing his workers' efficiency, this boss considers the purchase of a "feeding machine" to obviate the need for lunch breaks. As its test-subject, the strapped-in Little Tramp (hilariously) suffers a circling barrage of food (corn-on-the-cob, soup, a baked potato) mechanically thrust at his face, until the machine short-circuits. After this humiliation, the hungry Little Tramp is sent back to the assembly line and is unable to keep up with its ever-accelerating pace. Chasing an untightened bolt, he rides the assembly line into the factory's machinery, famously wound through its cogs. Rather than feed the worker, the industrial machine consumes him.[123]

After recuperating from his resulting nervous breakdown, the Little Tramp is released from a hospital into another of *Modern Times*' famous sequences. As he stands on a street corner, a passing truck drops a flag, which had marked the truck's oversized load. The Little Tramp picks it up, waving it at the driver to return. At this moment, a workers' protest march—banners proclaiming

"*Libertad*" (in Spanish) and "Unite"—rounds the corner behind the unsuspecting Tramp, who unintentionally becomes its flag-bearing leader. He is duly arrested, an "innocent victim" wrongly accused of being "a communist leader," according to the film's inter-title. As usual, Chaplin depicts the Little Tramp as a humanist whose very nature puts him at odds with inequity and injustice, which puts him squarely in line with the best US principles, a point Chaplin argues through *mise-en-scène*, with a portrait of Lincoln on the wall of the Little Tramp's jail cell.[124]

Meanwhile, the film introduces a waterfront "Gamin" (Paulette Goddard) who steals food for her unemployed father and hungry little sisters; she is a justified outlaw, taking from the rich to feed the poor. When the Little Tramp and the Gamin meet, they share a daydream of middle-class domesticity and material abundance; she fries a giant steak while he picks grapes from a vine that hangs outside their well-furnished home. With this dream in mind, the two move into a simple shack that the Gamin calls "paradise." But the Little Tramp still aspires to more, so he seeks gainful employment, first as a department-store night watchman and then as a singing waiter. Unfortunately, the inflexible social order frustrates the Little Tramp's aspirations at every turn, and the film ends with he and the Gamin again homeless but not hopeless. He tells her (and the inter-title tells the Depression-era audience), "Buck up, never say die. We'll get along," before they walk away together into a sunset.[125]

United Artists debuted *Modern Times* in Havana at the old Fausto in April 1936, extended for three weeks due to sold-out shows. It was a smash box office and critical success, just as Weiner predicted, given what he well knew about Cubans' affinity for Chaplin.[126] In the five-year wait for a new Chaplin film since *City Lights*, rescreenings of his old films had continued to draw big crowds, amid critics' exclamations of Chaplin's incomparable genius. When *Modern Times* arrived, Havana critics were ready to do the same.[127] In fact, even Valdés-Rodríguez came around to the Cuban critical consensus on Chaplin. By then, Valdés-Rodríguez had been promoted to resident film critic at *El Mundo*, a post he would hold for the next thirty-plus years (1936–67).[128] He used that mainstream newspaper's film page—among other venues—to articulate his highly politicized film criticism to a wider audience, albeit toned down from the Marxist diatribe that was "Hollywood: Sales Agent of American Imperialism." While the critic had previously lumped Chaplin with the rest of Hollywood's bourgeois apologists and imperialism boosters, he now wrote that Chaplin was a "genius" whose trademark "humanist critique" of contemporary social conditions was highly admirable. Perhaps it was

Chaplin's use of Soviet intellectual montage (which the critic greatly admired) in *Modern Times*—the aforementioned workers = sheep cut—that finally won him over. Or perhaps it was the Communist International's Popular Front policy from 1934 to 1939 (encouraging communists around the world to forge strategic alliances with liberal reformers); or perhaps it was his desire to reach *El Mundo*'s more general readership.[129] In any case, Valdés-Rodríguez embraced *Modern Times* as an opportunity to elaborate on what he considered to be its revolutionary content. He emphasizes the film's assembly line sequence and interprets its moral as follows: "Modern men find themselves proud of their conquests and inventions. But their imposing machinery standardizes everything. The human being, by virtue of such inventions, has made himself an automaton, who devotes his brain to serving a structure of gears and screws." Man is degraded and supplanted by the very machinery he created. Valdés-Rodríguez explains that the Tramp's nervous breakdown suggests the "insanity" of industrial capitalism, in which Man serves the machine rather than the other way around.[130]

Valdés-Rodríguez also highlights the protest march sequence in *Modern Times*. While he avoids explicit mention of the recent labor unrest in Cuba and Batista's brutal suppression of it, the PCC, or his own prison term of six months early in 1935, Valdés-Rodríguez likely has national and personal experiences in mind—and hopes his reader does too—when he describes Chaplin's attempt to flag down the truck driver which results in "accusations of being a Communist!" just because "he wanted to help a fellow man." Here, the critic translates this injustice into an indictment of capitalist society. As Valdés-Rodríguez explains, "The social order doesn't stop to ask questions. It is also a machine that causes injustices. To guarantee its existence, it does not hesitate to sacrifice the individual that is supposed to be its very reason to exist." The critic then moves on to interpret the Little Tramp and Gamin's shack—in contrast to their bourgeois daydream of consumer excess—as a socialist utopia. He writes, "We see the example of two simple human beings, who wish ill on no one. How easy it would be! A little modest house for the two, him and her, and food raised by hand . . . and in no greater quantity than is needed."[131]

Borrowing a page from his *minorista* colleagues, Valdés-Rodríguez appropriates this Chaplin film to his own politics. Like them, he prescribes a critical mode of spectatorship, writing, "The public who sees [Chaplin] laughs in the theater and then meditates. Not just a big laugh has been offered, but a lesson." For Valdés-Rodríguez's reader, that lesson is about the inhumanity of modern times, and the heroism of aspiring to an alternative.[132]

"A Great Slavery": Valdés-Rodríguez Decries the Emasculated Cuban Spectator

As always, Chaplin was an exception that proved the rule. Valdés-Rodríguez continued to argue that US-made films generally stupefied Cubans' aspirations for self-rule. Hollywood was an "audiovisual drug" that "numbs the longing for struggle" and the "liberating and rebellious impulse," he explained in a 1938 article, "*El problema social en el cine* [The Social Problem in Cinema]." Less obvious in its Marxist analysis than "Hollywood: Sales Agent of Imperialism," Valdés-Rodríguez's more lyrical portrait here of subordinated and demeaned Cubans—emasculated by both modern labor (especially for US companies) and Hollywood spectatorship—is also worth quoting at length.

> All these exploited workers, campesinos, employees, the office girl, the young errand boy, the bank teller, as well as the poor student, go to the cine every night after their hard workdays to forget the difficulties and miseries that overwhelm them, escaping the anguish and the rigor of each day in the shadows, not knowing that there awaits them, on the screen, the same thing. . . .
>
> By day, a monopoly over their bodies. By night, in the cine hall and by the magic of the silver screen, a monopoly over their spirits, their minds, their feelings. A great slavery more absolute and more difficult to combat. . . .
>
> There, in the cine hall, are Juan and Pedro, whose sinewy arms during the day lug cargo in the port and cut down and lift hundreds of *arrobas* of cane, or lay brick or mold cigar band after cigar band with skillful and light fingers. . . . [And] José, whose fingers during the day have passed over thousands and thousands of dollars, in the suffocating heat of the bank "window," under the harassment of demanding clients and the [danger] of a miscalculated sum which would be subtracted from his salary, already plenty small.[133]

Here, in Valdés-Rodríguez's appeal to so many physical sensations (exhausted limbs, touching fingers, suffocating heat), he works to disrupt Hollywood's transporting effect by reminding these overworked Cubans of their own bodies within their lived context, in which they are so relentlessly exploited, according to Valdés-Rodríguez.

Valdés-Rodríguez then goes on to describe the typical cine program, whose centerpiece is an imaginary Hollywood feature, which Valdés-Rodríguez describes as a formulaic cross-class romance about a poor young girl who manages to beguile a millionaire's son. Despite the girl's poverty, the son's father approves of their marriage; he "believes in democracy and liberalism," writes Valdés-Rodríguez in mocking derision. Moreover, the girl's bosses attest for her good character, because they are "honorable and kind men, with a human and paternal feeling for all their employees," he writes sarcastically of US bosses' supposed paternal benevolence. The only obstacle, then, is the arrival of "a foreigner," a stereotypically lusty Latino. But just as this villain is poised to pounce on the girl, she is saved by the police, who "lock up the villain" despite the lack of any evidence against him, the critic continues. Thus, the happy ending of marriage between poor girl and rich boy celebrates racialized law and order as well as class hierarchies, which are benign and surmountable by the worthy, according to the imaginary film's logic.[134]

For Valdés-Rodríguez, Hollywood's Good Neighbor efforts had not done enough to correct the derogation of Hispanics. But, for Valdés-Rodríguez, racism is simply a tool of the capitalist-imperialist class structure, the true object of the critic's deconstruction. He seeks to denaturalize it by explaining how Hollywood deludes Cuban audiences with these cross-class fantasies' false promises of upward mobility. Valdés-Rodríguez brings the reader back to the local context to clarify the (imaginary) film's ideological effect therein:

> For two hours Juan and Pedro and their respective female companions have forgotten their calamities and even think that perhaps it wouldn't be impossible that . . . their daughters . . . who they have been told look like Bette Davis might be proposed to by that handsome boy she met at the dance at *Centro Gallego*, the son of a wealthy family in Vedado. Why not? Isn't that what happened so naturally on the screen? . . . True they have been exploited for twenty or thirty years. But good heavens! One doesn't have to stop hoping. Maybe liberation comes by such subtle and amiable paths . . .
>
> . . . After all, [their daughter] is as beautiful as the girl in the movie and democracy and civilization have left behind many prejudices. . . . This is what Martí and [Antonio] Maceo died for, so that all would be equal. . . .
>
> So the group of beings that left part of their lives in their oppressive labor during the day, numb themselves through the silver screen's stupefactions by night, coming to reconcile themselves with those that exploit them to annihilation.[135]

According to Valdés-Rodríguez, Hollywood films dissembled the injustice of socioeconomic inequality and offered false promises of delayed rewards in exchange for submission to the status quo. And though Valdés-Rodríguez doesn't say so explicitly, Cuban readers knew that many of the bosses overseeing the "annihilation" of the Juans, Pedros, and Josés of Havana were US citizens or US corporations, which was especially insulting to Cuban manhood. In sarcastically comparing Martí's and Maceo's heroic struggle for liberty and democracy to Cubans' delusional individualistic material aspirations which they hoped to achieve through subordination, Valdés-Rodríguez is invoking revolutionary Cuban nationalism to shame his reader. Passive acceptance of such conditions—engendered through passive Hollywood spectatorship—made Cuban men no better than slaves.

"Great Application for Us": *Mr. Smith* Goes to Havana

By the end of the 1930s, the Cuban public was stirring once again, impatient for the new constitution and presidential elections they had been promised. Batista's image as a revolutionary man of the people had been tarnished by years of strongman tactics. And Batista was not the only political figure with a tainted record; politics in Havana continued to be characterized by well-publicized scandals and shifting alliances, including between Batista and the PCC, which he legalized in late 1938.[136] For many Cubans, the seeming duplicity and dirty-dealing in Cuban politics since 1934 increased the appeal of Grau, who had formed the Partido Revolucionario Cubano-Aútentico (PRC-A) in exile, and pointed to his "100 Days" government as proof of his singular "authenticity." In December 1938, Batista permitted Grau's return from exile, responding to new signals from Washington to revise his tactics. By then, Roosevelt's State Department found it increasingly difficult to support a man likened in the US press not only to Machado but also to Mussolini and Hitler.[137]

Pressed by the Cuban public *and* the US embassy to loosen his grip, Batista also finally allowed an election in November 1939 for delegates to a Constitutional Assembly. The results, in which Grau's PRC-A won a plurality, suggested a mandate for many objectives of 1933's "frustrated revolution." The resulting Constitution of 1940—the governing document of Cuba's Second Republic (1940–58)—was one of the most progressive in the Americas. It limited presidential terms to one; strengthened the legislative and judiciary branches; guaranteed various civil and labor rights; and called for free elections, including for the presidency, which would be held in July 1940 and would pit Grau against Batista. It also called for land reform, which would have hurt US sugar companies had provisions been enforced.[138] However, over the next two decades, successive Cuban governments largely subverted the Constitution of 1940, which nonetheless served as a powerful set of ideals for opposition groups to measure ruling Cubans' failures of revolutionary nationalism.

It was in this period of intense public debate about national ideals and governance that Frank Capra's *Mr. Smith Goes to Washington* premiered in Havana on February 5, 1940, at the Encanto, just two blocks away from the Capitolio, where the Constitutional Assembly convened five days later. *Mr. Smith* was the second in Capra's "Common Man trilogy," produced between *Mr. Deeds Goes to Town* (1936) and *Meet John Doe* (1941), all of them critical and popular hits in Havana.[139] All three are products of the Hollywood Left, with left-liberal Robert Riskin scripting *Mr. Deeds* and *Meet John Doe* while CPUSA member Sidney Buchman scripted *Mr. Smith*. Though Valdés-Rodríguez stretched the intent of *Mr. Deeds* when he argued that the film lays out "the need to redistribute wealth," these three Capra films do express serious critiques of capitalist inequality and greed (in US business, politics, and media) even while they are profoundly idealistic about US democracy and the ability of the Common Man—in the handsome form of Gary Cooper and/or Jimmy Stewart—to redeem it.[140] For Cuban audiences, in the throes of a national conversation about their own democracy, it would have been hard to miss *Mr. Smith's* sociopolitical critiques as well as analogies between contemporary developments in Havana and those depicted in the film.

In the film, Jefferson Smith (Stewart) arrives in Washington as a "Boy Rangers" youth leader appointed to a vacant Senate seat by the governor of a fictional western state. Dewy-eyed, Smith is naïve enough to "recite Jefferson and Lincoln," according to his cynical political mentor, Senator Joseph Paine (Claude Rains), who assures Jim Taylor (Edward Arnold), the bribing capitalist to whom Paine answers, that Smith can be made a reliable yes-man. But Paine underestimates the power of Smith's democratic idealism. In the film's aforementioned early montage, Smith escapes his handlers to tour Washington's most inspiring monuments, including the Lincoln Memorial, where Honest Abe seems to Smith to be "just sitting there like he was waiting for someone to come along." As the plot develops, the corrupting power of Big Money opens Smith's eyes and tests his faith, but Smith ultimately refuses cynicism. In the end, he becomes the "David" to Taylor's "Goliath," doing battle with political machinery, press censorship, and land speculation. In one of Golden Age Hollywood's most famous scenes, Smith embarks on a one-man filibuster in the US Senate. In the words of his love interest, Clarissa Saunders (Jean Arthur), Smith is the man Lincoln was waiting for, sent to redeem US democracy. Interestingly, Saunders connects Smith's idealism not only to US political history but also to an Hispanic literary tradition of social criticism: she calls him "Don Quixote Smith," a knight-errant equipped only with his vision of a better world.[141] This analogy to Quixote was elaborated by the Spanish title that Columbia Pictures gave the film for Cuba and other Spanish-speaking markets: *Caballero sin espada* (Knight without a Sword).

The promotion of the film in Cuba highlighted its critical content and its relevance to local politics. One advertisement that Columbia ran in Havana newspapers is especially telling. It features the photos of five Havana politicians, in a vertical line across the top of the ad, each of whose commitments to Cuban democracy and sovereignty were then under scrutiny: Batista; Grau; Gustavo Cuervo Rubio (Batista's running mate); Mario García Menocal (a hero of the Wars of Independence, whose subsequent presidency from 1913 to 1921 was embroiled in corruption); and Miguel Mariano Gómez (one of Batista's puppet presidents). The large text below the five photos reads, "All Will Agree that *Mr. Smith* Should Be Elected Senator."[142] Whether Columbia's office knew it or not, this ad offers at least two different readings. On the one hand, it might mean that these imminent public figures endorsed the film; they are the "All" for once in agreement about *Mr. Smith's* merits, however vehemently they disagree about everything else. On the other hand, given Cuban political scandals, the virulently contested records of these men, as well as the ad's mug-shot layout and the film's content, a more critical message finds expression: that the incorruptible *Mr. Smith* should be elected by the "All" of the Cuban electorate; that he would be a marked improvement over the usual Cuban suspects who had so corrupted the nation's ideals.

If Cuba's sociopolitical context facilitated the latter reading, Ichaso's review in *Diario de la marina* further encourages connections between the film's portrait of political corruption and Cuban politics. Having served in Grau's 100-Days government, Ichaso was a vociferous critic of Batista and supporter of Grau and the Aútenticos.[143] Perhaps coding a partisan reference to the PRC-A's pledge to make Cuban democracy more *authentic*, Ichaso opens his review by asking rhetorically whether idealism is "a virtue in politics?" He answers in the affirmative, explaining that Smith's idealism serves as an antidote to the treacherous "rogues" who have "supersaturated the [political] environment with guile and deceit."[144] Ichaso then explains that *Mr. Smith* reveals "the blemishes" in US politics, and that those 'blemishes'—more than its "happy end" (he writes in English)—should be of the "greatest interest" to Cubans. The film's exposé of political corruption, he elaborates, "has great application for us since unfortunately we also suffer from this wretchedness, only magnified, with even more damage to the country." This language highlights *Mr. Smith's* critical content and even, in a sense, translates the film into an "essay of national indignation," a ubiquitous Cuban genre in which Ichaso thrived.[145] Ichaso's synopsis of the film's plot goes on to suggest the specific "application" of the film's revelations in Cuba. Ichaso synopsizes that "a certain 'clique' of predatory politicians" appoint someone they believe they can "rely on as one more ally for their rackets, a monosyllabic senator" who will serve as an unthinking yes-man. Taylor and Paine want Smith to be their "puppet-congressman" who won't interfere with their "shady businesses, in which they divvy up a succulent profit margin." In this language, Ichaso gestures to Batista's puppet presidents; to corrupt Cuban politicians' and US companies' close relations; and to the prevalent practices of *botellas* (sinecures), kickbacks, and real estate speculation.

Thankfully, according to Ichaso, the film does not just reveal corruption, but also models "valiant" resistance in its face. Ichaso writes explicitly to demand Cuban identification with Smith's heroism: "Jefferson Smith, as *our* man is named" fights on behalf of the youth, a "true children's army" (perhaps connecting Smith and his Boy Rangers to Grau and the student revolutionaries of 1933). And though the corrupt powers unleash "every type of ruse and maneuver to impede" democracy, Smith perseveres. Ichaso cheers the masculine fortitude ("the physical strength") of Smith's famous filibuster in the US Senate (on which Cuba's own congressional chambers were modeled). According to Ichaso, Smith's filibuster "produc[ed] the most formidable and effective parliamentary obstruction that is recorded in the history of the North American Congress."[146]

Here conflating film fiction and US history, Ichaso's review also conflates film criticism and political endorsement. Ichaso all but announces his support of Grau. And given that the Constitutional Assembly—on which Ichaso had served as a delegate—had resurrected the Generation of '30's high hopes for Cuban democracy, it is not surprising that Ichaso chooses to highlight the film's early montage of lofty idealism. Ichaso writes, "Jefferson Smith's . . . first visit to the Capitol and to the Lincoln Memorial is used productively for well-edited passages of great cinematographic skill, along with the moral and civic elevation that are achieved implicitly."[147] Ichaso recognizes no paradox in borrowing the hypernationalist montage of *Mr. Smith* for "the moral and civic elevation" of *Cubans*. For him, the film inspires not genuflection before US influence but rather a virile freedom-fighting masculinity in defense of Cuban democracy.

As noted briefly in the introduction, Valdés-Rodríguez similarly appropriates *Mr. Smith* in his review in *El Mundo*. Like Ichaso, he highlights Smith's first visit to the Lincoln Memorial. Putting democratic idealism ahead of aesthetic rigor, the usually discriminating critic even calls the hokey early montage "the best part of the movie from the filmic point of view," particularly in the ways that Smith's "deep and palpable devotion prevails upon the spectator," the critic prescribes.[148]

To be clear, Valdés-Rodríguez appreciates the first Lincoln Memorial scene precisely for the contrast it sets up with Smith's second visit later in the film. As Valdés-Rodríguez describes it, "Jefferson Smith returns to the Lincoln Memorial defeated. . . . He says goodbye to the great figures [of the past] betrayed by the senatorial cronies and he sits dejectedly on his suitcases. . . . In the clear silence of the dusk we hear Jefferson Smith's dull sob, crying for the defeat of his ideal because it was among the founders' best." For Valdés-Rodríguez, this later scene captures the film's purpose: to make its viewers as clear-eyed as the disillusioned Smith.[149] Like Ichaso, Valdés-Rodríguez returns Cubans' attention from the film's happy ending—and the passivity it might engender—to the film's critical content.

After all, as noted in the Introduction, Valdés-Rodríguez argues that said corruption in US politics (which was something "*we* all know about") has infected Cuban politics and been "enlarged by the tropical environment," by residual *caudillismo* and *latifundia*, and by US companies operating on the island. After asserting that "Capra's brave film has an exemplariness and unique relevance" in Cuba, Valdés-Rodríguez concludes, "Therefore we recommend the film 'Mr. Smith Goes to Washington', despite some qualms that we have regarding certain patriotic . . . expressions [in it]."[150] In other words, Valdés-Rodríguez is aware of (and reticent about) the paradox of borrowing a US cultural product with distinct nationalist underpinnings in order to disarticulate US economic and political imperialism, and nonetheless finds it irresistibly effective as a tool. Like Ichaso, Valdés-Rodríguez translates *Mr. Smith Goes to Washington* into an essay of Cuban national indignation rather than a propagandistic paean to US democracy.

Conclusion

Five months after *Mr. Smith* debuted in Havana, Batista won the July 1940 presidential election, much to the relief of the US embassy. He did so by forging unlikely political alliances and by successfully positioning himself as a progressive torchbearer of revolutionary nationalism while, paradoxically, tapping into campaign coffers heavy with US companies' contributions.[151] Inaugurated on October 10, 1940, Cuba's Independence Day, President Batista would remain the United States' man in Havana during the coming war years, a period in which the stakes of US-Cuban ties, and of hemispheric solidarity generally, rose higher still for US policymakers.

In the seven years since the 1933 revolution, in the midst of a desperately needed economic recovery, Cubans had accommodated themselves to a military strongman and the restoration of US hegemony. But revolutionary nationalism was alive and well, exerting pressure on Batista to restore constitutional frameworks and to don civilian clothing (he "retired" from the military in order to run for president). Likewise, the Cuban public's acquiescence to US hegemony was qualified on the condition that the United States had sincerely reformed itself from wielder of the Big Stick to Good Neighbor, and from greedy Yankee capitalist to socially progressive New Dealer. The rapprochement of the United States and Cuba, then, was predicated not only on mutual prosperity but shared ideals about progressive *Pan*-American values (sovereignty, democracy, and economic opportunity) and shared ideals of heroic masculinity (commitment to fight for those values). In the mid- to late 1930s, US policymakers believed that Hollywood played an important role in forging these bonds with Cuba and other Latin American countries, so much so that US policymakers greatly elaborated their working relationship with the US film industry in the run-up to and during World War II, convinced that Hollywood and its representations of liberty-loving Pan-America would be the "strongest bonds" of hemispheric solidarity in the global War against Fascism. Their work, and Cuban reception of it, is the subject of the next chapter.

4

You Are Men! Fight for Liberty! Hollywood Heroes and the Pan-American Bonds of World War II

Just a few words from the Cuban national anthem: "Don't be afraid of the glorious death, because to die for your country is to live."

DESI ARNAZ, as a Cuban sailor in the US Navy, in *The Navy Comes Through*, 1943

Inspired by an elevated sentiment of continental fraternity and of solidarity with the heroic countries that combat gloriously to defend the Democracies . . . and against the barbarity, the cruelty and the horror of the totalitarian nations . . . we are all obliged to fight for Democracy.

CUBAN EXHIBITOR MANUEL RAMÓN FERNÁNDEZ, in *Cinema*, 1942

January 1942. In the Teatro América's lobby, high officials of Batista's administration mingle with Havana elites and film giro members—including Herbert White, Enrique López Porta, Charles Garrett, Enrique Perdices, and Henry Weiner.[1] Gathered for the premiere of Twentieth-Century Fox's *Week-End in Havana*, tonight's crowd crackles with an excitement stoked by plenty of advance publicity, including an Alice Faye lookalike contest, in which bleached-blonde Cuban women competed for a silver fox cape and a case of *Bourjois* perfume.[2] *Bohemia*'s pre-debut coverage of the film had been headlined "Hispanic-America Is Triumphing," evidenced by the astronomical Hollywood stardoms of *Week-End*'s Carmen Miranda and Cesar Romero.[3] As *Cine-Mundial* pointed out, the latter was José Martí's goddaughter's son, and so proud of that "noble Cuban ancestry" that he was trying to convince Fox executives to make a Martí biopic.[4]

Like so many prewar Good Neighbor Hollywood musicals, *Week-End in Havana* makes its argument for US-led Pan-Americanism on the basis of pleasure, romance, respect, and mutual prosperity. In an early montage of Havana's most iconic sites (e.g., Morro Castle, the Malécon, Oriental Race Track, the Capitolio), the movie represents Havana as a thriving and modern metropolis, as the film's US protagonists, Jay (John Payne) and Nan (Faye) arrive on a Pan-American Airways Clipper. The two then tour casinos and sugar fields, falling in love under the spell of Cuba's "enchanting rhythms," song lyrics explain. Along the way, Jay and Nan incidentally dump a fortune onto the laps of the film's two Cuban foils, played by Miranda and Romero, who share in the film's happy ending musical number.[5]

But a more sober and urgent argument for Pan-American solidarity was rising fast in early 1942 and was also amply evident at *Week-End in Havana's* Cuban premiere. Just four weeks earlier, in response to the Japanese attack at Pearl Harbor, the United States—and then Cuba (days later)—had declared war on the Axis powers. More and more, it seemed that the fate of the free world depended upon the mutual defense of the Americas. Thus the US government had created the Office of the Coordinator of Inter-American Affairs (OIAA), in August 1940, and the OIAA's Motion Picture Division had arrived in Hollywood by early 1941 to help the US film industry win Latin Americans over to hemispheric solidarity and defense. At the Teatro América's premiere of *Week-End in Havana*, signs at the entrance carried the OIAA slogan, "*America—Libre y Unida* [Free and United]." (That slogan—or sometimes "*Unidos Venceremos* [United We Will Win]"—would soon be added to the US studios' advertisements in Cuba and stamped on the pages of Cuban fanzines.)[6] And prominent signs at the box office announced that the night's proceeds would be donated to the Cuban-American Allied Relief Fund, run by US expats and prominent Cuban citizens, including chain exhibitor Edelberto de Carrerá.[7] As captured in the second epigraph above, another Cuban chain exhibitor, Manuel Ramón Fernández, rallied his compatriots to donate to this same fund in language that suggests that Cubans—in the film giro and elsewhere—enthusiastically embraced the wartime Pan-American freedom-fighting zeitgeist promoted by Hollywood, not least of all because of its consonance with revolutionary Cuban nationalism, as suggested by Desi Arnaz's line of dialogue from an OIAA-counseled film given in the first epigraph.[8] This chapter argues that Hollywood's wartime films in Havana played an important role in "elevating" the "sentiment of continental fraternity" that Fernández exhorts: the ideal of a hemispheric brotherhood duty-bound to freedom-fight, with US heroes leading the charge.

The period of World War II represents the high point of US-Cuban ties of singular intimacy. The war brought prosperity to the island. Though US tourism to Cuba declined from its prewar peak, the United States' voracious war machine made up the difference, requiring a steady diet of metals from Cuban mines and tons of sugar, at unprecedented prices. In exchange for this and millions of dollars in loans and military equipment, Batista offered the full cooperation of the Cuban navy; granted use of Cuba's military facilities; and allowed the construction of new US air bases on the island, crucial for the defense of Atlantic shipping lanes and the Panama Canal.[9]

But it was not just sugar, metals, arms, and money that flowed easily between the two countries during the war, tying them together. Hollywood films, especially now, served as an important binding agent, and not just the Good Neighbor musicals like *Week-end in Havana*. More than these, it was Hollywood's antifascist, prodemocratic films that touched a chord in Cuba. These films' intense romanticization of freedom-fighting masculinity as moral imperative sutured neatly onto Cuban revolutionary masculinity. Cubans looked up to and identified closely with the male heroes in these films. They wanted to be like them, in ways at least as consequential as Cuban women dying their hair to look like Alice Faye.

This effect wasn't entirely accidental. Many wartime Hollywood films were, in fact, designed to propagandize audiences—and not just domestic ones. To win Latin American hearts and minds, the OIAA worked with Hollywood on hundreds of shorts and feature films about the "U.S. War Effort" and the "American Way of Life." The Hollywood Left especially collaborated with the OIAA to win Latin Americans to the defense of freedom, which the OIAA posited as the very foundation of Pan-American identity, arguing that a shared "love of liberty" was the "strongest bond" between Americans, North and South.[10] This narrative, however, was confounded by Latin Americans' stubborn historical memory of US imperialism and US support of dictators in Latin America. Faced with this hypocrisy, some in the OIAA argued that the mistakes of the Big Stick and Dollar Diplomacy should be admitted and denounced, while others argued they should be ignored for a singular focus on the more recent Good Neighbor Policy. Others worried that future US policy might not look all that different from past policy and, thus, that too much "fulminating against the 'evils'" of dictatorships and too much proselytizing of democracy and national sovereignty might prove counterproductive to US interests in Latin America in the long run.[11]

This chapter explores this pivotal moment in both US-Cuban relations and Hollywood history, and their intersections. The first section covers the broader context of wartime US-Cuban relations, particularly through the rise of the OIAA and its Information Division, which represented Cuba as a model "sister republic" and Batista as a man learning democratic ways from US models. The second section canvasses the OIAA's work with the Hollywood Left, intent on representing the United States as the propagator of the progressive Four Freedoms throughout the hemisphere and on arguing that this "*Pan*-American Way" was a cause for which true men should be willing to give their lives. The third section hones in on the ways in which the OIAA's attempts to overcome Latin Americans' memory of US imperialism and US support of dictatorships shaped Hollywood war films. The fourth section returns to Havana to explore the film giro's embrace of Hollywood's Pan-American freedom-fighting antifascist propaganda. And the final sections examine Havana film critics' appropriation of Hollywood's wartime films, weaving them into revolutionary Cuban nationalism's freedom-fighting masculinity and democratic idealism, including its disdain for (US-supported) Cuban strongmen, suggesting that US policymakers were right to worry about the potential counterhegemonic effects of their hemispheric call to arms.

A Model Sister Republic: The OIAA, the Pan-American Free World, and Cuba

In the summer of 1940, as the Nazis rolled over Europe and assaulted Great Britain, and as imperial Japan flexed its expansionist muscle in Asia, President Roosevelt doubled-down on the Good Neighbor Policy, setting out to shore up his country's "own backyard." That August, Roosevelt created the OIAA, under Nelson Rockefeller, in order to coordinate the efforts of various government agencies and private industries in a policy objective of increasing urgency: "to strengthen the bonds between the nations of the Western Hemisphere."[12] To do so, the OIAA would have to combat Nazi propaganda that warned Latin Americans, according to OIAA analysts, that "the U.S. policy of so-called 'good-neighborliness' is merely a jumble of meaningless words" meant to cover up a proven history of economic imperialism and armed intervention.[13]

Thus, the OIAA came to focus much of its energies in its Information Division, which enlisted the United States' increasingly powerful communications media—the press, the radio, and the movies—for propaganda abroad to an unprecedented extent.[14] Noting that Latin Americans were tired of the phrase "Good Neighbor," OIAA propagandists decided to reframe their pitch using the "Four Freedoms," recently articulated in Roosevelt's January 1941 State of the Union address.[15] Indeed, left-liberals generally seized upon these Four Freedoms as the defining elements of the "American Way," a phrase just then rising to common usage and great cultural import. Intellectuals, artists, civic leaders, propagandists, and others characterized this unifying American Way—in sharp contrast to the Nazi Way—by the United States' commitments to civil liberties (freedom of expression), to religious and ethnic pluralism (freedom from discrimination), to a reformed capitalism that spread prosperity to all (freedom from want), and to the right to the peaceful self-determination of democratic nations (freedom from fear).[16]

While the Office of War Information (OWI, formed in 1942) also used the Four Freedoms to mobilize *US* citizens for the war, it was the OIAA's particular charge to persuade Latin Americans that this American Way was, in fact, the *Pan*-American Way, for which Latin Americans should also fight. In the summer of 1942, a two-page photo spread in the OIAA's new *Life*-like glossy magazine, *En Guardia* [On Guard] presented Latin Americans' choice in graphic terms: They could choose the Four Freedoms of "*El Mundo Libre* [The Free World]"—a world free from want, prejudice, political repression, and fear of military attacks—or they could choose "*El Mundo Esclavizado* [The Enslaved World]" offered by the Nazis—a world of starvation, racial and religious intolerance, political imprisonment, and conquest (see figs. 4.1 and 4.2).[17]

One needs look no further than Havana to appreciate the tenor and scale of the OIAA's Pan-American Free World pitch. There, the Cuban-American Allied Relief Fund alone circulated three thousand copies of *En Guardia* monthly, while the OIAA broadcast a steady stream of radio shows, including a number of regular programs and specials produced in Hollywood.[18] On Cuban Independence Day, October 10, 1942, for instance, Desi Arnaz, James Cagney, and Cesar Romero participated in a "Salute to Cuba" broadcast. And just two days later, on a Columbus Day broadcast, Linda Darnell and Ray Milland performed a sketch about a new bride sending her groom to war, "their dialogue built around freedom and liberty which the continents have always fought for since their discovery." The same broadcast featured Adolphe Menjou as a time-traveling Christopher Columbus, who calls "Hitler by telephone to inform him that the Americas stand for freedom and will not tolerate anything but that."[19] At the same time, the OIAA distributed pamphlets in Havana schools with titles like "True Heroes," which used comic strips to "depict the exploits of United States war heroes." The OIAA also filled Havana shop windows with posters by the thousands, with one series devoted to US political heroes like Jefferson and Lincoln, another to Pan-American soldiers, and another to the Four Freedoms as the defining principles for which these soldiers fought. And, finally, the OIAA's press department serviced seventy-one Cuban publications, including eighteen Havana newspapers, providing them with press releases, articles, and photographs.[20]

To facilitate the dissemination of all this OIAA "information," US businessmen in Cuba formed an OIAA Coordination Committee. Serving as chief of its Motion Picture Section was the film giro's own Charles Garrett, who took a leave from his new job as publicity chief in Paramount's Havana office.[21] In his OIAA post, Garrett arranged for the projection of US "non-theatrical" films (produced by the OIAA and/or other US war agencies), including in rural Cuba through the use of five mobile cinema trucks. Cubans saw US propaganda films (like "Victory for the Americas" and "The Basic Freedoms") in schools, town squares, government offices, and even on beaches. Garrett

FIG. 4.1. The OIAA represents the Four Freedoms offered to Latin Americans by the (Pan-)American Way. *En Guardia*, Year 1, no. 8 (Summer 1942). (Courtesy of Rockefeller Archive Center; FA789)

FIG. 4.2. In stark contrast to the Four Freedoms, the OIAA represents the deprivation, annihilation, repression, and fear offered to Latin Americans by the fascist Axis powers. *En Guardia*, Year 1, no. 8 (Summer 1942). (Courtesy of Rockefeller Archive Center; FA789)

reported great success, estimating that some 1,400 non-theatrical screenings reached 360,000 Cubans in 1944 alone, to say nothing of the OIAA's reach into Cuba's movie theaters through Hollywood entertainment films, as we will see.[22]

Cuba was a special target of OIAA propaganda, and not just because it was a strategic location for defense. After all, less than a decade before, the Platt Amendment had served as Exhibit A in Latin Americans' case against Yankee imperialism. Demonstrating that Cubans were now *choosing* the Pan-American Way should go a long way toward convincing other Latin Americans to do the same. This helps to explain why *En Guardia* repeatedly portrays Cuba as a model sister republic, presenting photographic evidence of its citizens fervently joining the war effort and enjoying all the benefits of its close ties with the United States. In September 1942, for instance, *En Guardia* ran a four-page article that represented US-Cuban relations (past and present) in the same rosy hues as had *Week-End in Havana*: US tourists enjoy and enrich the modern city of Havana; Cuba is amply rewarded for sharing the fruits of its "fertile lands" with US defense industries; and a photo captures a crowd gathered around a monument to the USS *Maine*, showing Cubans acknowledging their "debt of gratitude" to the US Empire of Liberty.[23]

Perhaps most importantly, *En Guardia* insisted on crediting *President* Batista for Cuba's successes. The article's first photograph is of Batista on the occasion of his presidential inauguration, captioned, "The Republic of Cuba has in its President Fulgencio Batista one of the greatest supporters of its progress." The body text cheers that Cuba is "under the direction of President Batista, who in nine years of work has built hundreds of schools" as well as health clinics and orphanages, passed laws to benefit farmers, stabilized the economy, and reduced inequality. *En Guardia* presents Batista as a populist reformer in the New Deal vein, never mind that he had ruled as a behind-the-scenes military strongman for most of the nine years *En Guardia* references. Glossing that recent past, *En Guardia* praises Batista's current build-up of Cuba's military—with US support—as evidence of Cuba's exemplary "bravery" in this fight to achieve "liberty for all the Americas in the coming centuries."[24]

En Guardia's representation of Batista captures the OIAA's attempt to spin the United States' continuing support of Latin American military dictators (also in the Dominican Republic, El Salvador, Guatemala, Nicaragua, and Venezuela), which threatened to undermine the OIAA's propaganda campaign. Batista represented a solution to the OIAA's conundrum. Having transformed from strongman to democratically-elected president, in fact, Batista represented the very personification of the Pan-American progress narrative that was an important part of the OIAA's pitch: that regrettable Old World *caudillismo* was evolving towards New World democracy under US tutelage.

"The Responsibility of Acting Likewise": Hollywood's Pan-American Freedom Fight

In order to convince Latin Americans of its Pan-American Free World pitch, the OIAA recognized it would need more than limited-circulation magazines, shortwave radio broadcasts, and even non-theatrical films. What was needed was Hollywood entertainment films, with their reach into Latin American cines and their unique ability to persuade without seeming to propagandize. Thus, early in 1941, the OIAA's Motion Picture Division (OIAA-MPD) set up an office in Hollywood and set out to enlist the US film industry toward winning Latin American hearts and minds to the War for Democracy. And Hollywood, it turned out, was eager to serve. At the OIAA's behest the film industry established an organization called the Motion Picture Society for the Americas (MPSA), which gathered the studio moguls on its executive committee, who, in turn, committed their Foreign Department chiefs—and later, their Story Department chiefs—to weekly meetings with OIAA-MPD representatives, in which they discussed how the film industry could best advance the OIAA's propaganda objectives. And the Production Code Administration (PCA) hired a Latin American "specialist," charged with reviewing scripts with two objectives in mind: first, to ensure that Hollywood's representations *of Latin America* did not offend Latin Americans; and second, to ensure that Hollywood's representation *of the United States* did not show the United States—"our own people, [our] government, our institutions or national ideals"—in "a bad light," in other words, in ways likely to confirm Latin Americans' negative preconceptions about Yankee ways and thus sully the United States' bid for hemispheric hegemony.[25] For this role, the PCA hired a Cuban-born NBC executive, Addison Durland, which the Cuban film trades noted with great pride. (Interestingly enough, Durland's interest in the cinema began at Valdés-Rodríguez's garage-wall screenings in the late 1920s.)[26] At the same time, the OIAA-MPD enlisted Hollywood actors and screenwriters to work on everything from political speeches and radio dialogue to film treatments and scripts.[27]

Like the Office of War Information's Bureau of Motion Pictures, the OIAA-MPD especially attracted the cooperation of the highly mobilized Hollywood Left.[28] After all, its members were inclined to work with the Roosevelt administration, increasingly optimistic that their vision of the (Pan-)American Way lined up with its New Deal vision: an increasingly inclusive democracy and a more equitable economic system. Perhaps even more importantly, members of the Hollywood Left were repulsed by the rise of fascism in Europe and began to argue that the United States and other democracies had the responsibility to fight for Freedom the world over. In the mid- to late 1930s, while much of the country clung to its interwar isolationism, they formed groups like the Hollywood Anti-Nazi League and the Motion Picture Artists' Committee to Aid Republican Spain.[29]

At the same time, in the late 1930s, the Hollywood Left had begun to make films that argued for US intervention. This trend began in 1938 with *Blockade*, a film about the Spanish Civil War, written by John Howard Lawson and produced by Walter Wanger (who would be made MPSA chief in 1941), which took aim at Spain's rising fascist General Francisco Franco and his forces. In *Blockade*, the suffering of Spanish civilians prompts Henry Fonda (playing a Spanish farmer turned anti-Franco resistance fighter) to ask famously, "Where is the conscience of the world?"[30] (See fig. 4.3.) In 1939, a young John Huston co-wrote *Juarez*, a Warner Bros. film that was both antifascist *and* Pan-American. About French imperial intervention in Mexico in the 1860s, *Juarez* works as a history lesson for present purposes, encouraging analogies between Napoleon III's extraterritorial ambitions and Hitler's, and celebrating Mexican president Benito Juarez (Paul Muni)'s resistance to French rule—with US support.[31] (*Juarez* was given a special premiere in Havana, attended by one of its Hollywood Left stars, John Garfield.)[32] Perhaps most famously, in October 1940, as the Battle of Britain raged, Chaplin released *The Great Dictator*, in which the horrors of Nazism compel him out of his trademark silence into a long speech urging all freedom-loving men to action. "You are men! . . . Fight for Liberty!" his character exhorts.[33] As if in response, the Hollywood Left put some of the industry's top masculine icons into military uniform in 1941. For instance, in *Sergeant York* (co-written by John Huston and Howard Koch), Gary Cooper portrays a conscientious objector turned decorated war hero of the Great War (like *Juarez*, a history lesson meant to mobilize Americans for the present war).[34] All of this is to say that, with the United States' official entry into the war at the end of 1941, the Hollywood Left was well disposed to help government propagandists pitch the War for Democracy to movie audiences—US and Latin American alike.

Thus, Hollywood Left screenwriters volunteered early and often for OIAA work, not least in penning original scripts for theatrical shorts and even features. At the same time, OIAA-MPD representatives (like OWI representatives) began to consult on feature films under consideration or in preparation at the studios, finding Hollywood Left screenwriters to be among their best collaborators. And the lists of 100-plus films on which the OIAA-MPD consulted clarify that the OIAA was at least as much concerned with representations of the United States as it was with representations of Latin America. Indeed, the OIAA-MPD lists of consulted films had a category for

FIG. 4.3. Havana's Cine-Teatro Fausto promotes Walter Wanger's antifascist film about the Spanish Civil War, *Blockade* (1938). *Around the World* 6, no. 5: 3. (Courtesy of Wisconsin Center for Film and Theater Research)

films about "Our Way of Life," which included *An American Romance*, *Going My Way*, *The Human Comedy*, *A Medal for Benny*, *The Ox-Bow Incident*, *Pittsburgh*, and *Thousands Cheer*. And they had a category for films about "Our Great War Effort," which included *Action in the North Atlantic*, *Bombardier*, *The Fighting Sullivans*, *Guadalcanal Diary*, *Manila Calling*, and *So Proudly We Hail!*[35] The majority of OIAA-MPD consulted films do contain "Latin American content," but it is usually "Incidental," that is, fleeting references and/or secondary characters—often suggested by the OIAA-MPD in the first place, which then allowed the OIAA-MPD to weigh in on the script generally, with the goal of "pointing the propaganda content to maximum effectiveness" for Latin American audiences.[36] Even beyond direct consultation on these 100-plus films, the OIAA-MPD endorsed other Hollywood feature films for "their promise to make important contributions to the Coordinator's Informational program in Latin America," because of their "pro-democratic theme," including *Casablanca*, *Air Force*, *Mrs. Miniver*, *Salute to the Marines*, and *Sergeant York*.[37]

While the OIAA-MPD consulted on many of the same scripts as the OWI, they argued that their work was not redundant. Shaping scripts for *Latin American* audiences, they argued, required special knowledge of "Latin American sensibilities."[38] For one thing, OIAA analysts reported that Latin Americans would be especially wary of obvious propaganda; it would be interpreted as proof that the United States was trying to manipulate them. Thus, it stood to reason that the continued inclusion of social criticisms of the American Way in Hollywood films would prove that the United States was not engaging in propaganda *and* that its citizens, unlike those under Nazi rule, enjoyed freedom of expression. Moreover, continued social criticism conformed to OIAA analysts' suggestions from the field that Hollywood films should show "some of our American National short-comings" in order "to counteract" Latin Americans' impression that US citizens "had a feeling of superiority towards them."[39]

However, one US "National shortcoming" was particularly thorny for the OIAA: racial discrimination. OIAA analysts in the field repeatedly worried about the ways that the maltreatment of Hispanics in the United States (e.g., around the Bracero Program and the Zoot Suit Riots) was reported in the Latin American press.[40] To counteract this bad publicity, the OIAA-MPD and MPSA settled on a simple "content directive": Hollywood should insert Hispanic soldiers into its many wartime multiethnic platoon combat films, ultimate proof that the United States did not look down upon them. The MPSA specifically laid out this objective in an early "Suggested Working Program": "If, for example, a Latin American boy, or one with a distinctively Latin American name, could be included in, say a group of American soldiers fighting in the war, such an indication would be helpful."[41] Once a Hispanic soldier was included in a film, the MPSA, the OIAA-MPD, and/or Durland at the PCA consulted on the script, working to "strengthen" that character's storyline and dialogue.[42]

Take, for instance, the two OIAA-MPD consulted war films in which Cuba's own Desi Arnaz appears as the token Hispanic serviceman: RKO's *The Navy Comes Through* (1942) and MGM's *Bataan* (1943). In the former, Arnaz plays a "Heroic Cuban character," according to MPSA notes.[43] When arriving for assignment to a US Navy gun crew, he proudly introduces himself, in rapid-fire Spanish, as "Patricio José Francisco Eduardo de la Vega Tarriba, Jr." and then good-naturedly accepts the Americanized version of his name, "Pat," immediately suggested by his Irish-American commander, Mike O'Mallory (Pat O'Brien). At this point, RKO's original script had Tarriba describe his hometown: "In Havana no one is asleep. They are drinking Daiquiris and dancing and making love." But the Cuban-born Durland, well versed in Cuban sensitivities, objected to this line, and compelled RKO to delete it. More problematic still was Tarriba's next line. When O'Mallory asks, "How is it a Cuban hotfoot like you comes all the way over here to join the United States Navy," the original script had Tarriba answer, "Why not? The U.S. made Cuba free, so I come here to free the United States." Durland objected strenuously to this exaggeration of Cuba's "debt of gratitude." He admonished RKO that "this statement is contrary to fact and should be changed to avoid giving offense to Cubans, especially since it will be uttered by a Cuban."[44] In response, RKO modified Arnaz's line as follows: "Well, the United States *helped to make* Cuba free so I come here to free the United States." Apparently appeased, Durland allowed the revised line as well as O'Mallory's response: "I think you got something there. Get on board, sailor," two sentences that pack a powerful ideological punch.[45] They affirm Tarriba's explanation of Cuba's (still substantial) debt to the United States and his distillation of US war aims (freedom); and they evidence the easy assimilation of Hispanics into the (Pan-)American Way on the condition of respect for US leadership.

Once he is "onboard" and traversing the Atlantic, Tarriba's easy assimilation into the inter-ethnic crew is facilitated by his firm grasp of Pan-America's common heritage of freedom fighting. After a Nazi U-boat attack kills a fellow sailor, Tarriba offers the following words of comfort: "No temáis una muerte gloriosa/Que morir por la patria es vivir." When pressed by a fellow sailor, Tarriba explains that these are "just a few words from the Cuban national anthem: 'Don't be afraid of the glorious death because to die for your country is to live.'"[46] With this line, Arnaz succinctly articulates the compatibility between Hollywood's wartime codes of Pan-American freedom-fighting masculinity and Cuban revolutionary nationalism, which is why it serves as this chapter's first epigraph.

In *Bataan*, too, Arnaz gets some choice lines about the Pan-American Way for which its soldiers were sacrificing their lives. In it, he plays Felix Ramírez, a Mexican American soldier, a Catholic, a proud US citizen, and a well-loved member of a multiethnic platoon in the Philippines. In camp one evening, Ramírez manages to rig a radio to pick up a US broadcast of the Tommy Dorsey Orchestra playing African American composer Sy Oliver's song "Well, Git It!" Hearing this swing music, associated as it was with the American Way's racial pluralism and its pleasures, Ramírez is overcome with pride.[47] He enthuses exuberantly, "That's good ole American! That's USA!" Later, when Ramírez is stricken with malaria, an Anglo-American private sacrifices his quinine pills to try (unsuccessfully) to save him and then translates Ramírez's dying words, the Latin prayer of contrition, into English.[48] Both gestures are meant to evidence the nondiscriminatory fraternal bonds of the US military and, by extension, of US society, in other words, to show that freedom from discrimination is a pillar of the (Pan-)American Way.

Another important part of the OIAA's Pan-American Free World pitch was that US hemispheric hegemony would bring prosperity and reduce economic inequality—and thereby spread freedom from want—by promoting New

Deal reforms throughout the Americas. Toward this end, the OIAA-MPD consulted on a number of films in the "Our Way of Life" category that celebrate labor-capital cooperation; in them, US capitalists are represented as benevolent leaders who had pulled themselves up from humble origins and who treat their workers like "partners," not least of all as US industry geared up to serve as the "Arsenal of Democracy," e.g., *Pittsburgh* and *An American Romance.* Much to the chagrin of the OIAA's Pan-American propagandists, however, a long history of US companies exploiting Latin American labor and natural resources could not be easily overcome. As the OIAA informed the MPSA, many Latin Americans refused to abandon their belief that "the *Americanos* were just a species of land-lubber pirates, hell-bent on looting the countries through which they slashed their way," leaving behind them a wake of want.[49] To address this perception, the OIAA-MPD suggested biopics about US citizens who went to Latin America to amass vast fortunes, sure, but along the way improved Latin Americans' lives. The most harebrained idea was for a feature about Samuel Zemurray, president of the United Fruit Company, much maligned throughout Latin America (including in Cuba) for land-grabbing, coddling repressive regimes, and violently repressing workers. The OIAA-MPD acknowledged that many Latin Americans believed that the United Fruit Company "typif[ied] U.S. methods of exploiting the other Americas." In fact, that was precisely why their Zemurray biopic would tell "another side to the story," namely Zemurray's rags-to-riches rise as a Russian immigrant to the United States and all "the physical good" that United Fruit had done to modernize Latin America's agriculture, transportation, communications, and health. According to the OIAA-MPD, a Zemurray biopic "would both demonstrate the US democratic theme of opportunities for all, and would underscore the good instead of the bad that has resulted from what has been termed 'dollar diplomacy.'" Wisely, however, the OIAA-MPD decided that United Fruit might "smack too much of Yankee imperialism," and it dropped the idea by the end of 1943.[50]

Indeed, the history of Yankee imperialism was the OIAA's greatest obstacle to convincing Latin Americans that US hemispheric hegemony would guarantee their freedom not just from censorship, discrimination, and want, but also from fear: from the types of violent territorial conquests and authoritarianism the OIAA associated with the Axis powers. Toward overcoming this obstacle, the OIAA-MPD emphasized—with the help of the Hollywood Left—the incomparable tyranny of Nazism. The OIAA-MPD counseled on and/or endorsed a number of Hollywood Left features depicting life under Nazi rule and heroic resistance against it. These included *Hitler's Children, The Cross of Lorraine, Five Were Chosen, For Whom the Bell Tolls, The Moon*

Is Down, *None Shall Escape*, and *Song of Russia*.[51] The OIAA-MPD also facilitated the Latin American distribution of additional Hollywood Left antifascist films, including *Confessions of a Nazi Spy*, *The Great Dictator*, and *Thirty Seconds over Tokyo*.[52]

Representatives of the OIAA-MPD and MPSA knew, however, that mobilizing Latin Americans *against* Nazism did not mean mobilizing them *for* US hemispheric hegemony. Reports from the field repeatedly cautioned them that, as one US citizen in Brazil put it, Latin Americans' "memory of McKinley-TR imperialism is all too green."[53] So the OIAA-MPD set out to revise that historical memory. They asked Hollywood screenwriters to work up a story treatment about the Mexican-American War that showed that "the U.S. didn't steal considerable territory" from Mexico in 1848, and to work up one on the Panama Canal that showed that the United States didn't steal Panamá from Colombia in 1903.[54] Neither of these two ideas materialized into finished films. Neither did a proposed short about the history of US policy in Latin America, whose evolving titles capture the US propagandists' struggle to spin the historical record: *Our Changing Attitude* was changed to *We Mean What We Say*, then to *Twenty-One Sisters*, and finally to *Your America–Our America* (borrowing Martí's phrase).[55] Along the way, OIAA-MPD representatives debated this short's content. Some argued that "we must level" with Latin American audiences about past "mistakes" and "the fault of our own money-grubbers," while others argued against addressing the past at all, arguing instead for a total focus on the postwar future. In the end, the final (but unproduced) script avoided discussion of US policy at all, instead chronicling a shared Pan-American history of anticolonial wars against Old World despotism and the liberty-loving heroes who led them.[56]

In fact, the OIAA-MPD believed Latin American anticolonial liberators of the nineteenth century—and especially their philosophical affinities and personal relationships with US leaders—were ripe for Hollywood dramatization, along the lines of *Juarez* (which had emphasized the Mexican leader's admiration for Lincoln). Thus, the OIAA-MPD asked writers to script theatrical shorts for a series it called "The Traditions of Freedom in Latin America," which would briefly chronicle the lives of Latin American anticolonial liberators. The OIAA-MPD explicitly laid out the intended spectator effects: "These subjects would tell how traditionally the countries of the other Americas have fought off foreign domination; and the peoples of America with this heritage have the responsibility of acting likewise under the present emergency."[57] From the start, the most promising candidate for this sort of treatment was the *Gran Liberador* Simón Bolívar, who was deemed worthy even of a feature biopic. In consultation with the OIAA, both MGM and Warner Bros. flirted with the idea, even surveying Latin Americans about who should be cast as Bolívar. (From Havana, votes came in for Jimmy Stewart and Robert Taylor.)[58] But both studios eventually demurred given the project's epic (and expensive) proportions and what the MPSA called too many "political complications." As OIAA consultants advised, Bolívar was regarded as a revolutionary hero *and* a military dictator after independence was achieved, and he had famously worried about the United States' growing imperialist ambitions in the nineteenth century.[59] A similar fate befell a proposed feature about Emiliano Zapata, a hero of the Mexican Revolution of the 1910s against successive Mexican dictatorships. When MGM proposed a Zapata biopic to the OIAA, Rockefeller himself was enthusiastic about it, but others were not. Durland advised that Zapata was too radical a figure, "his revolutionary activities" too "dangerous"; and the MPSA marked the proposed film "politically questionable."[60] Thus deterred, MGM shelved the idea for the time being.

The MPSA also considered Cuba's own José Martí for a feature biopic. Bringing Cesar Romero's proposition a step closer to fruition in 1943, the OIAA-MPD contracted writers to pen a treatment chronicling Martí's heroic life.[61] With the working title "The Flame of Freedom," the resulting twenty-seven-page treatment opens and closes in present-day Havana. At a military parade on Cuban Independence Day, an elderly man muses to his grandson about his friend José Martí. Here, the film flashes back seventy-five years to 1868, the year that Cuba's wars of independence began. A teen-age Martí writes poetry ("paeans to liberty") and political tracts ("extolling the virtue of a land free from the domination of foreign tyrants") for which the Spaniards imprison him. Once released from prison, Martí goes into exile in New York City, where he learns an unambiguous admiration for US democracy, according to the script. There, he also gains much financial and moral support for the cause of *Cuba libre*. After all, the script intones, US citizens recognized the "parallelism" between the Cuban wars of independence and the United States' Revolutionary War. United States' citizens could see that "the cause of Cuba is the cause of any heroic and liberty-loving people." With their help, Martí is able to return to Cuba. Like so many Hollywood war heroes, he lands on a beach to face the enemy, "charges through a hailstorm of bullets," and accepts death stoically, sure that his "sacrifice will not be in vain." Indeed, in their martyr's name, Cubans rise up and achieve independence.[62]

At this point, "The Flame of Freedom" script treatment flashes forward from 1898 to the present, neatly skipping over the Platt era, the 1933 revolution, and Batista's extraconstitutional rule of the 1930s. The grandfather and grandson "turn to the statue of Jose Marti, then to look down the Prado at the various evidences of a triumphant democracy . . . for which so much blood was shed and so many sacrifices made. The tramp of marching feet is again heard, as a squad bearing the presidential insignia comes across the central square, returning to the parade." The grandfather has the last word, articulating the lesson that history offers for the present: sometimes freedom requires a "[generation] of martyrs" so that future "generations may enjoy the fruit of their sacrifices."[63] Though the film was never produced, the treatment for "The Flame of Freedom" offers insight into Pan-American propagandists' romanticization of hemispheric freedom fighting, and the erasure of contradictory US policy in Latin America it required.

But US support of Latin American dictators was difficult to sublimate, as suggested by the problematic ending of "The Flame of Freedom": a military squad bearing Batista's "presidential insignia" makes for rather problematic "evidence" of "Cuba's triumphant democracy." Like *En Guardia's* representations of Batista, its inclusion suggests the OIAA's determination to spin Batista into the personification of democracy's US-led forward march in Latin America. Generally, however, the OIAA-MPD concluded that evading the issue of Latin American strongmen was more advisable than attempting to spin it. The MPSA screenwriters' guide contained a memo with this frank admission: "Dictatorship [is] a by-product of imperialism. That's why they [Latin Americans] fear the colossus of the North." Thus, the OIAA-MPD advised Hollywood writers *not* to "portray even fictitious presidents of fictitious Latin American republics as dictators."[64]

This strategy of evasion also explains why the OIAA-MPD counseled Warner Bros. to revise the screenplay for *To Have and Have Not* (1944). Ernest Hemingway's novel and Jules Furthman's original script were set in Cuba during the early 1930s, where protagonist Harry Morgan aids anti-Machado revolutionaries. But the OIAA worried that any association between dictatorship and Cuba might embarrass Batista. In February 1944, the OIAA-MPD suggested taking the story out of Cuba's past and setting it instead in French Martinique in the present, and to have Morgan (played by Humphrey Bogart) aid the French resistance against the Vichy.[65] Warner Bros. complied. Thus, in the produced film, when "Bogie"—reprising much about his famous character from *Casablanca*—lets himself be drawn out of cynical self-interest into the just cause of freedom fighting, no past (or present) Latin American dictators or US policies are implicated.[66]

Not only did the OIAA-MPD change the *setting* of Harry Morgan's exploits, its concerns about Latin Americans' historical memory likely also shaped his *characterization*—and that of so many Hollywood war heroes—as a *reluctant* warrior, not inherently belligerent but rather drawn in to the fight by the righteousness of the cause.[67] After all, as wartime Hollywood increased its output of combat films—and their glorification of US war production and weapons technologies—OIAA analysts warned that such films confirmed some Latin Americans' impression "that the United States is a militaristic nation."[68] One OIAA content directive put it plainly, "Over-emphasis of the might of the United States at war has the negative quality of reviving apprehension that great military powers develop strong imperialistic tendencies—thus an old fear could be made to live again in the other republics." The OIAA directive thus advised "diminished emphasis" on "U.S. War Might" and increased emphasis on the "decent, human, simple, sentimental" soldiers who abhorred war, but whose consciences had been awakened to the moral imperative of military action.[69]

In Hollywood's many OIAA-MPD–consulted combat films, US soldiers enlist to fight because they hate war not because they love it. As heavy-handed dialogue in the OIAA-MPD–consulted *Wake Island* puts it, US soldiers fight "to destroy destruction," and "to give eternal life to the ideals for which they die."[70] Not only do US servicemen die heroically for their peace-loving, democratic ideals, but they live by them, too. They are free of racial and class prejudice. Far from bloodthirsty, they coddle kittens, grapple with fear and their consciences, value human life profoundly, treat the enemy humanely, pray to God, goof around, fall in love, and miss their families. While film scholars have long recognized that these cinematic soldiers' emphatic likability was designed to solicit the identification of *domestic* spectators, it turns out that they were also designed to solicit the identification of *Latin Americans* as well.[71] As the examples of *The Navy Comes Through* and *Bataan* begin to capture, so too were their deaths. Not only meant to gird domestic audiences for unprecedented loss, onscreen US casualties had the added benefit of fulfilling an OIAA objective: to impress upon Latin Americans that the US war effort was a matter of selfless sacrifice, and *not* of self-serving conquest.

Perhaps most important toward breaking down Latin American distrust about enhanced US militarism, US soldiers in OIAA-MPD-consulted films are greeted as liberators rather than conquerors around the globe. For instance, in *The Story of Dr. Wassell*, in which Gary Cooper plays a US Navy doctor, the local women of Java fawn over US soldiers; and a wounded Chinese American man, upon seeing Dr. Wassell (who once did missionary work in China), says, "I see you're still helping those who cannot help themselves." Combat films set in the Philippines (which, like Cuba, became a "semi-sovereign" US possession after the War of 1898, until Japanese occupation in 1942) offered a special opportunity to reiterate the US Empire of Liberty and liberation, especially in contrast to the Japanese Empire of Enslavement. In *Bataan*, for instance, Filipino soldiers willingly give their lives under US command, "fighting shoulder to shoulder with Americans, [in order to] heroically stay the wave of barbaric conquest," as the film's prologue eulogizes.[72] These and other Hollywood war films put endorsements of US global interventions into the mouths—and actions—of United States' allies around the world.

In other words, whether in films about foreign antifascist resistance movements or about US soldiers in combat or even about nineteenth-century Latin American liberators, Hollywood's war heroes were designed with Latin American audiences in mind as well as domestic ones. Played by Hollywood's biggest stars, they were meant to solicit identification with this war for the (Pan-)American Way of freedom fighting. Indeed, these Hollywood heroes of (what would come to be known as) the "Greatest Generation" had a deep and lingering impact on *US* culture, and particularly on its ideals of masculinity. It should not be surprising, then, that Hollywood war heroes also deeply affected *Cuban* culture, given Hollywood's power within it and the particular congruence of Hollywood's wartime propaganda and revolutionary Cuban nationalism.

"An Elevated Sentiment of Continental Fraternity": Hollywood Heroes in the Giro

In the first weeks of 1941, a giant cut-out of Charlie Chaplin, posing as a military strongman, shook his fists at Havana's residents from atop the Radio Cine, where *The Great Dictator* would debut on January 20 (see fig. 4.4).[73] It had been five long years again since Chaplin's last film, *Modern Times*, had come to Havana; again, his new film was highly anticipated. *Cinema* had already devoted a great deal of coverage to what it was calling "The Biggest Event of the Year," including a photo of Weiner and Valcarce collecting the film reels at Havana's airport. United Artists arranged for a press preview, after which *Cinema* pronounced *The Great Dictator* to be "proof that the millions of small and decent human beings of the world . . . sooner or later are going to throw off tyranny's heavy chains." Perdices called it a brilliant "contribution to the cause that the democracies defend." He even declared that "To see it just once is not enough."[74] In his review for *El Tiempo*, Alejo Carpentier, who had returned to Havana from Paris in 1939, predicted that Chaplin's latest masterpiece "will do more damage to the totalitarian regimes than twenty pamphlets, than 100 volumes of propaganda, than 100 well-argued editorials." And in *El Mundo*, Valdés-Rodríguez deemed the film "brilliant," and Chaplin's final speech in it, "a fervent profession of democratic faith in Man."[75] At year's end, Havana's

FIG. 4.4. A striking billboard in Havana advertises Charlie Chaplin's *The Great Dictator*. *Around the World* 9, no. 1: 10. (Courtesy of Wisconsin Center for Film and Theater Research)

two new film writers' guilds, the Agrupación de Redactores Cinematográficos y Teatrales (ARTYC, founded in 1936) and the Federación de Redactores Cinematográficos y Teatrales (FRCT, founded in 1940), both ranked *The Great Dictator* on their annual top film lists, at fifth and seventh places respectively.[76]

In *The Great Dictator*, Chaplin plays two roles: the Jewish Barber and Adenoid Hynkel. The latter is the dictator of a fictional nation, "Tomaria," and an obvious analog for Hitler, whom Chaplin hilariously lampoons, all his hyperaggressive bluster an elaborate cover for his deep inferiority complex. Also played by Chaplin, the Jewish Barber is a slightly revised version of the Little Tramp: a profoundly good and innocent man persecuted by the powerful, in this case by Hynkel and his soldiers, who harass him, blow up his shop, and, ultimately, ship him to a concentration camp. When the Jewish Barber tries to escape, Hynkel's soldiers mistake him for Hynkel and force him to address a rally of Tomarians as their leader. It is here, in the film's ending, that Chaplin famously breaks his cinematic silence, speaking into an unmoving camera for over three minutes, soliloquizing against military dictatorships, racial hatred, and the industrial capitalism that seemed to have reared both. "Greed has poisoned men's souls, has barricaded the world with hate, has goose-stepped us into misery and bloodshed," the Jewish Barber passionately laments. He continues,

> Even now my voice is reaching millions throughout the world—millions of despairing men, women, and little children—victims of a system that makes men torture and imprison innocent people.
>
> To those who can hear me I say, do not despair. . . . The hate of men will pass, and dictators die, and the power they took from the people will return to the people.
>
> Soldiers, don't give yourselves to brutes. . . . Don't give yourselves to these unnatural men. . . . You are not machines! You are not cattle! You are men! You have the love of humanity in your hearts! . . . Don't fight for slavery! Fight for liberty!
>
> . . . .
>
> Then, in the name of democracy, let us use that power . . . let us fight for a new world—a decent world that will give men a chance to work—that will give youth a future, and old age a security. By the promise of these things, brutes have risen to power. But they lie! . . .
>
> Dictators free themselves but they enslave the people! Now let us fight to free the world. . . . In the name of democracy, let us all unite![77]

Cinema printed a translation of this rousing speech in its entirety, not once but twice, even before the film debuted in Havana.[78]

Thus began the flood of Hollywood antifascist, prodemocratic films into Havana's 109 cines, and the adulatory reception of such films in Havana's film giro, which was both a barometer and a director of Cuban public opinion by the early 1940s.[79] Havana's exhibitors, trade journalists, and film writers wholeheartedly embraced Hollywood's wartime films, and the propaganda about the (Pan-)American Way embedded in them. They promoted and recommended them, and translated their messages into the national discourse. Sometimes this translation was verbatim (as in the case of the Jewish Barber's speech from *The Great Dictator*), but more often Cubans put Hollywood's antifascist, prodemocratic fervor into their own words and more deeply insinuated it into the Cuban context, where the past decade had seen the popular overthrow of one strongman (Machado) and an ongoing debate about his successor (Batista). Cubans in the film giro made Havana cines, fanzines, and film columns effective sites for the dissemination of OIAA (and OWI) propaganda and, especially, for linking the Pan-American War for Democracy to revolutionary Cuban nationalism. As *Cinema* columnist and *ACRC* editor Pedro Pablo Chávez put it in 1942, the film giro could do much to stimulate "in our popular masses the desired war consciousness required by the gravity of the conflict." This effect was easy to achieve, he continued, given that "our forebearers' heroic example has planted in the Cuban people's subconscious a longing for democratic republicanism that . . . has come to be a votive lamp in our national life."[80]

One measure of the giro's adulatory reception of Hollywood (Left) propaganda is the wartime top film lists of the FRCT (comprised mostly of trade journalists) and the ARTYC (comprised mostly of film critics writing in mainstream newspapers and magazines, including Valdés-Rodríguez at *El Mundo*, Ichaso at *Diario de la marina*, Germinal Barral at *Bohemia*, as well as Perdices at *Cinema*).[81] Along with *The Great Dictator*, their top film lists included propaganda-infused war films like *Action in the North Atlantic*, *Casablanca*, *Going My Way*, *Lifeboat*, *The Mortal Storm*, *Mrs. Miniver*, *North Star*, *Sergeant York*, and *Watch on the Rhine*.[82] In 1941, the FRCT named Frank Capra's *Meet John Doe* that year's best film. In it, Gary Cooper plays an innocent American Common Man awakening to the threat of a would-be US fascist dictator and mobilizing "the People" against him in a radio speech that is double the length of the Jewish Barber's speech and equally lyrical in its prodemocratic antifascist exhortations.[83] Whether or not anyone noted the irony, the FRCT awarded *Meet John Doe* the first ever "Batista Trophy," a silver cup donated by the Cuban strongman-turned-president.[84]

According to their own accounts, Havana's film writers' special attention to Hollywood's antifascist war films matched the public's appetite for them. As Chávez explained in 1942, "We are at war, and war is the favorite theme in the spectating public's taste." And *Film Daily Yearbook*'s 1943 list of "top grossers" in Cuba—*Casablanca*, *Mission to Moscow*, *The Mortal Storm*, *Mrs. Miniver*, and *This Above All*—confirmed Chávez's impression. As did a survey conducted by Cuba's OIAA Coordination Committee in late 1942: "Action films showing war effort activities," it concluded, "are most in demand." And OIAA-MPD and MPSA representatives would have been cheered by Chávez's conclusion that such films were having the intended effect: "War movies are completely fulfilling their missions in terms of enthusing the [Cuban] public and carrying them down paths of heroism and sympathetic pronouncements about their faith and hope in the destiny of the democracies," he enthused. Cubans of today, he continued, were as eager to fight the "totalitarian catastrophe that threatens the world" as had been "our own Manuel Márquez Sterling," a Cuban hero of the wars of independence and the anti-Machado movement.[85]

As Chávez's lines suggest, not only did Havana's film writers commend Hollywood's antifascist, prodemocratic war films, but they also tended to reiterate—and even elaborate—their rhetorical excesses and to suture them onto revolutionary Cuban nationalism. The February 1942 entry of Cuba's new correspondent for *Cine-Mundial*, Luís Sánchez Amago, offers another representative example:

> In these moments of supreme transcendence for Humanity . . . this correspondence, written in the glow of the magnificent example of a Continent that rises as one . . . is mostly dedicated to exalting the cause of liberty to which we are enlisted, of which Washington, Bolívar, San Martín, Hidalgo and Martí, were glorious guardians in our hemisphere yesterday. . . . Profoundly convinced that it is better to die than to live abased, we could not, nor do we want to, withdraw from fulfilling a duty dictated by the most elemental sense of honor and responsibility, and we ready ourselves also to contribute our little part to the work of saving the world undertaken by América.

Like Chávez, Sánchez Amago links the current crisis to revolutionary Cuban nationalism's historical roots in freedom-fighting masculinity and *independentismo*, writing that the Cuban public's response to war was "proving that the Cuban of today, just like the Cuban of old" is "disposed to fight, without consideration of sacrifice" to secure "for our children a safe world in which honorable nations, big and small, and all human beings, humble and powerful, can develop and live with dignity, [and] without any fear of [extraterritorial] attacks."[86]

Throughout the film giro, this commitment to the fight—so often exhorted in the gendered language of "duty" and "honor"—was highly celebrated. Of course, the ultimate expression of that commitment was military service, and the Cuban film trades (like US ones) fell over themselves to congratulate movie star–enlistees, like Glenn Ford, Clark Gable, William Holden, Robert Montgomery, Robert Taylor, and Jimmy Stewart.[87] Desi Arnaz's enlistment in the US Army was a special point of pride, and an occasion for closing any distance between the United States' Empire of Liberty and revolutionary Cuban nationalism. *Cine-Mundial* noted that Arnaz would fight alongside North Americans, just as his own grandfather had fought alongside Theodore Roosevelt at San Juan Hill in 1898.[88] The Cuban trades also congratulated MGM's Havana manager, Eddie O'Connor, who proved his masculine mettle by enlisting in the US Navy of the "*gran nación amiga*," an occasion that called for a bon voyage luncheon at the Royal Palm Hotel attended by representatives from the US embassy and the film giro.[89] Acknowledging the primacy of the war effort, distributors and exhibitors pledged to reinstate any employee who left his job to join the military.[90]

Even short of taking up arms, war service of any kind was praised. For instance, the *ACRC* and *Cinema* lauded Charles Garrett's leadership of the OIAA's Cuba's Coordination Committee's Motion Picture Section, proof that he appreciated "the magnitude of the US war effort and the necessity of the closest union among our peoples to achieve the final victory."[91] And Hollywood film production, too, constituted commendable war service. In May 1942, the UNE presented a trophy to RKO Radio Pictures for the studio's contribution to "inter-American harmony" and, moreover, for fulfilling "the cinema's highest function: to maintain [our] unshakeable faith in the victory of the democracies."[92] And in September 1944, the Batista administration awarded the three Warner brothers with Cuba's National Order of Merit Carlos Manuel de Céspedes, another hero of the wars of independence.[93] The manager of Warner Bros.'s Havana office, Peter Colli, traveled to New York for the ceremony, a public expression of admiration that Colli had expressed privately in a letter to Harry Warner in 1940, praising him for his courageous leadership of the U.S. film industry's anti-Nazism.[94]

Havana exhibitors also proved eager to do their part. After Pearl Harbor, the cines in the movie barrio (bordered on the north by the Malecón sea wall) turned off their marquees for a full year, lest enemy boats exploit the bright lights that could be seen from as far as five miles out to sea.[95] And exhibitors' sacrifices did not end there. Air raids on Sundays cut into their best day for receipts; restrictions on transport of non-essential goods caused long lags in the arrival of Hollywood films to Havana; supply shortages and price hikes affected everything from projection carbons to electricity; and a wartime entertainment tax hit hard.[96] But Havana's exhibitors put on a brave face. They opened and closed each program with the Cuban national anthem, patriotic bookends (reminiscent of the singing of the same in Havana theaters during the first US occupation) that must have gone a long way toward "indigenizing" Hollywood's antifascist, prodemocratic fervor for Cuban audiences.[97]

Exhibidor's editor, Antonio Villazón Deus, rallied Havana exhibitors to these efforts, and explicitly linked them to revolutionary Cuban nationalism. For instance, in January 1943, he exhorted exhibitors to post more "*America libre y unida*" signs in their cines as follows: "Though not on the battlefront with the armies that clash, you can help the triumph of those that fight for the liberation of the world. . . . Use your word to make liberty shine. Remember what Jose de la Luz Caballero [nineteenth-century Cuban scholar admired by Martí] said, 'The word is stronger than the cannon.'" Like the Cuban exhibitor Manuel Ramón Fernández in the second epigraph above, Villazón Deus argued it was also Cuban exhibitors' patriotic duty to participate in fundraisers and, thus, "to Help the Glorious Armies that Fight in Defense of the Democracies."[98] On July 4, 1942, when all exhibitors and distributors were asked to donate 10 percent of that day's proceeds to the Cuban-American Allied Relief Fund, Villazón Deus even resorted to listing the names of those who failed to participate.[99] And this public shaming worked, at least according to Weiner, who warned his superiors in United Artists' New York office that *not* participating was inadvisable because likely to provoke "a very unfavorable and distasteful public reaction."[100]

Thus rallied, Cuban exhibitors and US distributors cooperated (along with other film giro businesses) on many fundraisers, for instance, at the premiere of *Week-End in Havana* (with which this chapter opened) as well at screenings of *The Great Dictator*, *Sergeant York*, and *This Is the Army*. At them, funds were raised for the American Red Cross, the US Army Emergency Relief Fund, the Cuban-American Allied Relief Fund, and the Cuban Foundation of the Good Neighbor.[101] A surviving playbill for a May 1943 benefit for the latter two Cuban organizations at the Teatro América premiere of MGM's *Mrs. Miniver* (about British civilians rallying in the face of Nazi attacks) further illustrates the tone of these events, and the translation of Hollywood antifascism into the Cuban context. The playbill's centerfold contains the premiere's schedule, which included, in this order: a Cuban and then US newsreel; the playing of the Cuban national anthem; an address by the president of the Cuban-American Allied Relief Fund; an address by US Ambassador Spruille Braden; and the playing of "The Star-Spangled Banner," to be followed by the main event, *Mrs. Miniver*. If the spectator found himself bored during this lengthy prologue to the feature, he might flip through the handbill's seventy-two pages, to admire the US and Cuban companies contributing to that night's benefit, and/or to read a rousing speech from *Mrs. Miniver*, reprinted in both Spanish and English, in which a rector eulogizes dead British civilians: "They will inspire us with an unbreakable determination to free ourselves and those who come after us from the tyranny and terror that threaten to strike us down! This is the people's war! . . . We are the fighters! Fight it, then! Fight it with all that is in us!"[102]

Also capturing the Havana film giro's enthusiastic reception, promotion, and local appropriation of Hollywood's wartime propaganda are the wartime editions of *Cinema*, now crumbling in Havana's José Martí National Library. Though many *Cinema* covers are missing from the collection, those that survive feature many OIAA-MPD-counseled films with immediately recognizable Pan-American content like *Rio Rita*, *The Three Caballeros*, *Tortilla Flat*, and *Week-End in Havana*; and editorials enthuse that "the movies tend to tighten the bonds of friendship between North and South America."[103] But the extant covers evidence an even more pronounced preference for Hollywood's antifascist films, including *Counter-Attack*, *The Cross of Lorraine*, *For Whom the Bell Tolls*, *A Guy Named Joe*, *Hostages*, *Mrs. Miniver*, *None Shall Escape*, *Thirty Seconds over Tokyo*, and *To Have and Have Not* (see fig. 4.5).

FIG. 4.5 On the cover of *Cinema*, June 3, 1945, the freedom-fighting hero (played by Humphrey Bogart) gets the girl (played by Lauren Bacall). From the collection of the *Biblioteca Nacional "José Martí,"* Havana, Cuba.

Inside the pages of *Cinema*, such films were highly endorsed, and their heroes' handsome faces ubiquitously printed. Over and over again, *Cinema* praised Hollywood's contribution to the "fight for a world free from dictatorial oppressors."[104] Editor Perdices' weekly column, "Son Cosas Nuestras," clearly evidences *Cinema's*—and the giro's—fervent embrace of Hollywood's Pan-American War for Democracy. In March 1941, Perdices writes approvingly that Hollywood "tries to inform our peoples [of] the reason that defending our lands, our beliefs, and our freedom, is worth the trouble."[105] Thereafter, Perdices proceeds to recommend Hollywood's antifascist films—especially those touched by the OIAA, the MPSA, the OWI, and/or the Hollywood Left—for promising both edification to moviegoers *and* box office success to exhibitors. And he especially lauds the freedom fighters in such films. He recommends *The Moon Is Down* for capturing the "moving" heroism of underground fighters in Nazi-occupied Norway, true men that would rather "rise up than be slaves." And he highly recommends the "magnificent" *Watch on the Rhine*, particularly praising Paul Lukas's portrayal of a European resistance leader determined "to fight for freedom at the cost of whatever sacrifices are necessary" and to convince his US relatives to do the same.[106] When US heroes did join the fight abroad, Perdices recommended these, too. He lauds Robert Taylor for his gritty personification of a US citizen who joins the "heroic" Russian people in their fight against the Nazis in *Song of Russia*, and Ray Milland as a heroic US pilot shot down over Nazi-occupied France in *Till We Meet Again*.[107]

No film, however, was more highly endorsed by *Cinema* than Paramount's *For Whom the Bell Tolls*, the OIAA- and OWI-consulted adaptation of Hemingway's best-selling 1940 novel about the Spanish Civil War.[108] The film arrived in Havana in January 1945, rolled out in grand premieres at the Encanto and Fausto.[109] Greatly anticipated, the film project had been tracked by *Cinema* and other Cuban periodicals for years. Early in 1942, for instance, they reported that Gary Cooper had been cast as Robert Jordan, the US idealist who joins leftist anti-Franco guerrillas in the Spanish sierra. Cubans were thrilled to learn that it would be Cooper, in all his Technicolor blue-eyed handsomeness, to embody the traits of the Hemingway hero: virile, courageous, stoic, graceful under pressure. And the Cuban trade press claimed to have been informed of Cooper's casting by no less an authority than Hemingway himself, the famous novelist who had recently made Havana his home. Indeed, in 1939, Hemingway had written much of *For Whom the Bell Tolls* in a Havana hotel room, mining his own recent experience of the Spanish Civil War, on which he had reported as a sort of celebrity war correspondent (as had Errol Flynn). By 1942, "Ernesto" had moved into his *Finca Vigía*, an estate a dozen miles outside of Havana. From there, Hemingway sought to enact his vision of heroism in person, launching patrols for German U-boats from his private yacht and orchestrating an amateur spy ring in search of Nazi sympathizers in Cuba. In fact, as he resided in his finca, Hemingway's personal history would intertwine with Cuba's at least through 1959, yet another nexus between Havana, Hollywood, and midcentury codes of masculinity.[110]

Feeling a certain ownership of *For Whom the Bell Tolls*, then, the Cuban trade press reported on the film adaptation throughout its production. The casting of two Cuban actors "*de nuestra raza* [of our race]" (Pedro de Cordoba and Lilo Yarson) as guerrillas was happily reported, as were the protestations made against the film by Generalissimo Franco (who had since won the civil war with some help from Hitler and Mussolini and who now ruled as Spain's military dictator).[111] As Weiner had noted during *Blockade*'s run in Havana, habaneros sided heavily with the leftist Republicans. So did Hemingway's novel and, to an even greater extent, the film.[112] In fact, the OWI had insisted on this, advising Paramount to minimize the novel's ambivalence about the Republicans' communist factions and to cut depictions of atrocities committed by them.[113]

Thus, in the version of *For Whom the Bell Tolls* that played in Cuba, the leftist guerrillas are depicted as unambiguously righteous underdogs, Franco's soldiers as evil murderers and rapists aided and abetted by Hitler, and Robert Jordan as proof positive that the United States' global role is a benevolent one. After expressing some doubts about Jordan's motives, the Spanish guerrillas come to trust him; and Jordan's subsequent actions prove that trust well founded. In charge of blowing up a strategically critical bridge, Jordan accomplishes his objective and, when fatally injured, insists on being left behind to gun down the enemy as his comrades-in-arms escape.[114]

Even before it reached Havana, *For Whom the Bell Tolls* was well received therein. Attending its New York premiere for *Cinema* in July 1943, María Garrett deemed it a "magnificent film," the "most interesting and moving" of our times. She has always loved Gary Cooper, she writes, but "in the role of Jordan, the North American adventurer who goes to the mountains of Spain, to hoist the flag of freedom, at the side of those that fight to free the country from the invader's yoke and from the terror of their own, Gary Cooper has re-conquered me one hundred times." *For Whom the Bell Tolls* honors "the immortal Spanish Republic (that someday will return)," she writes prescriptively; its spectators will "leave the theater with the desire to exclaim: 'Viva the immortal Spain of the invincible mountains!'"[115] For the next year, *Cinema* reported on the film's US box office success, and then gave the film the royal treatment as its Havana premiere approached.[116] *Cinema* published full pages of Paramount publicity, with many photos of Cooper as Jordan in heroic postures, "an American idealist" who "loves liberty" and bravely gives his life for it.[117] And, in mid-January 1945, when the film appeared at the Encanto and the Fausto, Cooper's sierra-weathered face graced the cover of *Cinema*, endorsing leftist freedom fighting (in ways that might make his postwar cold warrior-self cringe).[118]

Just four months later, in May 1945, Cooper's visage appeared again all over Havana, this time for the promotion of the aforementioned *The Story of Dr. Wassell*, which became a top-grossing film in Cuba that year.[119] In it, Cooper personifies a real-life US Navy doctor who, in 1942, heroically evacuated a dozen wounded US soldiers from Japanese-occupied Java. For his selfless courage, as Perdices pointed out in his adulatory review, Dr. Wassell had even been compared to Christ by the recently deceased President Roosevelt, whose April 1945 death was marked in Havana with a day of cine closings and, after they reopened, five minutes of silence during the Sunday matinee.[120]

As Allied victories swept over Europe, Perdices used *The Story of Dr. Wassell* to offer a positive postmortem of wartime Hollywood: "When history recalls . . . the great deeds of those that contributed to freedom, the men of the cinema will deserve special attention since they cooperated in so many ways, and at no time declined to brandish their weapon." And, not only did Hollywood's wartime movies mobilize spectators in the present, but they might continue to have utility into the future. Perdices continues, "Our sons and grandsons someday will find condensed in these [war films] the tragedies of a generation . . . that took up arms . . . in the fight in which all good men were united to achieve a better world."[121] Such films, Perdices hoped, might go on inspiring future generations of "good men," meaning freedom-fighting men, in Cuba. Like Havana theater critic Francisco Hermida writing in 1897, Perdices is not only (or even mostly) celebrating the cinema as a tool for recording history. Rather, he is constructing a national community around a shared vision of revolutionary masculinity refracted through a cinematic lens.

And yet, while Cubans in the Havana film giro seemed utterly taken in by Hollywood exhortations to manly self-sacrifice, they would not be made suckers. Behind all this Pan-American freedom-fighting enthusiasm, there remained a current of suspicion about US motives, ready to flare at any perceived slight. For instance, when the Cuban subsidiary of General Electric—vilified as the monopolistic Yankee "electric octopus" since the 1920s—raised electric rates in the summer of 1942 claiming it was a wartime emergency measure, Cuban exhibitors and the Cuban trade press cried foul. Perdices seethed at the Cuban Electric Company for war profiteering. He noted that "every freedom-loving man" in Cuba was lining up to "sacrifice his life rather than accept the enemy's yoke," but woe to the Yankee that sought to "take advantage of that selfless and patriotic sense of duty." He warned that "the Cuban people will not tolerate such abuse, because to do so would turn them into the slaves of those who oppress them and betray the very ideal that we defend."[122] In other words, even during this peak moment of US-Cuban cooperation, there was the occasional hint that all this propaganda to mobilize Latin Americans, including Cubans, for the Pan-American freedom fight could be appropriated within the local context in ways that could redound against US interests.

Fueling the Flame: Valdés-Rodríguez and Hollywood War Heroes

Like Perdices, his colleague (and wartime president) at the ARTYC, Jose Manuel Valdés-Rodríguez wielded significant influence in the film giro and beyond. Indeed, the film critic at *El Mundo* was in the midst of greatly expanding that influence. In 1939, he had begun to teach a class titled "*El cine: Industria y arte de nuestro tiempo* [The Cinema: Industry and Art of Our Times]" at Havana's Escuela Libre (Free School), which he founded with other onetime *minoristas*. Valdés-Rodríguez claimed it was the first academic course on the cinema to be offered in Latin America. In June 1942, Valdés-Rodríguez moved his course to the University of Havana, where it took its final shape: twelve projections and sixteen classes over a six-week period in the summer, in which students screened films and discussed their artistic merit and social significance.[123] As Valdés-Rodríguez told *Exhibidor* in 1942, the class was designed not only to elevate its students' appreciation of the world's best cinema but also "to clarify the role that the cinema plays as a social force in today's world."[124] Towards these ends, the class screened many Soviet and French films not widely exhibited in Havana, but also Hollywood films that were, especially those made by the Hollywood Left. During the war, Valdés-Rodríguez's picks included *Citizen Kane*, *The Grapes of Wrath*, *The Great Dictator* (and other Chaplin films), and *Watch on the Rhine*.[125] Over the next decade and a half, enrollment in Valdés-Rodríguez's course became a rite of passage for much of Cuba's next generation of film critics, filmmakers, and actors (many of them also revolutionary activists), as we will see.

To launch his course, Valdés-Rodríguez collaborated with the people he had only a decade before denounced as 'sales agents' of US imperialism. The Havana office of RKO loaned him its screening room, a small space that limited the course's enrollment to thirty students. Fox's office helped by funding ten scholarships for the course annually. And other US studios' Havana offices contributed free copies of films for class screenings and to build the university's film library, also recently founded by Valdés-Rodríguez.[126] In exchange, according to a United Artists report from Havana, Valdés-Rodríguez sometimes lent his "many talents and much power" as "one of Cuba's leading academic authorities on the Motion Picture" to help a studio promote one of its films by screening it for his students as well as professors and "others of importance in the cultural leadership of Cuba."[127] Indeed, not only did the once intransigent anti-imperialist now endorse certain Hollywood films, toast

Weiner, and hold classes in a local Hollywood office; in July 1941, he traveled to Washington, D.C., to meet with Nelson Rockefeller himself, in an interview arranged through the US State Department and the University of Havana. With Rockefeller's approval, Valdés-Rodríguez then moved on to New York to visit the Museum of Modern Art's new film library, from which he secured shipments of films for his course.[128]

During the war, Valdés-Rodríguez worked hard to appropriate Hollywood's OIAA-endorsed antifascism into the Cuban context. Take, for instance, his aforementioned adulatory review of *The Great Dictator*. He begins by comparing Chaplin's work to Martí's; both capture the "agony" of an artist-idealist unable to adapt to the world's less-than-ideal reality and, thus, inevitably drawn into battle with it. This (strained) comparison went a long way toward suturing the film's meanings to revolutionary Cuban nationalism. Valdés-Rodríguez then goes on to praise Chaplin's Hynkel character as a "brilliant" and "merciless caricature" of a dictator that is, nonetheless, realistic, portraying dictatorship with "psychological veracity and insight." At length, Valdés-Rodríguez then lists the realistic characteristics of Hynkel and Benzini Napaloni (the film's Mussolini caricature, played by Jack Oakie): "the monstrous hypertrophy of the self, the confused sexual status, the pretense, the lack of human sentiment, the expansive rage, the thundering verbosity, the frenzied activity, the abuse and harassment of his closest collaborators, his sense of superiority juxtaposed with his frailty and distrust in his own forces."[129] Here, Valdés-Rodríguez's description of Hynkel and Napaloni—power-hungry, self-aggrandizing, effeminate, insecure—drifts into something more. It suspiciously echoes contemporary critiques of Batista, who was said to be mercurial and insecure and who Cubans sometimes belittled as "*mulato lindo*," referring to his mixed race and his propensity to preen over his personal appearance (to be effeminate).

If dictators embody a perverted masculinity (are "unnatural men," as the Jewish Barber notes in his final speech), then the instinct to fight against them is a defining characteristic of "natural" men. That's why, Valdés-Rodríguez explains, Chaplin has no choice but to have the Little Tramp—slightly revised into the Jewish Barber—take action. "Without faltering, [Charlot] acts before reality in a way that is real, appropriate, consequential and just," Valdés-Rodríguez enthuses. Through his brave speech, Charlot "raises a hopeful voice to his brothers dispersed around the world."[130] Through unsubtle implication, Valdés-Rodríguez reminded Cuban spectators that they were included in this freedom-fighting fraternity and should act accordingly.

Valdés-Rodríguez continues this active appropriation of Hollywood Left antifascism in his review of *Keeper of the Flame* (1943). With ideas supplied by the OWI and a script by Donald Ogden Stewart, *Keeper of the Flame* opens with the fatal car crash of a rising US politician (and would-be fascist), Robert Forrest.[131] Steve O'Malley (Spencer Tracy), a newspaperman just back from reporting on European fascism, doggedly seeks the truth about Forrest's life and death. What O'Malley learns from Forrest's widow, Christine (Katherine Hepburn), is that Forrest, who rose from humble origins to become a Lincoln-like hero of the people, had been corrupted by power and his lust for more of it. "A traitor to his country" who "envied the dictators [and had only] contempt for democracy," Christine recalls, Forrest built an army of desperate followers, whom he disdained and whose basest impulses—xenophobia and economic self-interest—he exploited. Christine recognized that her husband had become like Hitler, and so she allowed him to die in the opening car accident, which she had the power to prevent. After revealing the truth to O'Malley, Christine dies at the hands of one of Forrest's lackeys, but the film ends triumphantly, with O'Malley penning her story for the public's enlightenment, as a US flag waves into a fade.[132]

As in his review of *The Great Dictator*, Valdés-Rodríguez forgives the inartistic heft of *Keeper of the Flame's* lengthy, propaganda-laced speeches because he agrees with their politics and because he believes they have a particular relevance in Cuba. Again seeming to gesture to then-president Batista's trajectory since 1934, he synopsizes the film as the story of a man (Forrest) who had once been "an organizer of collective movements for the public welfare; a man of steel will; the victor in whatever efforts he undertakes; a prototype of patriotism that constitutes the most exalted example for millions of men, women and children in his country." However, Forrest experiences a "transformation," abandoning his early democratic ideals in his lust for personal power. *Keeper of the Flame*, Valdés-Rodríguez writes, "points out how it is possible that a public man, who has displayed so much patriotism in past eras, takes advantage of the prestige and trust he enjoys to mislead the people along courses that betray the people's most beloved ideals." The critic explains that Forrest is "driven by his cult of himself [and] of force, . . . based on a fundamentally inhumane political theory [fascism], opposed in every way to pure democratic principles."[133]

Thankfully, *Keeper of the Flame* models heroic resistance to such despotic abuse of power, especially through the exercise of a free press. Valdés-Rodríguez especially lauds O'Malley, a "wise and tenacious journalist" who convinces Christine to reveal her husband's treachery by preaching to her "the very noble principle that fraud and pretense should always be exposed before the people, that they have enough strength to know the truth." Though truth-telling costs Christine her life, such are the sacrifices that we must be prepared to make to "keep the flame" of democracy alive, writes the critic. Echoing Spencer Tracy's character, Valdés-Rodríguez shares his democratic faith here in first person: "I firmly believe . . . that nobody can deceive the public for long." Democratic citizens have proven time and again that they will apply "sober but inflexible justice, to the [men] that try to use [their] influence to betray the basic principles of the nation," those of Cuba here implicitly conflated with those of the United States.[134]

Valdés-Rodríguez extracts a similarly mobilizing lesson from Warner Bros.' *Watch on the Rhine*. The film is based on the play by famous leftist Lillian Hellman about a Nazi resistance leader from Germany named Kurt Müller (Paul Lukacs) and his US-born wife, Sara (Bette Davis). Persecuted in Europe, they flee to Sara's childhood home outside of Washington, D.C. There, they find that their self-sacrificing devotion is not matched by Americans, who are instead blissfully unaware, self-absorbed, and, in at least the case of one US capitalist, willing to side with the Nazis for the right price. The film, then, dramatizes the conversion of Sara's mother and brother, Fanny and David Farrelly, to participation in the antifascist fight.[135] In his review, Valdés-Rodríguez is beside himself with praise: *Watch on the Rhine* departs from Hollywood's usual "dull escapism" to turn its "wide lens to debates on humanity's future." In this it is, in the critic's opinion, as good as "*Blockade*, Walter Wanger's unforgettable film." Like that film, the critic writes, *Watch on the Rhine* "point[s] out the duty of men and of nations of good will" to "defend democracy . . . threatened by the regressive and sinister forces of fascism," which the film attacks as "criminal, violent, antihuman and regressive." *Watch on the Rhine*, Valdés-Rodríguez continues, "portrays the lazy and careless attitude of many people . . . who are [nonetheless] capable of confronting the terrible plague [of fascism] when critical and illuminating circumstances demand it of them. . . . Ultimately, *Watch on the Rhine* exalts . . . the self-sacrifice, the intelligence and the bold heroism of those that fight against [fascism] from its very gestation." In fact, *Watch on the Rhine* offers "homage . . . to the antifascist fighters of the whole world," concludes Valdés-Rodríguez, especially those, it seems, who do not dither.[136]

In Valdés-Rodríguez's hands, the film also offers homage to Cubans, of past and future, who belong to this global brotherhood of heroes. The critic compares the character of Kurt Müller to Pablo de la Torriente Brau, a onetime attendee of Valdés-Rodríguez's garage wall screenings who was also a journalist and revolutionary activist against Machado, who died in 1936 fighting with the Republicans in Spain. Then the critic prescribes as much as predicts that "the deaths in the enormous [war] effort will not have been given in vain." He foresees the victorious return of "the alert and brave antifascist fighter[s]" to their homelands where they will continue to fight for "justice and collective welfare," fighting with "maximum selflessness in the name of a better world."[137] Indeed, a number of Cuban veterans of World War II would return to the island and eventually join the movement against Batista's dictatorship in the 1950s.[138] Havana film critics like Valdés-Rodríguez were among those who worked to keep their freedom-fighting commitments alive.

One final example of a Valdés-Rodríguez review further clarifies his use of Hollywood war heroes to fuel revolutionary Cuban nationalism. While the OIAA-MPD had insisted on moving *To Have and Have Not*'s setting out of Cuba's past (lest it reflect poorly on Batista), Valdés-Rodríguez moved its invocation of heroic freedom fighting back to Cuba's present and future. In his review of the film, which debuted at the Teatro América in June 1945, he summarizes its message as follows: "Without saying it explicitly, [it is] that fascism always provokes resistance from the best spirits, from the most strong and honest wills of whatever social strata." And then he sets out to make explicit what the film only implies: that good men—as exemplified by Bogart's Harry Morgan, with his "incorruptible moral vigor" and "strength of character"—refuse to be subjugated; they resist fascism instinctively. Valdés-Rodríguez writes,

> At heart these are the same motives that move intellectuals and writers . . . to launch themselves, nobly, into the brutal fight. . . . That irreducibility of the human spirit is the little factor that fascists around the world forget, convinced that brute force is enough to subjugate. This underestimation of man and his most noble faculties . . . has been enough to destroy fascism to date. And it will be one of the most powerful reasons for its final annihilation. Because it is not possible for humanity to accept a future of submission, surrender and defeat of spirit, which are all part and parcel of fascism.[139]

Here, Valdés-Rodríguez elaborates his Cuban reader's identification with Bogart's character, making him an exemplar of the global brotherhood of antifascist fighters, a righteous fraternity into which the critic includes "intellectuals and writers" and, thus, himself.

"The Exemplary Revolutionary Figure": Mirta Aguirre and Hollywood War Heroes

Perdices and Valdés-Rodríguez's ARTYC colleague Mirta Aguirre was not about to cede freedom fighting of the pen to *male* intellectuals and writers alone. Remembered today as an esteemed figure of Cuban literature, Cuban communism, and Cuban feminism, Aguirre wrote film reviews in the mid- to late 1940s and early 1950s, engaging in many of the same critical practices as her film writer colleagues but expressing them in a more radical tenor. Born in Havana in 1912 and radicalized by her participation in the anti-Machado student movement, Aguirre had joined the PCC in 1932 and went into exile in Mexico, where she joined that country's Anti-Imperialist League. She returned to Cuba in 1935, joined the Student Left Wing, and participated in the ill-fated general strike that March. In the late 1930s, she worked at various progressive publications and got her law degree. And in 1944, she was named film and theater critic at the communist newspaper *Hoy*, then enjoying the temporarily above ground nature of Cuban Communism.[140]

During her first years at *Hoy*, Aguirre joined her colleagues in embracing Hollywood antifascist films and their heroes. She used them to extrapolate the lesson that "those that most love peace, liberty, [and] the natural rights of every individual, are obliged occasionally to take up blood and violence to defend that which they love."[141] And she paid special attention to the antifascist films of the Hollywood Left. Aguirre recommended *Destination Tokyo* (co-written by Albert Maltz) for realistically portraying the stoic heroism of its US crew and the treachery of fascist regimes, which should be "banished from the world," she seethed. She recommended *Counter-Attack* (written by John Howard Lawson), especially for its depiction of "Russian heroism," this time exemplified by a Soviet guerrilla (played by Paul Muni) fighting Nazi occupation. And she found *None Shall Escape* (written by Lester Cole) and *Tomorrow, the World!* (written by Ring Lardner, Jr.) "useful" to argue that the soon-to-be defeated fascist regimes should be shown no mercy after the war.[142]

Aguirre's review of *Watch on the Rhine* captures much about the ways that she appropriated Hollywood Left antifascist films into the Cuban context. Like Valdés-Rodríguez, she highly recommended it and its "magnificent and very timely political message." The film, she explains, is about Müller's struggle to awaken an "America that still doesn't understand even remotely . . . the degree to which universal liberty and justice are in danger." While Valdés-Rodríguez had compared the character of Kurt Müller to a past Cuban revolutionary, Aguirre applies the lessons of his heroism to the Cuban present. She writes,

> Thousands of men and women still believe themselves above the bloody battle that divides the world today, still maintain a dangerous political naiveté that disallows them to recognize the enemy when he makes the slightest effort to hide his identity and even when he doesn't bother. [They] still shake their heads, as though faced with an exaggeration, when *here among us* someone says, for example, that certain attitudes of our public today . . . are oriented towards the initial roads of fascism; that the intent to "reorganize" the syndicates is nothing but totalitarian corporatism; that the persecution of this or

> that political group is nothing but the prologue of a terror that would extend to all Cubans.[143]

Here, Aguirre is referring not to Batista's abuses of power but to the threat she perceived in Ramón Grau San Martín, now the president-elect, having triumphed over Batista's handpicked successor in elections held on June 1, 1944. With a bitter history between Grau and Cuban Communists, the former now vowed to remove communist leaders from Cuba's powerful confederation of labor unions, the Confederación de Trabajadores de Cuba (CTC), and to reorganize the unions under his Ministry of Labor. This was the "intent" that Aguirre referred to as "totalitarian corporatism," while the persecuted "political group" she refers to is the Partido Socialista Popular (PSP), the new name adopted by the PCC in 1943.[144] Aguirre, in other words, is making Hollywood antifascism speak in defense of Cuban communism.

Aguirre prescribes for Cubans the same total conversion undergone by Fanny and David Farrelly in *Watch on the Rhine*: from apathy to awareness to activism. Aguirre stokes Cuba's collective consciousness, writing, "It is not enough that in a people these truths are comprehended by a thousand, ten thousand or a million citizens; . . . by one class or by one or various parties; but rather what is necessary . . . is that all the people, without exception, assimilate it." And then she uses the film to prescribe revolutionary action. The film's "lesson," she explains, is that

> the struggle has to be supreme, over all pretexts and justifications. In our way of life, the familiar is . . . a forceful fetter that prevents man—and woman—from every impetus of rebellion. To leave from the well-worn road represents the loss of a secure salary, the collapse of the home. . . . But Kurt Müller, the exemplary revolutionary figure of *Watch on the Rhine*, knows that there is no possible vacillation, that nobody has the right to procure for his house a fictitious peace and security when a whole country—a world—is wrecked in chaos. And so he brings his home into the vortex, risks his life, endangers his wife, and snatches from his children a carefree childhood in order to contribute to the salvation of his country's freedom and the defense of the liberty of all the peoples of the world.

Finally, Aguirre explicitly translates this mobilizing lesson from Hollywood—and its "exemplary revolutionary figure" of Kurt Müller—into the Cuban context. She writes, "Nobody knows in what moment the civic dignity of *Cubans* will be presented with the necessity of leaving behind this everyday calm life to fight for democracy, for the liberty of all."[145]

Like many Havana film writers, Aguirre was self-conscious about her role in mediating Hollywood's powerful influence on Cubans' worldviews. Instead of ignoring it, she sought to intervene in its influence, to make it speak for revolutionary Cuban nationalism. Indeed, Aguirre's review of *Watch on the Rhine* admits this strategy. She writes, "It does not have to be clarified that [the fight for freedom] will be decided by stimuli more deep and direct than can be contained by any movie. But, in moments of transcendent expectation, all—that which is read, that which is heard, that which is seen, even that which is dreamed—has importance. Therefore . . . that which can strengthen the moral fiber of a people in any sense will be emphasized."[146] Here Aguirre seems to summarize the efforts of Cuban film writers, including herself, to appropriate Hollywood antifascist films and their heroes to "strengthen" Cubans' "moral fiber," to fortify Cubans' freedom-fighting commitments to which they were honor-bound by their own history, and that of Pan-America more generally.

Conclusion

During World War II, US government propagandists together with Hollywood filmmakers argued fervently against dictatorships and for a progressive vision of the (Pan-)American Way, defined by the Four Freedoms and (Pan-) Americans' commitment to fight for them. This message spoke profoundly to Cubans, whose own historical heroes were those who raised arms for democracy and national sovereignty. Along with trade and military pacts, this freedom-fighting zeitgeist helped to buoy US-Cuban relations to their pre-1959 peak, binding the two countries together more tightly than ever.

Yet this wartime harmony was a tenuous one, which only temporarily patched together the essential incompatibility between US hemispheric hegemony and revolutionary Cuban nationalism. Tensions reemerged with the election of Grau to the Cuban presidency in 1944. Though watchful OIAA analysts had reason to hope that Grau's "antagonism" toward the United States and his "dangerously radical political theories" had "modified" with time, they noted that his ascension brought "uncertainties" to US-Cuban relations. As nervous as they were, OIAA analysts did cheer that the 1944 Cuban election, and Batista's and the US embassy's recognition of its results, were further evidence of Cuba's march along the path of democracy and the United States' commitment to that path.[147]

Wartime rhetoric had raised great expectations in Cuba, *and* among the Hollywood Left, that the United States had become a sincerer Good Neighbor and propagator of the Four Freedoms throughout the hemisphere, if not the globe. Expectations were so high, in fact, that disappointment was all but inevitable. And, indeed, the postwar brought profound disillusionment in both Havana and Hollywood. For one thing, the end of the war seemed to bring an end to the US government's acute interest in its southern neighbors. Despite OIAA leaders' protestations that a discontinuation of their efforts would confirm Latin Americans' suspicions about the United States' self-interestedness, the OIAA (along with the MPSA) was dissolved in April 1946; and the OIAA Information Division's work—including its collaboration with Hollywood—was scaled down and transferred to the State Department's new Cultural Division. Official postmortems of the OIAA claimed that it had united "the great American family [with] indestructible binds of a tradition of liberty" and that Hollywood had served as its strongest binding agent.[148] But, as the cold war emerged on the heels of the hot one, the US State Department turned its attentions from winning hearts and minds in Latin America to winning them in Europe and Asia. Worst of all, despite wartime denunciations of military dictators around the world, cold war US foreign policy would come to rely on them in Latin America more heavily than ever. In Cuba specifically, US policymakers' concerns about Grau and the PRC-Aútentico proved unfounded. Both the parties' administrations—Grau's and Carlos Prío Socarrás'—proved adequately abeyant to US interests and, relatedly, as corrupt as their predecessors. Given the Aútenticos' revolutionary roots, and the United States' wartime propaganda, Cubans were more dismayed than ever to see their democratic ideals betrayed by both.

The emerging cold war also brought disillusionment to the Hollywood Left, as the political climate in the United States turned against them. Many of its artists worried that they had created a monster by promoting the vision of a Manichean world in which the United States was an unimpeachable agent for Good, a vision now appropriated to the ends of conservative cold warriors.[149] In response, those leftist artists that survived an intense postwar Red Scare went on to create a "cycle" of films known as film noir, a type of film *defined* by its propensity to depict the United States darkly, or in a "bad light," and to offer ample evidence of discrimination, want, and fear within US society.

The importation of these film noirs into Havana, and the ways they were used to promote Cubans' long-held ambivalence about the United States and its "entrails" as well as to criticize contemporary Cuban politics and society, is the subject of the next chapter. Just as Hollywood films helped bind the "ties of singular intimacy" between Cuba and the United States during the war, Hollywood films would be appropriated to help break those bonds, refigured as chains, after it.

5

Breaking the Chains: Hollywood Noir in Postwar Havana, 1946–1952

August 1949. A crowd streams over the hemispheric map on the Teatro América's lobby floor. On the walls, large print on movie posters for Columbia Pictures' *We Were Strangers* reads "*FUERA LOS TIRANOS!* [Down with the Tyrants!]."[1] (See fig. 5.1.) Under this text, a chain in mid-rupture encircles the film's Spanish title, *Rompiendo las cadenas* (*Breaking the Chains*). The bottom half of the poster contains three dramatic stills from the film, under which a banner reads "*Patriotismo! Abnegación! Bravura!* [Patriotism! Self-Sacrifice! Bravery!]." Made in Havana for Columbia's branch office, this poster uses themes that had proven popular among Cuban audiences during and since World War II. This time, though, the appeal to Cuban moviegoers is even more direct, indicated in shorthand in the poster's third still, which features an action scene on the University of Havana's iconic stairway, La Escalinata. This time the film's freedom fighters are Cuban, namely fictionalized members of the ABC Revolutionary Society that had helped to overthrow Machado, the sixteenth anniversary of which *We Were Strangers*' Havana debut was timed to coincide.[2]

Inside Teatro América's auditorium, *We Were Strangers* opens with a prologue (in translation) on screen, transporting the viewer back to the early 1930s:

> Tyranny and brutality were making their debut in the world—again. Among the first casualties was the lovely island of Cuba. A clique of corrupt politicians led by President Machado drove all liberty from its tropic shores. They throttled its press, gagged its voice, hanged its soul, paralyzed its honor and reduced its people to beggary and despair. With gibbet and gun, they made a mockery of human rights and looted its industries and plantations. This is the story of the White Terror under which the island of Cuba cowered for seven years until its freedom-loving heart found its heroes—in 1933.[3]

FIG. 5.1. A locally made movie poster for John Huston's *We Were Strangers* (1949). (Author's collection)

This long first prologue, which links Machado to the "Enslaved World" offered by the recently vanquished Axis powers, is followed by a short second prologue that quotes Thomas Jefferson, "Resistance to tyranny is obedience to God," which links Cuban revolutionaries to Pan-America's freedom-fighting heroes of history. Thus, *We Were Strangers* announces its lineage from so much wartime Hollywood propaganda about a hemisphere bound together by its peoples' shared "love of liberty."

As the film's action begins, however, the moral clarity and idealism of the recent past give way to the ambiguity and growing disillusionment of the postwar present. Using conventions of film noir that he helped to develop, writer-director John Huston conveys a pessimistic mood. In sharp contrast to the Technicolor sunniness of *Week-End in Havana*, *We Were Strangers'* black and white Havana is shadowy, its iconic sites shrouded in darkness. The Capitolio appears at the end of a narrow street as revolutionaries flee Machado's henchmen in a late-night car chase. On La Escalinata, Machado's secret police gun down students. Much of the film takes place underground beneath Colón Cemetery, where the film's heroes dig a cramped tunnel as part of their plot to assassinate the dictator and his lackeys. Rather than a Pan American Airways flight arriving in the harbor by day, a cruise ship slinks guiltily out in the night, its US tourists afraid of getting caught in the revolution's crossfire. The film's protagonist, Tony Fenner (John Garfield), denounces its US passengers for, at best, abandoning the fight for freedom or, at worst, being on the wrong side of it. He seethes at them for "leaving Havana, leaving the heat and the crooked streets and the fear and the murder. That's it," he goes on, "Turn your back on them, the President and all his fat friends."[4]

Overall, *We Were Strangers'* depiction of the US role in Cuba is ambiguous. On one hand, along with that Jefferson quote, there is the character of Fenner, introduced as a US citizen who arrives in Havana to lead the Cuban rebels and who falls in love with one of them, a beautiful Cuban woman named China Valdés (Jennifer Jones), thus reiterating Pan-American bonds on the basis of US-led freedom fighting *and* interethnic romance. Further suggesting Cuba's "debt of gratitude," Fenner carries funds collected from US citizens sympathetic to the cause of *Cuba libre*. On the other hand, Huston managed to imply critiques of the US presence in Cuba, even if the conservative cold war climate in the United States precluded *explicit* critiques. In the film, Fenner's cover is that he is a US talent scout, visiting Cuba to pilfer its human resources and to enjoy its "cheap rum." "They're just here for our women" and "for money," complains one Cuban character of Yankees, while Fenner's Cuban co-conspirators articulate serious doubts about whether any US citizen can sincerely, selflessly fight for their cause.[5] Even the language in the prologue about the "loot[ing]" of Cuba's "industries and plantations" gestures to what many contemporary moviegoers (in both the United States and Cuba) knew of anti-Yankee sentiment in Cuba in the early 1930s and in the hemisphere more generally.

While ambiguous about the United States' role in Cuba, *We Were Strangers* is unambiguous about its denunciation of dictatorship and its endorsement of freedom-fighting masculinity. Intolerable tyranny is personified in the drunken, lecherous, and homicidal character of *la porra* chief, Ariete (Pedro Armendáriz), as sadistic as any movie Nazi. Thankfully, as one Cuban rebel proclaims, "the tyrants are strong but the cry of liberty is stronger." Patriots from all walks of life "swear in [their] hearts to make Cuba free" no matter the blood it costs. Rebels speechify on the need for "men [who] fight injustice wherever it appears" and finally decide that Tony Fenner is just "that kind of a man." Indeed, Fenner pays the ultimate price for *Cuba libre*, dying in China's arms. At this precise moment, the people rise up and overthrow Machado. Bells ring and Cubans celebrate in the streets, yelling "*Viva la Revolución!*" The screen fades to Columbia Pictures' Lady Liberty logo, as the lights come up in the Teatro América.[6]

For the most part, Cubans seemed to be flattered that a filmmaker as esteemed as Huston made a film that "glorifies Cuba," as one fan put it.[7] In *Cinema*, Perdices praised the film for "highlighting the unfaltering heroes persecuted by one of the most violent tyrannies of our time." He continued, "Many revolutionaries will feel proud to see themselves so well-represented."[8] Indeed, now in power, Auténtico party leaders, who had fought against Machado, believed the film burnished their (tarnished) revolutionary credentials. As a token of appreciation, Prío's administration sent crates of Cuba's best cigars to Huston.[9] Even Aguirre credited Huston for his intent "to honor the Cuban people's aspirations for liberty in those years." Yet, Aguirre was not willing to excuse Huston for the ways that the film "completely disfigured" the US policy that had supported the Machado regime or the ways the film raised the profile of one putschist plot (led by a US citizen, no less) over "the collective resistance" that really forced Machado out, as "*we* well know," she wrote prescriptively of the *Cuban* national audience. Invoking a phrase Aguirre uses frequently to describe the ways that Hollywood films could become more revolutionary than their makers intended, Aguirre writes that *We Were Strangers'* final moments "could not help but express" that the 1933 revolution was achieved through the mass mobilization of the Cuban people.[10]

We Were Strangers represents a culmination: It is the peak expression of Hollywood antifascism's congruence with revolutionary Cuban nationalism.

At the same time, as a strange hybrid between antifascist film and film noir, it captures the decline of the Hollywood Left's wartime idealism about the (Pan-)American Way into postwar disillusionment. The exhibition and reception of *We Were Strangers* in Havana, thus, makes a fitting opening to this chapter, which explores important shifts in Hollywood (politics, content, and business practices) and in US-Cuban relations, and how they related to each other.

This chapter's first section uses Huston's career to outline the Hollywood Left's political demise in the postwar US anticommunist crusade, but also the survival of the Hollywood Left's progressive social critiques in noirs and social problem films.[11] In postwar noirs, US society is no longer represented as an evolving model of freedom and equality, but rather as an unequal and inhumane society dictated by the almighty dollar and the scramble to get to the top of the heap. Working- and middle-class men are alienated, business and romantic partners duplicitous, and politicians and cops corrupt. In noirs, the male movie stars that Cubans adored in their roles as idealistic soldiers are recast as cynics and outlaws, as in the case with Garfield, who appeared as a noir antihero in *The Postman Always Rings Twice* (1946), *Body and Soul* (1947), and *Force of Evil* (1948) before his turn in *We Were Strangers*. (See fig. 5.2.) At the same time, a whole new crop of male actors (e.g., Marlon Brando, Kirk Douglas, Burt Lancaster, Robert Mitchum) became stars—and heroes to Cuban moviegoers—through their embodiment of 'tough guy' noir masculinity.

Coincidentally enough, noir's heyday overlapped with the two Aútentico administrations in Cuba: Ramón Grau San Martín's (1944–48) and Carlos Prío Soccoras's (1948–52), the subject of this chapter's second section. During their administrations, economic dependency on the United States and rampant political corruption limited the spread of postwar prosperity and agitated revolutionary Cuban nationalism. Havana's film giro during these postwar years—the subject of this chapter's third section—offers deeper insight into these developments, again tracing a trajectory from great expectations to deep disillusionment. In many ways, the giro began to devolve during this period from a site of US-Cuban bonding to a site of US-Cuban estrangement.

This chapter's final sections turn to Cuban reception of postwar Hollywood noirs and social problem films, which proved particularly popular with Havana moviegoers and critics. While the US government sometimes limited the exportation of noirs, such export controls rarely applied to Cuba. So, Cubans saw, and often preferred, the very films that confirmed what Martí had argued about the "violence, discord, immorality, and disorder" endemic to US society's "entrails." Attuned to this, Havana film writers set out to appropriate film noirs to fuel anti-Yankee, and anti-Auténtico, sentiments. They argued that

FIG. 5.2. John Garfield, on the cover of *Cinema*, March 28, 1948, promotes *Body and Soul*, a Hollywood Left film noir. From the collection of the *Biblioteca Nacional "José Martí,"* Havana, Cuba.

such films were true reflections of how far the United States had fallen from its Four Freedom ideals to its degraded reality and, thus, of how US imperial hegemony in Cuba amounted to a profoundly negative force. They used such films to launch diatribes against inequality and the abuse of power in the United States *and* Cuba, and to galvanize resistance through identification with their (anti)heroes.

In short, this chapter finds that representing the United States "in a bad light," along with "fulminating" against tyranny, had some of the counter-hegemonic effects about which US Pan-American propagandists had worried. The Hollywood Left's persistence in doing both during these years contributed to the reimagining of US-Cuban "bonds" into "chains," and to the idea that Cubans should break them, even before Batista's coup of March 1952.

Postwar (Mal)Adjustment: Huston, the Hollywood Left, Red Scares, and Dark Films

John Huston arrived in Hollywood in 1937, and he readily assimilated into its leftist circles. One of his first writing assignments was on the Pan-American antifascist film *Juarez* (1939), which well suited the lifelong aficionado of Mexico. He wrote rousing dialogue in the script margins about fighting tyranny and keeping "the cause of democracy alive!" Prewar, Huston also co-wrote *Sergeant York*, joined the Screen Writers Guild and its union drives, and participated in antifascist organizations; as such, he collaborated closely with CPUSA members, whom he later defended as "idealists," misguided about how to "improv[e] the social condition of mankind" but certainly not traitors intent upon the overthrow of the US government.[12] Promoted to writer-director in 1941, Huston transformed Dashiell Hammett's *The Maltese Falcon* into a prototype of noir and began his working relationship with Humphrey Bogart, two lefties who together shaped onscreen masculinity for years to come.

Bogart also appeared in Huston's next project: *The Treasure of the Sierra Madre*, about American gold prospectors consumed by greed in Mexico, a setting which put it within the OIAA's purview. In June 1942, Warner Bros. dutifully presented Huston's script to the PCA and OIAA to be sure it was "on safe ground" in "relation to the 'Good Neighbor Policy.'" Durland responded that it was not; he proclaimed it "unacceptable" for its "sordid" Mexican locales and characters, and the "derogatory statements" US characters made about them.[13] But it wasn't just Durland's disapproval that postponed *Treasure* for the next half-decade; it was also Huston's enlistment in the Army Signal Corps. While Huston's assignment was to produce morale-boosting propaganda, he translated his experiences on the front lines witnessing combat and heavy casualties into two films that the War Department found too demoralizing to release. Huston managed to salvage the first, *The Battle of San Pietro*, with various cuts, but could not do the same for *Let There Be Light*, a film about "shell-shock" that was supposed to show the wonders of psychiatric rehabilitation in US hospitals, but lingered too long on veterans' war-induced psychic distress for the US government's taste.[14]

Frustrated but increasingly determined not to compromise his artistic vision for anyone, Huston rewrote *The Treasure of the Sierra Madre* during his final months in the Army.[15] In August 1946, Warner Bros. sent a new script to the PCA, which approved it this time, albeit with further admonitions not to represent Mexicans negatively.[16] In truth, the PCA probably should have been more concerned about *Treasure's* representations of *US* citizens. After all, the film focuses on three Yankees, whose souls become perverted by their lust for gold. After toiling for weeks for a US oil company outside of Tampico and then being stiffed by their duplicitous US supervisor, two US expats, Dobbs (Bogart) and Curtin (Tim Holt), convince an old prospector, Howard (Walter Huston), to help them dig for gold in the Sierra Madre. Howard agrees, but warns Curtin and Dobbs that their "noble brotherhood" will not last if they strike gold, that they will turn on each other. And this is precisely what happens. When they strike it rich, Dobbs especially is unhinged by "gold fever." In a manic state, he plots to kill Curtin, but is, instead, killed himself by Mexican bandits. After the dust settles (and the gold literally blows away in the wind), Howard and Curtin have learned the film's lesson: that community and spiritual well-being are more important than individual material acquisition.[17]

Released in the United States in January 1948, and proclaimed one of the year's best films by critics in both the United States and Cuba, *The Treasure of the Sierra Madre* won Huston two Oscars. James Agee in *The Nation* proclaimed that "Huston, next only to Chaplin, is the most talented man working in American pictures," his style so admirably "masculine" and "virile" in this movie about the effects of greed on men's souls. Ominously, though, Agee worried about whether such socially critical filmmaking would be possible henceforth. *The Treasure of the Sierra Madre*, Agee concluded, proved "what it was possible to do in Hollywood . . . during the very hopeful period before the November [1947] freeze. God knows what can be done now."[18] Here, Agee is referring to the chilling effects of the postwar Hollywood Red Scare, part of a dramatically shifting political climate in the United States, in which "containment" of communism became the top priority of domestic and foreign policy. During this period, "the American Way" was reconstructed to reflect the *new* foreign enemy thought to pose an existential threat to the United States: the Soviet Union. The wartime language of the Four Freedoms—with its emphasis on civil liberties, racial pluralism, a fairer distribution of wealth, and the democratic self-determination of nations—gave way to the cold war language of Free Enterprise and its emphases on an anticommunist consensus (in which social criticism became suspect); ethnic assimilation; uninhibited corporate growth (rather than the protection of labor rights) as the source of prosperity and consumer abundance for all; and US interventions abroad to keep people free from communism. Congressional Republicans thrived in this climate, reviving their prewar House Un-American Activities Committee (HUAC) to attack the New Deal Left as a bastion of treasonous communists.[19]

In October 1947, HUAC made Hollywood one of its first postwar targets. The committee gathered files on films they suspected of leaning too far left (including *Counter-Attack*, *Juarez*, *Modern Times*, *Mr. Smith Goes to Washington*, and *Watch on the Rhine*) and subpoenaed over forty film artists. Nineteen of them (eventually whittled down to the famous "Hollywood Ten") were writers and directors deemed "unfriendly witnesses" because they refused to testify.[20] Now under investigation by Congress for being *un*-American, most of them had worked *with* the US government during the war—through the OWI and/or the OIAA—as spokesmen of the (Pan-) American Way, writing the antifascist, prodemocratic films that had been so popular in the United States and in Cuba. At the same time, film industry conservatives published a *Screen Guide for Americans*, which nicely captures the shift they advocated in Hollywood representations of the American Way. It admonished writers: "Don't Deify the 'Common Man,'" "Don't Glorify the Collective," and "Don't Smear the Free Enterprise System."[21]

For his part, Huston was outraged. He helped lead the Hollywood Left's liberal contingent in founding the Committee for the First Amendment (CFA) in defense of the Hollywood Ten's constitutional rights.[22] Many of Hollywood's biggest names signed CFA petitions, which denounced the HUAC "demagogues" and their fascistic strategies and which pledged to fight for "freedom of speech, freedom of thought, freedom of worship, and freedom from fear." Even an incomplete list of signatories conveys the breadth of the CFA's support among the industry's most recognizable male stars (e.g., Humphrey Bogart, Henry Fonda, John Garfield, Burt Lancaster, Audie Murphy, Gregory Peck, Edward G. Robinson, Jimmy Stewart, and Spencer Tracy) and filmmakers (e.g., Huston, Jerry Wald, Walter Wanger, and Billy Wilder).[23] A sizable contingent—including Bogart, Garfield, and Huston—flew to Washington to attend the HUAC hearings and pronounce *them* un-American.

But then came "the November freeze," as Agee called it. On the stand, the Hollywood Ten came across as strident and secretive, everything US citizens feared domestic communists to be; they were cited for contempt of Congress and sentenced to prison terms. Also called to testify, the president of the Motion Picture Association of America (MPAA, the new name for the MPPDA), Eric Johnston, and studio executives capitulated to HUAC, eager to establish that they, too, were determined to rout communists from the US film industry. In December 1947, the studios initiated an infamous blacklist of suspected communists and "fellow travelers" (liberals who had collaborated "too" closely with them). Under this assault, the CFA folded quickly, and many Hollywood liberals rushed to establish their anticommunist credentials. Some of them began the humiliating ritual of "naming names," while others left the country. Huston refused to cave in these ways, but his personal prestige seemed to save him from subpoenas and blacklists. So Huston turned his energies back to filmmaking and to showing Agee, and everyone else, what could be done even in this repressive environment.[24]

In early 1948, Huston began filming the classic noir *Key Largo*, which he co-wrote. In it, unemployed veteran Frank McCloud (Bogart) visits the widow (Lauren Bacall) of a war buddy and his father (Lionel Barrymore) in the Florida Keys, where they operate a hotel. In it, the three are forced by a hurricane to hole up with a handful of guests, most notably a sadistic gangster named Rocco (Edward G. Robinson). Tapping into long-standing associations between Cuba and US organized crime, Huston has Rocco operating out of Havana, just now returning to resume his US criminal empire.[25] At the time of production, Huston explained to a friend that the film expresses his postwar disillusionment, as well as his determination not to succumb to it. Capturing the mood of much postwar noir, and noting his surprise that Warner Bros. was letting him get away with it, Huston explains that "the central figure played by Bogart is a disenchanted, if not embittered idealist" who had believed the New Deal and the US war effort "would serve to uplift mankind." But now that the war is over, Huston continues, "He [McCloud] regrets the tremendous sacrifice of life of men of good will, as having been to no purpose, and he has resolved to live selfishly henceforward. . . . [Then] he comes up against a gangster (Eddie Robinson) who represents in miniature, the same evils he fought against in the war." Rocco, in other words, serves as a measure of the distance between wartime ideals and the postwar organization of US society around the individual pursuit of power and wealth.[26]

Key Largo is a representative film noir in many ways. For instance, its central characters—the disillusioned war veteran and the despotic gangster—were noir regulars. In many a noir, the Hollywood Left took the industry's movie stars out of uniform and plunked their characters into civilian life to great dramatic effect. While a number of them suffer the clinical signs of psychiatric distress that Huston documented in *Let There Be Light*, all of them suffer the psychic disorientation of adjusting from wartime idealism and male camaraderie to postwar society's venality and alienation. Indeed, with or without a veteran protagonist, noirs are obsessed with the theme of postwar masculine maladjustment. Working- and middle-class men are trapped, sometimes literally—e.g., boarded up in a hotel in *Key Largo* and stuck in a funhouse in *The Lady from Shanghai* (1947)—but more often figuratively, in noir's stultifying shadows and the machinations of the powerful. In many Hollywood Left noirs, (anti)heroes face off against mobsters and the shady businessmen and slippery politicians with whom they are linked. Sometimes noir (anti)heroes even win, as is the case in *Key Largo*, the conclusion of which reasserts a glimmer of wartime idealism. As Huston explains to his friend, "The climax comes [when Bogart's character realizes] that regardless of the outcome of the struggle, it is in the nature of man to go on fighting the good fight."[27] Bogart converts himself again to selfless hero, wins a gun battle against Rocco and his gunsels aboard a boat bound for Cuba, and returns to Bacall after the storm has passed.

But Huston's next noir, the equally prototypical *The Asphalt Jungle* (1950), denies the viewer any such happy ending. Co-written by Huston and the soon-to-be blacklisted Ben Maddow, *The Asphalt Jungle* is less optimistic about the recuperation of New Deal and wartime ideals. Set in a US city racked with crime and corruption, its plot revolves around a criminal heist conducted by a number of sympathetic working-class men, including Dix Handley (played by the soon-to-be HUAC-subpoenaed Sterling Hayden), who waxes poetic about the repossessed family farm he hopes to buy back with his portion of the heist's proceeds. This likable crew is double-crossed by the heist's financial backer, a corporate lawyer who is the film's true crook, Lon Emmerich (Louis Calhern). Lon plots to run off with the loot and his extramarital lover, Angela, played by Marilyn Monroe in her Hollywood speaking debut. Reflective of the intimate links between Cuba and Hollywood, Monroe as Angela gushes over the virtues of Havana as a tourist destination: "Isn't it romantic?" she coos about the trip Lon promises her. But Angela's dream dissolves into a bloody nightmare as Lon's deceit unravels the heist and the thieves are all shot up. In the film's final moments, Dix bleeds out at his family horse farm, his prelapsarian vision of America destroyed by a conniving capitalist's greed for more than his fair share.[28]

In many ways, the rise of film noir in the midst of the early cold war's repressive political climate is surprising. But Huston and other Hollywood filmmakers got away with them for a number of reasons even beyond their personal prestige. For one thing, noirs seemed to appeal to postwar audiences, hungry for greater realism and male-focused drama (but tired of combat films, which the studios mostly phased out). This made noirs too popular to stop producing, even as US government officials and industry conservatives admonished against their depictions of "the seamy side of American life."[29] Also, noirs were relatively cheap to make, an important consideration given the studios' postwar economic troubles. After the banner year of 1946, domestic box office fell precipitously as Hollywood faced new competition for Americans' leisure-time dollars (even before the rise of television) and foreign box office declined due to a global economic slump, the rise of the Iron Curtain, and remittance problems. Inexpensively produced, noirs could make a profit in the domestic market alone, a trend that filmmakers perpetuated by ever ramping up noirs' violence and sex, in defiance of the increasingly impotent PCA.[30]

Thus, studio executives were not overly concerned that noirs were often denied export, the self-policing of which now fell largely to the new Motion Picture Export Association (MPEA), a branch of the MPAA also presided over by Eric Johnston. Formed in 1945 to represent the major studios' collective interests in particularly difficult foreign markets, the MPEA counted on the help of the US Commerce and State Departments, more convinced than ever of Hollywood's capacity to sell the American Way abroad. In exchange, the MPEA promised to limit the export of films with a "'distorted' slant on American life" that might be used to foment anti-Americanism.[31] The MPEA tended to categorize noirs as such, especially those made by the Hollywood Left. Huston's *Key Largo*, for instance, was banned in Germany and Austria because it did *not* "giv[e] a positive and constructive picture of American life."[32] Neither did the Hollywood Left noirs *Boomerang!*, *Crossfire*, *Laura*, *The Lost Weekend*, *The Naked City*, and *To the Ends of the Earth*, which were all deemed "unsuitable for export" behind the Iron Curtain in 1949.[33] As noted above, export limits rarely applied to Cuba, which was considered securely within the ideological fold. *Key Largo*, for instance, premiered at Warner Bros.' new showcase theater in Havana (see below) in October 1948, as had *The Treasure of the Sierra Madre* just three months prior.[34]

In April and again in August 1948, Huston himself could be found in Havana, arriving to work on the script and then do some location shooting for *We Were Strangers*, which he made between *Key Largo* and *The Asphalt Jungle*.[35] In Havana, Huston's co-writer and future blacklistee Peter Viertel introduced him to Ernest Hemingway. The two became fast friends, engaging in duels of machismo: drinking, shooting, fishing, and nearly fist-fighting. (They also had dinner with Ernesto P. Smith, of Columbia Pictures, which had agreed to distribute the independently produced *We Were Strangers*.)[36] Hemingway regaled Huston with stories of the 1933 Cuban revolution and the still chronic corruption in Cuban politics, and he introduced Huston to Jim Kendrigan, the University of Havana's Irish-American football coach, much involved with "revolutionary" action groups still roiling on campus and beyond.[37] After these Havana visits, Huston concluded that the contemporary government of Cuba was utterly "corrupt" and its police forces repressive. He admired the anti-Machado revolutionaries, but noted that they had failed to bring democracy or independence to Cuba. Not least of all they had failed because of US interference, "especially [by] the industrialists, and sugar and fruit plantation owners," Huston noted, using language that suggests that the *We Were Strangers* prologue's implicit critique of the US presence in Cuba—"loot[ing] its industries and plantations"—was not accidental.[38]

Indeed, early drafts of *We Were Strangers* contained more explicit criticisms of the same. But when it seemed these would preclude US State Department approvals needed to film in Cuba, Huston toned them down. Further, the PCA insisted on rewrites that would emphasize that Machado's "tyrannical" power, and not US imperialism, was the 1933 revolution's target. Even still, Joseph Breen warned Columbia that the very subject matter would limit *We Were Strangers'* foreign distribution: "You will readily understand," Breen noted, "that a picture which sympathetically presents revolution by force may well meet with difficulty as regards its release in a number of countries."[39]

Breen was right: to make a film that celebrated armed revolution—especially in a film even vaguely critical of the United States' global role—was to invite controversy, and not just abroad. When *We Were Strangers* premiered in the United States in April 1949, cold warriors denounced it as Communist propaganda in which "the Americans are shown as nothing but money grubbers."[40] One critic deemed it especially dangerous "at a time when the Communist Party is attempting to persuade the people of . . . Latin America that the United States is an imperialistic nation and their enemy." This latter critic was especially outraged by the film's assertion, in her interpretation, that "wherever there is injustice in the world today, the solution is to revolt." She worried that *We Were Strangers* could "be interpreted as a call to direct action by revolution, against today's governments that are friendly to the United States." Violence and rebellion "are not in accord with the American way," she concluded, forgetting so much wartime propaganda that had argued that they were.[41] But the film's defenders had not forgotten. One Columbia Pictures executive wrote, "To say any revolution . . . indicates the work of Communists is to give that group far greater credit than they deserve. It certainly was not a group of Communists that inspired our own American revolution against tyranny in 1776." Nor had it been a group of communists that had inspired the Cuban wars of independence or its 1933 revolution, explained another Columbia executive, who lumped these events together in a continuum as "the Cuban struggle for independence and individual liberty from 1868–1934."[42]

We Were Strangers did not weather the controversy well. It did poorly at the US box office and Columbia abruptly withdrew it from domestic circulation.[43] Within three short years, Garfield was called to HUAC, blacklisted, and dead of a heart attack; and Viertel was blacklisted and forced to defend *We Were Strangers* before a military review board. The FBI flagged the film for its potential to inspire domestic radicals, and the State Department denied Huston's request to enter it into international film festivals.[44] And, just as Breen had predicted, foreign censors balked too. Convinced of *We Were Strangers'* subversive potential, Portugal's dictator and Egypt's king (both US allies) banned its importation into their countries.[45] And, along with Robert Rossen's *All the King's Men* (1949), it was denied exhibition permits in Argentina because, as *Variety* explained, "dictatorship is a sensitive subject down here."[46]

We Were Strangers was *not* denied export to or banned in Cuba. Nor did Columbia Pictures' Havana office or its local Cuban publicists shy away from its celebration of violent revolt. Along with the aforementioned movie posters, newspaper ads for the film featured Garfield gripping a machine gun, beside text that translates, "Daring without Restraint! Rebellion in its Glory!"[47] After all, as noted above, the country's ruling party, the Auténticos, welcomed the film's celebration of 1933 revolutionaries as a boost to their brand, much sullied by 1949. The sullying of that brand during the two Auténtico administrations is the subject of the following section.

A "Somber Picture of Corruption and Moral Decay": The Auténtico Years

As Grau took office in October 1944, there was much optimism in Cuba. The tide of World War II had turned, and Cubans had served meritoriously. The future would be won for Democracy, and Cuba had confirmed this by conducting some of the cleanest elections in its history. With US-Cuban rapprochement at its peak, Grau softened his anti-imperialist stance and visited Washington to meet President Roosevelt, the same president who had spurned him in 1933. On the strength of wartime sugar prices, the Cuban economy was booming. Cubans enjoyed one of the highest per capita incomes in Latin America and *the* highest per capita consumption of US goods, enjoying a prosperity the Auténticos pledged to spread through social programs and progressive labor laws.[48] At the same time, the Cuban tourist industry readied itself to rake in postwar US dollars, as more US citizens would have the time and money to take those "week-end in Havana" trips made so alluring by Hollywood. But Cubans' high hopes were to be dashed. The auspicious sugar market exacerbated the island's economic dependency on the United States; the tripling of government revenues invited more political malfeasance than ever; a rising tourism business enticed mobsters (US and homegrown); and the ascendance of the Auténticos precipitated a downward spiral of political violence.[49]

Neither Grau nor his successor, Prío, did anything to alter Cuba's reliance on sugar. There was no incentive to diversify the economy when sugar prices were so high, and the United States guaranteed purchase of the entire crop through 1947 and then starting again in 1950 with the advent of the Korean War. Underscoring Cuba's dependent position, the US government inserted a clause in the Sugar Act of 1948 that threatened quota cancellations if Cuba "denied fair and equitable treatment to United States citizens, their commerce, . . . and industry." This "good behavior clause" was needed, US policymakers argued, to "roll back" nationalist labor laws instituted by the Cuban constitution of 1940 and since won by the increasingly powerful Confederation of Cuban Workers (CTC).[50]

Indeed, Cuban labor had been making more demands since the founding of the CTC in 1939, under which the unions in Cuba's most important industries (including in the film giro) subsequently affiliated. While Cuban labor (like US labor) agreed to wage freezes and no-strike deals during the war, Auténtico campaign promises in 1944 unleashed a resurgence of labor demands. Once in power, the Auténticos sought to control labor—and wrestle its allegiances away from their communist rivals who largely controlled the CTC—by reorganizing the CTC under Grau's Ministry of Labor (recall Aguirre's review of *Watch on the Rhine*, in which she denounced this tactic as fascistic). When that failed, the Aútenticos took another tack. Rather than dismantle the CTC, they set out to undermine its communist faction and grow its Auténtico one, successfully usurping leadership of the CTC in 1947. While this strategy included no small amount of red-baiting, it also required that the Auténticos win over Cuban labor by advancing its cause, mandating (minimal) wage increases across various industries dominated by US companies, including in the film giro. But these increases barely allowed Cubans to keep up with inflation and the rising cost of living, as the price of US goods escalated with the United States' booming postwar economy.[51] And they fell far short of the Auténticos' campaign promises to address Cuban labor's grievances against these skewed dynamics. In the summer of 1949, Cuba's most popular radio show host and an Auténtico defector, Eduardo "Eddy" Chibás, excoriated the Auténticos for "restor[ing] the *chains* that bind the Republic to Yankee Imperialism," echoing a long-standing anti-imperialist trope.[52]

Yet, while the Auténticos seemed to bend to the United States' will on Pan-American economic policy, they consistently defied it on Pan-American foreign policy. As the cold war set in, the United States proved more willing than ever to support right-wing military dictators in Latin America, as long as they helped to contain leftist (and thus potentially communistic) movements in "our own backyard." But the Auténtico administrations continued to oppose such dictators actively, supporting exile movements against them in the Dominican Republic, Honduras, Nicaragua, and Venezuela. Most notably, in 1947, Grau's administration funded and facilitated an (aborted) expedition to overthrow Trujillo; for it, 1,200 Dominicans and Cubans, calling themselves the "Liberation Army of the Caribbean," amassed an arsenal of weaponry, organized themselves into battalions named after Cuban revolutionary heroes, and practiced beach landings in eastern Cuba. And in 1949, Prío's administration supported a second eight-hundred-man strong (aborted) plot against Trujillo. Participants in these plots included Spanish Civil War and World War II veterans, while even nonveterans claimed to be inspired by those righteous crusades against Franco and the Axis powers respectively.[53] Others were recruited (by football coach Kendrigan and others) from the ranks of athletes and "toughs" at the University of Havana, young Cubans (including the twenty-one-year-old Fidel Castro) eager to become men of action, to prove their grit, and to take up arms against tyranny. "We are romantics devoted to the cause of liberty," one participant explained to a *Bohemia* reporter.[54]

Contributing to this zeitgeist, a number of backlogged Hollywood Left combat films reached Havana through 1946, for example, *The Story of G.I. Joe*; *Counter-Attack*; *Back to Bataan*; and *Pride of the Marines* (starring Garfield).[55] For a few years after 1946, World War II combat films disappeared, but Hollywood briefly revived the genre in the early 1950s. Tweaked to gird audiences for the cold war against global communism, these films still revolved around their soldiers' masculine resolve to fight for Freedom. And they still received a great deal of attention in Havana. Take, for instance, John "Yon" Wayne's early postwar combat films. *The Sands of Iwo Jima*—starring Wayne as a tough-as-nails marine sergeant who leads a squad of men, and ultimately sacrifices himself, on that heavily fortified Japanese island—did big box office in Havana in April 1950.[56] Wayne plays a similar role in the Guadacanal-set *Flying Leathernecks*, which opens with a voiceover assuring audiences that "our country, then as always, would fight against aggression and all the aggressors that challenge the rights of free men." To promote *Flying Leathernecks*, and the similarly themed *Operation Pacific*, Wayne himself appeared in Havana in May 1951, which was the cause for much celebration in Havana fanzines.[57] In other words, Hollywood continued to fuel the Pan-American freedom-fighting zeitgeist that strengthened Cuba's self-professed freedom fighters. Cuban recruits to the "Liberation Army of the Caribbean" *and* Auténtico leaders seemed convinced of their Pan-American "responsibility" to fight for freedom. In fact, when US State Department officials admonished the Cubans to stand down, President Prío retorted in August 1949—as *We Were Strangers* played in Havana—that Latin American movements against dictators were part of "an historical process" that World War II had accelerated and that "democracy" was Pan-America's defining principle.[58]

Ironically enough, however, the Auténticos seemed to do everything they could to undermine democracy in their own country. Indeed, a succession of spectacular scandals plagued both Grau's and Prío's administrations, with high-profile officials plausibly accused of graft, nepotism, patronage, vote buying, bribery, obstruction of justice, and the embezzlement of millions. They were also accused of complicity with the criminal underworld, including US mafioso. Late in 1946, allegedly with the Grau administration's consent, Meyer Lansky—who set up shop in Cuba to run rum during the Prohibition years, then switched to overseeing legal gambling operations under Batista's reign in the 1930s and early 1940s—invited Lucky Luciano (the model for *Key Largo's* Rocco) to Havana. There, Lansky and Luciano held a gathering of US mobsters at the Hotel Nacional in order to carve up the licit and illicit businesses (i.e., gambling, prostitution, and drugs) that exploding US tourism made so profitable. The US government, the Cuban Congress, and the Havana press demanded Luciano's expulsion, but Grau refused for months, fueling accusations that the Cuban president was complicit with mobsters.[59]

When Grau finally did deport Luciano in March 1947, Havana was hardly rid of "*gangsterismo*." Instead, the city seemed to teem with homegrown gangsters, whose (even closer) ties to Auténtico officials went way back. During the 1933 revolution, Grau and Prío had fought alongside a number of revolutionary action groups, like the ABC Society featured in *We Were Strangers*. After Batista's 1934 coup, these (ever-reorganizing) action groups conspired against Batista and his puppet presidents; a number of them allied with the exiled Aútentico party. Now in power, the Auténticos owed various debts to these action groups and their trigger-happy members, who came to be known as *pistoleros* (the same word Cubans used for movie gunsels). Beyond their past debts, the Auténticos found that these pistoleros were presently useful in checking the power of the army (full of Batista loyalists), in manning the plots against Trujillo, and in intimidating communists in the CTC. So, the Auténticos granted funds and important government posts, including in the police forces, to members of the Socialist Revolutionary Movement (MSR) and the Insurrectional Revolutionary Union (UIR). Despite this lofty nomenclature, these action groups devolved into little more than rival gangs, largely operating from the University of Havana campus, where they ran a thriving black market and drug trade and recruited student leaders, whose incorporation, in turn, corrupted and bloodied student life. (For instance, football coach Kendrigan was associated with the MSR, and Fidel Castro with the UIR.)[60] These rival groups then engaged in spectacular shootouts and assassinations, for instance, on La Escalinata (the one featured in *We Were Strangers*) and outside of the Cine Resumén in the movie barrio (where the MSR's leader had been catching a flick). Indeed, what happened inside and outside the cines seemed to blur. In Havana's press, bold headlines and images of bullet-riddled cars and bloodied bodies seemed ripped from noir scripts and stills.[61] The pistoleros' "sensational assaults [seemed] right out of the movies," one Cuban later recalled.[62]

Cuban educators and local leaders of the Catholic Church also noted similarities between the behaviors of the pistoleros and Hollywood depictions, and they assigned some blame for the former on the latter. Joining a rising chorus of concern about juvenile delinquency around the world, they sought to check what they considered to be Hollywood's corrosive effect on Cuban youth.[63] They pressured Grau to form a Children's Censor Board in 1945, charged with designating films appropriate, or not, for minors, a demographic said to compose as much as 90% of *cine de barrio* audiences during weekend matinees and holidays.[64] Citing cinema's unique capacity to influence young spectators, and noting cinema's (noir-ish) shift to "pessimism" and "immorality"—and to "exalting the outlaw [and] the gangster"—the Children's Censor Board "prohibited for minors" all films that contained "scenes of robbing, murders, terror, crime or marked sensuality," all noir trademarks.[65]

It was in the midst of all these developments, in the fall of 1945, that an eighteen-year-old Fidel Castro arrived at the University of Havana, just one of many students drawn into the pistolero fray.[66] By then, like so many in his generational cohort, Castro had already ingested plenty of Hollywood masculinity. As a child growing up in eastern Cuba, he had spent his spare dimes at the local cine on Sundays.[67] And his peers at the all-male Jesuit boarding school he attended in Santiago de Cuba recall watching Hollywood movies with Castro, and idolizing John Wayne and Gary Cooper (an actor that a contemporary Cuban film giro employee described as "demonstrat[ing] masculinity to those of us in life who work at being men").[68] Arriving in Havana, Castro set out to imitate his generation's onscreen heroes. He began to associate with campus pistoleros and took to packing a gun; and he joined the plot against Trujillo in 1947 (and told dramatic, self-mythologizing tales of swimming ashore, through shark-infested waters, with a machine gun strapped to his back after the mission failed).[69] Back on campus, Castro wore dark suits and spoke rousingly against the Auténtico's degradation of Cuban democracy. He and another student traveled to Manzanillo, where they stole the Demajagua Bell, an important national symbol from Cuba's wars of independence. They paraded it through the streets of Havana to symbolize that a new generation of "freedom fighters" was taking up the "task of achieving independence and justice," Castro speechified.[70]

At about this time, Castro found a mentor in radio personality Eddy Chibás and joined his new political party, the Cuban People's Party-Ortodoxo, which promised to be more nationalist and anti-imperialist than the Auténticos. Castro campaigned for Chibás in the 1950 congressional elections, in which Chibás won a senate seat. But Castro's apprenticeship was shortlived. On air on August 5, 1951, Chibás denounced Auténtico corruption one last time, shouted "People of Cuba, rise up! People of Cuba, wake up!" and then shot himself in the stomach. When Chibás died eleven days later, Castro at his bedside had well learned the importance of charisma, showmanship, and the grand gesture in appealing to a Cuban audience.[71]

Picking up the fallen leader's torch, Castro used radio broadcasts to reiterate Chibás's accusations against the Aútenticos. He published sensational exposés in the Havana press about "the somber picture of corruption and moral decay" that was postwar Cuba. In one article, Castro evoked a noir criminal caper as he described shady government payoffs to pistoleros, who collected their illicit cash under cover of night à la *The Asphalt Jungle*, which MGM had premiered in Havana with a six-theater roll-out just a year and a half prior.[72] In another article, Castro evoked a noir private eye as he described sneaking onto Prío's estate to snap pictures of the president's ill-begotten wealth, including a lavish swimming pool, recalling to mind the set of *Sunset Boulevard*. In other words, Castro seemed to intuit Hollywood's influence on the generation of Cubans he sought to lead. Consciously or not, he appropriated narratives and imagery from Hollywood antifascist war films and noirs, both genres with special resonance in Auténtico-era Havana.

(Not So) Happy in Havana: US-Cuban Relations in the Postwar Film Giro

In April 1951, Paramount premiered *Sunset Boulevard* at the Teatro América, with a sold-out crowd spilling into the aisles.[73] (See fig. 5.3.) In this most famous of noirs, Austrian-born Jewish émigré and Hollywood Leftist director Billy Wilder seemed to announce the decline of Hollywood's Golden Age. Wilder does so with both loving nostalgia and critical disdain, through the film's story of an aging silent era star, Norma Desmond (Gloria Swanson), and her pathetic delusions of a comeback.[74] In Havana, audiences would have been quick to recognize Swanson; after all, she had been a familiar figure in the 1920s: on screen, in fanzines, and even in person, sharing cocktails with the Cuban president.

FIG. 5.3. A playbill for *Sunset Boulevard*'s run at the Teatro América in April 1951. Note the stamp (*bottom right*) announcing the kick-off of Paramount Havana's twenty-fifth anniversary. (Author's collection)

Further given their singular intimacy with Hollywood, Cubans might have especially appreciated *Sunset Boulevard*'s homages to a bygone film era (like Desmond's impersonation of the Little Tramp) *as well as* its characterization of contemporary Hollywood's studio system as stiflingly commercial and inhumane: its struggling and cynical screenwriter (William Holden) dead in the pool and its discarded actress destined for a mental asylum. As one attendee of Paramount's special preview for Havana film writers explained, *Sunset Boulevard* was "a very honest movie, that bares the real-life and cruel side of 'show business,' made by people that know that business at its core."[75]

Echoing their minorista predecessors, Cuban film writers—who also knew the US film business "at its core"—were also growing cynical about it. In the film giro as elsewhere in Cuba, a declining economy after 1948 threw fundamental inequalities into stark relief. As revenues shrank and tensions rose, Cubans in the giro had growing cause to doubt Hollywood's good neighborliness and to see exploitation where they had once seen opportunity, for self and country. Though this section focuses on deteriorating relations between the US studios and their Cuban office employees in Havana, it is worth noting that relations between the US studios and Cuban exhibitors also soured. For instance, the US studios' Havana offices accused the Cubans they hired as box office "checkers" (who tallied ticket sales) of conspiring with Cuban exhibitors to under-report receipts precisely because the checkers' loyalties lie with their Cuban compatriots.[76] Indeed, the importance of national allegiances seemed to rise as the discourse of transnational mutualism fell. In the late 1940s and early 1950s, the language of conflict displaced the language of familial intimacy in the film giro, and the movie barrio became "*el sector de las luchas* [the sector of battles]." In *Cinema*, Pedro Pablo Chávez lamented, "For more than thirty years, the Cuban film sector was among the most tranquil in the country's many commercial activities. . . . But now our peaceful sector has turned fractious, feverish, and agitated."[77]

The postwar period had begun auspiciously enough, as Cuba's economy boomed. In 1946, the film business in Cuba was up as much as 30 percent from the previous year.[78] With so much money to go around, it was easy to dispel any grumbling about the northward flow of profits. As one Cuban salesman for United Artists put it, notably appealing to *Cubanidad*, the film business in Havana employed an estimated 2,500 Cubans, whose salaries represented "MONEY THAT STAYS IN CUBA" and feeds Cuban families.[79] According to the US studios' own accounts, the Cubans they employed in their branch offices were particularly content. In 1945, Warner Bros. boasted in the *ACRC* that its offices were characterized by "Camaraderie" and, in 1947, Paramount proclaimed its employees "Happy in Havana."[80] (See figs. 5.4 and 5.5.)

FIG. 5.4. In a Cuban film trade journal, Warner Bros. boasts of the (transnational) "Camaraderie" in its Havana office, led by Peter Colli (top photo, second from left). *ACRC 1945–46*. (Courtesy of the Cuban Heritage Collection, University of Miami Libraries, Coral Gables Florida)

HAPPY IN HAVANA Here is the full Havana force of Paramounteers, plus such visiting 'celebrities' as George Weltner, A.L.Pratchett, Louis Lazar and Lennart Bjorck. They all look well and content in the Havana headquarters. Depicted in the scene are, kneeling: R.A.Pratchett, T. Morera, G.Renaud, L.Domínguez, P.Serrano, P.Rosete, F. Marín, R.Sobrado, A.Mavilla, J.de la Torre. Seated: C.Pulido, B.Trinidad, J. Queipo, M.Rosado, S.Pérez, J.R.de Marín, M. Queipo. Standing: M.Aragón, A.Betancourt, F. Cuervo, V.Lastra, O.Hernández, F.Marín,Jr., R.Martínez, J.Mendizábal, P.Marín, D.Pernas,Jr. E.Cuervo, I.Marchal, M.E.Rodríguez, Teresita García, Mr. Weltner, Mr. Pratchett, R.L.Graham, A.Sastre, Mr. Bjorck, Mr. Lazar, M.Avila, P. Galindo, A. Cruz, F. Pantoja -- and Americo Rosenberger, back from Mexico on a visit.

FIG. 5.5. Paramount's International Department proclaims its Cuban office employees "Happy in Havana." *Paramount International News*, March 1947. (From the periodicals collection of the Margaret Herrick Library, Academy of Motion Picture Arts and Sciences)

Endorsing this impression of happy transnational camaraderie, Hollywood's top movie idols again arrived in Havana to promote their movies and/or enjoy Cuban vacations. Along with the aforementioned John Wayne, star visitors during this period included Montgomery Clift (twice), Gary Cooper, Errol Flynn (twice), Van Johnson, Robert Mitchum, Dick Powell, and Edward G. Robinson.[81] "Such visits do more to tighten cordial relations between the Americas than many diplomatic missions," enthused *Variety*, describing mobs of fans greeting Tyrone Power and native-son Cesar Romero, who arrived together at the Havana airport in 1946.[82]

A feeling of Pan-American fellowship was also promoted by the visits of Hollywood executives, who continued to serve as models of successful businessmen and Good Neighbors in the Cuban film trades. Many came during this period to celebrate their studios' silver anniversaries in Havana and thus to celebrate US-Cuban bonds. In April 1946, United Artists celebrated its twenty-fifth anniversary in Cuba and, with it, Henry Weiner's. The *ACRC* reminded Cubans that they "owe a debt to 'old Henry,' that they will never be able to repay, a debt of a patriotic character since Weiner is a veteran of the Spanish-Cuban American War." And *Cinema* again bestowed national belonging on Weiner: "he is Cuban because he fought for our independence."[83] The next April, Twentieth-Century Fox president Spyros Skouras arrived to mark Fox's silver anniversary, hosting a banquet for six hundred people at the Hotel Nacional and prompting *Cinema* to declare Skouras a visionary businessman and a "goodwill ambassador," driven by the "best intentions of the Good Neighbor policy."[84] And the culminating event of Paramount's silver anniversary celebration was a luncheon for over four hundred guests at the Club Mulgoba. Addressing Cuban exhibitors, journalists, and government officials in a speech translated and reprinted in *Cinema*, Paramount president Barney Balaban enthused about the history of freedom fighting at the heart of the "enduring friendship" between the United States and Cuba. "As a boy," he intoned, "I was thrilled by the struggle of your people to win the priceless blessings of freedom. As an American I was proud of the role played by my own country in your fight for independence." Balaban went on to describe how Paramount films, business practices, and businessmen in Cuba had strengthened that friendship. Before turning over the podium to Arthur Pratchett, who flew in from Mexico, Balaban enthused: "We are proud that you judge us through men like Pratch. . . . Men like these *are* Paramount."[85]

In the mid- to late 1940s, all this transnational optimism and prosperity also inspired another rash of cine renovation, consolidation, and construction. Enthusiastic about new technologies in sound, projection, and cooling, Cuban exhibitors made long-delayed updates, which the Cuban trades ballyhooed as proof yet again of national "progress."[86] José Valcarce and Edelberto de Carrerá continued to add cines to their circuits, which peaked at six and sixteen respectively.[87] They were joined by Enrique Vázquez, who owned the next largest chain with five cines.[88] (See fig. 5.6.) Two dozen new cines went up in Havana, radiating westward and southward from the movie barrio into residential neighborhoods and the increasingly important district of Vedado. Consistent with international architectural trends, most of these "modern" cines were variations on a large concrete box, for example, the Alameda, the

FIG. 5.6. The cines of the Vasquez Circuit in Havana. *Clockwise from left*: Vanidades, Neptuno, Lira, Majestic, and Ritz. *ACRC 1945–46*. (Courtesy of the Cuban Heritage Collection, University of Miami Libraries, Coral Gables, Florida)

Arenal, the Ambassador, the Astral, the Atlantic, the Avenida, the Florida, the Miramar, the Santa Catalina (fig. 5.7), and the Tosca. The peak of this postwar boom came at the end of the decade with the construction of the massive 6,500-seat Teatro Blanquita in the posh suburb of Miramar. Designed for stage spectacles, the Blanquita was also used for movies, including re-releases of *Gone with the Wind* and Chaplin's *City Lights* as well as United Artists' new releases. Cubans loved to boast that the Blanquita was the world's largest theater, further evidence of their nation's place in the ranks of the most civilized countries.[89]

The US studios sensed opportunity in Havana's thriving exhibition business, and they were particularly eager to avail themselves of it at this moment, in which the US Justice Department was poised finally to divest the studios of their domestic theater chains in an antitrust case that had lasted nearly a decade. Ever since the case had been filed in the late 1930s, the Hollywood studios had considered that overseas theaters might help them offset their anticipated losses. And Havana, as usual, was top of mind. During the war, Fox, MGM, and United Artists each tried (unsuccessfully) to lease or build a movie house in the movie barrio.[90] At the end of 1944, it was Paramount

FIG. 5.7. The Cine Santa Catalina in the barrio Santo Suárez, Havana, circa 1947. The most visible movie poster (*right*) promotes a Mexican film, but the partially obscured movie poster (*left*) promotes *Maldita mujer*, the Spanish-language title for *Dead Reckoning*, a Columbia Pictures noir starring Humphrey Bogart. (Courtesy of the Cuban Heritage Collection, University of Miami Libraries, Coral Gables, Florida)

that first succeeded, when it leased the eight cines of the Smith circuit, giving the studio three first-runs (including the Encanto and Fausto) as well as five subsequent-run movie theaters.[91]

Warner Bros., too, was eager to get into exhibition in Havana. In mid-1945, studio executives began negotiating with Goar Mestre, the Cuban-born, Yale-educated head of Cuba's largest radio network (CMQ) who was building

FIG. 5.8. Warner Bros. opened the Teatro Warner in Vedado in December 1947. The marquee advertises *Los Amantes*, the Spanish-language title for Columbia Pictures' 1949 film noir *Shockproof*. (Courtesy of the Cuban Heritage Collection, University of Miami Libraries, Coral Gables, Florida)

a commercial complex in the heart of Vedado. In his plans for this "Radiocentro," Mestre included a movie theater, which Warner Bros. contracted to lease for the next twenty years.[92] To be named the Teatro Warner, the cine's design was modern-minimalist, its four-story rust-colored façade embellished only with a large sign that read "Warner." (See fig. 5.8.) Inside, the auditorium was outfitted with 1,600 seats, a stage, a grand piano, and space for a thirty-four-piece orchestra (to accommodate the still government-mandated live acts), as well as RCA's latest sound and projection systems; and the lobby boasted a concession stand, the very latest in US exhibition trends.[93] In December 1947, President Grau—who had laid the theater's first stone back in March 1946—returned to hobnob with Warner Bros. executives at the cine's opening gala. In the meanwhile, Warner Bros. had also acquired the twenty-year-old Cine Prado, renovating it and renaming it the Cine Plaza.[94]

Unfortunately for Warner Bros., the studio's entry into Havana exhibition seemed to cause nothing but headaches. Construction delays and cost overruns as well as disputes about the lease caused tensions—and derogatory stereotypes—to flare. Condescension crept into Warner executives' correspondence; they balked at Mestre's hot-headed "Latin temperament" and his presumption to know more than they did about "any peculiar customs and habits" of Havana moviegoers. Warner executives had decades of exhibition experience, they reminded Mestre, and he would do well to appreciate their "advice and counsel [which was worth] incalculable dollars and cents."[95] For his part, Mestre resented having his "business judgment" impugned and leveled a (somewhat veiled) accusation of Yankee imperialism. Mestre wrote that if Warner Bros. would agree to just a little more in annual rent, it would help "revis[e] the bad reputation generally that US motion picture companies have among Cuban business men, simply because they are regarded as tough and cold-blooded organizations." Eager to prove themselves "reasonable and conscientious business men," Warner executives agreed to $7,500 more in rent per year.[96]

Quickly, however, Warner Bros.' executives came to regret this concession, if not the whole endeavor. Pre-opening turned out to be just the beginning of the Teatro Warner's troubles, not least of all because the movie business in Cuba began to decline in mid-1948 as the Cuban economy slumped.[97] Moreover, Warner Bros.' entry into Havana exhibition increased its exposure to growing postwar labor agitation and to a sector of giro labor—movie theater employees—generally more militant than their compatriots employed in the studios' distribution offices. While the former had unionized during the heady days of the 1933 revolution and had participated in revolutionary strikes (see chapter 2), the latter only unionized in 1939, which was the year that both unions were officially recognized by the Cuban government and that both affiliated with the CTC.[98] During the war, the unions made no-strike commitments, but the film giro workers revived their demands toward war's end. For instance, in June 1944, the theater employees of the Smith circuit asked for raises and engaged in a bit of political theater to publicize their grievances to cine patrons: the women stopped wearing makeup and the men stopped shaving. Smith yielded when these same employees threatened a wildcat strike in August (one month before Smith got out of the exhibition business by leasing his circuit to Paramount).[99]

In early 1946, the separate unions of cines' employees and distributors' employees consolidated into the Federación Nacional De Sindicatos Cinematográficos de Cuba, or Film Giro Syndicate.[100] Citing the current "conditions of splendor in the movie business" in Cuba in contrast to their stagnant wages, members of this Film Giro Syndicate marched on the Presidential Palace to demand a 30 percent salary increase and a $4 minimum wage giro-wide, just as the Auténticos were vying to wrestle labor's allegiances from the communist leaders of the CTC.[101] At about the same time, projectionists at the Teatro Payret launched a wildcat strike, closing that theater for a month. In response, the CTC's rising Auténtico faction—along with the exhibitors of the UNE—rejected the projectionists' "radical" tactics and accused them and the CTC's communist leaders of being "Stalinist agents" who threatened Cuba's "national sovereignty," because they sought "to disturb the peace [in service to] the ambitions of foreign powers."[102] But it seems the Auténticos hadn't fully won this anticommunist argument with the rank and file. When communist CTC leaders were arrested, Film Giro Syndicate members walked out, forcing all Havana cines to close for a day in July 1946. Under pressure, Grau's administration did mandate 5 to 10 percent raises for movie theater employees by summer's end, while distributors' office employees threatened sit-down strikes to win similar concessions.[103]

Indeed, despite Warner Bros.' and Paramount's claims of happy camaraderie in Havana, their Cuban office employees agitated continually throughout this period for better wages, better benefits, and safer working conditions. As a result, they won further government-mandated raises averaging 30 percent in May 1948, and 15 percent in February 1952.[104] Still, they complained that they were hardly keeping up with the rising cost of living. And even as the US studios grumbled that the Cuban giro unions were "causing untold business hardships" and costing "large sums in revenue," they tellingly congratulated themselves that "our wage patterns will still be below general average comparable work [in] any other important American industry" operating in Cuba.[105]

In any case, as Warner Bros.' records show, union participation was high in the film giro, as was the US studios' dismay about it. All of Warner Bros.' twenty-seven theater employees belonged to the Film Giro Syndicate while fifteen of its twenty-five distribution office employees did.[106] Warner Bros.' men in Havana—including Peter Colli (now promoted to regional supervisor but still headquartered in Havana)—constantly found themselves answering their New York office superiors' vexed queries about Cuba's labor laws: yes, the Havana office could only be open from 8 am to 1 pm during summer months; and yes, government-mandated raises and benefits would have to be honored. They likewise explained that, in order to fire a Cuban employee, the company had to file for an "*expediente*" from Cuba's Labor Ministry, which was very rarely granted. Further, not only did the Aútentico's Labor Ministry tend to side with Cuban employees and their union, so did the country's courts during the Aútentico years.[107] Indeed, in at least three separate cases, Warner Bros. was ordered to reinstate or pay considerable settlements to fired theater employees, even one who was caught twice helping himself to salary advances from the theater's petty cash.[108] In March 1951, this latter case caused Warner Bros.' International Department chief, John J. Glynn, to snap, "Haven't we got any rights in that God d___ country at all?"[109]

With labor and legal expenses up and revenues down, Warner Bros. decided to unload its Havana theaters by the end of 1951. (Plagued by the same troubles, Paramount had recently sold all its leases back to Smith, who turned around and sold most of them to Carrerá.)[110] Effective January 1, 1952, Warner Bros. sold its Teatro Warner lease back to Mestre. The large "Warner" sign was removed and replaced with one that read "Teatro Radiocentro." Unable to find a new lessee for the Cine Plaza, Warner Bros. continued to operate that cine at a loss until closing it in 1954.[111]

Thus, the US studios ended their brief postwar venture into Havana exhibition. But they still had to contend with growing problems in their distribution offices, problems that were especially vexing in this difficult moment of studio belt-tightening. Seeking to cut expenses that had been "overlooked" in "the lush of good times," the US studios' foreign (often renamed "international" now) departments sent increasingly sharp memos demanding salary freezes, personnel reduction, bonus discontinuations, and expense account reductions. They admonished their managers abroad to "plug" all "operational deficiencies," to "cut everything to the bone and even more."[112]

Caught between pressure from their increasingly stingy companies *and* their increasingly adversarial employees, the US studios' branch office managers were hard-pressed to mediate conflicts between them. And it didn't help that the studios' wartime and postwar reorganization created continual turnover among those managers, whose brevity of tenure limited their capacity to ameliorate the mutual distrust. Warner Bros.' promotion of Colli to regional supervisor in 1948 precipitated a quick succession of two Havana managers (John Jones and Geza Polaty) until Colli reclaimed the post in 1954.[113] At Paramount, after Jacob Rapoport was relocated to Panama in 1942, the Havana office cycled through three managers until, in 1947, Arthur Pratchett's Havana-born son, Robert, claimed the post, which he would hold for a decade.[114] And MGM cycled through five managers from 1942 to 1956, when Eddie O'Connor successfully requested reassignment to the post, citing his love of Cuba.[115] Though "Pedro" Colli, "Roberto" Pratchett, and "Eduardo" O'Connor all demonstrated their respect for *Cubanidad*, most postwar US managers seemed to regard Havana as a career stepping stone rather than as a place to put down roots, to make friends and family, to "go native" à la Henry Weiner.

Indeed, Weiner's retirement in 1952 can be said to mark the end of the era of "Cubanized" US manager-patriarchs benevolently heading the giro family. As early as December 1946, United Artists' Foreign Department had determined that Weiner was no longer "the ideal man for the job in Havana."[116] While studio executives recognized that forcing Weiner to retire would cause him to "die of a broken heart," the studio's financial straits precluded such sentimental consideration. Weiner, they determined, was "weak." In part, this was attributed to his seventy years of age: "his burden should be shifted to the shoulders of a younger man," they argued.[117] But, in other part, the home office deemed him too soft on his Cuban employees, for whose salary raises and vacation pay he still fought (and even snuck) despite the studios' new efficiency program.[118] After almost thirty years of running United Artists' Havana office, Weiner seemed unwilling to submit to what New York called its "intensified supervision" over its foreign offices, a sort of micromanagement made necessary by falling revenues and made possible by advances in travel and communications.[119] In March 1952, just days before Batista's coup, New York sent a representative to audit the Havana office and to manage Weiner's transition to "elderly statesman" (aka "special consultant"). Effective June 1, Weiner handed over his post to his longtime Cuban assistant manager, José Del Amo.[120]

Cubans in the giro lamented the passing of a more amicable era and sympathized with Cubanized US managers, like Weiner, as vulnerable to the whims of the US companies, which were proving themselves insensitive to the local environment. In 1950, Perdices described the plight of those US managers—"who had earned the trust and sympathy of those with whom they work here" but now had no choice but to enact the harsh efficiency programs of their companies, "which want to dictate orders from afar"—using language that echoed long-standing Cuban complaints about their own *semi*-sovereignty. Perdices wrote,

> The trustworthy man, who should have ample leeway to do what he sees fit for the company's benefit, instead has his personal agency reduced.
>
> . . . To expect to keep picking abundant fruit by 'reducing seeds' is just an infantile idea of [penny-pinchers] who practice the policy of the good neighbor looking only to their own house. . . .
>
> . . . To run a business well one has to acclimate to the environment, and to achieve that here, one cannot have to ask permission from "papa" like children every time one wants to solve a problem.[121]

Here, Perdices mobilizes the gendered rhetoric of revolutionary Cuban nationalism that emerged so often when Cubans chafed at patronizing US power, here associated with undemocratic rule and extraterritorial power ("dictate orders from afar"). It is unnatural and ultimately counterproductive for US bosses to emasculate their employees by denying them autonomy. It is the former that are acting like "children" (being "infantile") rather than the latter, who are "trustworthy" men. Here, too, film business practices become an opportunity to assert that the Good Neighbor Policy's rhetorical mutualism belied US self-interest ("looking only to their own house").

By early 1950, when Perdices wrote these lines, the US studios' good neighborliness was profoundly in doubt, and US-Cuban camaraderie in the film giro coming apart. As if to underscore this cultural shift, the US studios initiated a physical one. That summer, their Havana offices undertook a collective exodus to a new complex they built jointly in a neighborhood called Almendares, where rent was cheaper and construction codes looser. Located for decades in the movie barrio in Central Havana, the US studios' offices had occupied the ground floors of nineteenth-century tenement buildings whose upper floors were crowded with boarders. The storage of highly combustible films in these offices represented a serious public safety risk. A number of recent fires—including one in Fox's office and another in Universal's, which killed two children—made the issue a new focus of municipal authorities and a major grievance of the Film Giro Syndicate, which cited unsafe working conditions. In 1948, the Havana managers warned their superiors in New York that a long overdue "crackdown" on fire codes was imminent and, worse yet, that another lethal fire (a public relations disaster) was likely, if something wasn't done.[122] By the end of 1949, the Hollywood studios had agreed to the expense of new offices, secured a whole block on Calle Almendares, and begun construction. Sadly, though, the studios had not acted quickly enough. Columbia's office caught fire in the early morning of May 11, 1950, burning nine residents. Outraged that the US companies had proven so disastrously careless with Cuban lives, *Cinema* noted that it was only thanks to heroic Cuban firefighters that the whole neighborhood didn't burn.[123] Thus, it was with a sense of relief that, at the end of 1950, the US studios each moved to Almendares, into identical one-story, bright blue "*casitas*" complete with well-appointed office spaces, temperature-controlled storage vaults, projection rooms, and shipping quarters.[124] (See fig. 5.9.)

Over the next few years, most film giro businesses had no choice but to follow their economic bloodline out to Almendares, with plenty of grumbling about the cost and inconvenience.[125] The US companies coined this new area "Filmcentro" or, sometimes, the "Centro Fílmico." But Cubans began calling it "*la Corea*" [Korea] (after the contemporary conflict in Asia) to connote their sense of displacement in a strange new place. And the nickname stuck. As the old movie barrio emptied of giro offices, Cubans extended their pun and renamed that vacated area "Parallel 38." Thus, they suggested that the once amiably transnational area around Calle Consulado [Consulate Street], connoting cooperation through trade, had been reduced to a sort of no-man's-land, connoting (whether they knew it or not) a division of nations.[126]

FIG. 5.9. Photos show Paramount's new bungalow-style office located in the "Filmcentro." Note the signage that reads "Paramount" over the office's front door (*center top*). *Paramount International News* 9, no. 2 (February 12, 1951): 21. (From the periodicals collection of the Margaret Herrick Library, Academy of Motion Picture Arts and Sciences)

"A Film's Success Says a Lot about Its Public's Psychology": The Popularity of Noir

In February 1949, Paramount sent a special executive team to Havana to plan the promotion therein of Billy Wilder's *A Foreign Affair* (1948), a film set in postwar US-occupied Berlin, where US soldiers fuel prostitution and a thriving black market.[127] Though billed as a dark comedy, Wilder's depiction of war-ravaged Berlin exudes the noir sensibility Wilder had already mastered in *Double Indemnity* (1944) and would soon turn on Hollywood itself in *Sunset Boulevard* (1950). For instance, in one scene set in the shadowy offices of the US Occupation Forces at night, Captain John Pringle (John Lund) explains the harsh realities of the postwar world to US congresswoman Phoebe Frost (Jean Arthur). To Frost's naïve notion that a US soldier should exemplify the American Way at all times, Pringle responds with a succinct distillation of Hollywood Left disillusionment: "Oh, that one. You expect him to be an ambassador, a salesman of goodwill. You want him to stand there in the blackened rubble . . . with an open sample case of assorted freedoms, waving the flag and giving out the Bill of Rights. Well, that's not the way it works." US soldiers had done and seen terrible things during the war, and sometimes, now, they "scrape those fine, shiny ideals," Captain Pringle explains.[128]

Not surprisingly, the US Department of Defense was not amused. They denounced *A Foreign Affair* for its denigration of US occupation forces, while the MPEA banned its exhibition in a number of foreign markets.[129] In Havana, on the other hand, Paramount's executive team decided to emphasize the film's controversial aspects, placing pretty "cigarette girls" in Havana cines to hand out cigarettes labeled "black market."[130] Seemingly unconcerned that their "exploitation scheme" might remind Cubans of the black market and sex tourism in their own country (both phenomena commonly attributed to Yankees), Paramount's executive team was simply concerned with which promotional practices would draw Cubans to the box office.

After all, Cubans preferred films that "tackled rough and risqué themes," as one of *Bohemia's* film writers, Miguel de Zarraga, put it in 1950, an assertion borne out by advertisements in Havana newspapers. In them, it is clear that the Hollywood studios put a great deal of stock in the selling power of noir's generic markers: criminal intrigue, illicit sex, dramatic action, and gun-wielding men. In fact, Warner Bros.' Havana office asked New York to stop sending so much advertising material for "[melo]dramas, musicals, and comedies" just "because this kind of pictures are very much liked in the States"; this pattern did "not apply to Cuba," the Havana office noted, specifically mentioning a noir, *White Heat*, as the type of film Cubans preferred.[131] And a survey of Cubans conducted by *Cinema* in 1948 corroborates this predilection. Top picks for best US films of the year leaned toward noir (*Gilda*, *Mildred Pierce*, *Nora Prentiss*, *Possessed*) and top actor picks leaned toward noir regulars (Alan Ladd, Ray Milland, Edward G. Robinson, and Glenn Ford).[132]

Another measure of noir's popularity is found in the film giro's virulent response to the Children's Censor Board, whose rulings against noirs "gravely injured the film business in Cuba," according to outraged distributors and exhibitors.[133] In an article in *Cinema* boldly headlined "DICTATORSHIP," Charles Garrett denounced the board's decisions as arbitrary and "dictatorial."[134] Others writing in *Cinema* criticized the board as hypocritical for singling out the cinema when the press was equally guilty of sensationalizing crime and violence, especially in its coverage of "the killers and thieves inside and outside of Cuban political circles."[135] And though *Cinema's* editor, Perdices, conceded that the movies might be "giving dangerous 'tips' in delinquency to inexperienced children," he defended Hollywood against accusations that it was *the* source of their bad behaviors. At least in Hollywood films, Perdices argued, crime and immorality were punished, whereas in Cuban society, criminals enjoyed impunity and illicit sex was promoted by the tourist industry.[136]

Generally speaking, *Cinema* was a good barometer of postwar reception trends, just as it had been a good barometer of wartime trends. In it, noirs replaced antifascist films for disproportionate coverage. Beginning especially in 1947, noirs feature heavily on (surviving) *Cinema* covers. And Perdices' weekly column, "Son Cosas Nuestras," evidences an even greater preference for noir. During the Auténtico era, he recommended over fifty noir titles, including the following Hollywood Left noirs, *Double Indemnity*, *Body and Soul*, *The Lady from Shanghai*, *Possessed*, *A Foreign Affair*, *They Live by Night*, *Knock on Any Door*, *All the King's Men*, and *Sunset Boulevard*. Such noirs, he promised, would "satisfy the taste of the most exacting fans and the economic aspirations of the exhibitor."[137] As evidence, Perdices often noted a noir's impressive first-run returns and/or its bankable noir elements: realism, violence, and hardboiled men of action.

While evidencing noir's popularity in Havana, Perdices's column also offers a glimpse into the ways that Cuban film writers translated the Hollywood Left's postwar cynicism into Cuban discourse, just as they had translated its wartime optimism into the same. Take Perdices's discussion of Edward Dmytryk's *Till the End of Time* (1946). Debuting at the Teatro América in August 1947, it is a dark drama about a group of US veterans struggling with psychological trauma and profound physical injuries.[138] Before introducing the film, Perdices describes the postwar disillusionment that is its subject: "The war left *us* an unexpected bequest. *We* are defeated spiritually. Uncertainty curbs every aspiration and for those that heroically gave their blood for liberty, the sacrifice they made has not yet been justified"; the US's official rhetoric about the ideals for which they fought has proven "a major deception." Having argued that *Till the End of Time* reflects a reality with relevance to a Cuban national audience of "us" and "we," and having once again romanticized freedom-fighting masculinity ("heroically gave their blood for liberty"), Perdices synopsizes the film as a story about US veterans suffering unemployment, alcoholism, and racial discrimination, about their coming to realize that they do not live in a land free from want, prejudice, or fear. *Till the End of Time* "shows *us* painful episodes that cause *us* to meditate," Perdices concludes prescriptively.[139]

Perdices similarly suggests that the noir *The Street with No Name* (1948)—about the FBI's work to bring to justice a gang of criminals and a corrupt police commissioner—has relevance to Cubans. Perdices praises the film as a realistic portrayal of gangsters in "an *authentic* atmosphere," he noted, (perhaps coyly) linking the film's subject to the *gangsterismo* rampant in Auténtico-era Havana. He goes on to argue that the postwar rise of gangsterism is an effect of the war: men trained by their governments in the use of arms are now unwilling to put those arms down, having developed a taste for gunplay. Often, corrupt public officials "also belongs to these groups of gangsters," Perdices notes, apropos Cuban reality as much as the cinematic representation in question.[140] Indeed, while many of Perdices's columns *imply* connections to be made between noir and the Cuban context during the Aútentico era, he was occasionally explicit about them. Perhaps the best example is found in his discussion of the gangster noir *The Enforcer* (1951). Lauding the character played by Humphrey Bogart as an "incorruptible" assistant district attorney intent on prosecuting gangsters, Perdices writes, "How sorely *we* lack a public servant of this caliber! What a shame that a similar figure doesn't arise *here*!"[141]

As the following section explores, Perdices was not alone in employing such strategies. Film critics writing in mainstream Havana periodicals also disproportionally recommended noirs and Hollywood Left social problem films, and implicitly and explicitly appropriated their disillusionment and their sociopolitical critiques.

"A Severe Critique of Contemporary Society": Postwar Cuban Film Criticism

In April 1948, Havana exhibitor Edelberto de Carrerá rolled out Charlie Chaplin's *Monsieur Verdoux* with great fanfare in his five best cines, a full seven years since Chaplin's last film, *The Great Dictator*, had debuted in the city.[142] By then, Chaplin was feeling the chill of the Hollywood Red Scare. And though he was never subpoenaed to testify before HUAC, he was often the subject of its inquiries; he would be hounded by the FBI, threatened with deportation, and ultimately exiled from the United States by 1952, developments followed closely by the Havana press.[143]

Certainly, *Monsieur Verdoux* reflects this dark moment for Chaplin and the Hollywood Left. In it, the Little Tramp is revised further. From the determinedly hopeful Jewish Barber in *The Great Dictator*, he is now transformed into the Frenchman Henri Verdoux (Chaplin), a man turned cynical—and homicidal—by a cynical and inhumane modern world. Most disturbingly, and most resonant with noir, he is dead. Like Joe Gillis in *Sunset Boulevard*, Verdoux narrates his tragic story from beyond the grave: After the stock market crash of '29, he was suddenly unemployed, despite having served as a dutiful bank teller for thirty-five monotonous years. Unable to find another job to provide for his beloved family, he becomes an *homme fatale*, spending the next decade (hilariously) seducing wealthy women, taking their money, and killing them. But Verdoux's life of crime catches up with him, and he is arrested, tried, and ultimately sentenced to death. Two short speeches that Verdoux gives at film's end—to a jury and a reporter—are a good measure of how far Chaplin has moved away from the determined idealism expressed in *The Great Dictator's* final speech. Verdoux tells his jury, "As a mass killer, I am an amateur by comparison" to munitions manufacturers. "As for being a mass killer, does not the world encourage it? Is it not building weapons of destruction for the sole purpose of mass killing? Has it not blown unsuspecting women and little children to pieces?" he asks rhetorically. Later, when a reporter admonishes him against such cynicism, Verdoux responds, "To be idealistic at this moment would be incongruous," explaining that "robbing and murdering people" are at the heart of "many a big business." The film ends with Verdoux's state execution.[144]

In the United States, most reviews of *Monsieur Verdoux* ranged from mixed to negative; many found Chaplin's social criticisms too strident this time, especially those about "the ruthlessness of business," one US critic complained.[145] But in Havana, critics continued to be overwhelmingly laudatory. The ARTYC and the FRCT respectively named *Monsieur Verdoux* the first and third best US film shown in Cuba in 1948, with only Elia Kazan's *Gentleman's Agreement* (about anti-Semitism in the United States) and Huston's *The Treasure of the Sierra Madre* outranking it on the FRCT's list.[146] In periodicals across the political spectrum, Havana film critics continued to esteem Chaplin a genius, elevating him to artist-philosopher whose great insights into capitalist modernity should be taken seriously.

For instance, in *Diario de la marina*, Ichaso describes *Monsieur Verdoux*'s title character as another iteration of "Charlot," "the clowning conscience of a suffering and convulsive epoch." Here again, Ichaso appropriates the Little Tramp to a Hispanic critical tradition; in past films, the critic explains, Charlot was like "Don Quixote," strolling naively through "the landscape of modern times." But his innocence is now dispelled, Ichaso explains. After "thirty years of honest employment," Charlot (as Verdoux) is "thrown out on the street . . . faced with hunger and misery." Want and fear finally provoke him to criminality; "The unfortunate tramp of yesteryear is the dangerous tramp of today." His soul has been corrupted, which is why Chaplin, the artist, has no choice now but to kill Charlot, the character. The film's "social implications," Ichaso explains, are that a man singularly devoted to "justice, liberty, and love" can no longer survive the "unhinged humanity" of today's "twisted world."[147]

Ichaso's friend Valdés-Rodríguez is even clearer about the "social implications" of *Monsieur Verdoux*.[148] In *El Mundo*, he writes that *Monsieur Verdoux* offers "less smiling" critiques of the same social ills Chaplin has always denounced: "violence, injustice and society's indifference towards the misfortunes of the weak and small, [as well as] the impunity of the great, rich and powerful." Like *Modern Times*, *Monsieur Verdoux* is, in short, a "severe critique of contemporary society." Henri Verdoux, Valdés-Rodríguez explains, is "a new version of Charlot, as if the old vagabond had acquired a new personality, the consequence of radically transformative circumstances." "Unhinged" by a "dehumanizing society," he has become "an aseptic, methodical and rationalized murderer, like the great armament consortiums, the industrialists and traffickers in death." That "contemporary society has converted the pure and almost angelic figure of Charlot" into a coldhearted killer for cash is a terrible measure of "the great politico-economic, material and spiritual crisis" of the modern world. Having announced the film's sociopolitical message, Valdés-Rodríguez then offers a brief synopsis, describing Verdoux's unemployment ("after thirty years of irreproachable service"), his laudable determination to support his family, his turn to crime (driven by "the criminal arrangement of society"), and his surrender to the authorities. The critic then focuses attention on, and endorses, Verdoux's final speeches, so much more "succinct and cutting" than the closing "pep talk" of *The Great Dictator*, Valdés-Rodríguez writes.[149]

As these two reviews begin to suggest, film critics writing in mainstream Havana periodicals revived minorista strategies during this postwar era, including in their special reverence for Chaplin. They also now returned to denunciations of most Hollywood films as banal and imperialistic. This trend is clearly evidenced in a series of *Cinema* interviews, conducted at the end of 1948, with Havana's most important critics, including Valdés-Rodríguez and Ichaso, as well as Don Galaor at *Bohemia*, Francois Baguer at *El Crisol*, and Leandro García at *El País*. Asked to pontificate on the contemporary film scene, they spoke of Hollywood's *superior* resources but *inferior* product, because its films were usually made with financial gain rather than art or social commentary in mind. Thus, Hollywood's "monopoly" on the island demeaned the Cuban national audience, García explained, "causing our spiritual deformation and intellectual disorientation." Yet, like the minoristas, these Havana critics made exceptions of Hollywood's most progressive and critical films and filmmakers. In these *Cinema* interviews, the example given repeatedly was Huston's *The Treasure of the Sierra Madre*.[150]

Indeed, Havana critics seemed especially loyal to the Hollywood Left as it suffered the Red Scare. They interpreted attacks on Chaplin and the Hollywood Ten as proof of US democracy's degradation. Valdés-Rodríguez repeatedly declared HUAC and the industry blacklist to be "absurd," constituting an abuse of personal liberties that "mutilated and deformed" artistic expressions.[151] In November 1947, Aguirre used her column to denounce HUAC and to cheer the artists (specifically naming Bogart, Garfield, Peck, and Robinson) who fought the "fascist" committee's "truly anti-American, anti-democratic activities." Given Hollywood's powerful influence, Aguirre warned that HUAC's attempts to squelch the Hollywood Left represented a "danger to culture in our hemisphere" and to "Latin American democratic consciousness."[152] By 1950, Aguirre lamented that HUAC and the blacklist had effectively repressed the "political thought" of Hollywood's "progressive elements," such that the "super-enchained Hollywood of today is incapable of producing anymore anything similar to *Watch on the Rhine*."[153]

Perhaps the annual top film lists of the ARTYC and the FRCT are an even better measure of critics' souring on the US film industry. From 1946 through 1951, Latin American and European films crowded out Hollywood, while those US films that did make the lists tended to be Hollywood Left noirs, including *The Asphalt Jungle*, *Crossfire*, *The Killers*, *The Lost Weekend*, *A Place in the Sun*, *Spellbound*, *The Strange Love of Martha Ivers*, *Strangers on a Train*, *Sunset Boulevard*, *Undercurrent*, and *The Window*. Havana critics' allegiance to the Hollywood Left is also evident in their selections of its social problem films, including *Gentleman's Agreement*; *Home of the Brave* and *Intruder in the Dust* (both about antiblack racism); and *Give Us This Day* (about poverty and labor grievances).[154]

Serving as ARTYC president again in 1949, Valdés-Rodríguez was by now respected as *the* preeminent authority on the cinema in Cuba, and his influence was only growing.[155] During this period, along with continuing to write reviews for *El Mundo*, he founded the University of Havana's Cinema Department and convinced the university to renovate the Enrique José Varona Amphitheater for film screenings. Valdés-Rodríguez also continued to teach his summer school class and began, in 1949, to hold his Cine de Arte sessions: bimonthly film projections open to the public. In Cine de Arte's program notes, prefilm lectures, or postfilm discussions, Valdés-Rodríguez made it a point, he later explained, to focus on a film's "explicit or hidden political meaning."[156] He continued to express his low opinion of most Hollywood films and his high opinion of other national cinemas. But, again, he made exceptions, and the US films he did select for Cine de Arte screenings leaned toward Hollywood Left noirs. These included *The Asphalt Jungle*—described in program notes as being about "the sickly ambition for money and power" that was "characteristic of the unhinged urban centers of our times"—as well as *The Killers*, *The Lost Weekend*, *Phantom Lady*, *The Strange Love of Martha Ivers*, and *The Window*. And Cine de Arte sessions screened other films of the Hollywood Left, regardless of genre, including Chaplin's *The Gold Rush* and *Monsieur Verdoux*; Huston's *Juarez* and *The Treasure of the Sierra Madre*; Elia Kazan's *Gentleman's Agreement*; and Edward Dmytryk's *Give Us This Day*.[157]

In this work, Valdés-Rodríguez profoundly influenced the next generation of Cuban film critics and filmmakers. Onetime students of his summer course include Guillermo Cabrera Infante, Enrique Pineda Barnet, Julio García Espinosa, Alfredo Guevara, José Massip, Walfredo Piñera, and Nelson Rodríguez, a group that would go on to shape Cuban film criticism during Batista's coming dictatorship, lead the cine-club movement, and create the post-1959 Cuban film industry. Many of them also regularly attended Valdés-Rodríguez's Cine de Arte screenings, and brought their friends, including Tomás Gutiérrez Alea, who would become post-1958 Cuba's most internationally renowned filmmaker.[158] Among them, too, was Mario Rodríguez Alemán, who graduated from Valdés-Rodríguez's course and started as resident film critic at *Mañana* in 1949.[159]

Rodríguez Alemán's *Mañana* columns offer clear evidence of Valdés-Rodríguez's influence. Like his mentor, Rodríguez Alemán worked to increase Cuban audiences for European and Latin American cinema, wresting his compatriots away from "Hollywood's daily chain" of mediocre and redundant films, with their "stupid" scripts and their predictable "'*happy ends*.'"[160] Like his mentor, too, Rodríguez Alemán made exceptions of Hollywood Left noirs and social problem films—which he praised for overcoming the newly restrictive "bonds of North American censorship"—and he appropriated their social critiques. For instance, he praised both *Act of Violence* and *Knock on Any Door* for their portrayals of a psychologically traumatized veteran and a juvenile delinquent respectively, proclaiming both characters to be representative of Twentieth-Century Man, whose degraded condition reflected the "moral failings of contemporary society." As just one more example from September 1949, Rodríguez Alemán declared *Flamingo Road*—a noir about patronage, graft, and embezzlement in politics in the US South—to be a realistic portrayal of "the miserliness of rich society that dirties politics, with its machinations and tricks, in order to obtain power and wealth." This was true not only in the United States but also in "every country of the world," Rodríguez Alemán laments. That Cuba was a prime example would have been clear to the young critic's reader.[161]

In other words, Havana critics writing in mainstream periodicals especially favored noirs and Hollywood Left social problem films, and they interpreted them for their readers as true reflections of the US "entrails" and their ill-effects in Cuba.[162] As the following section explores briefly, this practice of recommending Hollywood's most critical films, appropriating their critiques of the United States, and elaborating their significance within the Cuban context, was most pronounced in Aguirre's reviews in *Hoy*.

"The Despicable Neighbor": Aguirre Appropriates Noir Visions of the United States

As yet another (more radical) practitioner of "looking up," Aguirre argued in this period that the United States' own cinematic self-representations revealed the United States to be "The Despicable Neighbor."[163] A well-respected colleague of mainstream critics, Aguirre remained a member of the ARTYC in Havana, where anticommunism never reached the fever pitch it did in the United States, despite the Auténticos' best efforts.[164] Albeit framed in Marxist-Leninist terms, her interpretive practices cohered to, and most explicitly articulated, widespread critical approaches to Hollywood in postwar Havana.

Take Aguirre's review of *Monsieur Verdoux*. As reverent as Valdés-Rodríguez and Ichaso (she compares the film to Francisco Goya paintings), she likewise highlights the film's final speeches, in which "Chaplin concentrates the social message of the film": that "the capitalist world itself engenders crime." "*Monsieur Verdoux*," she writes, "is the work of a great artist that is fed up with the rottenness and hypocrisy that surrounds him." However, while Henri Verdoux and Chaplin himself might be resigned to their fates, Aguirre cannot countenance such fatalism. Her beef with the film is that Verdoux does not "turn his inconformity, his hate, his longing for justice, [and] aspirations for improvement into the forging of great collective struggles for the renovation of that world." And though Aguirre thus declares the film short of its subversive potential, she notes that US congressmen and the League of Decency felt differently. "The U.S. high bourgeois have recognized the importance of the attack and have not been able to hide their ire against it [the film]," she concluded, offering high praise indeed.[165]

Interestingly, Aguirre was cognizant that US cold warriors' attempts to censor the Hollywood Left included export restrictions. In 1950, she explained that US government officials worried that films that "evidence the deficiencies and imperfections of US 'democracy'" were thought to play right into the hands of Soviet propagandists. She elaborates, "To allude to 'gangsterism,' to unemployment, to the existence of racial prejudices against blacks and Jews, to the corruption of the North American political machinery, etc., are things that [are] consider[ed] subversive and that . . . should be prohibited; or that, at least, should not leave the geographic limits of the Union."[166] And maybe US officials weren't entirely wrong to worry about these representations of the United States "in a bad light," as Aguirre and other Havana critics' reviews suggest.

Take Aguirre's review of *From This Day Forward* (1946). Like Dmytryk's aforementioned *Till the End of Time*, this dark film (written and directed by men soon to be blacklisted) chronicles veterans' struggles to adjust to civilian life in uncaring US cities, to adjust to institutional injustice, unemployment, economic insecurity, and emasculation.[167] It is, according to Aguirre, about the disappointments experienced by men "who took up arms to fight for a better and more just world" only to be treated not even like "human being[s] in the New York of skyscrapers." These men feel "defrauded" and "swindled" to find that their war service has not earned them the "dignity of existence" for which they fought. In "the world driven by supply and demand," Aguirre summarizes, returning veterans find both want and fear.[168] In Aguirre's hands, two other Hollywood Left films about "mentally unhinged" veterans, *Somewhere in the Night* (1946) and *Shadow in the Sky* (1952), also indict "the capitalist world" as an "unhappy world," where "the only legitimized aspirations of man are mercantile" and where man is surrounded "with fear from every direction" because of "unemployment, war, absence of civil liberties, racial persecutions, etc."[169]

For Aguirre, a film did not have to focus on a maladjusted veteran for it to illuminate US betrayals of wartime promises. This is evident in her review of the noir *Mildred Pierce*, in which Mildred (Joan Crawford) struggles to provide her children with all the material luxuries of a burgeoning consumer culture, which ultimately instills a murderous greed in her spoiled daughter.[170] According to Aguirre, the film is "an excellent representation of the capitalist world" with all its "tragedy born through the love of money"; it is "a portrait . . . of the world in which *we* are still condemned to live." "All the dirt of society has been waved before *our* eyes, giving *us* an extremely repulsive spectacle," she explains. It only remains for the critic to extrapolate for the Cuban audience the "more vigorous social criticism" from which the film shies.[171]

Again and again, Aguirre relied on Hollywood noirs to project the 'dirty,' damning truth about US society and to use them to advocate action. As with *Mildred Pierce*, many of the noirs Aguirre liked were those intent on showing the dark side of material "success" in the postwar world. For instance, Aguirre highly recommends *The Big Clock* (1948), a film (co-written by future blacklistee Harold Goldman) that dramatizes the plight of the emasculated Organization Man of postwar America, trapped in what the film's protagonist (Ray Milland) calls "this rat race," treated by his boss like a mere machine, "a clock with springs and gears instead of flesh and blood."[172] Aguirre praises *The Big Clock* as a true and "lamentable depiction of the newly-coined slavery implicit in the regime of the salaried, in which liberty is merely, in truth, the right to die of hunger if such is the pleasure of some business magnate." The film, for Aguirre, is about the United States' "egomaniacal" bosses and "the frightened existence of [their] subordinates."[173] Her review thus works to disarticulate the narrative of success through subordination to US companies that circulated in the film giro, as elsewhere in Havana.

Aguirre appropriated noirs not only to denounce US capitalism but also to denounce US foreign policy and its cold war expansionism. For instance, just as the US Defense Department and the MPEA had worried, she used Wilder's *A Foreign Affair* to launch a screed against "capitalist rottenness," the moral failings of US occupation authorities, and the "dirty 'democratic' entrails of Yankee warring."[174] Aguirre's review of *Intrigue* (1947), a noir about a US veteran (George Raft) running contraband in Shanghai, works similarly. *Intrigue*, she writes, "cannot help but show objectively that the principal persons responsible for the turbid business [of global black markets] are often North American citizens."[175]

Finally, like other Havana critics, Aguirre used noirs about political corruption to condemn the same in both the United States and Cuba. Like Perdices, Aguirre emphasizes *The Street with No Name*'s exposé of postwar gangsters and especially "the complicity of high figures of the State, of politicians, judges, and policemen" with them. "Complicity," she continues, "of which we have had very clear proofs in Cuba to this very day."[176] And like Rodríguez Alemán, Aguirre interprets *Flamingo Road* as a true reflection of political corruption in the United States. "The description of the North American political world, *seen from the entrails*, is correct," she writes. Thus, for Aguirre, the film "fails not for that which it says but rather for that which it silences," she writes, namely the "restless forces and reformers, each day more numerous, [that] the movie omits completely, in its pessimistic, partial, and unacceptable focus."[177] Again, Aguirre rejects noir's fatalism and turns the film into an opportunity to imagine into being and mobilize said "restless forces."

Indeed, their numbers did seem to be growing among frustrated Cubans in the fall of 1949, when this review appeared. After almost a year in power, Prío's administration had stymied the Cuban courts' efforts to prosecute the Grau administration's many crimes; Prío's own administration was itself accused of corruption and had done little to curb *pistolerismo*. Students marched; Ortodoxo rallies grew; and Chibás, and others, flung sensational accusations of graft on his radio show and in the press.[178] This dissidence also found expression in Havana's film columns, as the reviews of one final postwar Hollywood Left noir demonstrate.

Willie Stark Goes to Havana: The Critical Reception of *All the King's Men*

With the Spanish title *Decepción*, (ex-CPUSA member) Robert Rossen's *All the King's Men* debuted in Havana at the Teatro América on July 17, 1950, in the midst of one of the Auténticos' most sensational scandals.[179] Less than two weeks earlier, six masked gunmen had stormed the Cuban Supreme Court and stolen evidence files for an investigation of Grau and his ministers, accused of embezzling some $174 million.[180] Chibás accused Prío himself of masterminding the plot, while *Bohemia* accused the Auténticos of undermining the Cuban public's already weak "faith in their government."[181] That same month, Ichaso lambasted the Auténticos' betrayal of the 1933 revolution's top objective: democracy "without caudillos."[182] Given this context, it is no surprise that *All the King's Men*, about a populist politician turned corrupt demagogue, was a hit in Havana and was appropriated by Havana film critics to condemn Cuban demagoguery in ways that implicated Batista and especially the Auténtico presidents.[183]

In *El Mundo*, Valdés-Rodríguez noted the film's well-deserved Oscars and the screenplay's source in Robert Penn Warren's novel based loosely on the life of Louisiana governor Huey Long. The critic then synopsized the film hence: "It presents the life of a demagogue, his rise without scruples, and his fall." Willie Stark (Broderick Crawford) comes to politics "a humble" and "sincere man," but he lacks a deep well of moral courage to stave off the corrupting influence of the "*caciques* [political bosses]." So, "the political machinery brings him to accept . . . pacts and compromises in order to gain power, and then to maintain it."[184]

In *Cinema*, Perdices explicitly noted that *All the King's Men*'s subject of demagoguery "is very familiar to us." Cubans would easily recognize, he suggests, the characterization of Stark as a populist turned "demagogue": "a man of incredible persuasion and magnetism, sweeping the masses along with him with promises of better days," and then betraying those promises in the pursuit of ever-more power. Willie Stark is "a self-made man" whose "excessive power turned him into an egomaniac." Its profound relevance to Cubans guaranteed its "commercial" success, Perdices assured exhibitors.[185]

In *Bohemia*, De Zarraga also explicitly linked *All the King's Men*'s subject to the Cuban context. He writes, "[*All the King's Men*] is a majestically successful film from its first scene to its last. It is a novel subject in a standard of rather monotonous American production and is treated with more audacity than is the custom in Hollywood; it clearly addresses the dirtiness and vulgarity of politics. And it meditates profoundly on how *we* are ignorant of the profane in the matter, those of *us* that still go in good faith to deposit *our* votes in the ballot box." Here, in referring to elected officials' betrayals of voters' trust, De Zarraga is not employing a universal "we" as much as a Cuban one.

Like Valdés-Rodríguez's and Perdices's, De Zarraga's synopsis seems designed to draw parallels between the film's plot and the corruption of the Aútenticos. When *All the King's Men* begins, he explains, Stark is an "honest, honorable man that wants to clean up public administration. The old politicians cheat the people, keeping for themselves the funds intended to improve roads, schools and hospitals." At first, the established politicians laugh at the young Stark's idealism, but when they come to understand his appeal to "the popular masses," they coopt him, drawing him into their "deceitful system." And, though "the people do their part and elect him governor," De Zarraga writes, Stark fails them. "Just as he had during the campaign, once in power, he makes pacts and offers"; he becomes wealthy through graft; and he sets up "obstacles to the opposition, silencing attacks of the press and radio." He becomes as corrupted as the democracy he set out to purify, or make more authentic; he has become, in short, "a dictator." And if the reader still missed it, De Zarraga's last line makes it painfully clear that *All the King's Men* is to be read as a meditation on Cuban politics: "How often *our* votes result in a post-electoral Stark!"[186]

As usual, Aguirre's review of *All the King's Men* in *Hoy* was the most explicit, and specific, about how the film's lessons should be applied in Cuba. From it, she extrapolates "a truly accusatory allegation" that might even "exceed its makers' intentions," she writes.

> The film is stupendous as a picture of the politico-social corruption within capitalist environments; stupendous as a portrait of venality and the trampling of [civil] liberties [and] of the methods that many dictators use to obtain . . . public sympathies; and stupendous, also, as a description of the great political fraud that constitute these "messianic" figures that, through demagogic clamor, successfully take in the masses. . . .
>
> It would be well worth it for many well-intentioned and candid members of the PPC [Chibás's Ortodoxo Party] to see *All the King's Men* and analyze . . . its similarities with certain happenings of our national political life.[187]

In other words, after generalizing about the corruption of popular democracy endemic to "capitalist environments" illuminated in the film, she argues a very specific application of the film's lessons in contemporary Cuba. Not only are Batista, Grau, and Prío false "messiahs" like Willie Stark, but so is Chibás, the "messianic" leader of the Ortodoxos, who also happened to be an outspoken anticommunist, so no friend of Aguirre's.[188]

As stupendous as she considered the film, Aguirre nonetheless finds it lacking. *All the King's Men*, she laments, is "a great fresco of darkness, despair, defeat, and impotence, . . . an exhortation to cross one's arms." The film is "defeatist, a sapper of enthusiasm and of the determination to struggle, designed to demonstrate the innateness of human corruption," and therefore the "futility" of trying to change anything. Thus, Aguirre considers it her job to extrapolate what she calls the film's "revolutionary content." Though "louts" like Willie Stark clearly existed in Cuba, this did not mean that Cubans had to admit defeat. Aguirre writes, "If in the capitalist world the honest politician is always defeated . . . this just goes to show that the only thing to do is to attack the organization of this world at its base."[189] So once again Aguirre converts a Hollywood film's perceived fatalism into a starting point from which to advocate revolution.

Unfortunately for Aguirre and her dissident peers, as the political climate grew increasingly tense in Cuba, such subversive iterations were decreasingly tolerated by Prío's administration. The following month, in August 1950, it temporarily shut down *Hoy* and began to censor the radio, including Chibás's popular radio show. Cuban journalists vociferously denounced the suppression of free speech, and Chibás committed his on-air suicide in August 1951, a dramatic act interpreted by many Cubans as a heroic act of martyrdom.[190] Facing a wave of labor and student strikes, Prío threatened to unleash his police to restore the peace. In Havana cines, Auténtico-payrolled pistoleros beat Cubans who whistled their disapproval when Auténtico leaders appeared in newsreels.[191] Early in 1952, as June presidential elections neared, the Ortodoxo candidate ran well ahead of the Auténtico candidate in national polls. Cuba's once and future dictator Fulgencio Batista ran a distant third.[192]

Conclusion

The Hollywood Left's disillusioned visions of the United States found especially receptive audiences in Havana during the Auténtico-era. Noir's dark perspectives on the (Pan-)American Way rang true to many Cubans' own experiences. Aware of this special resonance, Havana film critics extracted social critiques from noirs and Hollywood Left social problem films and used them to denounce US imperial hegemony as well as Cuban political corruption, *and* to celebrate the type of men that fought such forms of tyranny and injustice.

On March 10, 1952, Batista usurped power in a military coup, claiming he was only temporarily instituting martial law, in order to restore the order and democracy that the Auténticos had so thoroughly undermined. But few Cubans were naïve enough to take such claims at face value. In fact, the coup immediately sparked an insurrectionary movement that would grow throughout the 1950s. In that movement, Hollywood's freedom-fighting masculinity and its depiction of US social ills would continue to be invoked. As we will see in the following chapter, film criticism was especially useful during Batista's regime from 1952 to 1958, as film columns and new cine clubs became veiled sites for revolutionary calls to action.

6

Rebel Idealism: Hollywood in Havana during the Batistato, 1952–1958

> It is commonly said in Latin America that a military government is a normal way of life. I think that isn't true. I think the people don't like them. The people . . . have not yet learned to fight them effectively. But they're learning and I believe our propaganda during the war made an intangible contribution to that learning.
>
> FRANCIS JAMIESON, Ex-Chief, OIAA Information Division, November 1952[1]

> A week ago, a citizen . . . presented himself in a police station to report that he had heard the impresario say to a spectator in the lobby: A revolution is projected. The authorities hastened to investigate the place in question, finding that what was projected was a movie [about] a revolution.
>
> ENRIQUE PERDICES, *Cinema*, July 1954

August 1952. In Havana newspapers, advertisements for Twentieth-Century Fox's *Viva Zapata!* announce the arrival of a "REBELDE IDEALIST! [Idealistic Rebel!]." In them, Marlon Brando-as-Emiliano Zapata strikes various poses embodying Hollywood visions of Pan-American freedom-fighting masculinity: crying out for justice for the people, sword drawn atop a bucking stallion, leading a charge of armed men. (See fig. 6.1.) Appearing less than five months after Batista's military coup, these ads are part of a month-long local publicity campaign that have highlighted *Viva Zapata!*'s celebration of armed revolt against Latin American dictatorships, seemingly unafraid of censorship from the new regime.[2] Even as Cubans throughout Havana begin to plan for insurrection, *Viva Zapata!* now plays in five of Edelberto de Carrerá's cines, offering Cuban audiences one last gasp of Hollywood Left Pan-American freedom-fighting idealism.

First conceived of at MGM in consultation with the OIAA in the early 1940s, and later adopted by John Steinbeck and director Elia Kazan as a mutual passion project at Fox in the late 1940s, *Viva Zapata!* struggled for a decade to come to life at all. By the time it did, it bore the marks of its long and difficult gestation: a paean to Pan-American freedom fighting twisted into an anticommunist parable. Fearful that Kazan and Steinbeck's early scripts might contain a whiff of communist sympathies, Fox executives insisted on revisions. Brando's Zapata could not be some militant Marxist ideologue but rather had to be an admirer of US democracy and a reluctant warrior, compelled to take up

FIG. 6.1. In an advertisement for *Viva Zapata!* Marlon Brando-as-Emiliano Zapata embodies progressive Hollywood's vision of Pan-American freedom-fighting masculinity. "Viva Zapata!" Pressbook, Twentieth Century Fox, held at the Cinemateca, ICAIC, Havana, Cuba.

arms in the people's undeniably righteous struggle against successive Mexican dictators, who morph into would-be Stalinists in the finished film.[3] Brando's Zapata consistently resists the temptation to abuse his own power, in stark contrast to men like his corrupted ex-revolutionary colleagues (Presidents Díaz, Huerta, and Carranza). "A strong people don't need a strongman," Brando's Zapata speechifies, just before he is assassinated and thus made a martyr for the irrepressible spirit of Democracy, as his freed white stallion symbolizes in the film's final image.[4]

While film scholars have spilled much ink over the historical inaccuracies and political confusion of *Viva Zapata!*, contemporary mainstream Havana film writers did not.[5] They ignored all the anticommunist caveats coded into the film and duly appropriated it as an unambiguous endorsement of revolution against Latin American dictatorships. Perdices thrilled that *Viva Zapata!* was filled "marvelously with the ideals of the great revolutionary hero of our sister Mexican Republic, Emiliano Zapata, who fought against tyranny . . . and knew how to fill the heart of his people with the love and respect for liberty and justice that can only thrive in a democracy." Valdés-Rodríguez wrote that *Viva Zapata!* was "a song exalting the dispossessed *campesino* [Zapata] who quickly became the leader of a broad, profound and undeniably justified movement"; it "affirm[s] the undying nature of ideals of goodness and justice." Valdés-Rodríguez especially pointed his reader to a scene in which *campesinos* gather to free Zapata from *federales* who have captured him: "Men have arisen from all over, peaceful but resolved, [becoming] a growing human flow," the critic lyricizes about mass mobilization.[6] Ichaso declared Kazan one of Hollywood's best directors, and *Viva Zapata!* one of his best films.[7] Finally, writing in *Carteles*, Guillermo Cabrera Infante did note *Viva Zapata!*'s historical inaccuracies, but proclaimed it emotionally rousing nonetheless: "When he [Zapata] dies riddled with bullets . . . one feels what all of Mexico must have felt when it heard the news. The spectator has been moved."[8]

Indeed, Cuban spectators did seem to be moved by *Viva Zapata!* In Havana, the film's enthusiastic *critical* reception was matched by its enthusiastic *popular* reception. Even as the film did disappointing US box office, it did well in Havana, playing for extended runs in Carrerá's cines before moving on to Havana's subsequent-run cines. In fact, it did such good box office—in a decidedly down market, no less—that it set a bar to which other films' receipts were compared.[9] *Viva Zapata!* and its star seemed to resonate especially with a rising generation of "rebel idealists" in Cuba, as did so many Hollywood freedom-fighting films and their heroes in the 1940s and 1950s. Fidel Castro himself specifically self-identified as a Brando à la Zapata type. In fact, after Batista's ouster early in 1959, Castro signed over the film rights to his life story to Hollywood producer Jerry Wald, requesting that none other than Brando be cast to play him (from a script he hoped none other than Ernest Hemingway would agree to write).[10]

This final chapter covers the seven years of Batista's dictatorship (the *batistato*), which saw the rise of a new generational cohort, the "Centennial Generation" (after the hundredth anniversary of Martí's birth), dedicated to achieving revolutionary Cuban nationalism's elusive objectives of democracy and true sovereignty. It is about how Hollywood shaped this generation's ideas of revolution and how they shaped Hollywood to their revolutionary ends. The first section covers the historical context in Cuba, describing the widespread insurrectionary movement against Batista, which especially attracted youths whose participation was inspired, in part, by the Hollywood movies on which they had been raised. The second section covers the historical context in Hollywood, using Elia Kazan's career to explore the continued stifling of leftist filmmakers, but also the survival of freedom-fighting masculinity and progressive social criticism within their films, Hollywood trends that Cuban moviegoers and critics continued to appreciate. The third section explores developments in the Havana film giro that evidence Cubans' growing support for armed revolt and their growing disillusionment with US imperial hegemony. As escalating political unrest came inside the cines (a serious phenomenon that Perdices hints at facetiously in the second epigraph above), Cuban box office receipts fell even further than they had during the Auténtico years.[11] And the US studios' relations with Cubans in the giro continued to deteriorate, so much so that at least one studio (Warner Bros.) called in Batista's police to break up a wildcat strike; and another (Paramount) closed its Havana office for good. More than ever, the business practices of the Hollywood studios came to appear greedy, inhumane even, and contrary to the best interests of Cubans, as individuals and as a national community.

During this period, even the tone of Hollywood star visits changed. For instance, when Brando arrived in Havana in 1956, he seemed to intuit and channel Cubans' shifting attitude toward Hollywood. In an interview with Guillermo Cabrera Infante for *Carteles*, Brando ingratiated himself by declaring himself an aficionado of *Cubanidad*, and he was received as "un amigo" precisely because he did *not* present himself as a salesman of Hollywood or the American Way. (See fig. 6.2.) Brando joined Havana film writers in denouncing the negative depiction of their city in *Guys and Dolls* (1955), in which he said he regretted having starred, and generally struck a rebellious pose against the US film industry, which he derided for its greater interest in making money than art, unlike the European film industries that he (and Havana film critics) considered superior.[12] Brando complained of being perverted into a commercial product and hounded by the paparazzi like "an animal in the zoo." Brando told Cabrera Infante that he survived by clinging to role models like Charlie Chaplin, a subversive choice given Chaplin's recent forced exile.[13]

It seems that Brando knew his audience. Cabrera Infante was part of a new generation of activist film critics who, like their minorista predecessors, made Cuban ways of seeing Hollywood a part of their revolutionary movement: identifying with Hollywood's freedom-fighting heroes, appropriating its critical insights about the American Way, and highlighting its more unsavory business practices. Indeed, it was during the *batistato* that these critical strategies were most fully elaborated and integrated into revolutionary

FIG. 6.2. Guillermo Cabrera Infante watches as Marlon Brando plays a Cuban *tambor* in Havana. *Carteles*, March 1956. (Courtesy of the Cuban Heritage Collection, University of Miami Libraries, Coral Gables, Florida)

Cuban nationalism, as this chapter's final sections show. From fanzines and mainstream periodicals to the radical press, film columns were made venues for anti-Batista, anti-imperialist mobilization that survived various waves of censorship. Furthermore, this practice moved beyond the printed page, as critics and activist youth forged a cine-club movement, which sought to build a critical, even insurrectional public sphere. According to one contemporary Havana film critic, the cine-club movement was "another form of fighting" against Batista. Indeed, this "cultural" form of fighting literally translated into armed action, as members of at least one cine club formed a clandestine cell of an insurrectionary group.[14]

Rebels with a Cause: The Centennial Generation and the Batistato

In the early hours of March 10, 1952, tanks rolled from Camp Columbia army headquarters outside of Havana to the Presidential Palace two blocks east of the Prado. While Havana slept, General Batista grabbed power. Claiming a national emergency caused by Auténtico misrule, Batista promised to restore democracy, eventually. But first he postponed the upcoming June election, dissolved Congress, and suspended the constitution. Within hours, Batista was assuring the US embassy that he would protect US interests and be avidly anticommunist. In return, the US State Department recognized Batista's regime within days.[15] This despite the fact that, as Warner Bros.' Havana manager, Geza Polaty, cabled New York, "the mass of the [Cuban] population don't seem to be in accord with the new change of government, and above all, the way (military) it was done."[16] In scenes that echoed the 1933 revolution (and its depiction in *We Were Strangers*), students demonstrated at the Escalinata, and Cubans from all walks of life began to organize clandestinely.[17] The Centennial Generation began to envision themselves taking up the torch of revolutionary nationalism.

Among them was Fidel Castro, who immediately denounced Batista's coup as an illegal seizure of power. At first gathering in Ortodoxo party offices in the old movie barrio, Castro and his Ortodoxo action group soon went underground and branched out into outlying Havana neighborhoods to connect with, and create, insurrectionary cells of like-minded youth.[18] (Castro also worked as an extra in some Mexican-Cuban co-productions filmed in Havana during this period. In 1959, *Variety* would quip that "instead of a real-life 'hero,' he dreamed of being a screen hero," and suggested that only Castro's failure at the latter caused him to turn his attention fully to the former.)[19] In the first year after Batista's coup, Castro's group and other insurrectionary organizations in Havana—like the Movimiento Nacional Revolucionario (MNR) and the Acción Armada Aútentica (Triple A)—met secretly in private residences and even, at least once, in a cine.[20] Especially attracting youth, they culled participants from the working and middle classes, including aspiring young professionals and white-collar employees of US companies.[21]

By mid-1953, some 160 of them had agreed to follow Castro in an attack on the army's Moncada Barracks in eastern Cuba (hoping to do better than another group's failed attack on Camp Columbia which had resulted in the arrest of twenty conspirators in April).[22] The Moncada assault took place on

July 26, 1953, with even more disastrous results: over sixty *moncadistas* were killed during or after the ill-conceived plot. But the defeat in battle proved a public relations victory. Stories of the young martyrs' courage, and their egregious torture and summary execution by Batista's troops, moved the Cuban public. It also made Castro a household name and gained new recruits to his organization, now called the 26th of July Movement (M267). After all, the *moncadistas* and their daring leader conformed neatly to Cubans' ideal of heroic men of action.[23]

Thus began Castro's cult of personality in contemporary US and Cuban media narratives and, subsequently, in US and Cuban histories of the 1950s insurrection, a tendency encouraged (even made state policy) by Castro's Revolutionary Government after 1958. "Fidel-as-hero" satisfied both US and Cuban audiences' Hollywood-whetted appetite for narratives revolving around a few freedom-fighting good guys—and especially their top-billed leader—overcoming impossible odds to triumph over the bad guys.[24] Thus, histories of the 1950s insurrection tend to follow Castro: from the Moncada assault to his subsequent trial and "History Will Absolve Me" defense; from his two years in prison (1953 to 1955) to his exile in Mexico (1955 to 1956), where he met another rebel celebrity in Ernesto "Che" Guevara; and, especially, Castro's leadership of a ragtag guerrilla army in the Sierra Maestra mountains in eastern Cuba (1956 to 1958).

Recently, historians working in the United States have begun to expand beyond this emphasis on Castro and the *sierra* campaign to reassert the crucial role of thousands of Cubans who participated actively in insurrection in Cuba's major cities, especially Santiago de Cuba and Havana, to say nothing of the many more Cubans who aided and abetted them, providing material support, safe houses, and medical care. The M267 had a large urban component (referred to as the *llano* [the plains] in contrast to the *sierra*), but the M267's *llano* was just one of at least a half dozen such insurrectional groups, including the aforementioned MNR and Triple A as well as University of Havana students' Revolutionary Directorate (DR).[25] There were so many, in fact, that it is difficult (and not necessary here) to track their various and shifting acronyms. Suffice it to say that participation in, and complicity with, the urban insurrection was widespread, and that the various groups agreed on the need for violent action to oust Batista, if not on any post-Batista political program, about which these groups were decidedly vague.[26] For the most part, the insurrectionist groups and communist party leaders treated each other with mutual suspicion, which began to ease only in mid-1958.[27] In other words, the Cuban insurrection of the 1950s was *not* communist-led. As one insurrectionist in the Triple A later recalled, "The only Marx I knew was Groucho."[28]

No matter the organization they joined, or what little they knew about competing political doctrines, insurgent Havana youth did know that they were putting themselves at great risk. In their demonstrations, marches, and student strikes, they were subject to arrest, police beatings, and even death. Potentially even more risky were their clandestine activities: recruiting and raising funds, printing propaganda, smuggling arms, planting bombs, and conspiring in assassinations and any number of ill-fated plots, like the DR's attack on the Presidential Palace in March 1957, in which a cine doorman was implicated and over forty conspirators were killed.[29] As the insurrection grew, so did the brutality of Batista's attempts to quash it. The regime repeatedly instituted martial law, increased censorship, and suspended classes at universities. Suspected insurrectionists were subject to raids, searched indiscriminately, rounded up by Batista's secret police (the SIM), tortured, and sometimes executed, their battered bodies left on city streets to deter other would-be rebels.[30]

So why did so many young Cubans join the movement at such peril? Until recently, the cultural sources of this collective mobilization were as underexplored as Castro's personal motives were overexamined. The revolutionary movement has long been treated as if it were an inevitable response to socioeconomic factors or, even more often, as if some mystical force beyond historians' purview: a "growing crescendo of popular insurrection" that was "in the air."[31] More recently, however, historians have begun to examine the role of cultural norms of masculinity in compelling young Cuban men into armed action.[32] Relatedly, in a study of Cuban historical memory, Louis A. Pérez, Jr., has convincingly argued that decades of Cuban commemoration of the *mambises* and the Generation of '30—in stone, text, and imagery—inspired the Centennial Generation's "romantic longings" to perform similarly heroic acts in the name of *la patria*. Reading 1950s insurrectionists' own first-hand accounts, Pérez finds them constantly invoking their historical predecessors, and he concludes that this generation of Cubans "joined an expanding insurgency as a matter of legacy, disposed to discharge duty long consecrated in the narratives of nation."[33]

This seems indisputably true, but insurrectionists' first-hand accounts and biographies likewise suggest that many of them were also "disposed to discharge duties long consecrated in"—and norms of masculinity glorified in—*Hollywood* narratives, ones that had been sutured onto those Cuban national narratives for decades, as I have shown. In insurrectionists' accounts, it is clearly *de rigueur* to cite Martí; and many former insurrectionists are far too serious-minded (and later dogmatically anti-Yankee) to recall the US cinema as a source of inspiration. And yet, throughout the remembrances of insurrectionists (whether since disillusioned by the Revolution or still committed to it), there are hints that their ideas about armed revolution, and their visions of themselves enacting it, were shaped not only by the Cuban heroes in their school lessons, but also by the Hollywood heroes they revered onscreen. They recall countless childhood and adolescent hours spent in the cines and being deeply impressed by Hollywood war films, noirs, and Westerns.[34] They describe additional countless childhood hours reenacting the scenes they saw in the cines, pretending to be cowboys and especially Allied soldiers, shooting at imaginary Nazis. And like their US counterparts, their formative role playing was facilitated by holiday and birthday gifts avidly desired and joyfully received: toy guns, cartridge belts, miniature lead soldiers.[35]

Over and over again, insurrectionists recall that they were attracted to the movement not because of any well-formed political convictions (beyond anti-Batista outrage) but rather because of a vague predilection for "dash and adventure" and "a romantic and idealized vision of the fight."[36] Once they joined, they continued to view the insurrection through a Hollywood lens. Like many of his insurrectionary peers, M267 *llano* leader in Havana, Carlos Franqui, wrote in his diary, "It was all like something out of a movie," referring to underground meetings and harrowing encounters with Batista's police. He also noted that he and his fellow insurrectionists consciously modeled acts of sabotage on those of anti-Nazi resistance fighters in Europe, some of them likely learned in all those wartime Hollywood Left films.[37] And Hollywood movies were not just a part of the Centennial Generation's past, but also of its present. A number of first-hand accounts recall that insurgent youth continued to find time for going to the movies even in the midst of their clandestine activities; and they recall mixing discussions of those movies in with their discussions of the contemporary Cuban context.[38]

Some of the insurgents were aware, at least in retrospect, that their "revolutionary self-image" was informed by Hollywood. To some extent, they were acting a part: they recall shoving pistols in their belts "movie-style" (though one's pocket served better) and pulling pins out of grenades with their teeth just like "they did in the cinema" (though such a move was seriously unsafe).[39] And while the antifascist movie heroes of the 1940s were etched on their psyches, they were also affected by the most recent crop of Hollywood rebels, like Marlon Brando and James Dean, perhaps more angst-riddled and self-consciously "cool" than their predecessors but equally tough. Cuban rebels "wanted to be like James Dean," one underground activist recalled.[40] One insurrectionist in Santiago, in fact, seemed to have achieved that goal in the eyes of his peers, who honored him with the nickname "James Dean" [Jorge] Sotus.[41]

Like previous generations, the Centennial Generation found no contradiction in their admiration for Hollywood heroes and their movement's growing anti-Americanism.[42] Just as in previous decades, Cubans sutured norms of heroic masculinity from US cinema onto revolutionary Cuban nationalism, even as US imperial hegemony increasingly became a target of their revolt, figured as a major source of Cuba's past and present woes. After all, the US government's recognition of Batista underscored US policymakers' willingness to put US financial interests and US national security ahead of their (rhetorical) commitments to Cuban democracy. Most egregiously, US officials supported Batista with increased military aid and equipment, which Batista turned against Cuban citizens, a source of outrage to many. Further, rumors abounded that the FBI was assisting Batista's secret police and that the CIA was aiding his draconian Bureau for the Repression of Communist Activities (BRAC).[43]

At the same time, a stagnating economy heightened Cubans' frustration with their economic dependency on the United States. When the Korean War ended in 1953, the international sugar market declined, prices plummeted, and domestic US sugar producers successfully lobbied the US government to decrease its purchase of Cuban sugar. As a result, the Cuban economy fell into a recession, which was deepened by the ongoing political unrest.[44] As profits declined for US (and Cuban) companies in Cuba, they initiated wage decreases and layoffs that the CTC proved unwilling to contest, because its leaders had cozied up to the Batista regime, which was eager to maintain US investments. In response, rank-and-file workers increasingly sought redress outside of the CTC; they turned to more militant (including communist) labor leaders locally, and launched wildcat strikes and street demonstrations, often quashed by Batista's police. Thus radicalized, working-class Cubans increasingly supported the insurrection, not least of all through collaboration with insurrectionary groups on national general strikes.[45] At the same time, middle-class Cubans were also increasingly vulnerable to salary freezes and layoffs, and felt the inequities of US-Cuban relations more intensely than ever. In the 1950s, salaried Cuban employees and professionals made less than one-fifth what their US counterparts made while being charged premiums for the imported consumer goods to which they aspired. Exacerbated by rising inflation, soaring real estate prices, and high rates charged by US utilities companies, the cost of living in Havana was among the highest in the world.[46]

To make matters worse, Batista's campaign to increase US tourism in order to boost the faltering economy further soured Cubans on the Yankee presence on their island. In areas where US tourists congregated (i.e., hotels, restaurants, and clubs), darker-skinned Cubans were barred entry, so as not to offend the segregationist sensibilities of US southerners.[47] Whether or not a Cuban personally experienced the sting of this discrimination, many were inclined to interpret it as an offense against *Cubanidad* and evidence of North Americans' racially charged condescension. Batista's efforts to boost tourism also reinvigorated gambling, prostitution, and the US mafia's presence in Havana. To help manage the city's casinos, Batista put his old friend Meyer Lansky on the government payroll. Lansky, in turn, invited his mob associates to operate those casinos, and the hotels and nightclubs to which they were attached. In exchange for bribes and kickbacks, Batista's regime granted loans, licenses, and tax incentives to help US mobsters build new properties. In 1956, Lansky opened the twenty-one-story Hotel Riviera on the Malecón, with megastar Hollywood hoofer Ginger Rogers headlining its casino's floor show. And in 1957, Florida mobster Santos Trafficante, Jr., opened the nineteen-story Hotel Capri and Sans Soucí casino, where aging Hollywood gangster George Raft greeted patrons at the door.[48]

Perhaps not surprisingly, then, Hollywood began again to emphasize associations between Havana and illicit activities in a rash of films, including in the aforementioned *Guys and Dolls* and the B-noir *The Big Boodle* (1957), which brought Errol Flynn back to Havana to shoot on location.[49] And once again, as Havana film critics noted, Hollywood's "portray[al of] Havana as a Mecca of vice" and "a sordid place" full of gangsters, seedy nightclubs, and brothels offended many Cubans.[50] But so did the vice itself, and the way it degraded Cubans, a debasement increasingly associated in the public mind with US influence. Cubans found evidence of their neighbor's debased nature and debasing influence not only in Havana casinos and vice districts, but also in the Havana film giro and in the Hollywood movies made by leftist artists playing at local cines.

Beloved Rogues: Kazan and the Survival of Hollywood Progressives

One Hollywood filmmaker who continued to make movies exploring the United States' "entrails" was Elia Kazan. A Greek immigrant raised in New York, Kazan first came to Hollywood by way of the Group Theatre, a centerpiece of the Popular Front New York theater movement in the 1930s. Joining the Group in 1932, Kazan also joined its CPUSA unit from 1933 to 1935, leaving it after becoming disenchanted with the CPUSA's inartistic ideological rigidity and its top-down structure. Party membership, however, was not a requisite to move in New York's leftist theater circles or to cross over from them into overlapping Hollywood Left circles. In the mid to late 1930s, Kazan made a number of trips to Southern California to act in Hollywood Left films, including Wanger's *Blockade* (though the production's long delays kept Kazan out of the finished film). But it was back in New York that Kazan was starting to make a name for himself as a stage director, particularly as a self-professed "left-wing intellectual" type who preferred plays with "social content."[51] By 1944, he had scored several Broadway hits and had caught the attention of Twentieth-Century Fox, which contracted Kazan to direct five films over the next five years. The first was *A Tree Grows in Brooklyn*, adapted by Hollywood Left screenwriters. Two were noirs—*Boomerang!* and *Panic in the Streets*—and the other two were social problem films: *Gentleman's Agreement*, about anti-Semitism; and *Pinky*, written by Dudley Nichols and Philip Dunne, about antiblack racism.[52]

Between films, Kazan continued to direct New York stage productions, including some of the most important plays of the postwar American theater renaissance, most famously, Arthur Miller's *All My Sons* and *Death of a Salesman* and Tennessee Williams's *A Streetcar Named Desire*, starring newcomer Marlon Brando as Stanley Kowalski. Launched thus into stardom, Brando reprised the role of Kowalski in the film adaptation, which Kazan directed for Warner Bros. in 1951. By then, Kazan was a darling of theater and film critics, not only in the United States but also in Havana, where his films were guaranteed spots on critics' annual top film lists. During these years, Kazan's prestige as an Oscar-winning artist and bankable big-name director, like Huston's, seemed to insulate him (temporarily) from the chilling effect of the Red Scare. Consciously defiant of it, Kazan continued to grapple with social problems from a left-liberal perspective.[53]

In this defiance, Kazan found a willing partner in Fox's studio head, Daryl F. Zanuck, who loved to make sellable drama out of controversial issues. In 1949, they set out to revive the idea of a Zapata biopic, which Kazan had been contemplating since 1943, when he began jotting notes during the heyday of OIAA–Hollywood Pan-Americanism. After the war, Kazan learned that his friend John Steinbeck shared his interest and had even written a story outline. By then, MGM was also reviving the Zapata idea, despite one MGM executives' admonition that "Zapata is a goddamn commie revolutionary." But MGM dropped the Zapata idea again in 1947, when HUAC subpoenaed Lester Cole, the screenwriter they had assigned to it. Undeterred, Zanuck bought the rights from MGM in 1949 and set Kazan and Steinbeck to work on a script with the working title *The Beloved Rogue*.[54]

As they did so, the chill of the cold war climate was intensifying. Atomic espionage trials made the existential threat of domestic communists seem very real indeed, and Senator Joseph McCarthy arrived on the scene in 1950 to lend his name to the growing anticommunist hysteria. By this time, many ex-communists and fellow travelers, including Kazan, had come to denounce communism, not least of all in light of postwar revelations about Stalinism. As Kazan and Steinbeck wrote and rewrote the Zapata screenplay, they struggled with expressing their leftist but also anticommunist politics.[55] In drafts, Kazan kept pushing what he saw as an analogy between Zapata and Lincoln, while Zanuck insisted on dialogue that analogized Zapata to Jefferson.[56] But all of this tortured tinkering made the film's telling of the Mexican Revolution—already compressing a decade of complicated Mexican politics into a two-hour biopic—even more confusing to contemporary US critics and audiences, who largely rejected *Viva Zapata!* And the anti-Stalinist rewrites did nothing to save Kazan from HUAC. Two months after *Zapata*'s US release, in April 1952, Kazan appeared before the committee and named the names of people he had known to be CPUSA members in the mid-1930s, an act derided by many of his leftist colleagues as cowardly. Kazan defended himself in a *New York Times* advertisement, arguing that the US government had the right to know all it could about the "dangerous and alien conspiracy" that was Communism.[57]

Despite the controversy thus swirling around Kazan, he continued to work prodigiously on stage and screen, and he continued to imbue his films with critical social content. By early 1953, he had begun collaborating with Budd Schulberg (who had also named names to HUAC) on an original screenplay for *On the Waterfront*, about a corrupt union in the Port of New York. When all the major studios passed on the project (not least because they feared that the State Department would advise against its foreign distribution), Kazan turned to Sam Spiegel, independent producer of Huston's *We Were Strangers*. Once financing was secured, Brando agreed to play Terry Malloy, *On the Waterfront*'s ex-boxer turned longshoreman who becomes disillusioned with the tyrannical mobsters who control his union, mobsters for whom he once worked and for whom his brother still does. After much soul-searching, Malloy decides to inform on the mobsters to a crime commission, knowing he will be denounced by them as a "stool pigeon" (a story that spoke to parallels in Kazan's and Schulberg's decision to name names).[58] The role made Brando an icon of American masculinity, both physically tough and morally principled, incapable of *not* acting in the face of injustice, of *not* rebelling against abusive power. (Perhaps Castro—himself a reformed gangster—had Brando's Malloy in mind as much as Brando's Zapata when he made his casting suggestion to Jerry Wald in 1959.)

Released in the summer of 1954, *On the Waterfront* redeemed Kazan from the professional and personal low of *Viva Zapata!*'s poor box office returns and his HUAC testimony. *On the Waterfront* did big US box office and garnered eight Oscars. (It was released in Havana in December, just as that city's dockworkers were tangling with corrupt leaders in the CTC.)[59] Kazan then turned his attention to Warner Bros.' adaptation of Steinbeck's *East of Eden* and to the other young actor he would help make a role model to rebellious youth around the world, James Dean, whose next film was *Rebel without a Cause*. After *East of Eden*, Kazan's next two films were the independently produced *Baby Doll* (1956) and Warner Bros.' *A Face in the Crowd* (1957), with screenplays by Tennessee Williams and Budd Schulberg respectively.[60] While *Baby Doll* is a sexual farce designed to show off Williams's characteristically withering depictions of the US South, *A Face in the Crowd* is a more profound social satire that takes on the rising Age of Television, and the new medium's potential for manipulating public opinion and undermining democracy. In it, Andy Griffith plays "Lonesome" Rhodes, a charismatic, guitar-picking, Arkansas-born hillbilly who rises up through local radio to become a huge national star, building an adulatory fan base charmed by his (increasingly inauthentic) folksiness. Growing arrogant and contemptuous of his audience, Rhodes begins to wield his influence to endorse useless consumer products and even to back a presidential candidate. Rhodes spirals toward megalomaniacal demagoguery until a colleague exposes him on air as the false populist he is.[61]

Kazan's ability to make films so profoundly critical of US society in the cold war's increasingly conservative political environment is partially explained by the idiosyncrasies of biography. But his continued success, and that of other socially critical leftist filmmakers, was also an effect of broader developments in the US film industry. These were bad years for the Hollywood studios, the end in fact of their Golden Age. To their recent difficulties (HUAC, forced divestiture of their theaters, trade barriers, and the postwar rise of European film industries) was added the death knell: the precipitous rise of television ownership, which took off in 1952. In response, Hollywood increasingly emphasized its capacities to offer what the small screen in the family home could not: grand spectacles and adult themes. In terms of spectacle, the studios made more films in color; introduced 3-D; and developed a number of widescreen formats (i.e., CinemaScope, Cinerama, and VistaVision), for which the studios produced big-budget biblical epics and sprawling Westerns.[62] In terms of adult themes, the film industry countered television's family-friendly and politically centrist programming with more violence, more sex, and more controversial topics, hoping to tantalize audiences back into theaters. This was especially true among the growing number of independent production companies. Along with Kazan's *Baby Doll* and *A Face in the Crowd*, examples of independently produced films include many a noir (e.g., *Kiss Me Deadly*, *The Killing*, *The Big Knife*, and *Sweet Smell of Success*) and social problem dramas (e.g., *The Defiant Ones* and *Riot in Cell Block 11*).

These were the films that Havana critics recommended as exceptions to the rule of Hollywood's banality in this era. But before we get there, the following section explores the effects of the US studios' decline in the Havana film giro, where Hollywood's financial (and reputational) losses were exacerbated by political unrest.

Death of a Salesman (of American Imperialism): The Demise of the Film Giro

Back in Havana, the film giro that had struggled during the Auténtico years deteriorated further during the *batistato*. With box office receipts now consistently in decline, the US and Cuban film trades declared the Cuban film business in full "crisis" at the end of 1953.[63] Admissions declined again, a full 30 percent, in 1954, due to Cuba's stagnating economy and "the uncertain political situation" which posed "Cubans' traditional love for a democratic form of government" against "a military regime," explained the Cuban correspondent for the *Film Daily Yearbook*.[64] At the same time, by mid-decade, the rise of television that plagued Hollywood in the United States also came to Cuba, which had Latin America's highest number of TV sets per capita; on them, Cubans could now watch old Hollywood movies (which the US studios sold to Cuban broadcasters) in their own homes.[65] And even as Cuban box office receipts shrank overall, Hollywood's market share in Cuba sank as low as 50 percent, as Cuban demand grew for Mexican and, especially in Havana, for European cinema. In 1957, the growing political unrest kept even more Cuban moviegoers away, making it the "worst year yet" for the film giro, whose members called for tax relief to prop up what they insisted was a vital part of the national economy.[66] In short, the golden years of Hollywood in Havana, and of its role as US-Cuban bond, ended in the decade *before* Castro's Revolutionary Government nationalized the country's cines and expropriated the Hollywood distribution offices.

At the beginning of this period, some first-run Havana exhibitors sought survival through the projection of strength. For one thing, they continued to consolidate into chains. Of Havana's half-dozen cine chains, Carrerá's was the largest, consisting of twelve first-runs (down from its peak of sixteen in the late 1940s), followed by Mestre's Radiocentro Circuit's six cines and the América circuit's five.[67] The latter added two new cines in Vedado in 1952: the 1,500-seat Cine 23 y 12 and the 1,700-seat Teatro Rodi, an "ultramodern" theater that was the latest "pride of Cuba" (see fig. 6.3). The Rodi's opening night premiered MGM's *Quo Vadis*, one of Hollywood's big-budget biblical

FIG. 6.3. The "ultramodern" Teatro Rodi in Vedado represents the latest "pride of Cuba." *ACRC 1952–53*. (Courtesy of the Cuban Heritage Collection, University of Miami Libraries, Coral Gables, Florida)

epics; it was attended by Batista's wife, who was apparently untroubled by any analogies to be made between her husband and the tyrannical Emperor Nero.[68] Havana exhibitors also opened smaller venues for screening European and art films, including the 450-seat Cine Capri in the old movie barrio and the 900-seat Cinema La Rampa in Vedado.[69] Finally, in July 1958, Carrerá opened the last Havana cine of the republican era: the 1,400-seat Gran Cine Acapulco in Vedado Heights. Its opening night's feature was Fox's *The Young Lions*, a film about World War II soldiers, directed by (Hollywood Ten member) Edward Dmytryk and starring Brando and Montgomery Clift. Carrerá also announced that he would open a "ranch" next to the cine, where children could ride ponies "like real '*cowboys*,'" capitalizing on and encouraging Cubans' habit of identifying closely with their onscreen heroes.[70]

These new cines, however, represent exceptions to the rule: more Havana cines were boarded up than were constructed during the *batistato*.[71] Declining market conditions prompted what Perdices described as a "ruthless" survival-of-the-fittest struggle. First-run exhibitors (fretfully) gambled on the expense of adapting their cines for Hollywood's ever more spectacular widescreen formats, projection equipment, and sound systems.[72] "*Renovarse o Morir!* [Update or Die]," one ad for CinemaScope put it starkly.[73] Some of these innovations did (temporarily) attract audiences, and were vaunted as proof of Cuba's modernity.[74] So was an "*auto-cine*" (drive-in) that opened on the outskirts of Havana in 1955, the Vento, with two more opening in 1958: La Novia del Mediodia and the Tarará.[75] But other expensive exhibition novelties were dismal failures, like 3-D, which required headache-inducing glasses that Havana moviegoers disliked and critics deplored.[76] And, for most cine de barrio exhibitors, such costly adaptations were not even an option; instead, they tried to survive by lowering admission prices and/or decreasing employees' wages.

Even in the cines that did manage to adopt Hollywood's increasingly engrossing exhibition technologies, there seemed less escape than ever from the disruptive national context outside their doors. The insurrection came inside the cines in the form of rebels who used their darkness to rendezvous undetected and/or used their stages to deliver impassioned speeches against Batista, detection be damned.[77] At other times, rebellious expressions were more spontaneous, more like murmurs of dissent becoming collective. For instance, immediately following the Moncada assault, as rumors swirled about Batista's soldiers torturing and executing the *moncadistas*, a correspondent for *Variety* observed that "when first reports of the revolt were reaching Havana, and before censorship was fully instituted, the América circuit was coincidentally showing *Crisis*," a MGM drama about a despicable dictator of a fictional Latin American country, President Farrago (José Ferrer), who undermines free elections, assassinates his opponents and imposes martial law because, as Farrago seethes, a weak people need a strong leader. According to *Variety's* correspondent, the Havana audience he observed recognized analogies between the film and the contemporary Cuban context. *Crisis*'s dictator seemed "not-so-imaginary" in Cuba in 1953 and "the lines spoken in the picture evoked bitter laughter in the audience."[78] In years to come, too, Batista's image in newsreels regularly provoked angry hisses from Havana audiences.[79]

Indeed, there is evidence scattered throughout the historical record that the rebelliousness surging outside the cines came inside and affected moviegoing and reception practices. By many accounts, Cuban moviegoing devolved back to the unruliness of early exhibition spaces. In the 1950s, Perdices complained often about a loss of decorum in the cines, especially griping about disruptive youth who snuck into films prohibited for minors, smoked (despite posted prohibitions), chatted loudly, and burst out sexual innuendos whenever the occasion arose.[80] In memoirs, Cubans recall audiences that made loud smooching noises to parody love scenes; sent up cheers for that which they approved and hisses for that which they did not; and generally talked back at the screen, loudly rejecting implausible character and/or plot developments.[81] As one Cuban remembers, "We took pride in thinking that we were too clever, too slick and alert, to have some gringo moviemaker get away with that."[82] And film-by-film reports from Paramount's Havana office during this period confirm Havana moviegoers' unruliness. Much to that office's chagrin, Cuban audiences laughed at over-the-top anticommunist propaganda and rejected "sentimental pictures" with "too much 'sweetness'"; instead, they demanded "action," "gun-play," "'blood and thunder.'"[83]

As in other moments of heightened revolutionary nationalism, Cuban audiences were also in no mood for offenses against *Cubanidad*. For instance, Paramount's office reported that Havana audiences ran an effective word-of-mouth campaign against *Mambo* (1954), when its titular Cuban music and dance proved inauthentic.[84] And Cubans' so-called super-sensitiveness was even more inflamed by *Santiago* (1956), a Warner Bros. movie about the "Spanish-American War." In it, Alan Ladd plays an American gunrunner named "Cash" Adams who smuggles guns to Cuban rebels in 1898. Despite his cynical professions of single-minded self-interest, Adams is won over to the Cubans' struggle for freedom, not least of all through his love of a beautiful *mambisa* (played by an Italian actress rather than a Cuban one). Converted to the cause, Adams risks his life to sneak through Spanish-patrolled waters to the besieged *mambí* leader Antonio Maceo, who like José Martí (played by US character actor Ernest Sarracino), barely figures in the story.[85] Released in the United States in July 1956, *Santiago* provoked protests in Havana even before the film arrived there. Cuban historians denounced its many inaccuracies and its subjugation of Cuban heroes to US ones, not least through the film's denigration of Martí "as a near ludicrous fat man." The Teachers Union of Cuba protested to the US embassy, asking that Warner Bros. not be allowed to distribute the film—so "detrimental to our patriotic feelings"—in foreign markets. In August, the US embassy reported "an almost daily barrage of criticism" in the Havana press and even from the insurrectionary group MNR. Perdices warned Warner Bros. to tread carefully: "The Cuban feels love for his country and never, in any moment, forgets the men that fought for it."[86]

At the time, Warner Bros., and the other US studios, could ill afford additional problems in the Cuban market. The insurrection was "playing havoc on box office take," Colli had explained to Warner Bros. executives in New York just a few months earlier.[87] This is hardly surprising since the insurgency had literally exploded into movie theaters by mid-decade. In early summer 1955, rebels planted bombs in six Havana cines, including the Cine Infanta near the University of Havana and the Cine Tosca in the Víbora neighborhood, the latter allegedly the work of Fidel Castro's brother, Raúl. In 1957, insurgents planted bombs in at least four more Havana cines, including the Teatro Radiocentro (the old Warner), which was the site of a bomb attack again in February 1958.[88] In response, police took to regularly searching youth in cines, and spectators reported that the possibility of a bomb weighed heavily on them as they tried to enjoy the show.[89] In other words, cine bombings "terrorized audiences, which is precisely the point," explained *Film Daily Yearbook*'s Cuba correspondent. Indeed, the objective of the rebels—who called ahead with warnings to avoid civilian casualties—was to disrupt everyday Cuban life and, with them, the economy. Toward this social and economic disruption, insurgents also sabotaged the transport of goods, which cost the US studios hundreds of lost films. And they dynamited Havana's electrical grid and called national general strikes, both of which also closed Havana cines, as did curfews whenever Batista invoked martial law.[90] Moviegoing was further deterred in mid-1958, when the M267's Radio Rebelde issued a "No 3 Cs" directive to those Cubans wanting to express their support for the insurrection: no cines, no *compras* (shopping), and no cabarets.[91]

As the film business suffered, the already frayed transnational camaraderie in the film giro tore further. Discord grew between Cuban exhibitors and the US distributors, especially as the latter began to demand higher box office percentages and rental fees to try to offset the down market. When exhibitors balked, the US companies' international departments insisted on intransigence from their Havana managers: "Stick to the answer NO. We have the pictures and they need us more than we need them," came the instruction from Warner Bros.[92] In response to this us vs. them mentality, Cuban exhibitors complained that they were shouldering the burden of trying times, even while it was the US companies whose product was in decline, they accused.[93] Fed up with the US companies' terms and seeking better products, even Havana first-run exhibitors began to contract with more European distributors, prompting the Hollywood offices to threaten contract cancellations.[94]

The US companies' relations with their Cuban office employees also soured further. From executives in the United States came additional orders to cut operating costs. In contrast to previous eras when local friendships were considered "good business," the US studios reprimanded their Havana managers for treating their "employees like one big family," for being too softhearted when employees, who had served for two, even three decades, requested sick leaves.[95] Like other US companies operating in Cuba's declining economy, the Hollywood studios especially pushed for wage and staff reductions. After all, the payroll was the "biggest item of controllable expense," Warner Bros. International Department reminded its Havana office, repeatedly requesting lists of personnel and their duties, and even sending an auditor to ensure the staff was "streamlined."[96] The giro's grumblings about such measures again found their way into Perdices's column, in which he criticized US studio executives who "dictate drastic orders from abroad," rescinding their local managers' authority and damaging the hard-earned goodwill they enjoyed with local exhibitors and employees.[97]

Faced with the studios' efficiency measures, Cuban giro employees turned to their individual unions and their umbrella organization, the CTC-affiliated Film Giro Syndicate.[98] However, in the film giro, as in many industries, the grievances of rank-and-file workers exceeded the CTC's willingness to address them. As a result, wildcat strikes erupted in the US studios' Havana offices. For instance, in February 1953, the US companies converted a number of existing percentage basis contracts to flat rental fee contracts, in part to transfer all risk to the exhibitor and, in other part, to save on the cost of paying box office checkers, whose jobs were obviated by flat rental fees. The checkers' union cried foul, arguing that the US companies still had to pay their checkers on staff for the converted contracts, per Auténtico-era precedent. The conflict reached a climax when all of Warner Bros. employees engaged in a "spontaneous" work stoppage in solidarity with Warner Bros.' checkers. "All hell broke loose in our office," Geza Polaty (manager) wrote to Colli (regional supervisor), complaining that more militant leaders in the Film Giro Syndicate were agitating their usually docile office staff. Polaty called in Batista's police to break up the illegal strike action. This left the checkers little choice but to agree to mediation with the US studios through Batista's Ministry of Labor, which ruled in the US companies' favor, overturning the more labor-friendly Auténtico-era precedent.[99]

In fact, during the *batistato*, the US studios' Havana Film Board had reason to boast that it had "some weight with [Batista's] Government" in squashing labor demands.[100] But temporary victories had longer-term costs: namely to enhance the appeal of the Film Giro Syndicate's more radical factions, who rose as part of a general wave of labor militancy that began in mid-1956. That summer and fall, the syndicate's members elected a slate of more militant leaders, who demanded 25 percent salary increases in the giro's distribution offices. The US companies balked that they could not afford such raises under present economic conditions, but sit-down strikes in their offices pressed the issue. Early in 1957, a Cuban lower labor court reviewed the Hollywood studios' books in Havana and determined that their profit margins *did* allow for small salary bumps. Outraged, the US companies appealed their case to the Cuban Supreme Court, which ruled in their favor in October 1958, just two months before Batista's ouster. The US companies cheered at having saved thousands of dollars, unable to know that not only would the impending Revolutionary Government reverse this ruling and force the US companies to back-pay these denied raises, but also that their perceived stinginess would be counted heavily against them in the post-1958 settling of accounts.[101]

During the *batistato*, the film giro proved a highly stressful place to work, to an unhealthy and even deadly degree. One victim of the giro's stresses was José Del Amo, Weiner's replacement at United Artists' Havana office. With the company for over twenty-seven years beginning in the late 1920s, Del Amo had risen from clerk to booker, to salesman, to assistant manager, and now to the top spot. But the strain proved too much, and Del Amo died suddenly in March

1954; he was only forty-eight years old. "Those who worked at his side say that the position killed him," noted the *ACRC*, blaming the pressures of corporate masculinity generally and United Artists' efficiency measures specifically for Del Amo's demise: "He was the first to arrive in the office, and the last to leave. Night after night, he stayed late in his office, doing tasks that others should have done, in that way saving the Company the expense of new employees."[102] Describing a remembrance held in United Artists' office, Valdés-Rodriguez wrote in *Cinema* about the special bond of friendship and respect between the highly capable Del Amo and Weiner, who had been "a father figure" to Del Amo and now mourned him "as if he has lost a son of his own flesh and blood."[103]

Sadly, Weiner did not have to wait long to join his Cuban "son." Less than two years later, in January 1956, the "dean" of the film giro died of heart failure at age eighty. He was buried in the city's famous Colón Cemetery, and his death became yet another occasion to celebrate revolutionary Cuban nationalism, this time in the context of the 1950s insurrection. Eulogizing his "fraternal friend" in *Cinema*, Valdés-Rodríguez wrote, "In Cuban land, for which he fought bravely and which he loved as his own, rests forever Henry Weiner, who was an upright, good and simple man; a reliable and loyal friend; an honest, indefatigable and vigilant employee; a cordial and humane boss; [and] a responsible citizen willing to put his very life on the line when he believed it necessary to defend ideals of human progress only possible in a climate of liberty and justice."

In his eulogy, Valdés-Rodríguez also reviewed Weiner's biography again, this time with anti-Batista as well as anti-imperialist subtext. Born in Bohemia under Austrian imperial rule, the critic recalled, Weiner had immigrated to the United States, seeking political freedoms and material opportunity. Then, in 1898, "the rumor of a nearby country, small like his native Bohemia and likewise oppressed, agitated his restless zeal for liberty and the pursuit of happiness. So Henry Weiner joined the North American army and came to war in Cuba, in an unequivocal and extremely generous act for the liberty of this small and brave people, for the island's absolute independence without obstructions." Remembering Weiner's life, Valdés-Rodríguez concluded, should reinvigorate his giro colleagues' own commitments to the Pan-American democratic ideals that "animated" Weiner and the *mambises*.[104]

Despite such exhortations, however, the days of mutual Pan-American devotions in the film giro were over. As if to announce this, Paramount permanently closed its Havana office in March 1958, citing abysmal Cuban box office receipts and the high cost of operations under conditions of political unrest. Adding salt to the wound, Paramount refused to pay severance to its Cuban employees, many of who had worked for the company for over twenty-five years (one employee for thirty-eight).[105] Cubans in the giro were outraged. Charles Garrett (then head of publicity at Fox's Havana office) expressed the general sentiment. Explicitly appropriating moral codes prescribed in Hollywood's own narratives, he wrote in *Cinema*, "Many say that heart and feelings don't matter in the world of business. But we are in a business that presents on the world's screens stories in which love, justice and the good always triumph. The bosses of Paramount should think about the plots of some of their movies; they should think a little about those who have faithfully served the company for more than a third of a century and that now, in difficult times, are thrown to the street."[106] Cubans in the giro pointed to Paramount's healthy Wall Street stock price and the extravagant productions it still churned out as proof that the company could afford to withstand some "difficult times" in a market from which they had, after all, extracted considerable profits during better days. They also pointed to Paramount's own history in Cuba, particularly during the Depression and Machado's reign, when Arthur Pratchett had bravely helmed the ship and the company had recognized that "economic sacrifice would have to be shared by all."[107] In contrast, Paramount's departure now was interpreted as proof of the United States' exploitative self-interest and corporate cowardice. Paramount was forsaking Cuba and the giro family precisely when it mattered most.

Meanwhile, at least some *Cubans* in the giro were willing to put their necks out for *Cuba libre*. For instance, in Havana, a traveling film equipment salesman for Western Electric used his equipment bags to smuggle medicine to sierra rebels in eastern Cuba.[108] And Teatro Radiocentro's projectionist showed a French film without cutting scenes of a revolutionary uprising as ordered by Batista's interior minister.[109] In fact, Havana exhibitors continually risked provoking the regime's ire by showing Cuban newsreels that publicized (and heroicized) the insurrection. For this audacity, Cuban newsreel makers were repeatedly arrested and charged with inciting "native passion."[110] Among others in the giro, Perdices jumped to the newsreel makers' defense, wielding the language of revolutionary Cuban nationalism. To accept such censorship would be "a betrayal of those ideals for which Martí fought with such passion," he argued in 1953.[111]

Indeed, Perdices repeatedly voiced his opposition to Batista's dictatorship and his advocacy of resistance, albeit often in veiled terms given the prevailing climate of censorship. Just six days after Batista's coup, Perdices wrote about an MGM noir, *The Unknown Man*, explaining that the film is about a city's "criminal empire" and a "self-sacrificing" man (played by Walter Pidgeon) so utterly "devoted" to "justice" that he is willing to risk his life to oppose that empire. For Cubans, Perdices continues, the film is "of great instruction in these days in which [some men are] seduced by greed to obtain, illegally, wealth and power from the shadow of a palace in which men present themselves as 'saints' while using evil like 'devils.'"[112]

Though Perdices's columns are rife with such anti-Batista subtext, one more example will have to suffice here. In 1957, on the occasion of the May 20 national holiday commemorating the founding of the Cuban republic, Perdices again seemed to encourage revolutionary action. His column begins with the lyrics of a Cuban folksong: "*Si Maceo volviera a vivir, y a su patria otra vez contemplara* [If Maceo came back to life, and contemplated his country once again]." Perdices then trails off, writing simply, "you know the rest." As his Cuban reader did likely know, the lyrics continue, "*de seguro la vergüenza lo matara* [the shame would surely kill him]." And yet, not all hope was lost, continued Perdices. "There are patriots today that have not lost hope of seeing Cuba made a paradise where brothers are united [in] patriotism. . . . In spite of . . . the reprisals they suffer, they don't faint away but persevere. . . . They are true heroes that sacrifice everything. . . . They are untiring patriots that are giving new birth to that which we hold dear."[113] Though Perdices here is purportedly referring to struggling Cuban exhibitors, Cuban readers in 1957 must have understood such language to be an endorsement of the insurrection and its "heroes."

In fact, throughout its pages, *Cinema* reflects the burgeoning (and fomenting) of rebellion against the status quo in the film giro and in Havana generally. For one thing, in 1953, Perdices began reprinting reviews by esteemed critics like Valdés-Rodríguez, Ichaso, and Rodríguez Alemán, as well as by relative newcomers like Walfredo Piñera (critic for *Diario de la marina* and various Catholic publications); and Rene Jordan (critic for *Bohemia*). These reviews displaced the overwhelming predominance of Hollywood publicity in *Cinema*, notably turning the publication's focus to more critical modes of film reception. At the same time, *Cinema* enthusiastically promoted Havana's cine-club movement and the radical cultural society "Nuestro Tiempo." In these ways, *Cinema* became part of a cross-referencing intellectual network that supported insurrection. A closer look at film criticism during the *batistato*—published in Havana periodicals, and practiced in classrooms and in cine clubs—further illuminates that network's efforts toward that end.

David(s) versus Goliath: Mainstream Havana Critics Endorse Insurrection

From the pages of *El Mundo* and especially from the University of Havana's campus, Valdés-Rodríguez continued to be a major influence on this intellectual network. At the latter, he still headed the Cinema Department, held his Cine de Arte sessions, and taught his summer course, where he privileged European cinema but also continued to show films (old and new) made by the Hollywood Left.[114] During the *batistato*, Valdés-Rodríguez's students compared him to Martí and enthused about his lively classes where "everyone opines with total freedom."[115] This freedom of speech was possible because the university campus enjoyed (nominal) autonomy from Batista's police, at least until it was closed for the duration in November 1956 due to its students' and faculty's insurrectionary activities.

Like Perdices, Valdés-Rodríguez also expressed his support for insurrection in his film reviews, in (thinly) veiled terms. In *Cinema* in 1954, he praised a Mexican-Cuban coproduced biopic about Martí as respectful to "the dream of independence and the indomitable *mambí* spirit shared by generations" and for keeping "alive the ideal of liberty and democracy, of respect for the popular will, [and] of the rejection of governments of force."[116] And Hollywood Left films continued to prove amenable to similar uses, albeit with a little more work. In January 1955, Valdés-Rodríguez still found an ally in Walter Wanger, whose *Blockade* (1938) was much admired by the critic. In his review of Wanger's 1954 film, *Riot in Cell Block 11*, written while the surviving *moncadistas* were in prison, the critic appropriates the film's denunciation of unjust incarceration and corrupt authorities. However, he does not agree with what he deems the film's apparent squeamishness about armed revolt: "[The film] does not allow that we accept the use of violence and insurrection to rectify very grave facts."[117] Clearly, faced with the grave fact of Batista's dictatorship, Valdés-Rodríguez did.

One last Valdés-Rodríguez review will suffice to suggest their tenor during the *batistato*. It is of Stanley Kramer's *The Defiant Ones* (1958), about an angry black man (played by Sidney Poitier), who has been treated like a second-class citizen his whole life, and a bigoted white man (played by Tony Curtis). The two men escape prison, but are chained together and must learn to coexist. By film's end, they have overcome their mutual animosity and come to recognize their common humanity.[118] As usual, Valdés-Rodríguez used this film to spotlight the US "entrails" that the film exposed, particularly the "inhumanity, absurdity, iniquity, and barbarity of [racial] discrimination." But he also used *The Defiant Ones* to borrow inspiration ("a new hopeful spirit") from the emerging Civil Rights Movement in the United States for analogous "Cuban struggles" for democracy and sovereignty. This film is about "the spirit of resistance to transcend the negative circumstance in which one is found," Valdés-Rodríguez explains. It is about "the vindicating fight that brings together millions of souls yearning for justice and equality in the living reality of their individual and collective existence." It is about men "made brothers in frustration and pain," forged into a "virile fraternity."[119]

By the time he wrote this review, Valdés-Rodríguez was in his sixties. Though he was not ready to retire, his onetime students increasingly picked up his torch, asserting themselves as film critics and founding progressive cultural institutions while also participating in insurrectionary activities. Rodríguez Aléman continued to write reviews for *Mañana*, even as he worked with the DR and later the M267, printing subversive anti-Batista literature (for which he was arrested four times during the *batistato*). Cabrera Infante wrote film reviews for *Carteles* and cofounded Nuestro Tiempo, even as he safehoused insurgents hiding from Batista's police in his family apartment, helped transport arms, and wrote for the underground press. And Tomás Gutiérrez Alea wrote film reviews for Nuestro Tiempo's publication, even as he held clandestine meetings and hid rebel fugitives in his apartment.[120] Taken together, these former students of Valdés-Rodríguez overwhelmingly promoted European neorealist cinema, whose sociopolitical engagement they admired, and bashed Hollywood for vapidity and denigrating racial and national stereotypes, while highlighting those US-made films that persisted in progressive critiques of US society.

As always, Havana film critics stood by Chaplin even, or especially, as he was persecuted by US cold warriors. When Chaplin's last US-made film, *Limelight*, premiered in Havana in 1953 (in a "splash" release in ten Havana first-run cines), Havana critics used the occasion to condemn Chaplin's ill-treatment by the US film industry and government, and to explain yet again that Chaplin's films "exposed the entrails of the society in which he lives" and "made the common man a hero in the midst of a social system hostile to him."[121] Retrospective cycles of Chaplin's films offered by cine clubs were also made opportunities to bring Chaplin's critiques of capitalist modernity and the Little Tramp's instinctual underdog rebelliousness to bear into the *batistato*.[122] The Little Tramp refused to be defeated. "Small and mischievous, he always beats the crushing giant—David against Goliath," Rodríguez Alemán cheered.[123]

Even as Mario Rodríguez Alemán wrote these lines in *Mañana* in October 1953 (and when *Cinema* reprinted them in January 1954), his brother, Eduardo, was in prison for participating in the Moncada assault, a clear case of David against Goliath in many Cubans' minds. Shortly thereafter, Mario himself was put in charge of printing underground pamphlets of Castro's famous courtroom speech, "History Will Absolve Me," in which Castro condemns Batista, political corruption, and socioeconomic inequality in Cuba; links these problems to the abuses of US corporations operating on the island; argues for the legitimacy of armed revolt against the dictator; and even implores Cuban soldiers to mutiny.[124]

It was in this context that United Artists' re-released Chaplin's *The Great Dictator* in Havana in January 1954, and that Rodríguez Alemán, and other Havana critics, re-viewed it. As had *Cinema* during World War II, Rodríguez Alemán in *Mañana* reprinted large portions of the Jewish Barber's final speech, this time asserting them in (implicit) defense of the *moncadistas*, perhaps even in defense of Castro's defense. He writes,

> He who studies *The Great Dictator* closely will find in Chaplin a capable defender of liberty. . . . He says, "Soldiers! Don't give yourselves to brutes, to men who despise you, enslave you . . . He adds: "You are not machines! You are men! You have the love of Humanity in your hearts!" . . . And to the people he says, "You, the people, have the power to make this life free and happy. . . . Then, let's use this power, let us all unite."[125]

Here it seems the young critic, Mario, fancies himself wielding his pen against the regime while his brother, Eduardo, had chosen to wield arms.

Mario Rodríguez Alemán kept up this tactic throughout the *moncadistas*' nineteen-month imprisonment. In a September 1954 review, he translates the protagonist of Walt Disney's *Rob Roy, the Highland Rogue* (1953) into a model for Cuban rebels. He writes, "The great Scottish rebel . . . had the laudable impudence to fight against England and to demand for his people a higher and less abusive type of government. . . . Against base tortures, against all that made Scottish life unbearable then, Rob Roy took up arms. . . . [He] was made into such a terrible warrior that the King of England had to accept him one day in his court and listen to his grievances." In Rodríguez Alemán's description here, Rob Roy sounds a lot like the young Castro in Batista's courtroom, "representing [not only himself but] a national spirit of great significance."[126]

Eduardo and the other *moncadistas* were released in May 1955, but Mario's job was not done. He continued to use his film column to celebrate armed revolt and sometimes even explicitly to denounce Batista's rule.[127] And he continued to commend Hollywood films that, according to him, "reaffirm ideas about liberty" and "the act of liberation," with "vital men" in "heroic rebellion against their oppressors."[128] In 1957, as Cubans grew increasingly angry about US arms shipments to Batista, Rodríguez Alemán also used Hollywood war films to criticize the US's cold war militarism, its constant "experimenting with the most brutal of weapons."[129] In other words, Rodríguez Alemán used Hollywood films toward the very counterhegemonic interpretations about which OIAA representatives had worried.

Guillermo Cabrera Infante was another onetime student of Valdés-Rodríguez's who used film criticism to promote the insurrection (though he would later disagree with the Revolution's directions and leave the island in the mid-1960s). As a boy, Cabrera Infante spent as much time as he could in Havana cines, utterly obsessed with Hollywood movies, according to his own diagnosis. In 1948, he won a scholarship to Valdés-Rodríguez's film course. That same summer, he and some of his peers from the course cofounded the Cine-Club de La Habana, setting out to project European and art cinema. In 1951, encouraged by Valdés-Rodríguez, he also cofounded the cultural society Nuestro Tiempo (into which the Cine-Club de La Habana's functions were folded) and the Cinemateca de Cuba—a film library devoted to acquiring and projecting the masterworks of international cinema. Though the Cinemateca dissolved in 1956, it held important retrospectives in the early 1950s, including of US noirs. From 1954 to 1960, Cabrera Infante also served as *Carteles*'s film critic, using the pseudonym G. Caín. Eventually, his film reviews caught the Batista regime's attention, which began to censor his column in 1958.[130] In one example of the sort of writing that irked the regime, Cabrera Infante used a June 1957 review of the Italian film *Anni facili* (1953) to compare Batista to Mussolini and to write that "good people always oppose dictators, now as in the time of the Caesars."[131]

Like his colleagues, Cabrera Infante avidly promoted European cinema. However, as a longtime devotee of Hollywood, Cabrera Infante also maintained his connoisseurship of certain US-made films. In February 1958, much to Cabrera Infante's delight, a Havana cine re-released (the recently exiled) Jules Dassin's *Brute Force* (1947), another Hollywood Left film about a justified prison revolt, this one starring Burt Lancaster. Cabrera Infante's review became an occasion to recall the "vanishing" Hollywood Left, lament its artists' treatment by HUAC, and criticize the suppression of civil liberties in the United States generally. Cabrera Infante also used it to offer coded comparisons between Batista and *Brute Force*'s tyrannical "powers that be," including its "reactionary warden." The "savage, cold-blooded, inhumane punishment" practiced by prison guards "becomes the policy of the prison. That is: the nation," for which the film's prison serves as an "allegory," according to Cabrera Infante. And if the allegory's applicability to Cuba is unclear, Cabrera Infante writes of the prison, "what is it: an island?" He then writes that the film's prison warden is symbolic of "Nazism, fascism, or whatever it may be called in any country that may suffer from this pseudo-philosophy of brutal force and terror." Under such force, it is to be expected that heroes—like Lancaster's character—will be driven to violent revolt by their "dynamic despair."[132]

Seven months later, in August 1958, Cabrera Infante again risked the regime's ire in his review of *Touch of Evil*, directed by Orson Welles, who was another Hollywood Left filmmaker and wartime Pan-Americanist.[133] Often described as the last classical noir, *Touch of Evil* is the story of a corrupt policeman, Captain Hank Quinlan (played by Welles), and his authoritarian reign of injustice, which includes planting evidence to inculpate innocent suspects (a common accusation against the Batista regime). Cabrera Infante's laudatory review highlights the film's denunciation of a "police state" in which policemen become "judge, jury and executioner all at once." The moral of the story is that "'absolute power corrupts absolutely,'" the critic writes, but the people's "struggle for decency and justice" will prevail. Written in the Cuban insurrection's final months, the subtext of this review seems unsubtle indeed.[134]

Cabrera Infante also used his film column to denounce abusive *colonial* power and to cheer the rise of decolonization globally and, in doing so, to critique (implicitly) US imperialism. His review of MGM's *Something of Value* (1957) about British colonial Kenya becomes an opportunity to explicate "the imperialist problem." He describes the history of Africa's colonization by the British, its effect of establishing "a system of exploitation of the natives," and the righteousness of revolt against it. Cabrera Infante explicitly compares the "rebel uprising" of Kenyan anticolonialists to the Boston Tea Party, and implicitly to the Cuban rebel movement and its growing anti-imperialism. Cabrera Infante ends his review by giving the film's Kenyan rebel leader the last word and then translates it into the Latin American context: "'The whole colored world burns with the fever of revolt, with fire for freedom.' This means Africa. But it also means Asia, Oceania and, above all, America."[135] And, in the Americas, as Cubans well knew, the imperial power in question was the United States.

"Rooting through the Fetid Entrails": Mainstream Critics and the American Way

That is why the imperative that Cubans know "the truth about the United States," as Martí put it, continued to preoccupy Havana film critics. And toward highlighting US "entrails," Hollywood dramas set in New York City continued to be particularly useful. For instance, Rodríguez Alemán recommended MGM's *Executive Suite* (1954), a film that he praised for leaving "Wall Street exposed" and for spotlighting the "human and social consequences" of US corporate culture, which encouraged men to "sell their souls" in the name of "ambition and greed."[136] Perhaps even more revealing, and therefore useful, was *The Bachelor Party*, a dark drama about five Manhattan office employees and their financial and psychological woes.[137] *Cinema* featured *The Bachelor*

Party on its cover and United Artists held a special screening for critics, including Valdés-Rodríguez, Rodríguez Alemán, and Piñera, whose high praise helped to make it a box office hit.[138] Piñera deemed it "a devastating testimony" of life in the United States that "parades before us the common man's profound disappointment today, his essential bankruptcy of moral values and his spiritual disorientation." It "is a series of slaps on the conscience of the spectator," showing us these men's "doubts and frustrations . . . faced with limited salaries and a bureaucratic, mechanized, circumscribed life." Likewise, Cabrera Infante praised *The Bachelor Party* for its "importance as a social document." It reveals "the daily agony of strained budgets," "poverty and misery," and "the nightmare that lurks behind every dream" in modern cities, offering "a minute description of the ugly side" of US corporate culture, particularly its emasculation of white-collar workers.[139] In a succinct description of the usefulness of such socially critical Hollywood films to Cuban critics, Rodríguez Alemán proclaimed *The Bachelor Party* a film of "an essentially nationalist character, but of a denunciating and critical nationalism."

Havana critics' appropriation of one last film set in Manhattan illustrates the way that Hollywood content—in addition to its giro business practices—confirmed Cubans' disillusionment with the American Dream. The film in question is *Sweet Smell of Success*, a noir written by famed leftist playwright Clifford Odets. Cabrera Infante writes in April 1958 that *Sweet Smell of Success* is "very illuminating at its rotten core," as it follows its characters "rooting through the fetid entrails" of the New York theater world. Writing just weeks after Paramount had closed its Havana office and refused to pay severance packages, Cabrera Infante finds that *Sweet Smell of Success* confirms the degradation of humanity within US show business practices and the capitalist rat race more generally. According to the critic, the film condemns "men's deadly race in search of success, like mad greyhounds after an elusive [and] fickle golden hare." It follows "the little machinations and great treacheries of [its protagonist, Sidney Falco] to get up the steep ladder of success. He lies, steals, flatters, corrupts, creeps and crawls to try to get ahead." It shows the depths to which Falco (Tony Curtis), a young publicity agent, is willing to sink to become a "self-made man" [given in English]. Falco "stoops in order to rise," Cabrera Infante writes. Most damning is Falco's prostration before the "megalomaniac" gossip columnist J. J. Hunsecker (Burt Lancaster)—whom Cabrera Infante deems a "fascist"—to secure positive reviews for his clients. In Cabrera Infante's review, Hunsecker sounds not unlike Batista for his "reactionary stance and fake patriotism," his use of the "corrupt police" to terrorize his opponents, and his anticommunist red-baiting to defame them. "Absolute power corrupts absolutely," the critic admonishes once again.[140]

Havana critics also embraced Robert Aldrich's *The Big Knife*, another noir about the ugly side of US show business, this time set in Hollywood. Adapted from a Clifford Odets play, *The Big Knife* offers a scathing rebuke of the dehumanizing effects of the studio system through the rise and fall of an A-list actor, Charlie Castle (Jack Palance), and the tyranny of studio boss Stanley Hoff (Rod Steiger), who cares only about the bottom line and is willing to sacrifice his actors' souls (and lives) to make money. Hoff and Castle's own agent bully and blackmail their big star into locking himself into another seven-year studio contract. Based loosely on the life of John Garfield, as at least one Havana critic pointed out, *The Big Knife* suggests that the beleaguered, alcoholic, and ultimately suicidal Charlie Castle is haunted by his sense of having sold out, not least of all in having abandoned his Hollywood Left roots.[141] He had come to the film industry idealistically espousing political and artistic populism, but has devolved into a maker of commercial slop, estranged from the few artists still creating worthwhile films: "Kazan, Huston, Wyler, Wilder, Stanley Kramer," *The Big Knife* argues, in a list with which Havana critics would have agreed.[142] Cabrera Infante praises the film's penetrating critique of Hollywood's profit-driven "psyche" and its corrosive effects on humanity and art, as most artists who want to succeed are forced to "renounce [their] ideals in exchange for deals." *The Big Knife* shows that Hollywood is a "hell" that "deforms the nature of those who serve it, as if a machine twisting its key screw."[143]

But perhaps the most widely praised Hollywood film about corrupt US show business practices was Kazan's aforementioned *A Face in the Crowd*, which debuted in Havana early in 1958. Valdés-Rodríguez writes that *A Face in the Crowd* "is not the first time that the North American cinema has denounced failings within institutions, customs, and even within the very nation, but rarely has it gone so deeply and clearly into an evil, so unequivocally." Valdés-Rodríguez describes Lonesome Rhodes's ascent to TV stardom, aided by "unscrupulous" promoters and "commercial firms" who together hypnotize a public that is "unprepared to defend themselves from such influences." Valdés-Rodríguez declares the film an "invective directed against the misuse of the great mediums of information" and against overly credulous, even naïve audiences unschooled in the sort of critical spectatorship to which the critic had devoted his life.[144]

In Cabrera Infante's review of *A Face in the Crowd*, which he entitled "The Demagogue," he interprets the film as an "indictment" of demagoguery that spoke directly to the Cuban context. Cabrera Infante describes Rhodes as a "nobody transformed into a dictator of public opinion" who can handpick "political candidates." Seeming to leave the film well behind him, Cabrera

Infante decries despotic rulers who claim the right to decide who has "the right to life, work and freedom and who deserves calumny, prison and scorn." The United States tends toward this "American fascism," Cabrera Infante argues, listing as examples Joseph McCarthy, Huey Long, and William Randolph Hearst. The critic then reminds the reader that this critique of US demagoguery is also found in Welles's *Citizen Kane*, which is, in Cabrera Infante's summation, the story of the "*homo americanus*," "the powerful lord, smiling with a knife under his capitalist cloak, . . . champion of right-wing causes and imperialism." Finally, Cabrera Infante uses *A Face in the Crowd* to reiterate the film's rejection of such demagogues and their self-serving argument that the weak-minded masses require an "iron-fisted leader."[145]

Rodríguez Alemán also appropriated *A Face in the Crowd* into the context of the *batistato*. He declared it "daring and honest"; "a tenacious denunciation" of a gullible public; and "a piercing study of a demagogue, his public posturing and his 'inside.'" The film is "not only about a man capable of dragging the multitudes behind him, but also about a society that blindly trusts this man . . . and votes for the candidate that he supports." This last line suggests an analogy to Batista's handpicked presidential candidates throughout the 1930s and, more recently, a sham of a Cuban election held in 1954 designed to legitimize Batista's rule, as well as an election he was promising to hold in 1958. Rodríguez Alemán argues that *A Face in the Crowd* should be seen for its "message of great social import and its useful political sense."[146]

Pressing Matters: Film Criticism in the Radical Press during the Batistato

For the half year that *Hoy* remained open after Batista's coup, Aguirre continued to use her film reviews in its pages much as she had during the Auténtico years. For instance, she used Kazan's *Viva Zapata!*—to which she devoted three full days of her column—to extrapolate from it a prorevolutionary message while also correcting its historical inaccuracies, particularly its "distorting and deceptive" representation of the United States as a "pure, noble and disinterested" model of democracy that inspired Mexican revolutionaries.[147] In her reviews generally, Aguirre continued to teach her readers how to "read between the lines" when watching Hollywood films, a habit which was "useful in a political sense," she explained.[148] She continued to debunk films that "sing of Yankee 'superiorities,'" perpetuate racism, or celebrate the United States' role as "the world's policeman," which had led repeatedly to "Yankee occupation of our country," she reminded her readers.[149] She continued to recommend US noirs, from which "the fetid North American social atmosphere can't help but pop out here and there."[150] And she continued to denounce what she considered antirevolutionary films. For instance, three months after Batista's coup, she argued that MGM's *The Sellout*—about a corrupt sheriff who coerces and terrifies citizens into submission—was designed "to show the public the infinite quantity of problems . . . that befall people who, instead of staying quiet in their homes, leaving the world to turn, make an effort to set it right." Movies, she wrote, should instead "be directed toward encouraging the public to choose to fight against the banditry prevailing in official spheres."[151] In fact, it was critical rabble-rousing like this that prompted Batista to shutter *Hoy* for good in the fall of 1952. By then, Aguirre's tolerance for watching bad Hollywood films was exhausted.[152] Thus, when she moved over to the new communist newspaper, *La Última Hora* [The Final Hour], Aguirre was happy to cede the role of film critic to her colleague José Massip, the Harvard-educated son of Ortodoxo activists who also happened to attend Valdés-Rodríguez's summer course in 1949, through which the young Massip was integrated into the cross-referencing intellectual network under consideration here.[153]

As film critic for *La Última Hora*, Massip set out to "weaken Hollywood's ideological influence in our country" not least of all by promoting European neorealist cinema as an "antidote." European films were "bombshell[s]," while Hollywood films were "molasses cand[ies]" inuring spectators with their gummy sweetness. Most Hollywood films should "get on the nerves of the spectator with even a rudimentary sensibility," said Massip.[154] Hoping to grow and gird that category of more critical spectators, Massip endeavored to teach his readers to see Hollywood's shameless commercialism and its mind-numbingly predictable formulas, which proved that the United States was "a society where the conditions of life . . . practically annul the possibilities of cultural and intellectual development." Hollywood was particularly despicable now that "the fascist purging perpetuated by [HUAC] . . . has degraded Hollywood even more, artistically and morally, and has left talented screenwriters and directors without work or in prison."[155] He prods his reader to see Hollywood's obfuscation of class conflict; its disdain for nonwhite peoples; and the imperialist ideology foisted by "the concept of the Yankee superman" who sweeps into all corners of the globe to rescue lesser peoples "*tarzanacamente*," he writes in a sarcastic Cubanization of Tarzan.[156]

In this, Massip builds upon what he saw as Cubans' own rebellious instincts as unruly spectators. In his March 1953 review of Paramount's *Thunder in the East*, he writes about a fellow moviegoer who yelled at the screen, "my neighbor in the half-light of the cinema [who] was strident in his loquacity." Massip is thrilled that this "wise" moviegoer vociferously rejected so much about *Thunder in the East*, set in India shortly after independence in 1947, in which a mercenary American gunrunner (Alan Ladd) rides in to save remaining British ex-pats (and moderate Indians) from militant Indian rebels.[157] Regarding the Yankee superman cliché, Massip writes that his fellow moviegoer's "description of Alan Ladd cannot be improved upon: 'This guy is an American asshole.'" Massip then prods his reader to better understand what bothered his fellow moviegoer instinctually: that the film soft-pedals not just British colonialism but also "North American imperialism" and that it vilifies those "patriots that fight against the colonial yoke."[158]

It is only the rare Hollywood film, then, that Massip recommends. For instance, he praises *Death of a Salesman*, *Detective Story*, and *Come Back, Little Sheba* for daring to explore "the frustration of the North American middle class," and its members' inability to "understand and control their destiny." Massip writes that even though these films fail to "signal the objective social causes of that frustration," they do at least reveal that "the rosy North American paradise [is] out of order."[159] Such socially critical films, though falling short of the radical conclusions Massip would have preferred, were "sufficient to make naïve people, who have believed the tall tales about the ideal conditions of life in the United States, think for a good while," he writes prescriptively.[160]

Like its predecessor *Hoy*, *La Última Hora's* offices were closed by Batista's regime in the summer of 1953. By then, Massip was already serving as president of the Cinema Section of the radical cultural society Nuestro Tiempo, which he had cofounded in 1951 with Cabrera Infante, (M267 *llano* leader) Franqui, and Gutiérrez Alea, among others. This cultural society, and its monthly publication of the same name, set out to fashion a radical cultural consciousness among a wide public that would lead to sociopolitical transformations. In this, its members were cognizant of inheriting the mission and methods of the minoristas, continuing "the journey that we must complete in our time [*nuestro tiempo*]," they noted.[161] Nuestro Tiempo's membership became a who's who of Cuba's intellectual and artistic elite, including, in its Cinema Section (in addition to the founders listed above), Aguirre, Julio García Espinosa, and Rodríguez Alemán.[162] Among Nuestro Tiempo's five hundred members, only a small minority knew of the cultural society's affiliation with the PSP, though the majority of them voted repeatedly to defend Cuban communists against Batista's repression.[163] Many Nuestro Tiempo members were tortured, imprisoned, and/or exiled for their anti-Batista activism through the society and its publication, including Massip, who was arrested more than once.[164] Yet *Nuestro Tiempo* was published without interruption from April 1954 until August 1959, not least of all because it was publicly supported by prominent intellectuals and journalists, including Ichaso, Mañach, Marinello, Perdices, Roa, and Valdés-Rodríguez, who jumped to *Nuestro Tiempo*'s defense whenever its critiques of Batista brought the wrath of the regime upon it.[165]

As president of the society's Cinema Section, Massip had many responsibilities. He polled members to compile the society's annual top ten film lists (dominated by European cinema, as were the lists of the ARTYC and FRCT); cosponsored panels with the ARTYC and various emerging cine clubs; and arranged the society's monthly film screenings, which essentially operated as a cine club. Valdés-Rodríguez's Cinema Department cosponsored some of these screenings, which took place in the Varona Amphitheater, while others were held in the new 450-seat Cine Capri and later in the 800-seat Cine Neptuno, in order to accommodate growing numbers.[166] Nuestro Tiempo's screenings favored European neorealism, but they also showed Hollywood Left films, for example, exiled filmmaker Edward Dymtyrk's grim tale of working-class exploitation and misery set in New York City tenements, *Give Us This Day* (1949).[167] Along with numerous Chaplin cycles, Nuestro Tiempo also screened *The Asphalt Jungle*, *The Big Knife*, *Blockade*, *Death of a Salesman*, and *Sunset Boulevard* (to name a representative few), using copies rented to them by the US studios' offices.[168]

Finally, Massip wrote reviews for *Nuestro Tiempo*, and commissioned his fellow Cinema Section members to do the same. Together, they recommended only those Hollywood films that showed uglier truths about the American Way, including Kazan's *On the Waterfront*, *Baby Doll*, and *A Face in the Crowd*, as well as *The Bachelor Party*, *The Big Knife*, *Blackboard Jungle*, *The Defiant Ones*, and *The Harder They Fall*. Such films offered "a crack from where to scrutinize aspect[s] of North American society," writes Massip. In the case of *Baby Doll*, this crack allowed a glimpse at "the [racist] deep South," giving Massip a chance to remind his reader of Emmett Till's assassination in Mississippi in 1955. "Seek and find what there is in *Baby Doll*," writes Massip in direct address, emphasizing that Cuban spectatorship should be an act, in an active and almost anthropological sense, of scrutinizing US society.[169] Following this line, other *Nuestro Tiempo* critics prompted Cubans to *see* "[North Americans] devoured by their struggle to attain the basic necessities of existence"; "the absurdity of racial discrimination"; and US businessmen "disposed to use whatever method necessary to make profits, including blackmail, violence and [association with] professional gangsters."[170] In the Hollywood Left's critiques of the US film industry itself, as in *The Big Knife* and *Sunset Boulevard*, *Nuestro Tiempo*'s critics encouraged Cubans to *see* "the degradation of film art" by "vacuity, mediocrity and a small-minded world fallen to its knees before the altar of money."[171]

Like his colleagues past and present, Massip held up Chaplin as the Hollywood Left's most exceptional filmmaker. When *Nuestro Tiempo* rescreened *Modern Times* in 1956, Massip proclaimed it to be the film that transformed Chaplin into the profound social critic "who would become the object of a fierce persecution" by US conservatives. It was in *Modern Times*, which Massip proclaimed "a critique of our contemporary society," that the Little Tramp became less a clown and more "Charlot the common man, a hero in a hostile environment." Massip specifically recalls to his readers' minds the feeding machine sequence, with the Little Tramp "trapped in the intricate machinery [that] thrusts lunch at his mouth through the most ludicrous processes." This is hilarious slapstick, Massip concedes, but even a little bit of analysis "makes *us* understand that the scene [is] part of *Modern Times'* powerful sociopolitical satire. Let's not forget that this scene ends abruptly with the workers declaring a strike," writes Massip, mischaracterizing the plot to argue that Chaplin is not just criticizing but also suggesting that action should be taken.[172]

Though Chaplin belonged in a category unto himself, Elia Kazan was another favorite of *Nuestro Tiempo*'s cinephiles. *A Face in the Crowd* was one of only two Hollywood films, along with *The Defiant Ones*, to make the society's top ten film list for 1958, and García Espinosa reviewed it glowingly in *Nuestro Tiempo*. With *A Face in the Crowd*, he writes, Kazan "has been able to penetrate with great insight and profundity into the complicated and dense labyrinth that is his country's reality." As in the case of his colleagues' reviews elsewhere, however, García Espinosa's review seems to be as much about contemporary Cuba's "reality" as is it is about the United States'. Directly addressing the Cuban reader, he writes, "Ask yourself: 'What does Kazan tell us in his latest movie?' He shows *us* how an ignorant *campesino*, thanks to his powerful personal magnetism, can transform himself overnight into a true monster of popularity before a naïve public. . . . The movie seems to want to say to this naïve and hysterical public . . . 'Distrust your idols. Without you realizing, they are making you into their idiots.'"[173] Indigenizing the film, García Espinosa manages to turn *A Face in the Crowd* into a critique not only of US society but also of Batista *and* of uncritical media consumption in Cuba.

Nuestro Tiempo also recommended Kazan's *On the Waterfront* and made use of it within the local context. In his January 1955 review, Gutiérrez Alea praised highly its truthful exposé of corrupt unions and exploited workers in the United States. But his review also became an opportunity to reject *On the Waterfront*'s "dangerous generalization" that "the workers submit passively to this situation since the only one capable of reacting and fighting against [the union boss] is the [film's] priest." This generalization of labor's passive submission was one that revolutionary activists could not countenance, as M267 *llano* activists worked to incorporate the labor movement into the insurrection. Thus, Gutiérrez Alea redirected *On the Waterfront* from a potential source of defeatism into a message promoting working-class activism against Batista.[174]

For the most part, though, *Nuestro Tiempo*'s critics denounced Hollywood as banal and imperialistic, its stupefactions to be resisted. For instance, Massip joined the chorus of protest against Warner Bros.' *Santiago*, which (despite those protests) premiered in Havana in December 1956. Massip writes in *Nuestro Tiempo* that *Santiago* was "an offense to our national dignity." While the film's historical inaccuracies were despicable, worse yet was "the mentality [the film] wants to engender," modeling Cuban prostration before the "*made in Hollywood* North American 'superman,'" compared to whom "the nation's [Cuba's] great heroes are mere pygmies" or "subheroes." According to Massip, *Santiago* repeatedly portrays *Cuban mambises* passively accepting insults: US "gangster" gunrunners call them "the scum, the thieves and the pickpockets of Havana and Santiago," without provoking a response. Even (the "caricature" of) Martí is "submissive, servile," doing nothing to protest the North Americans when they insult Martí himself, his soldiers, and the Cuban women who are vulgarly eroticized in the film. As such, *Santiago* reiterates Hollywood's "pernicious" tendency to look down on other peoples and encourages them to accept their own denigration. Outraged, Massip concludes that "two roads remain to us: we can receive these insults with the submissive resignation of the Cuban 'patriots' of the film or we can do what these patriots really would have done if some petty thief had dared to raise their hand against him."[175] For *Nuestro Tiempo*'s reader, the choice, by then, was an obvious one.

"Another Form of Fighting": Havana's Cine-Club Movement

Following the examples of Valdés-Rodríguez's Cine de Arte sessions, the Cine-Club de La Habana, and the Cinemateca's and Nuestro Tiempo's screenings, Havana youth began forming neighborhood cine clubs in 1953. Among them were the Cine-Club Católico, which held screenings at the 500-seat Cine Duplex in Central Havana, and the Cine-Club Lumière, which held screenings at the 900-seat Cine Alba in Marianao. Nuestro Tiempo and Valdés-Rodríguez eagerly promoted these cine clubs as broadening the more critical and active civic sphere they sought to create.[176] In December 1956, as the invited speaker at a Havana suburb's small university's new cinema department and its cine club, Valdés-Rodríguez recalled his own history of working to bring higher forms of cinema, spectatorship, and citizenship to Cuba and praised this new generation for doing the same with its cine-club movement, even in this "period of violence in which we find ourselves" provoked by "the frustration of the *mambí* ideal." Valdés-Rodríguez's own generation, he recalled, had "also hoped that, sooner or later, a new republican era rectified of painful defects would begin."[177]

The largest of these cine clubs was Cine-Club Visión, begun by youth in the working-class barrio of Santos Suarez in 1956, with the help of some Nuestro Tiempo emissaries, including Gutiérrez Alea and Alfredo Guevara. Among Cine-Club Visión's founders were a number of youth who would become filmmakers after 1958, including Nelson Rodríguez, who was the youngest at age fifteen. At the time, Rodríguez had just graduated from Valdés-Rodríguez's summer course and set out consciously to share what he had learned with his neighborhood. He and his peers went from door to door to sell tickets to the Cine-Club Visión's first function, collecting enough money to rent their 1,300-seat neighborhood cine, the Apolo, as well as a couple of movies from giro distributors. They thought hard about what films to show, finally agreeing on *Umberto D.*, an Italian neorealist film about the poverty and suicidal desperation of a retired worker. Rodríguez remembers their logic in this choice: "That's what moved us: films that critiqued social problems [would] help open the eyes of the people to a reality very similar to ours, [and would suggest] that society had to change in some way." In other words, their titular "Visión" was related to the minoristas' and subsequent Havana critics' ideas about 'teaching eyes to see.' But Rodríguez also recalls that he lobbied for balance in the cine club's first program. He argued that they needed to offer spectators something cheerful to offset the grimness of *Umberto D.* So, they picked *Tonight and Every Night*, a 1945 Columbia Pictures musical starring Rita Hayworth about a theater troupe during the bombing of London.[178]

Despite (or because of) this incongruent double billing, Cine-Club Visión's first event was a great success. Thereafter, their monthly screenings continued to pair a European or Latin American neorealist film with a Hollywood film, though they became more selective about the latter, following the critical predilections of the day. Among their selections were Kazan's *A Streetcar Named Desire*, *On the Waterfront*, and *East of Eden*; as one Cine-Club Visión member recalled, they had "great respect for Elia Kazan as an artist."[179] They also included Stanley Kubrick's *Paths of Glory* and his noir *The Killing*; Welles's *Touch of Evil* and *Mr. Arkadin*; as well as *The Bachelor Party*, *The Big Knife*, *Blackboard Jungle*, *The Defiant Ones*, *A Face in the Crowd*, *Rebel without a Cause*, and *Sweet Smell of Success*.[180]

Postscreening debates led by Cine-Club Visión members often turned into discussions about the need for social change in Cuba and even, in guarded language, support for the insurrection. However, fear of infiltration by *chivatos* (informers) meant such discussions were characterized by discretion and coded subtext. Since 1959, its members have retrospectively described the Cine-Club Visión's political orientation as Marxist; but, if this was the case, very few who attended its screenings knew it. As Rodríguez recalls, some members and attendees were more conscious of "the club as a form of political action" than others. The postscreening debates, in fact, became a way for more radical members to vet others who might be of the same mind. Cine-Club Visión member Manuel Pérez remembers being so designated and eventually invited into a smaller subset of the cine club, which met to discuss the insurrection in each other's apartments. Having come to trust each other in this smaller group, some went on to collaborate on clandestine operations, such as collecting funds for the M267.[181] This development—of a cine club spinning off an insurrectionary cell—seems a fitting culmination, indeed, to decades of Havana intellectuals fomenting critical film spectatorship toward the construction and mobilization of revolutionary Cuban nationalism.

Conclusion

Batista fled Cuba on January 1, 1959. (Hollywood gangster George Raft was right behind him; rebel soldiers at the airport asked for Raft's autograph *and* ripped open the lining of his suitcase to ensure he was not absconding with ill-begotten funds.)[182] Batista's departure set off a jubilation that lasted at least through January 8, when Castro and his rebel compatriots rolled into Havana, with US and Cuban newsreel crews capturing their heroes' welcome. But habaneros did not have to see these images projected onscreen to recognize the spectacle as an eminently cinematic one: the freedom-fighting good guys had overcome great odds to best the tyrannical villain. The Hollywood culture that was such a pervasive part of habaneros' everyday lives had prepared Cubans to see, and celebrate, the scene in this way. To Cuban audiences in early 1959, the tall, articulate, idealistic, and virile Fidel Castro might have seemed like a Cuban amalgamation of Jimmy Stewart in *Mr. Smith Goes to Washington*, Errol Flynn in *Robin Hood*, Charlie Chaplin in *The Great Dictator*, Gary Cooper in *For Whom the Bell Tolls*, John Garfield in *We Were Strangers*, and Marlon Brando in *Viva Zapata!* and *On the Waterfront*. (Corroborating this latter analogy, *Waterfront* scenarist Budd Schulberg arrived in Havana in January to write a profile of Castro for *True Magazine*.)[183] Recognizing a freedom fight in its own image, Hollywood rushed to put together scripts about the dramatic Cuban insurrection and its dashing leader; among the producers vying to make such a bankable hit were Jerry Wald (at Fox) and Sam Spiegel, independent producer of *We Were Strangers* and *On the Waterfront*. *Film Daily Yearbook*'s Cuba summary of 1959 cheered, "Cuba is a small but modern and freedom loving nation that will not tolerate tyranny, as proved by the success of the poorly armed rebels commanded by Dr. Fidel Castro."[184]

But the freedom-fighting insurrection of the 1950s, just like that of the 1930s, had not just taken aim at the nation's strongman. Cubans were mobilized for fundamental changes in Cuban politics, society, and culture, not least of all in their relation to US imperial hegemony. In the coming months and years, many middle-class and elite Cubans would come to disagree with Castro's Revolutionary Government, not least with its total break with the United States. However, during the mid- to late 1950s, many Cubans—including those working in the Havana film giro—had reason to agree with the revolutionary movement's growing anti-imperialism. As I have argued throughout *Hollywood in Havana*, US films and Hollywood business practices were used to strengthen the public perception that the so-called American Way, though admirable in its ideals, was bad for Cuba and Cubans in its real practices. For decades, Havana film writers had elaborated Martí's practice of critically examining the "entrails" of US society and US imperialism's negative effects in Latin America generally and Cuba specifically. While Martí made his observations while living in exile in the United States at the end of the nineteenth century, Havana film writers and moviegoers of the twentieth century had assessed US society and US global expansionism without having to travel more than a few blocks to the nearest cine, while Cubans working in the film giro had done the same in Havana office spaces. In these cines and office spaces, Cuban ambivalence about the American Way was fostered by the United States' own cinematic self-representations, by Hollywood business practices, and by Cubans' particular ways of seeing and interacting with them.

Havana film writers served as more than just arbiters of cultural taste; they were intentional political actors. In so many of their columns, teaching Cubans how to interpret a movie, or even how to understand a development in the film giro, was really about teaching Cubans how to interpret the national condition. Cuban intellectuals working as film critics endeavored to create a national interpretive community that not only saw films but also Cuban politics and US-Cuban relations the ways they did. And Havana film writers sometimes even rallied Cuban spectators-cum-citizens to *act* on those shared visions. This is not to say that Havana film writers or cine clubs singlehandedly mobilized Cubans for the 1950s insurrection. Rather *Hollywood in Havana* begins to demonstrate, in concrete ways, that revolutionary sentiment in Cuba was *not* just "in the air" or something born inevitably of the contradictions of capital. Even less so was it born of one man, namely Castro, which is a crucial insight as that one man exits the stage of Cuban history. Rather, revolutionary Cuban nationalism was nurtured through decades of intellectual intervention in Cuba's everyday cultural fabric, woven through as it was with Hollywood influences.

Havana's spectator-citizens did experience "Americanization," but in a way far more complex than that term generally conveys. The term is usually used to connote the inculcation of desire for US products, and with it, consumerist sensibilities and capitalist ideology. But, in Havana—and surely elsewhere around the globe—that Americanization also inculcated desires, expectations, and even demands (backed by arms) for economic opportunity, political liberties, racial equality, and true national sovereignty. In the context of the Americas, the term (in its most idealistic iterations) even connotes a shared tradition of anti-authoritarian, pro-independence freedom fighting. In other words, Americanization can run directly counter to US policy and US corporations that have contravened sovereign nations (economically, politically, and militarily) and supported repressive dictatorships throughout Latin America and the world. Further, Americanization is not unidirectional or homogenous, emanating from a consistent set of directives issued in Washington; rather, "US influence" comes at least as much from exported popular culture as it does from state policy. Nor is it passively received. Whether or not critiques of the so-called American Way are "coded" into US media texts at the point of production, consumers and critics abroad are able to "decode" them to counterhegemonic purposes within local contexts, actively reshaping Americanization to their own ends.

In terms of US-Cuban relations specifically, such a rethinking of Americanization allows us to move beyond cold war formulations in which the Cuban Revolution is figured as a rejection of all things (North) American. *Hollywood in Havana* argues that the Cuban Revolution's fervent anti-imperialist *independentismo* was not a simple reaction against the US embassy or US corporations on the island, but rather an embrace of the United States' own ambivalent self-imaginings. Perhaps more than a rejection of all things (North) American, Revolutionary Cuba—at least in its infancy—was a refracted reflection of the United States' own conflicted self, a self whose idealism *and* critical introspection were projected on a daily basis for decades on Cuban movie screens. This brings us back to the photograph of Castro standing before the Lincoln Memorial with which we began. To the reader of *Hollywood in Havana* it should now make all the sense in the world that Cuban revolutionaries in 1959 would quote José Martí *and* Frank Capra in the same breath, mobilizing revolutionary Cuban nationalism through a particular practice of looking up at the American Way developed for more than half a century.

EPILOGUE

The Show Goes On: Hollywood in Havana after 1958

> I already paid for my ticket and I want to see how the movie ends.
>
> CUBAN CITIZEN, critical of the Revolution, when asked why he doesn't leave the island, 1999

Summer 1968. A crowd of Havana moviegoers is packed into the 1,400-seat auditorium of the old Cine Atlantic, by then renamed the Cine de Arte ICAIC (later still to be renamed the Cine Charles Chaplin in the 1980s). Onscreen, the Little Tramp is strapped in the feeding machine, hilariously struggling.[1] But this is not yet another rescreening of Chaplin's *Modern Times*, though there would be plenty more of those. Rather, this is the premiere of a Cuban documentary short, *Por primera vez* [For the First Time], about a mobile cinema truck sent by the state-run Cuban Institute of Cinematographic Art and Industry (ICAIC) to introduce the marvels of the cinema to an audience of uninitiated *campesinos* in a remote village in eastern Cuba. *Por primera vez* ends with scenes from the village's screening of *Modern Times*, intercutting shots of Chaplin onscreen with shots of the new spectators' laughing faces, looking up, eyes agleam. Watching *Por primera vez* back in Havana, as if traveling in time to witness their own urban predecessors' first cinematic encounters, Havana spectators are meant to marvel at the deprivations of a precinematic people and to cheer ICAIC for initiating their rural compatriots into modernity through learning how to watch a classic Hollywood movie—*not* some ICAIC propaganda film or socialist bloc feature. Perhaps ICAIC workers had explained to the villagers that their laughter should be followed by a more serious meditation on Chaplin's commentary on US society and capitalist modernity. Even absent such prescriptions, ICAIC's very selection of *Modern Times* reiterated (to the villagers *and* the Havana audience) a critical practice developed over several decades, that of emphasizing progressive Hollywood's social criticisms and its invocations to see and resist un-freedom. Nor was ICAIC's use of mobile cinema something entirely new, but rather it followed the precedent of José Casasús's mule cart at the end of the nineteenth century and the OIAA mobile cinema trucks during World War II. Thus, despite its title, *Por primera vez* captures historical continuity as much as it does a break from the past, contradicting the tendency to think of 1959 as the point of total rupture in Cuban film culture, as in so many things Cuban. Despite the Revolutionary Government's virulent denunciation of all things Yankee, its cultural leaders continued to use US films to construct a national community around particular ways of seeing—and "Cubanizing"—Hollywood into the 1960s and beyond, albeit under significantly altered conditions.

In fact, many of the Havana intellectuals we have been following in the previous pages shaped the Revolutionary Government's film policy. In 1960, Valdés-Rodríguez re-initiated his summer course and his Cine de Arte sessions at the reopened University of Havana. For the latter, along with a majority of European films, he selected a handful of old Hollywood films, like Chaplin's *The Gold Rush*, as well as 1950s Hollywood noirs.[2] He also continued to write reviews for *El Mundo* (state-run after 1960), until he retired in 1965. In April 1971, the University of Havana and ICAIC held a celebration at the Varona Amphitheater of Valdés-Rodríguez's long and illustrious career, just six months before his death. Raúl Roa, then serving as Castro's foreign minister, delivered the homage, recalling his friend's garage door screenings as the roots of critical film reception in Cuba, pronouncing him a "pioneer" of Cuban film criticism and a true revolutionary for his participation in the movements against Machado and Batista.[3]

By then, a number of Valdés-Rodríguez's ex-students were prominent leaders at ICAIC, including Alfredo Guevara (who served as its first president, 1959–83), Tomás Gutiérrez Alea, Julio García Espinosa, José Massip, Nelson Rodríguez, and Enrique Pineda Barnet, among other veterans of Nuestro Tiempo and the cine-club movement. Founded in March 1959 as the Revolutionary Government's first cultural institution, ICAIC's stated objectives were to elevate Cuban spectatorship and fulfill the dream of a national film production industry. Convinced of the cinema's incomparable power to shape Cuban public opinion, they set out to use it to "make the revolutionary spirit deeper and clearer." To do so, ICAIC's founding document enthused that they would *not* have to forgo the type of action-packed plots and valiant characters they knew Havana's Hollywood-schooled audiences demanded: "Our history, a true epic of liberty since the dawn of the struggle for independence and the formation of a national spirit, represents a great source of themes and heroes capable of being incarnated on the screen."[4] In other words, they recognized that revolutionary Cuban nationalism was eminently cinematic, and in ways that had long been shaped by Hollywood.

At the same time, ICAIC sought to limit Cubans' exposure to Hollywood's worst films. In the fall of 1959, an ICAIC censor board replaced the Comisión Revisora and the Children's Censor Board, and it immediately prohibited a number of films, including Warner Bros.' *Santiago*. Thereafter, the list of outlawed Hollywood films grew, prohibiting especially those deemed to glorify imperialism and/or to encourage racial discrimination.[5] By the end of 1959, rumors circulated that ICAIC would also impose quotas to curtail Hollywood's screen time and would mandate the exhibition of ICAIC-made films. Concerned that this would devastate the film business in Cuba, the Film Giro Syndicate implored ICAIC president "*compañero* [Alfredo] Guevara" to reconsider. Invoking *Cubanidad*, they conceded that a sustained Cuban film production industry was long overdue (given Cubans' great talents), but nonetheless pleaded that limiting Hollywood's market share would do great harm to "8,000 Cuban families who live off of the motion picture activities of the American motion picture distributing companies."[6] For the time being, ICAIC demurred, in concession to the syndicate *and* Havana's Hollywood-addicted public, from whom they feared a less polite reaction.

Still, seeking to lessen Hollywood's influence, ICAIC centralized the efforts of Havana's neighborhood cine clubs into the state-run Cine-Debate-Populares, led by Mario Rodríguez Alemán.[7] Held at various Havana cines (e.g., the old Campoamor and Payret), Cine-Debate-Popular screenings were used to promote ICAIC productions, but other national cinemas were also represented, especially European neorealist and "exceptional" Hollywood films. The latter were usually those same US films that had been shown in the 1950s cine clubs: for example, *The Bachelor Party*, *The Defiant Ones*, *A Face in the Crowd*, *Paths of Glory*, *Sweet Smell of Success*, and *Touch of Evil*. Predictably enough, the Cine-Debate-Populares' printed programs repeatedly invoked Martí's "entrails of the monster" phrase and used words like "accuse," "expose," and "condemn" the US "*way of life*" (written in English) to prescribe particular interpretations.[8]

The ICAIC also rescreened *Viva Zapata!* in one of its Cine-Debate-Popular sessions in October 1960, a pivotal month for Hollywood in Havana and for US-Cuban relations generally. By then, Castro had interpreted his evident popularity as a mandate to consolidate moral authority and power in his person. With revolutionary nationalist fervor running high, he set out to ensure that "his" movement would not be "frustrated" by Cubans less "authentically" revolutionary than he. Among its first acts, the Revolutionary Government decreed rent and utilities reductions, salary increases, and the seizure of properties owned by *batistianos* (onetime allies of the dictator). Officers of Batista's army were tried before revolutionary tribunals; some were executed. In May

1959, just after Castro's US tour, the Agrarian Reform Law nationalized large landholdings, including those held by US citizens and corporations, such as the United Fruit Company. United States' stakeholders were deeply alarmed, but they weren't the only ones. Plenty of Cubans, too, became disenchanted of the Revolution and its top-billed star, who was still at the national narrative's center for them, but transformed from "Fidel-as-hero" to "Fidel-as-villain." Counter-revolutionary plots developed, on the island and among exiles in the United States. (One writer in *Variety* even suggested Castro should watch *We Were Strangers* as "a refresher course" about the sort of conspiracies that might be brewing against him.)[9] In response, Castro doubled down on the Revolution's radical tact, arming civilian-militias to resist counter-revolutionaries and to prepare for an impending US invasion. As moderates fled the government (and the country), Cuban communists grew their power and influence. Anti-Yankee sentiment intensified. To shift away from the island's economic dependence on the United States, the Revolutionary Government sold a large portion of its sugar harvest to the Soviet Union, which US policymakers interpreted as a provocation. A tit-for-tat deterioration of US-Cuban relations followed swiftly, including Cuban expropriation of US properties and, in October 1960, the implementation of the US trade embargo (from which Hollywood films were exempted, because the US State and Commerce Departments still believed in their unique "binding" capacity).[10]

In this context, *Viva Zapata!* was made an endorsement of rigidifying revolutionary intransigence. Its Cine-Debate-Popular program announces, "Zapata was right. Arms had to be left with the *campesinos* not taken from them; the army had to be liquidated; there was no way to try to civilize it, to inculcate in its members a respect for civil power; the *latifundios* had to be cut up and [the revolutionaries] could not expect that capital horded in other lands would submit to a law of reform. . . . Zapata was a *campesino* and he knew that one couldn't compromise." In other words, in Havana in 1960, Brando's Zapata was fully transformed from an anticommunist (Pan-)American Jeffersonian to an anti-imperialist redistributive revolutionary who inspires armed resistance against both local despots *and* US hegemony. Recognizing the paradox of borrowing from a product of US culture to reject the United States' presence in Cuba, the Cine-Debate-Popular program explained that Kazan and Steinbeck were admirable leftists who had been thought "crazy" to make *Viva Zapata!* at the time and that their movie went "as far as possible in a film produced from 'within the entrails of the monster.'"[11] (Interestingly enough, and apropos films' unfixed meanings, in 1963 Steinbeck advocated *Viva Zapata!*'s re-release in the United States in order to "point up the parallel to Cuba," by which he meant the parallel between Castro-as-tyrant and a number of characters in the film: Mexican revolutionaries-turned-despotic strongmen.[12] Perhaps, ICAIC found this latter interpretation too readily apparent: at some point, ICAIC stopped showing *Viva Zapata!* just as it began to exclude *The Great Dictator* from Chaplin retrospectives.)

By that same month, October 1960, the Revolutionary Government had nationalized Cuban television stations.[13] On one of them, Mario Rodríguez Alemán began broadcasting old movies on "*Cine en TV*," a program that would run for nearly two decades. Predictably, Rodríguez Alemán favored European and (increasingly) Soviet-bloc cinema, but he also showed old Hollywood Left films. As Carlos Eire (who would soon leave Cuba) later recalled, he and his friends groaned about Cuban state television's constant replaying of Edward Dmytryk's unrelentingly grim *Give Us This Day*.[14] (Into the twenty-first century, Cuban television programs such as "*24 Veces por Segundo*" and "*La Historia del Cine*" continued to show carefully chosen US films, only after a critic prepared the audience with lengthy prescriptions of how to interpret them. On a research trip in 2004, for instance, I caught MGM's 1954 drama *Executive Suite*.) In that same pivotal month of October 1960, the Revolutionary Government also nationalized Cuban cines, starting with forty-two movie theaters in Havana, and turned their operation over to ICAIC, which began dictating rental terms far less favorable to Hollywood's distribution offices.[15] (Eventually, ICAIC renamed a number of Havana cines: e.g., the Radiocentro became the Yara; the Blanquita became the Karl Marx; and the Atlantic became the Cine de Arte ICAIC.)

By the fall of 1960, the US studios' Havana offices had weathered nearly two years of revolutionary changes. As early as mid-January 1959, they reported that "an extremely nationalistic group of Cuban exhibitors" demanded changes in rental terms, while the Film Giro Syndicate's "radical elements" demanded that all distribution offices' managers and assistant managers had to be Cuban nationals; and the Film Giro Syndicate joined the (now PSP-controlled) CTC's call for 20 percent salary increases for all Cuban workers. Calling these demands an "ambush," the US studios considered themselves lucky to hold the syndicate's gains to 10 to 15 percent raises, given the fate of other US businesses operating in Cuba.[16] At the same time, throughout 1959 and into 1960, the US studios faced substantial new taxes (aka "contributions" to the Revolution); the slowing of remittances to a trickle; the assignment of an ICAIC "supervisor" to each of the Hollywood offices; and even the brief arrest of some of the US managers.[17] Dismayed, the US studios' Havana Film Board complained that they held no sway with "the two Guevaras," meaning "Alfredo" (who was president at ICAIC) and "Che" (who was president at the Banco Nacional de Cuba).[18] Not surprisingly then, most of the Hollywood managers had left or were leaving Cuba by late 1960: Smith (Columbia) retired and moved to Puerto Rico; Colli (Warner Bros.) transferred to Spain; and O'Connor (MGM) resigned.[19] Not far behind them were plenty of Cuban exhibitors and white-collar Cuban employees of the US studios' offices.[20]

The US companies limped along, hoping even to survive the severing of US-Cuban diplomatic relations that came in January 1961, proclaiming it still "too early to tell."[21] But then, in March 1961, the Revolutionary Government froze Hollywood's remittances and stopped payment on existing contracts. In mid-May 1961, just weeks after the US's failed Bay of Pigs invasion, the Revolutionary Government seized the US studios' offices and assets. ICAIC confiscated the film reels in their vaults, and revolutionaries climbed atop the studios' blue casitas in Filmcentro, taking sledgehammers to their trademark signs.[22]

Not that this was the end of Hollywood in Havana, even if it *is* the end of *Hollywood in Havana*. After some initial efforts to wean the Havana public from its Hollywood habit entirely, and to exhibit Soviet bloc cinema in its place, ICAIC quickly gave up, opting instead to control the supply. Cubans still clamored for Hollywood films, so ICAIC borrowed a page from Cine-Club Visión's double-billings: As bait, ICAIC offered an old Hollywood film, e.g., *Robin Hood* (1938) and *How to Marry a Millionaire* (1953), before each socialist bloc film. But Havana audiences simply walked out after the Hollywood film, forcing ICAIC to tweak its tactic: they reversed the order, so that audiences had to sit through the socialist film if they wanted a seat to enjoy the American one.[23]

Indeed, into the twenty-first century, life on the island is still run through with Hollywood influences. Even the existential conundrum to stay or to leave gets expressed in movie terms, as suggested by the expression, "*Voy por* [I'm going to] *la Yuma*" (after the 1957 Hollywood Western *3:10 to Yuma*) and the epigraph above.[24] Even now, when dissident Cuban blogger Yoani Sanchez writes to complain about the inadequacy of the Revolutionary Government's recent opening of "entrepreneurial" opportunities, she invokes Chaplin's Little Tramp as a destitute window repairman in *The Kid* as a common reference point.[25] Cubans continue to watch old and new Hollywood films on state-run television and in old cines, with ICAIC still controlling selections, leaning as ever toward Hollywood films that expose the monster's entrails. In short, ICAIC's policymakers do not seem to fear that Cuban viewers will be "Americanized" in any facile way. Instead, they believe that Cuban viewers, especially with a little guidance, will continue to engage in the multivalent practice of looking up through Hollywood: recognizing structural flaws in the so-called

FIG. E.1. In 2004, the Cine La Rampa promotes *21 Grams* (2003), a dark US-produced drama directed by Mexican director Alejandro González Iñarritú. (Author's photo)

American Way, identifying with heroic underdogs, and perceiving abusive US power as the greatest threat to Cuban sovereignty. But, as Yoani Sanchez's dissident blog suggests and as decades of pre-1959 Cuban film criticism established, such appropriations can be turned—like the sling of David—to mobilize Cubans against those who would degrade *Cuba libre*, who would make Cubans un-free, within the country as much as outside of it.

Abbreviations of Frequently Cited Sources

Cuban Periodicals

Available from US lending libraries unless otherwise noted

ACRC	*Anuario Cinematográfico y Radical Cubano* (at CHC)
DDLM	*Diario de la marina*
EM	*El Mundo*
LUH	*La Última Hora* (at ILLH)
NT	*Nuestro Tiempo* (at ILLH)
RA	*Revista de Avance*

US Periodicals

Available from US lending libraries unless otherwise noted

ATW	*Around the World* (at United Artists Collection)
CM	*Cine-Mundial*
EG	*En Guardia* (at RFA-RAC)
FD	*Film Daily*
FDY	*Film Daily Yearbook*
MPD	*Motion Picture Daily*
MPN	*Motion Picture News*
MPW	*Moving Picture World*
NYT	*New York Times*

Archives

CHC	Cuban Heritage Collection, University of Miami, Coral Gables, Florida
HBSBL	Harvard Business School Baker Library, Boston, Massachusetts
ICAIC	Instituto cubano de artes y industrias cinematográficas, Havana, Cuba

ILLH	Instituto de literatura y lingüística, Havana, Cuba
MHL	Margaret Herrick Library, Academy of Motion Picture Arts and Sciences, Beverly Hills, California
MPSA	Motion Picture Society for the Americas records
MPAA	Motion Picture Association of America general correspondence
PCA	Production Code administrative records
RFA-RAC	Rockefeller Family Archives, Rockefeller Archive Center, Sleepy Hollow, New York
WBA	Warner Brothers Archives, Cinematic Arts Library, University of Southern California
UAC	United Artists Collection, Wisconsin Center for Film and Theater Research, Madison, Wisconsin

Notes

Introduction

1. *Mr. Smith Goes to Washington*, dir. Frank Capra, written by Sidney Buchman (Columbia Pictures, 1939).

2. Teresa Casuso, *Cuba and Castro*, trans. Elmer Grossberg (New York: Random House, 1961), 208.

3. Phil Casey, "Castro Promises Cuba Will Honor Agreements," *Washington Post*, April 20, 1959, A1; Dana Adams Schmidt, "Castro Rules Out Role as Neutral; Opposes the Reds," *New York Times* (hereafter *NYT*), April 20, 1959, A1, A5; and "Humanist Abroad," *Time*, May 4, 1959, 27–28.

4. J. L. Pimsleur, *The New Leader*, September 30, 1957, as quoted by Van Gosse, *Where the Boys Are: Cuba, Cold War America and the Making of a New Left* (New York: Verso, 1993), 55. Gosse discusses Castro's appeal *in the U.S.* in the 1950s, including the role of Hollywood masculinity in shaping that appeal.

5. LeRoi Jones, as quoted by John A. Gronbeck-Tedesco, "Reading Revolution: Politics in the U.S.-Cuban Imagination, 1930–1970" (PhD diss., University of Texas at Austin, 2009), 269, fn. 464.

6. *The Truth about Fidel Castro Revolution*, dir. Victor Pahlen (1959; Fenix Producciones: Image Entertainment, 2002), DVD. On Flynn's 1938 trip, see *Bohemia*, April 3, 1938, 12–13, 95.

7. Pablo Medina, *Exiled Memories: A Cuban Childhood* (Austin: University of Texas Press, 1990), 109–10. On the guerrillas' reception, see Louis A. Pérez, Jr., *The Structure of Cuban History: Meanings and Purpose of the Past* (Chapel Hill: University of North Carolina Press, 2013), 213–14.

8. For an exhaustive catalog of the United States' cultural influence in republican Cuba, see Louis A. Pérez, Jr., *On Becoming Cuban: Identity, Nationality, and Culture* (Chapel Hill: University of North Carolina Press, 1999).

9. Carlos Franqui, *Diary of the Cuban Revolution*, trans. by Georgette Felix et al. (New York: Viking Press, 1980), 162, 47, 64; and Francisco José Moreno, *Before Fidel: The Cuba I Remember* (Austin: University of Texas Press, 2007), 137.

10. Enrique Pineda Barnet, interview by author, Havana, Cuba, June 11, 2004.

11. "Castro Biopic via Jerry Wald," *Variety*, April 29, 1959, 1.

12. For the term "Cuban nationalist masculinity," see Emilio Bejel, *Gay Cuban Nation* (Chicago: University of Chicago University Press, 2001), xvii. On the nascent field of gender studies in Cuba, see Denise Quaresma De Silva and Oscar Ulloa Guerra, "The Study of Masculinities in

Cuba," *Cuban Studies* 42 (2011): 227–38. On the importance of Cuban revolutionary heroes in Cuban culture, see Louis A. Pérez, Jr., *Structure*.

13. José Martí, "Letter to the Editor of *The Evening Post*," March 25, 1889, reprinted in *José Martí: Selected Writings*, ed. and trans. Esther Allen (New York: Penguin Books, 2002), 263–64. My study, like many others, is indebted to Benedict Anderson's *Imagined Communities: Reflections on the Origin and Spread of Nationalism* (London: Verso, 1983), about the rise of nationalisms since the late eighteenth century, their discursive constructions and their great emotional power.

14. "Exclusivo: Actividades de Fidel en Washington," *Revolución*, April 20, 1959, 15. Korda is most famous for his iconic photo of another masculine "star" of the Cuban Revolution, Ernesto "Che" Guevara.

15. Christopher Loviny, ed., *Cuba by Korda* (Melbourne: Ocean Press, 2006), 74.

16. José Martí, "Letter to Manuel Mercado," May 18, 1895, reprinted in Esther Allen, ed. and trans., *José Martí: Selected Writings* (New York: Penguin, 2002), 347.

17. José Martí, "The Truth about the United States," in *Patria*, March 23, 1894, in *José Martí: Selected Writings*, 329–33. For "clear-eyed," see Martí, "To Cuba," *Patria*, January 27, 1894, in *José Martí: Selected Writings*, 323. On Martí's writings about the United States, see Susana Rotker, *The American Chronicles of José Martí: Journalism and Modernity in Spanish America* (Hanover: University Press of New England, 2000).

18. Emphasis added. Valdés-Rodríguez, review of *Mr. Smith Goes to Washington*, *El Mundo*, February 6, 1940, 6. All translations from Spanish-language sources are my own, unless otherwise noted.

19. The term "contact zone," coined by Mary Louise Pratt in *Imperial Eyes: Travel Writing and Transculturation* (London: Routledge, 1992), is borrowed by Gilbert M. Joseph to describe the focus of a groundbreaking "cultural turn" anthology that explores complex U.S.-Latin American relations in varied sites of "material and discursive interaction." See Joseph, "Close Encounters: Toward a New Cultural History of U.S.-Latin American Relations," in *Close Encounters of Empire: Writing the Cultural History of U.S.-Latin American Relations*, ed. Gilbert M. Joseph, Catherine C. Legrand, and Ricardo D. Salvatore (Durham, NC: Duke University Press, 1998), 3–46. Indeed, *Close Encounters* belongs to a growing body of work in the fields of history, American studies, and US foreign relations that look more deeply into the globalization of US power and, especially, dynamic local encounters with it. Studies in this vein within Latin American contexts include Eric Zolov, *Refried Elvis: The Rise of Mexican Counterculture* (Berkeley: University of California Press, 1999); Michael Gobat, *Confronting the American Dream: Nicaragua under U.S. Imperial Rule* (Durham, NC: Duke University Press, 2005); and *Holiday in Mexico: Critical Reflections on Tourism and Tourist Encounters*, ed. Dina Berger and Andrew Grant Wood (Durham, NC: Duke University Press, 2010).

20. "Eric Johnston Calls U.S. Films Instruments for World Freedom in Fostering Democracy and Creating New Economic Desires," *Motion Picture Export Association Newsletter* 4, no. 12 (December 30, 1949): 8, Periodicals Collection, Margaret Herrick Library, Academy of Motion Picture Arts and Sciences, Beverly Hills, California (hereafter MHL).

21. Castro biographies have been legion. The most reputable recent entry is Leycester Coltman's *The Real Fidel Castro* (New Haven, CT: Yale University Press, 2005). Many biographies and studies of the Revolution are preoccupied with *when* Castro became a communist, thus seeking to explain the Revolution's anti-Americanism in analyses of Castro's psyche (or his education, religious training, Galician heritage) and/or his contact with Marxist texts and/or colleagues;

see Lionel Martin, *The Early Fidel: Roots of Castro's Communism* (Secaucus, NJ: Lyle Stuart, Inc., 1978).

22. Aside from seeking the roots of the Revolution's anti-Americanism in the person of Castro, traditional approaches to US-Cuba relations have sought them in the botched policies of the US Department of State; for instance, see Thomas G. Paterson, *Contesting Castro: The United States and the Triumph of the Cuban Revolution* (New York: Oxford University Press, 1994); and Jules Benjamin, *The United States and the Origins of the Cuban Revolution: An Empire in an Age of National Liberation* (Princeton, NJ: Princeton University Press, 1990).

23. This phenomenon has been described aptly by Greg Grandin, "Your Americanism and Mine: Americanism and Anti-Americanism in the Americas," *American Historical Review* 111, no. 4 (October 2006), 1042–66.

24. In English, the authoritative text is Michael Chanan, *The Cuban Cinema*, rev. ed. (Minneapolis: University of Minnesota Press, 2004). In Cuba, decades of research recently culminated in Arturo Agramonte and Luciano Castillo's four volumes of *Cronología del cine cubano* (La Habana: Ediciones ICAIC, 2011–16), in which the distribution and exhibition of US films are covered but treated mostly as impediments to the pre-1959 Cuban film production that is their scholarship's focus.

25. Andrew Higson's "The Concept of National Cinema," *Screen* 30, no. 4 (October 1989): 36–47, first expanded the definition of a national cinema from a nation's film *production* to call for more qualitative studies of a nation's film *consumption*, exploring the ways actual audiences make use of films to "construct their cultural identity" in the local context. Film historians responded to this call; see, for instance, Yuri Tsivian, *Early Cinema in Russia and Its Cultural Reception*, trans. Alan Bodeger (Chicago: University of Chicago Press, 1998); and Thomas J. Saunders, *Hollywood in Berlin: American Cinema and Weimar Germany* (Berkeley: University of California Press, 1994). In applying this expanded definition in a Latin American context, I am indebted to Laura Isabel Serna's *Making Cinelandia: American Films and Mexican Film Culture before the Golden Age* (Durham, NC: Duke University Press, 2014).

26. This tendency has its roots in the central role of feminist theory in film studies and particularly Laura Mulvey's essay "Visual Pleasure and Narrative Cinema, *Screen* 16, no. 3 (Autumn 1975): 6–18, which argued that classical cinema reifies patriarchal ideology through the male gaze and its objectification of women. Later, feminist film scholars set out to recover a wider array of interpretive strategies employed by female (and gay) film viewers, and thus founded the growing field of film reception studies. See Miriam Hansen, *Babel and Babylon: Spectatorship in American Silent Film* (Cambridge, MA: Harvard University Press, 1991); and Lauren Rabinowitz's *For the Love of Pleasure: Women, Movies, and Culture in Turn-of-the-Century Chicago* (New Brunswick, NJ: Rutgers University Press, 1998). For global reception of Hollywood femininity, see Marina Dahlquist, ed. *Exporting Perilous Pauline: Pearl White and the Serial Film Craze* (Urbana: University of Illinois Press, 2013).

27. See E. Ann Kaplan, *Looking for the Other: Feminism, Film, and the Imperial Gaze* (New York: Routledge, 1997).

28. For "symbolic emasculation," see Mayra Beers, "Murder in San Isidro: Crime and Culture during the Second Republic," *Cuban Studies* 34 (2003): 100. On the crucial role that late nineteenth-century constructions of masculinity *in the U.S.* played in US intervention, see Kristin L. Hoganson, *Fighting for American Manhood: How Gender Politics Provoked the Spanish-American and Philippine-American Wars* (New Haven, CT: Yale University Press, 1998).

29. "The Platt Amendment," reprinted in *Neighborly Adversaries: Readings in U.S.-Latin*

American Relations, ed. Michael LaRosa and Frank O. Mora, 2nd ed. (Lanham, MD: Rowman & Littlefield, 2007), 65–66. On national humiliation, see Pérez, *Structure*, 123–24.

30. For more on sociopolitical developments in the Plattist Republic, see Louis A. Pérez, Jr., *Cuba under the Platt Amendment, 1902–1934* (Pittsburgh: University of Pittsburgh Press, 1986).

31. Ibid.

32. Ibid.

33. See Louis A. Pérez, Jr., *Cuba: Between Reform and Revolution*, 2nd ed. (New York: Oxford University Press, 1995), 214–20.

34. For instance, see Ella Shohat and Robert Stam, *Unthinking Eurocentrism: Multiculturalism and the Media* (London: Routledge, 1994), esp. chap. 3: "The Imperial Imaginary," 100–136.

35. Louis A. Pérez, Jr. "Incurring a Debt of Gratitude: 1898 and the Moral Sources of United States Hegemony in Cuba," *American Historical Review* 104, no. 2 (April 1999): 356–98.

36. See, for instance, Reinhold Wagnleitner, *Coca-colonization and the Cold War: The Cultural Mission of the United States in Austria after the Second World War*, trans. Diana M. Wolf (Chapel Hill: University of North Carolina Press, 1994), esp. chap. 8; and Victoria de Grazia, *Irresistible Empire: America's Advance through Twentieth-Century Europe* (Cambridge, MA: Harvard University Press, 2005), esp. chap. 6.

37. The mechanisms of this government support have been well-documented; see Emily S. Rosenberg, *Spreading the American Dream: American Economic and Cultural Expansion, 1890–1945* (New York: Hill & Wang, 1982), esp. 99–103; Kristin Thompson, *Exporting Entertainment: America in the World Film Market, 1907–1934* (London: BFI, 1985); John Trumpbour, *Selling Hollywood to the World: U.S. and European Struggles for Mastery of the Global Film Industry* (Cambridge: Cambridge University Press, 2002); and Ian Jarvie, *Hollywood Overseas Campaign: The North Atlantic Movie Trade, 1920–1950* (Cambridge: Cambridge University Press, 1992). On Latin American markets, see Gaizka S. de Usabel, *The High Noon of American Films in Latin America* (Ann Arbor: UMI Research Press, 1982).

38. Pérez, *On Becoming Cuban*, 311, 327. Pérez explains that Hollywood "motion pictures contributed to an anomalous condition in which North American modalities could encourage lifestyles, foster consumption patterns, and shape popular tastes independent of the capacity of national structures to sustain the material base for these practices and preferences"(292). In *The Origins of the Cuban Revolution Reconsidered* (Chapel Hill: University of North Carolina Press, 2006), 16, historian Samuel Farber makes a similar argument about the role of US media in engendering revolutionary discontent: "Modern means of communication are . . . relatively easier to extend and disseminate than means of production and distribution. As a result, the expectations for consumption may rise faster than the means to satisfy them . . . [in] a world divided by have and have-not nation states." In *Contesting Castro*, Paterson similarly argues that Cubans "grew embittered because, although incorporated into the U.S. consumer culture, they could not sustain the standard of living to which they aspired" (35).

39. Gustavo Pérez Firmat notes that Pérez does not give enough consideration to "the specificity of Cuban appropriations," in his review of *On Becoming Cuban*, in *Cuban Studies/Estudios Cubanos* 31 (2003): 181.

40. The Frankfurt School's sense of mass culture as instrumentalist tool of high capitalism is captured famously in Max Horkheimer and Theodor W. Adorno, "The Culture Industry: Enlightenment as Mass Deception," *Dialectic of Enlightenment* (1944; reprint, New York: Continuum, 2002). In film studies, apparatus theorists argue that cinema technologies inherently promote capitalist ideology. See, for instance, Jean-Louis Baudry's "Ideological Effects of the Basic Cinematographic Apparatus," *Film Quarterly* 28, no. 2 (Winter, 1974–75): 39–47. David Bordwell,

in *Narration in the Fictional Film* (Madison: University of Wisconsin Press, 1985), argues that classical Hollywood cinema typically solicits identification with America, capitalism, patriarchy, and whiteness.

41. See Frederic Jameson, "Reification and Utopia in Mass Culture," 1979, reprinted in *Signatures of the Visible* (New York: Routledge, 1992), 29. Exploring early cinema, Lary May, *Screening out the Past: The Birth of Mass Culture and the Motion Picture Industry* (Chicago: University of Chicago Press, 1980), concludes that the notion that Hollywood films are always mechanisms of "social control" is inadequate to the historical record, vii. For an insightful study of Hollywood's mixed message in a later period, the 1940s, see Dana Polan, *Power & Paranoia: History, Narrative and the American Cinema, 1940–1950* (New York: Columbia University Press, 1986).

42. For important studies of the Hollywood Left, see Larry Ceplair and Steven Englund's *The Inquisition in Hollywood: Politics in the Film Community, 1930–1960* (Garden City, NY: Anchor Press, 1980); and Lary May, *The Big Tomorrow: Hollywood and the Politics of the American Way* (Chicago: University of Chicago Press, 2000). I use the term "Hollywood Left" instead of "Hollywood Popular Front" intentionally. The latter smacks of Communist duplicity, a "front" used to hide a conspiratorial subversion of the US government directed by the Soviet Union itself. It has been rendered derogatory by cold war anticommunist crusades and threatens to entangle us in those crusades' preoccupation with who was a "Red" and when. Particularly in relation to US-Cuba relations, it risks diminishing a broader story about transnational cultural exchange into the limited, and limiting, question of when and via what influences Fidel Castro turned to Communism after 1959. That being said, because CPUSA membership (however brief) *is* one measure of a film artist's commitment to progressive causes (but not of the degree of progressive idealism and social criticism s/he injected into a film), I tend to note the affiliation but not dwell on it.

43. George Lipsitz, *Time Passages: Collective Memory and American Popular Culture* (Minneapolis: University of Minnesota Press, 1990), 17.

44. Frank Capra, *The Name above the Title* (1971; reprint, New York: Da Capo Press, 1997), 260; Eric Smoodin, *Regarding Frank Capra: Audience, Celebrity and American Film Studies, 1930–1960* (Durham, NC: Duke University Press, 2004), 17, 20, 121, 130–33, 137; and Michael P. Rogin and Kathleen Moran, "Mr. Capra Goes to Washington," *Representations*, no. 84 (Autumn 2003): 215.

45. Colin Shindler, *Hollywood in Crisis: Cinema and American Society, 1929–1939* (London: Routledge, 1996), 87–95.

46. May, *Big Tomorrow*, 87–89; and Wes D. Gehring, *Populism and the Capra Legacy* (Westport, CT: Greenwood Press, 1995).

47. See Rogin and Moran, "Mr. Capra Goes to Washington"; and Joseph McBride, *Frank Capra: The Catastrophe of Success* (New York: Simon & Schuster, 1992).

48. See Janet Staiger, *Interpreting Films: Studies in the Historical Reception of American Cinema* (Princeton, NJ: Princeton University Press, 1992), and *Perverse Spectators: The Practices of Film Reception* (New York: New York University Press, 2000). See also Judith Mayne, *Cinema and Spectatorship* (London: Routledge, 1993). And the series of anthologies edited by Melvyn Stokes and Richard Maltby for the British Film Institute: *American Movie Audiences: From the Turn of the Century to the Early Sound Era* (1999); *Identifying Hollywood's Audiences: Cultural Identity and the Movies* (1999); and *Hollywood Spectatorship: Changing Perceptions of Cinema Audiences* (2001).

49. My use of the term "coded" refers to Stuart Hall's seminal ideas about cultural reception laid out in "Encoding/Decoding," in *Culture, Media, Language: Working Papers in Cultural Studies*

(1972–1979), ed. Stuart Hall et al. (Birmingham: Centre for Contemporary Cultural Studies, 1980), 128–38. On female viewers, see note 26 above; and Kathy Peiss, "Cheap Theater and the Nickle Dumps," chap. 6 in *Cheap Amusements: Working Women and Leisure in Turn-of-the-Century New York* (Philadelphia: Temple University Press, 1986); and Nan Endstadt, "Movie-Struck Girls: Motion Pictures and Consumer Subjectivities," chap. 5 in *Ladies of Labor, Girls of Adventure: Working Women, Popular Culture, and Labor Politics at the Turn of the Century* (New York: Columbia University Press, 1999). On African American audiences, see Jacqueline Stewart, *Migrating to the Movies: Cinema and Black Urban Modernity* (Berkeley: University of California Press, 2005).

50. "Alternative public spheres" is from Hansen, *Babel and Babylon*, 92.

51. "Indigenize" is from Ella Shohat and Robert Stam, "Film Theory and Spectatorship in the Age of the 'Posts,'" in *Reinventing Film Studies*, ed. Christine Gledhill and Linda Williams (London: Oxford University Press, 2000), 383. For various case studies, see *Hollywood Abroad: Audiences and Cultural Exchange*, ed. Melvyn Stokes and Richard Maltby (London: BFI Publishing, 2004). See also Anat Helman, "Hollywood in an Israeli Kibbutz: Going to the Movies in 1950s' Afikim," *Historical Journal of Film, Radio, and Television* 23, no. 2 (2003): 153–63.

52. See, for instance, James Burns, "Watching Africans Watch Films: Theories of Spectatorship in British Colonial Africa," *Historical Journal of Film, Radio and Television* 20, no. 2 (June 2000): 197–211; Charles Ambler, "Popular Films and Colonial Audiences in Central Africa," in Stokes and Maltby, *Hollywood Abroad*, 133–57; and Ruth Ben-Ghiat, "The Italian Colonial Cinema: Agendas and Audiences," *Modern Italy* 8, no. 1 (2003): 49–63.

53. Especially on business practices, see Priya Jaikumar in "Hollywood and the Multiple Constituencies of Colonial India," in Stokes and Maltby, *Hollywood Abroad*, 88–89. See also Hiroshima Kitamura, *Screening Enlightenment: Hollywood and the Cultural Reconstruction of Defeated Japan* (Ithaca, NY: Cornell University Press, 2010), which offers a fine-grained study of Japanese citizens' (including exhibitors, journalists, and fans) engagement with Hollywood content and business practices during the United States' postwar occupation, mostly uncovering the ways that it supported the "Americanization" of Japan, but occasionally hinting at Japanese grumblings and grousing.

54. Indeed, it is likely that studies of differentiated Cuban film audiences (i.e., via race, religion, and class) would be as fruitful as studies of differentiated US audiences have been.

55. Chanan, *Cuban Cinema*, 87; and *Anuario Cinematográfico y Radical Cubano* (hereafter *ACRC*) *1956*, 114. Cited editions of the *ACRC* are from the Cuban Heritage Collection, University of Miami, Coral Gables, Florida.

56. See, for instance, the oral histories in Oscar Lewis, Ruth Lewis, and Susan M. Rigdon, *Four Men: Living the Revolution: An Oral History of Contemporary Cuba*, vol. 1 (Urbana: University of Illinois Press, 1977). On kissing, see Medina, *Exiled Memories*, 56. See also Guillermo Cabrera Infante's autobiographical *Infante's Inferno*, trans. Suzanne Jill Levine (New York: Harper & Row, 1984), in which references to Havana moviegoing practices and/or Cuban appropriations of Hollywood culture appear on nearly every page.

57. While I rely heavily on Havana's longest-running fanzine, *Cinema* (1935–62), there were countless (mostly fleeting) Cuban fanzines, including *Celuloide*, *Cine-dial*, *Cine-fans*, *Cinegráfico*, *Cinemanía*, *Cintas y estrellas*, *Film*, *Filmópolis*, *Films Selected*, *Magazine del Cinéfilo*, *Hollywood*, *La Pantalla*, and *La revista del cine*.

58. My analysis of the film giro is informed by Thomas O'Brien, *The Revolutionary Mission: American Enterprise in Latin America, 1900–1945* (New York: Cambridge University Press, 1996), especially his case study analyzing the US-Cuban encounter through General Electric's Cuban subsidiary. See also Pérez, *On Becoming Cuban*, 394–95, 401, and also 220–34 (on the US-Cuban

encounter in US-owned sugar mills); and Julio Moreno, *Yankee Don't Go Home: Mexican Nationalism, American Business Culture, and the Shaping of Modern Mexico, 1920–1950* (Chapel Hill: University of North Carolina Press, 2003).

59. Pérez, *Cuba under Platt*, 37.

60. This accusation was often launched against Cuban exhibitors, but also against Cuban employees of US studios who were deemed "too friendly with the [US] Manager" and thus apt to sell out their fellow union members. See *Exhibidor*, January 10, 1940, 1. All cited copies of *Exhibidor* are from the Instituto de literatura y lingüística, Havana, Cuba (hereafter ILLH).

61. On the *guayabera* as a conscious symbol of Cuban nationalism, see Charles D. Ameringer, *The Cuban Democratic Experience: The Auténtico Years, 1942–1955* (Gainesville: University Press of Florida, 2000), 136.

62. Pineda Barnet, interview by author.

63. Cabrera Infante, *Infante's Inferno*, 54, 89.

64. One Cuban described whistling at the screen "a *criollo* tradition in times of bad governments." *Bohemia*, September 30, 1951, 59.

65. See reports on *Casanova's Big Night* (1954), *Tropic Zone* (1953), and *War and Peace* (1956); Foreign exchange reports—Cuba 1952–1957, Paramount Pictures Production Records, Special Collections, MHL.

66. A handful of film scholars have also understood film critics in this way. See Staiger, *Interpreting Films*, 58, 91. And Anna Everett, *Returning the Gaze: A Genealogy of Black Film Criticism, 1909–1949* (Durham, NC: Duke University Press, 2001); and Saunders, *Hollywood in Berlin*. Smoodin, *Regarding Frank Capra*, weaves critics throughout his discussion of the "rhetorics of reception" that shaped interpretations of Capra's films.

67. For a brief discussion of the role of the *pensador* in Cuba, see Rotker, *American Chronicles of José Martí*, 18, 20, 25. For an exception to the general neglect of Latin American film critics as *pensadores*, see Jason Borge, *Latin American Writers and the Rise of Hollywood Cinema* (New York: Routledge, 2008). See also his previous *Avances de Hollywood: Critica cinematografica en Latinoamerica, 1915–1945* (Rosario, ARG: Beatriz Viterbo Editora, 2005). The only English-language study I know of that focuses on *Cuban* film criticism is Hector Amaya, *Screening Cuba: Film Criticism as Political Performance during the Cold War* (Urbana: University of Illinois Press, 2010), about the highly conscious revolutionary nationalism in *post*-1959 criticism; Amaya ignores the phenomenon's pre-1959 roots.

68. Louis A. Pérez, Jr., interview by author, Chapel Hill, NC, March 31, 2005; and Franqui, *Diary*, 162, 165.

69. Ernesto Che Guevara, *Episodes of the Cuban Revolutionary War, 1956–1958*, ed. Mary-Alice Waters (New York: Pathfinder Press, 1996), 365.

70. Carlos Eire, *Waiting for Snow in Havana: Confessions of a Cuban Boy* (New York: Free Press, 2003), 208, 7, 210.

Chapter One

1. Eduardo Quiñones, "Crónica de la Habana," *Cine-Mundial* (hereafter *CM*), April 1922, 201. *Way Down East*, dir. D. W. Griffith (United Artists, 1920).

2. José Manuel Valdés-Rodríguez, "El Cine: Su proceso creador; el montaje," *Revista Lyceum*, September–December 1939, 3. On his biography, see Romualdo Santos, "Historia de una pasión cinematográfica," in José Manuel Valdés-Rodríguez, *El cine: Industria y arte de nuestro tiempo*, ed. Olga Marta Pérez (La Habana: Editorial Letras Cubanas, 1989): 5–25.

3. On the less-transporting effects of early film production and exhibition, see Hansen, *Babel and Babylon*, 33–34. On the "localizing" of meanings this allowed, see "Introduction," in Stokes and Maltby, *Hollywood Abroad*, 9.

4. Ada Ferrer, *Insurgent Cuba: Race, Nation, and Revolution, 1868–1898* (Chapel Hill: University of North Carolina Press, 1999), 141–42; and Pérez, *Cuba: Between Reform*, chap. 7.

5. Enrique Agüero Hidalgo, "*Revolviendo papeles viejos*," *Cinema*, April 27, 1941, 17. All copies of *Cinema* are from the *Biblioteca Nacional "José Martí*," Havana, Cuba. See also María Eulalia Douglas, *La tienda negra: El cine en Cuba [1897–1990]* (La Habana: Cinemateca de Cuba, 1996), 9.

6. Francisco Hermida, *La Unión Constitucional*, January 26, 1897; Ancieto Valdivia, *La Lucha*, January 1897; unknown author, *El Hogar*, January 31, 1897; and unknown author, *La Caricatura*, February 11, 1897, all reprinted in the first appendix, Arturo Agramonte and Luciano Castillo, *Cronología de cine Cubano*, 1897–1936 (La Habana: Ediciones ICAIC, 2011), 1:388–93.

7. Valdivia, *La Lucha*, in Agramonte and Castillo, *Cronología*, 390.

8. Chanan, *Cuban Cinema*, 47; and Douglas, *Tienda negra*, 9.

9. Emphasis in the original. Hermida, in Agramonte and Castillo, *Cronología*, 1:389.

10. Agramonte and Castillo, *Cronología*, 1:35–39.

11. Federico Villoch, *La Caricatura*, Havana, April 18, 1897, as quoted by Agramonte and Castillo, *Cronología*, 1:46.

12. Douglas, *Tienda negra*, 11, 222; and Pérez, *On Becoming Cuban*, 284.

13. Charles Musser, *The Emergence of the Cinema: The American Screen to 1907*, vol. 1 of *History of the American Cinema* (New York: Charles Scribner's Sons, 1990), 247.

14. Ibid., 248–49, 258, 281; and Charles Musser, *Before the Nickelodeon: Edwin S. Porter and the Edison Manufacturing Company* (Berkeley: University of California Press, 1991), 127–34.

15. Pérez, *Cuba under Platt*, 34–72.

16. Mariola Espinosa, *Epidemic Invasion: Yellow Fever and the Limits of Cuban Independence, 1878–1930* (Chicago: University of Chicago Press, 2009).

17. Pérez, *On Becoming Cuban*, 107, 129.

18. Ibid., 115–25. On the imposition of US business practices and "US corporate culture" during the occupation, see O'Brien, *Revolutionary Mission*, 207.

19. United States Military Governor Leonard Wood, as quoted by Marial Iglesias Utset, *A Cultural History of Cuba during the U.S. Occupation*, trans. Russ Davidson (Chapel Hill: University of North Carolina Press, 2011), 74.

20. Ibid., 34–35, 44–49, 73.

21. Agramonte and Castillo, *Cronología*, 1:75–76.

22. Douglas, *Tienda negra*, 15; and Iglesias Utset, *Cultural History*, 27–28.

23. Douglas, *Tienda negra*, 14; and Agramonte and Castillo, *Cronología*, 1:77.

24. Iglesias Utset, *Cultural History*, 61.

25. Pérez, *Cuba: Between Reform*, 187, 197–99; and Pérez, *Cuba under Platt*, 154, 187, 189. On Cuban protest, see also Luis E. Aguilar, *Cuba 1933: Prologue to Revolution* (Ithaca, NY: Cornell University Press, 1972), 19.

26. Pérez, *On Becoming Cuban*, 125–29, 137–38; and Joseph L. Scarpaci, Roberto Segre, and Mario Coyula, *Havana: Two Faces of the Antillean Metropolis*, rev. ed. (Chapel Hill: University of North Carolina Press, 2002), 53.

27. Rachel Carley, *Cuba: 400 Years of Architectural Heritage* (New York: Whitney Library of Design, 1997), 143–47.

28. Douglas, *Tienda negra*, 18; see also *Cuba y América: revista ilustrada*, May 13, 1906, 111.

29. Raúl Rodríguez, *El cine silente en Cuba* (La Habana: Editorial Letras Cubanas, 1992), 83; Hector García Mesa, *Cine latinoamericano, 1896–1930* (Caracas: Consejo Nacional de la cultura, 1992), 154; and A. Hyatt Verrill, *Cuba, Past and Present* (New York: Dodd, Mead, 1914), 106.

30. Rodríguez, *Cine silente*, 40–41, 50; and García Mesa, *Cine latinoamericano*, 147.

31. "Diez Anécdotas del Cine Cubano," *ACRC 1946–47*, 97; Agramonte and Castillo, *Cronología* 1:145–47; and Raymond Fielding, "Hale's Tours: Ultrarealism in the Pre-1910 Motion Picture," *Cinema Journal* 10, no. 1 (Autumn 1970): 34–47.

32. Rodríguez, *Cine silente*, 74; and Douglas, *Tienda negra*, 28.

33. Agramonte and Castillo, *Cronología*, 1:81, 97, 104, 106, 113–14.

34. Agramonte and Castillo, *Cronología*, 1:89, 97, 105, 124; T. Philip Terry, *Terry's Guide to Cuba* (Boston: Houghton Mifflin Co., 1926), 54; García Mesa, *Cine latinoamericano*, 149, 152; Rodríguez, *Cine silente*, 57–58, 61, 63; and Douglas, *Tienda negra*, 24, 30, 73.

35. This portrait of early exhibition in Havana is derived from Rodríguez, *Cine silente*; and Agramonte and Castillo, *Cronología*, vol. 1. For the US practices they mirrored, see Douglas Gomery, *Shared Pleasures: A History of Movie Presentation in the United States* (Madison: University of Wisconsin Press, 1992), 18–19; and Eileen Bowser, *The Transformation of Cinema: 1907–1915*, vol. 1 of *History of the American Cinema* (Berkeley, University of California Press, 1990), 13–18, 125–26.

36. On the US market, see Bowser, *Transformation of Cinema*, 23.

37. Rodríguez, *Cine silente*, 79–80; and León Primelles, *Crónica cubana, 1915–1918* (La Habana: Editorial Lex, 1955), 100.

38. Though scholars have debated the actual class and ethnic makeup of early US cinema audiences (see Stokes and Maltby, *American Movie Audiences*, 2–8), contemporary Americans *perceived* it as "lowbrow."

39. Enrique Fontanills, "Crónica," *El Hogar*, September 12, 1897, reprinted in first appendix in Agramonte and Castillo, *Cronología*, 1:403.

40. Rodríguez, *Cine silente*, 60, 63; and Renée Méndez Capote, *Memorias de una cubanita que nació con el siglo* (La Habana: Editorial UNIÓN, 1964), 170, 172.

41. Primelles, *Crónica cubana*, 213.

42. Méndez Capote, *Memorias*, 172.

43. "Diez Anécdotas del Cine Cubano," 86, 90. The film was the Cuban-made *El Rescate del Brigadier Sanguily*; one Spanish spectator protested the representation of Spaniards cowardly fleeing Cuban *mambises*, and the brawl ensued.

44. Agramonte and Castillo, *Cronología*, 1:178; and Méndez Capote, *Memorias*, 173. Some Havana exhibitors did show multireel features before the war, especially Italian epics, but most preferred shorter films. Film pirates even cut D. W. Griffith's *Intolerance* into four episodes to be shown as a serial; see "Pirates More Active," *Film Daily* (hereafter *FD*), January 16, 1919, 1.

45. Agramonte and Castillo, *Cronología*, 1:291; and Antonio Kapcia, *Havana: The Making of Cuban Culture* (Oxford: Berg, 2005), 87.

46. Rodríguez, *Cine silente*, 73; and Agramonte and Castillo, *Cronología*, 1:102.

47. Méndez Capote, *Memorias*, 170; Agramonte and Castillo, *Cronología*, 1:88. On the *danzón* and Cuban nationalism, see Iglesias Utset, *Cultural History*, 56–60. On accompanists' standard repertoire, see Tsivian, *Early Cinema in Russia*, 80.

48. Arturo Agramonte and Luciano Castillo, *Entre Vivir y Soñar* (Camagüey: Editorial Ácana, 2008), 137.

49. Agramonte and Castillo, *Cronología*, 1:82–87, 159. On translated inter-titles, see Thompson, *Exporting Entertainment*, 48.

50. Enrique Agüero Hidalgo "Los 'parlantes' que antaño 'sincronizaban," *Cinema*, February 1944, 5, as quoted by Agramonte and Castillo, *Cronología*, 1:86, 87.

51. Valdés-Rodríguez in 1967, as quoted by Agramonte and Castillo, *Cronología*, 1:116.

52. This language is from a film poster for *La manigua* (1915); reprinted in Eduardo G. Noguer, *Historia del Cine Cubano: Cien Años 1897–1998* (Miami: Ediciones Universal, 2002), 13.

53. On this plethora of *mambí* commemoration, see Pérez, *Structure*, 141–44.

54. Gerben Bakker, *Entertainment Industrialised: The Emergence of the International Film Industry, 1890–1940* (Cambridge: Cambridge University Press, 2008), 227.

55. "Facts and Comments," *Moving Picture World* (hereafter *MPW*), December 2, 1916, 1299. On exports to Latin America, see Thompson, *Exporting Entertainment*, Table A.III, 216.

56. Ortega appears as director on *Cine-Mundial*'s masthead for the first time on June 1917, 273. Ortega also wrote for it under the pseudonym Jorge Hermida; see *International Motion Picture Almanac 1937–38*, 674.

57. W. Stephen Bush, "A Note of Warning to Producers," *MPW*, May 13, 1916, 1135. "Our Cuban colony" is how United Artists' board of directors referred to Cuba in 1921; as quoted by Usabel, *High Noon*, 19.

58. On ship service, see Ricardo G. Mariño, "El Mercado Cubano," *CM*, May 1916, 195. On plane service, see "Pathé News," *FD*, December 22, 1920, 1393.

59. Pérez, *On Becoming Cuban*, 281.

60. O'Brien, *Revolutionary Mission*, 210; and Mary Speck, "Prosperity, Progress, and Wealth: Cuban Enterprise during the Early Republic," *Cuban Studies* 36 (2005): 51.

61. Pérez, *Cuba under Platt*, 230–31, 265.

62. "Export Items," *MPW*, October 1917, 530; see also US Commerce Dept., *Selling in Foreign Markets*, 1919, 468, Harvard Business School Baker Library, Boston (hereafter HBSBL).

63. *MPW*, "Here is 'Cine-Mundial,'" December 18, 1915, 2154.

64. The *Campoamor* first opened as a Cuban-built and -owned stage theater in November 1915; see Primelles, *Crónica cubana*, 97. On Universal's lease, see "In the Courts," *FD*, February 3, 1921, 2; and "Stewart Attachment Off," *Variety*, April 21, 1922, 39.

65. "Diez Anécdotas del Cine Cubano," 98.

66. Eduardo Quiñones, "De la Habana," *CM*, March 1917, 135.

67. Emphasis original. "Circulares de pieles rojas," *Cuba Cinematográfica*, October 15, 1916, 4, as quoted by Agramonte and Castillo, *Cronología*, 1:158.

68. "Adopts American Program," *FD*, November 30, 1918, 2.

69. Marcelo Pogolotti, as quoted by Agramonte and Castillo, *Cronología*, 1:180. On "combination titles," see "Central America Deal," *Variety*, December 14, 1917, 1; and *Film Daily Yearbook* (hereafter *FDY*) *1924*, 393.

70. Quiñones, "Crónica de la Habana," *CM*, February 18, 1918, 89.

71. Agramonte and Castillo, *Cronología* 1:155, 179, 230–31; and a Havana poll cited in "Happy Combine Preferred by George Walsh," *Motion Picture News* (hereafter *MPN*), October 16, 1920, 3037.

72. United Artists' office opened next to the Cine Verdun on February 15, 1921, and consistently had about thirteen employees; see Joaquín Baez-Miró, "Henry Weiner toda una institucion de la Cia. United Artist de Cuba," *Cinema*, June 15, 1952, page numbers not given. On Fox's office, see Eduardo Quiñones, "Bienvenidos a Cuba," *CM*, November 1922, 616. On MGM's, see *ACRC 1946–47*, 132. On Warner Bros.', see "Cuba toma el turismo en serio," *CM*, September 1925, 539. Paramount first rented films through the Caribbean Film Co. of Havana; "Central America Deal,"

Variety, December 14, 1917, 1. The office reorganized under the name Paramount in 1926; *Paramount International News*, September 28, 1951, 5, Periodicals Collection, MHL.

73. For addresses, see *FDY* 1927, 960. Confusingly, Havana streets often have two names. In the early twentieth century, many were rechristened with names honoring revolutionary heroes, e.g., Consulado was renamed Estrada Palma, Industria was renamed Raímundo Cabrera, and Águila was renamed Rafael M. de Labra. But many of these didn't stick, and Cubans continued to refer to them by their old names. For a list, see Terry, *Terry's Guide*, 154, 196.

74. On Columbia, see "Along the Rialto," *FD*, December 22, 1931, 4. On RKO, see *FDY* 1937, 1206.

75. All three also worked at Warner Bros.' Havana office (Lichtig in 1925, Brookheim in 1926, and Liebeskind in 1929). On Litchtig (variously spelled) in Havana, see "King to Cuba," *FD*, December 28, 1918, 1; and "Cuba toma el turismo en serio," *CM*, September 1925, 538–39. On Lichtig's heritage, see Bernard Lichtig, passport application, July 20, 1917, *U.S. Passport Applications, 1795–1925* [database on-line], Lehi, UT: Ancestry.com, 2007. On Brookheim and Liebeskind in Havana for Universal, see "Brookheim Goes to Cuba Exchange," *Universal Weekly* 24, no. 11. Liebeskind was born in 1894 in a part of Russia that is now Poland; see Nathan Liebeskind, World War I draft registration card, New York, New York; Roll: 1786813; Draft Board: 152, *U.S., World War I Draft Registration Cards, 1917–1918* [database on-line], Provo, UT: Ancestry.com, 2005.

76. See "Goldstein Going to Cuba," *FD*, October 3, 1926, 11. On his heritage, Louis Goldstein, passport application, January 29, 1920, *U.S. Passport Applications, 1795–1925* [database on-line], Lehi, UT: Ancestry.com, 2007.

77. Usabel, *High Noon*, 36. On Ehrenreich's heritage, see Max Ehrenreich, passport application, December 6, 1922, *U.S. Passport Applications, 1795–1925* [database on-line], Lehi, UT: Ancestry.com, 2007. Weiner's career and background are covered in greater detail in chapter 3.

78. Robert M. Levine, *Tropical Diaspora: The Jewish Experience in Cuba* (Gainesville: University Press of Florida, 1993).

79. On "pioneers," see "Cuba's Pic Industry to Honor UA Manager," *FD*, July 24, 1941, 1. On their various troubles, see Usabel, *High Noon*, 35–37; and Eduardo Quiñones, "Crónica de la Habana," *CM*, May 1918, 270. Universal's first Havana office was destroyed in a fire; "Film Property Destroyed," *FD*, October 31, 1918, 648; and the RKO office had a fire in 1932; "RKO Cuban Fire," *FD*, March 3, 1932, 8.

80. Ehrenreich to W. W. Hines (UA head of sales), undated, f. 5, b. 12, f. 14, b. 212, series 2A, United Artists Collection, Wisconsin Center for Film and Theater Research, Madison (hereafter UAC).

81. "Typhoid Kills Universal's Cuban Manager," *MPN*, January 14, 1928, 127.

82. "Pictures and People," *MPN*, August 4, 1928, 351.

83. Eduardo Quiñones, "Crónica de la Habana," *CM*, December 1920, 1014. On taxes and tariffs, see "Trade Chiefs Visiting Havana to Get Cuban Film Concession," *Variety*, January 20, 1922, 38. On film piracy, see "Cuba after Film Pirates," *FD*, September 14, 1923, 7; and Usabel, *High Noon*, 33. On censorship, see *FDY* 1924, 393.

84. "United front" is from John Jones (Havana manager), to J. J. Glynn (foreign chief), November 22, 1949, 2, f. Film Boards, b. 16671B, Warner Bros. Archives, Cinematic Arts Library, University of Southern California, Los Angeles, CA (hereafter WBA). For the Cuban Film Board's founding, see "Exhib.-Distributor War in Cuba," *MPN*, July 10, 1926, 131. For its renaming, see Agramonte and Castillo, *Cronología*, 1:276.

85. On these booking practices generally, see Richard Koszarski, *An Evening's Entertainment:*

The Age of the Silent Feature Picture, 1915–1928, vol. 3 of *History of the American Cinema* (Berkeley: University of California Press, 1990), 71–72. On the other practices, see Usabel, *High Noon*, 48, 62.

86. On price and date of sale, see Primelles, *Crónica cubana*, 523. On seating capacity, see Ad, Caribbean Film Company, *CM*, January 1920, 57. For another picture, see Eduardo Quiñones, "Crónica de la Habana," *CM*, March 1920, 339. On its reopening as a Warner deluxer, see *Bohemia*, June 7, 1931, 43.

87. "Havana First Run for 1'st National," *FD*, August 26, 1925, 4.

88. Eduardo Quiñones, "La Habana languidece," *CM*, October 1925, 629; and Primelles, *Crónica cubana*, 100.

89. "South American Boom," *Variety*, January 17, 1919, 57; and "Cuba on the Boom," *FD*, July 26, 1919, 144.

90. "Business Progressing in Cuba," *FD*, August 5, 1923, 2. On Liebeskind, see "Liebeskind Opening First in Cuba," *FD*, October 28, 1926, 3. On Kent's chain, see Pérez, *On Becoming Cuban*, 283. See also "Saenger in Havana," *Variety*, December 16, 1925. For Fox's ambitions for a Havana theater, see "Amusement Stock Quotations," *Variety*, February 3, 1926, 35.

91. "Siege" is from Luís García Ortega, "Finura japonesa y el dulce azucar cubano," *CM*, December 1927, 992. On the proposed ordinance, see Eduardo Quiñones, "¡Ese Calor de la Habana!" *CM*, September 1926, 586.

92. See *FDY* 1924, 393; *FDY* 1927, 960; *FDY* 1929, 1017; *FDY* 1930, 1013; *FDY* 1931, 1014; and Thompson, *Exporting Entertainment*, Table A.IV, 219. For market rank by volume, see "Foreign Markets Are Changing," *FD*, September 2, 1927, 8.

93. "Havana Popular," *FD*, February 11, 1931, 8.

94. On the *Wilson* and *Roosevelt*, see Eduardo Quiñones, "Crónica de la Habana," *CM*, January 1920, 126; and April 1920, 415, respectively. On the *Edison*, see "Three New Houses for Cuba," *FD*, May 12, 1921, 4.

95. Luís García Ortega, "Bullanguera Habana," *CM*, July 1928, 586; and "Powell Returns to Studio," *FD*, February 19, 1929, 10.

96. On Swanson, see "Cable Note," *FD*, February 3, 1924, 3; and *Social*, February 1924, 59. On Rogers, see Gustavo Pérez Firmat, *The Havana Habit* (New Haven, CT: Yale University Press, 2010), 40. On Mix, see "Cuba Fetes Mix," *Variety*, February 12, 1930, 5; and *Carteles*, February 23, 1930, 24, 64–65.

97. Eduardo Quiñones, "Crónica de la Habana," *CM*, August 1920, 718; April 1921, 282; and May 1922, 255.

98. Serna, *Making Cinelandia*, 92.

99. On the similar development of fan culture in Mexico in the 1920s and the ideological work it did, see Serna, *Making Cinelandia*. On the development of the star system and the ideological work it does generally, see Richard Dyer's seminal *Stars* (London: BFI, 1979).

100. As late as 1918, Quiñones complained that the Cuban press pays "scarce attention" to cinema; Eduardo Quiñones, "Crónica de la Habana," *CM*, July 1918, 412. In 1919, Ramón Becali [aka Lady Godiva] began a column, "Averiguador Cinematográfica," in *La Noche*; see Douglas, *Tienda negra*, 41. Maria M. Garrett wrote "Crónica Cinematográfica" in *El Fígaro*; and Enrique Agüero Hidalgo [aka Henry McDorin] wrote "Secretos del Cinema" in *La Libertad*; see Arturo Agramonte and Luciano Castillo, *Ramón Peón: El hombre de los glóbulos negros* (La Habana: Editorial de Ciencias Sociales, 2003), 8–21.

101. *Carteles*, September 25, 1925, 1.

102. *Social*, May 1928, 93.

103. Ad, Santos y Artigas, *CM*, January 1921, 74. For Zayas, see Enrique Agüero Hidalgo, "*Revolviendo papeles viejos*," *Cinema*, December 1948-January 1949, pages not numbered.

104. Gypsy, "El Arte Silente," *Bohemia*, October 30, 1921, 16.

105. Eduardo Quiñones, "Crónica de la Habana," *CM*, January 1922, 32; February 1922, 87; and January 1923, 36; and Agramonte and Castillo, *Entre vivir y soñar*, 49.

106. Agramonte and Castillo, *Cronología*, 1:261.

107. "New Methods in Havana," *Variety*, March 3, 1926, 23; and "Loew Breaks Cuban Record," *Variety*, March 10, 1926, 1. On MGM's selling its lease after a year, see Eduardo Quiñones, "Facil victoria," *CM*, March 1927, 240.

108. Agramonte and Castillo, *Cronología*, 1:289.

109. "Encanto Brings Atmospheric Design to Cuba," *MPN*, October 6, 1928, 1048–49 (including photos); and Rene Canizares, "Chatter in Havana," *Variety*, September 12, 1928, 2.

110. Gerardo del Valle, "*Cines de moda*," *Bohemia*, April 22, 1928, 7; 74. On *Bohemia* as leading Havana periodical, see José G. Ricardo, *La imprenta en Cuba* (La Habana: Editorial Letras Cubanas, 1989), 141–42.

111. Speck, "Prosperity, Progress, and Wealth," 53–54.

112. Emphasis added. Del Valle, "*Cines de moda*."

113. Gypsy, "El Arte Silente," *Bohemia*, October 30, 1921, 16.

114. Koszarski, *An Evening's Entertainment*, 41–43.

115. As quoted by Agramonte and Castillo, *Cronología*, 1:250

116. "Exhib.-Distributor War in Cuba," *MPN*, July 10, 1926, 131; and Usabel, *High Noon*, 62–63.

117. For the offense Cubans took to another US-made film about the Spanish-American war, see "Mimic War in Cuba for Yankee 'Movies,'" *NYT*, November 6, 1913, 11.

118. *Cuba Cinematográfica*, January 15, 1917, 7, as quoted by Agramonte and Castillo, *Cronología*, 1:165. On the debut theaters, see Primelles, *Crónica cubana*, 404. On the "Rowan Myth" generally, and Cuban resentment toward it, see Ambrosio Fornet, "The Perpetual Alibi: Mythology and Mythomania in the Discourse of '98," *Journal of Latin American Cultural Studies* 9, no. 1 (2000): 21.

119. Douglas, *Tienda negra*, 38.

120. According to its director, *Cytherea* represented Cuba as "hot" and "filthy"; George Fitzmaurice, "The Next Advance," *FD*, June 22, 1924, 97.

121. "Cuba in Uproar Over 1st Nat'l Films," *Variety*, August 6, 1924, 19.

122. "Delay in Cuba," *FD*, October 6, 1926, 1, 6; "Cuban Decree," *FD*, January 23, 1927, 5; and "Federal Censorship in Cuba," *MPN*, October 9, 1926, 1367. On Mexico, see Serna, *Making Cinelandia*, 154–79.

123. "Pictures and People," *MPN*, August 4, 1928, 351.

Chapter Two

1. *City Lights*, written and directed by Charles Chaplin (United Artists, 1931).

2. García Mesa, *Cine latinoamericano*, 163.

3. "Havana House Wired," *Variety*, December 26, 1928, 6; Usabel, *High Noon*, 78; and Agramonte and Castillo, *Cronología*, 1:292–93.

4. "Protest Against Talkies," *NYT*, July 24, 1929, 30; and "Film Machine Trade Rises," *NYT*, August 14, 1929, 43. By 1932, 123 of Cuba's 400 cinemas were wired for sound, with these updates concentrated in Havana; see Usabel, *High Noon*, 81. For a photo of the Teatro Prado advertising

its sound capacities, see "Havana Up-To-The-Minute with Modern Ballyhoo," *Motion Picture News* (hereafter *MPN*), September 7, 1929, 929.

5. "Cine con ruido," *Carteles*, June 9, 1929, 16.

6. Iglesias Utset, *Cultural History*, 84.

7. Emphasis added, Jorge Mañach, *El Excelsior-El Pais*, May 3, 1929, as quoted by Rodríguez, *Cine silente*, 134–35. The *New York Times* reported that the talkies *were* spreading English-language "Americanisms" like "O.K." and "all right" in Havana; see "English in Cuba," *NYT*, June 18, 1931, 26.

8. For the history of Cuban protest against the Cuban Electric Company, see O'Brien, *Revolutionary Mission*, chaps. 8 and 9.

9. Robert Whitney, *State and Revolution in Cuba: Mass Mobilization and Political Change, 1920–1940* (Chapel Hill: University of North Carolina Press, 2001), 53, 55, 68; and Pérez, *Cuba under Platt*, 270–73, 283–84.

10. Pérez, *Cuba under Platt*, 284–96.

11. "Manifesto del Grupo Minorista," *Carteles*, May 22, 1927, 16, 25.

12. In 1927, Machado's government tried suspected communists, including Carpentier. In 1930, Marinello was imprisoned and then exiled to Mexico; *Revista de Avance* was discontinued; see Pamela Maria Smorkaloff, *Readers and Writers in Cuba: A Social History of Print Culture* (New York: Routledge, 1997), 41–42.

13. Francine Masiello, "Rethinking Neocolonial Esthetics: Literature, Politics, and Intellectual Community in Cuba's *Revista de Avance*," *Latin American Research Review* 28, no. 2 (1993): 3–31. On *Carteles*, see Ricardo, *La imprenta en Cuba*, 163. On *Social*, see Smorkaloff, *Readers and Writers in Cuba*, 39–40.

14. Juan Marinello, "Arte y política," *Revista de Avance* (hereafter *RA*), January 15, 1928, 5–7.

15. Ichaso, "Cinema y deportes," *RA*, June 15, 1928, 157.

16. Cinefan, "Notas del Celuloide," *Social*, November 1931, 22; and June 1932, 27; 64. Despite this expressed disdain, *Social* and *Carteles* continued to print plenty of Hollywood-provided publicity during these years.

17. Borge, *Latin American Writers*, 95. Elsewhere, Borge speculates that Latin American intellectuals used pseudonyms when writing about film in part for political cover and in other part to avoid being considered sell-outs by their fellow intellectuals, see Borge, *Avances de Hollywood*, 17.

18. Cinefan, "Notas del Celuloide," *Social*, April 1932, 22–24.

19. "Bourgeois spectator" and "intelligent spectator" are from Cinefan, "Notas del Celuloide," *Social*, December 1932, 41; and February 1931, 52, respectively

20. Cinefan, "Notas del celuloide," *Social*, March 1932, 22–23; and June 1932, 26–27.

21. Cinefan, "Notas del Celuloide," *Social*, April 1931, 66.

22. Cinefan, "Notas del Celuloide," *Social*, June 1932, 25–27.

23. Cinefan, "Notas del Celuloide," *Social*, June 1931, 62.

24. On Mañach's role in the ABC, see Whitney, *State and Revolution*, 85. On the ABC's politics, see Samuel Farber, *Revolution and Reaction in Cuba, 1933–1960: A Political Sociology from Machado to Castro* (Middletown, CT: Wesleyan University Press, 1976), 52–59.

25. J.M.R., review of *Underworld*, *RA*, July 15, 1928. For a discussion of the tradition of banditry as expression of revolutionary Cuban nationalism, see Louis A. Pérez, Jr., *Lords of the Mountain: Social Banditry and Peasant Protest in Cuba, 1878–1918* (Pittsburgh, PA: University of Pittsburgh Press, 1989).

26. On Ichaso's role in the ABC, see Whitney, *State and Revolution*, 85.

27. Ichaso, review of *The Crowd*, *RA*, August 15, 1928, 224.

28. *The Crowd*, written and directed by King Vidor (MGM, 1928).

29. Emphasis added. Ichaso, review of *The Crowd*.

30. Roberto González Echevarría, *Alejo Carpentier: The Pilgrim at Home* (Ithaca, NY: Cornell University Press, 1977), 34–61.

31. Carpentier, "La cinematográfia de avanzada," *Carteles*, November 4, 1928, reprinted in *El cine, décima musa* (Mexico City: Lectorum, 2013) 33–38.

32. Carpentier, "Las campeonas de *sex appeal*," *Carteles*, December 25, 1932; and "El cine en la nueva Rusia," *Carteles*, October 7, 1928, reprinted in *El cine, décima musa*, 97–103, and 26–32 respectively.

33. Carpentier, "La cinematográfia de avanzada," 34, 36.

34. Carpentier "El cine en la nueva Rusia," 27.

35. Luís Ortega García, "Por las calles de la Habana," *CM*, May 1928, 450; and Rodríguez, *Cine silente*, 138–40.

36. Carpentier, "Las tristes consecuencias de una película malsana," *Carteles*, July 17, 1932, reprinted in *El cine, décima musa*, 83–90.

37. Carpentier, "Man Ray," *Social*, July 1928, reprinted in Alejo Carpentier, *Crónicas* (La Habana: Editorial Letras Cubanas, 1985), 1:81.

38. Carpentier, "La cinematografía de avanzada," 35.

39. "Cronología," in Valdés-Rodríguez, *El cine*, 439–40; and Agramonte and Castillo, *Cronología*, 1:297. For his Fausto resignation, see Rene Canizares, "Chatter in Havana," *Variety*, May 8, 1929, 6. For more of these screenings' attendees, see Valdés-Rodríguez, "En torno a los cine-clubes," *Cinema*, December 2, 1956, 12–13.

40. Douglas, *Tienda negra*, 53.

41. José Manuel Valdés-Rodríguez, "Grand Hotel: Una crítica," *Social*, February 1933, 27–28.

42. "Cronología," in Valdés-Rodríguez, *El cine*, 440–41; and Raúl Roa, "José Manuel Valdés Rodríguez," *Bohemia*, April 2, 1971, 56–57.

43. José Manuel Valdés-Rodríguez, "Hollywood: Sales Agent of American Imperialism," *Experimental Cinema* 1, no. 4 (1932): 18–20, 52–53.

44. Ibid., 19.

45. Emphasis in original. Ibid., 20.

46. Emphasis in original. Ibid., 20. Of Chaplin, he writes, "there is no real attempt to present and analyze the inner source, the *social source*, of [the Little Tramp's] condition and status as a lumpenproletariat."

47. Ibid., 53.

48. Eduardo Quiñones, "Crónica de la Habana," *CM*, November 1918, 731; and January 1922, 32.

49. On *The Circus* debut at the Teatro Prado, see Luís García Ortega, "Bullanguera Habana," *CM*, July 1928, 625. Actually, *The Circus* first came to Havana with President Calvin Coolidge via steamship in route to the Sixth Pan-American Conference; see "Pictures for President on His Round Trip to Havana," *Variety*, January 11, 1928, 3.

50. See, for instance, "Luces de la Ciudad," *Bohemia*, April 12, 1931, 38.

51. Ichaso, "Cinema y deportes," *RA*, June 15, 1928, 157.

52. Carpentier, "Glosas de un festival Chaplin," *Carteles*, December 16, 1928; "La cinematografía de avanzada," *Carteles*, November 4, 1928; and "Charles Chaplin in Paris," *Carteles*, May 31, 1931; all reprinted in *El cine, décima musa*, 47, 34, 77. Even the most dogmatic denouncers of US imperialism made an exception of Chaplin's work. For instance, Julio Antonio Mella—founder of the Federation of University Students (FEU) and cofounder of PCC and its

Anti-Imperialist League—wrote, "Yankee cinema, *with the exception of films like those of Chaplin*, has been used for militarist propaganda and for forming the mindset of new generations in the bloody cult of Wall Street's Olympian gods of finance." Emphasis added, Juan Antonio Mella, "O Octubre," *Tren Blindado* (Mexico, 1928), reprinted in *Cine Cubano* 54/55 (March-April 1969): 111.

53. Cinefan, "Notas del Celuloide," *Social*, July 1931, 43.

54. Borge, *Latin American Writers*, 76.

55. Mañach, "El Cameraman," *RA*, March 1929, 89.

56. Carpentier, "Glosas de un festival Chaplin," 45–46.

57. Ibid., 47.

58. Cinefan, "Notas del Celuloide: Máximo Gorky vs. Charles Chaplin," *Social*, December 1932, 41.

59. Ichaso, "Cinema y deportes," *RA*, June 15, 1928, 158.

60. Carpentier, "Glosas de un festival Chaplin," 45.

61. Aguilar, *Cuba 1933*, 116, fn. 1.

62. Roa, *Orto*, July 1929, 14–15, as quoted by Rodríguez, *Cine silente*, Appendix, 198–99.

63. Wenceslao Gálvez y del Monte, *Costumbres, sátiras y observaciones* (La Habana: Rambla, Bouzay y Cia., 1932), 121–23.

64. "Cuban Depression Cut 1929 Receipts," *FD*, March 2, 1930, 12; *FDY* 1931, 1015; and "Machado Regime Hurt Cuban Film Imports," *Variety*, September 26, 1933, 17. Hollywood's market share declined to 80 percent, with German and French films making gains; see Rafael W. Bornn, "Motion Picture Distribution in Cuba," *Motion Pictures Abroad*, US Dept. of Commerce, July 13, 1932, 2, HBSBL.

65. "Few Spanish Versions Being Shown in Cuba," *FD*, August 19, 1931, 1.

66. "News from the Dailies," *Variety*, December 24, 1930, 37.

67. Cinefan, "Notas del Celuloide," *Social*, February 1931, 51–52; and Usabel, *High Noon*, 83.

68. Earle M. Holden, "A Famous Havana Hop!," *MPN*, October 18, 1930, 74.

69. Bornn, "Motion Picture Distribution in Cuba," 3.

70. See Cinefan, "Notas del Celuloide," *Social*, February 1931, 52; and April 1931, 64–65. On these "version" films, see Lisa Jarvinen, *The Rise of Spanish-Language Filmmaking: Out from Hollywood's Shadow, 1929–1939* (New Brunswick, NJ: Rutgers University Press, 2012).

71. "Cuban Urges Ban on English Talkies," *NYT*, October 26, 1929, 36; *FDY* 1931, 1014; *FDY* 1933, 983; and Usabel, *High Noon*, 36.

72. Agramonte and Castillo, *Cronología*, 1:349–50; "Down Havana Way," *FD*, August 29, 1933, 3; and Rene Canizares, "Cuba," *Variety*, October 23, 1934, 60; and December 4, 1934, 60.

73. Jarvinen, *Rise of Spanish-Language Filmmaking*, 88. The *Comisión Revisora* demanded to screen any movies depicting "Mexican life;" see *FDY* 1932, 1019.

74. "Cubans Resent Scenes in Pathé's 'Her Man,'" *MPN*, October 18, 25; and "Cutting Havana Reference," *MPN*, November 8, 1930, 48.

75. Emphasis added, *Bohemia*, November 22, 1931, 42–43.

76. "'Cuban Love Song' Protested in Havana," *NYT*, December 19, 1931, 16.

77. "Cuba Objects to 'Love Song,'" *FD*, December 21, 1931, 4; "Cuban Exhibs Demand That Metro Scrap Its 'Cuban Love Song' Film," *Variety*, January 5, 1932, 11; and "Cuban Film Shelved," *Variety*, January 12, 1932, 11. The PCA denied MGM's request to re-issue the film in 1937, citing the "tremendously unfavorable reaction abroad, particularly in Cuba." See Joseph I. Breen to Louis B. Mayer, March 31, 1937, "Cuban Love Song" file, Production Code Administration Records (hereafter PCA), Special Collections, MHL.

78. Emphasis added. Herron to Jason Joy, December 22, 1931; and Joy to Herron, January 13, 1932. Both in "Cuban Love Song" file, PCA, MHL.

79. Whitney, *State and Revolution*, 81–98. "Yankee meddling" is from a radical student manifesto that Whitney (89) quotes.

80. In Hollywood, according to rumor, Buck Jones taught this Cuban, Manuel Benítez, "how to quick draw his pistol"; see Frank Argote-Freyre, *Fulgencio Batista: From Revolutionary to Strongman* (New Brunswick, NJ: Rutgers University Press, 2006), 152.

81. Whitney, *State and Revolution*, 100–105; and Aguilar, *Cuba 1933*, 171–75.

82. Jorge Mañach, "Revolution in Cuba," *Foreign Affairs*, October 1933, 46–56.

83. Whitney, *State and Revolution*, 119–20; and Argote-Freyre, *Fulgencio Batista*, 110–35.

84. Gilles Mora, *Walker Evans: Havana 1933* (New York: Pantheon, 1989), 8–23. In addition to *Havana Cinema, 1933*, Evans also took a photograph entitled *Cinema*.

85. "Cuban Rumpus Shutters Pix," *Variety*, August 15, 1933, 17; "Along the Rialto," *FD*, August 17, 1933, 4; and Rene Canizares, "Chatter in Havana," *Variety*, September 19, 1933, 51.

86. "All Havana Theatres Ordered Shut Down," *Variety*, November 14, 1933, 1; 3; "Martial Law in Havana Again," *Variety*, January 19, 1934, 2; and *FDY* 1934, 1019.

Chapter Three

1. Arturo Agramonte and Luciano Castillo, *Cronología del cine cubano*, vol. 2, *1937–1944* (La Habana: Ediciones ICAIC, 2012), 315. For a photo of the Teatro América's lobby floor, see Alejandro G. Alonso, Pedro Contreras, Martino Fagiuoli, eds., *Havana Deco* (New York: W. W. Norton & Co., 2007), 142–43.

2. "Un esplendido almuerzo-homaje ofrecieron a Henry Weiner," *Cinema*, September 21, 1941, 17. Here, *Cinema* published the same photo (fig. 3.2) used by United Artists' Foreign Department newsletter, *Around the World* (hereafter *ATW*), vol. 9, no. 3: 3. All editions of *ATW* are from boxes 2–3, series 12D, UAC.

3. Ibid.

4. David F. Schmitz, *Thank God They're on Our Side: The United States and Right-Wing Dictatorships, 1921–1965* (Chapel Hill: University of North Carolina Press, 1999).

5. For a succinct articulation (and endorsement) of this phenomenon, see Luís Sánchez Amago, "Lo que pasa en Cuba," *CM*, June 1942, 299.

6. Roosevelt, First Inaugural Address, March 4, 1933, reprinted in Richard Polenberg, *The Era of Franklin D. Roosevelt: A Brief History With Documents* (Boston: Bedford/St. Martin's, 2000), 40–44. On the relationship between the Great Depression and the Good Neighbor Policy, see Frederick B. Pike, *FDR's Good Neighbor Policy: Sixty Years of Generally Gentle Chaos* (Austin: University of Texas Press, 1995).

7. Historian Mark Berger considers this "long-standing tension between the idea of the Americas (North and South) as a historical unity" and Latin America as a "sub-America" to be a key characteristic of "Pan-American liberalism"; *Under Northern Eyes: Latin American Studies and U.S. Hegemony in the Americas 1898–1990* (Bloomington: Indiana University Press, 1995), 15, 17, 42.

8. See Greg Grandin, *Empire's Workshop: Latin America, the United States, and the Rise of the New Imperialism* (New York: Metropolitan Books, 2006).

9. Argote-Freyre, *Fulgencio Batista*, 144–45, 170, 188–89, 193.

10. Irvin Gellman, *Roosevelt and Batista: Good Neighbor Diplomacy in Cuba, 1933–1945* (Albuquerque: University of New Mexico Press, 1973). For more on how US policymakers dealt with

this contradiction, see Eric Paul Roorda, *The Dictator Next Door: The Good Neighbor Policy and the Trujillo Regime in the Dominican Republic, 1930–1945* (Durham, NC: Duke University Press, 1998).

11. As quoted by Gellman, *Roosevelt and Batista*, 164.

12. Argote-Freyre, *Fulgencio Batista*, 208, 225–29; and Whitney, *State and Revolution*, 12.

13. Argote-Freyre, *Fulgencio Batista*, 125, 134–37, 142–47, 202–22 247.

14. See Rene Canizares, "Cuba," *Variety*, October 23, 1934, 60.

15. Roa to Pablo de la Torriente Brau, June 5, 1936, as quoted by Pérez, *On Becoming Cuban*, 295.

16. Argote-Freyre, *Fulgencio Batista*, 156–57, 165–77, 236; and Whitney, *State and Revolution*, 16, 122–48, 157–58, 167.

17. Whitney, *State and Revolution*, 135, 84; and Gellman, *Roosevelt and Batista*, 170.

18. Pérez, *Cuba: Between Reform*, 280–81.

19. As quoted by Argote-Freyre, *Fulgencio Batista*, 147.

20. Press Release, "Commerce Department Creates New Motion Picture Trade Promotion Unit," US Commerce Dept., June 30, 1937, HBSBL.

21. "U.S. Pix Up in Cuba," *Variety*, February 12, 1935, 31; Harold S. Tewell, "The Cuban Motion Picture Industry," in *Motion Pictures Abroad*, U.S. Commerce Dept., July 15, 1935, 8, HBSBL; "Film Exports Aided by Trade Agreements," *FD*, September 19, 1935, 8.

22. "A Better Break for Films Via American Trade Agreements," *FD*, July 20, 1939, 12; and Carl E. Milliken (Foreign Dept. Chief, MPPDA) to Joseph McConville (Columbia), January 6, 1942, reel 7, from the Motion Picture Association of America general correspondence, MHL.

23. Tewell, "The Cuban Motion Picture Industry," 6.

24. "The Motion Picture Production Code," 1930, Appendix, in Leonard J. Leff and Jerold L. Simmons, *The Dame in the Kimono: Hollywood, Censorship, and the Production Code*, 2nd ed. (Lexington: University Press of Kentucky, 2001), 300.

25. Brian O'Neil, "The Demands of Authenticity: Addison Durland and Hollywood's Latin Images during World War II" in *Classic Hollywood, Classic Whiteness*, ed. Daniel Bernardi (Minneapolis: University of Minnesota Press, 2001), 363.

26. Usabel, *High Noon*, 41–43; and "Cuban Squawk on WB Picture in Spain," *Variety*, June 12, 1935, 13. On Hollywood's self-interest in revising its representations, see Ruth Vasey, "Foreign Parts: Hollywood's Global Distribution and the Representation of Ethnicity," in *Movie Censorship and American Culture*, ed. Francis G. Couvares (Washington: Smithsonian Institution Press, 1996).

27. See, for instance, Adrián Pérez Melgosa, "Hemispheric Romances at the Cinematic Contact Zone," in *Cinema and Inter-American Relations: Tracking Transnational Affect* (New York: Routledge, 2012), 76–105; and Philip Swanson, "Going Down on Good Neighbors: Imagining *América* in Hollywood Movies of the 1930s and 1940s," *Bulletin of Latin American Research* 29, no. 1 (2010): 71–84.

28. "Hot in Havana," *Variety*, May 1, 1934, 21.

29. "Hollywood Inside," *Variety*, December 5, 1934, 2; and January 2, 1935, 2.

30. "PAR's 'Rumba' is a Pain to Cuba," *Variety*, March 6, 1935, 25; "Approves 'Rumba,'" *FD*, March 19, 1935, 7; and "Internationalism a Hard Denominator," *FD*, March 21, 1935, 10.

31. "U.S. Pix Blow Cuba if Censorship Sticks," *Variety*, June 30, 1936, 1; and "Cuba Retreating on Censorship Front," *Variety*, July 29, 1936, 1.

32. Pérez Firmat, *Havana Habit*, 73–76. On the vogue of Cuban music in the States from the 1930s through the 1950s, see Pérez, *On Becoming Cuban*, 198–218.

33. "Sergio Orta: Cubanizando a Hollywood," *Bohemia*, November 23, 1941, 36–37, 57–58.

34. *ACRC 1940–41*, 1.

35. For a montage of stars' personal salutations, see *Bohemia*, December 28, 1941, 12.

36. On "trade-fan magazine," see Weiner to Walter Gould, February 3, 1937, unnumbered folder, b. 39, Z Accessions, UAC. *Cinema* was published every Saturday, and it could be found on newsstands, in subscribers' homes, and in waiting rooms in doctors' and dentists' offices throughout Havana.

37. Emphasis added. Perdices, "Son Cosas Nuestras," (hereafter SCN), review of *That Night in Rio*, July 20, 1941, 3. Despite being born in Madrid, or more likely because of it, Perdices was a vocal enthusiast of *Cubanidad*; for his origins, see Agramonte and Castillo, *Cronología*, 1:354.

38. Perdices, "SCN," review of *Blood and Sand*, *Cinema*, November 2, 1941, 3.

39. Desi Arnaz, *A Book* (New York: Warner Books, 1976), 7–128.

40. *ACRC 1940–41*, 1. See also "Un Cubano Triunfa en Hollywood," *Cinema*, December 1, 1940, 17; and "De Cuba vino el mozo y se caso con la bella," *Bohemia*, January 19, 1941, 70–71.

41. Maria M. Garrett, "Desi Arnaz escribe la primera pagina de la historia de Cuba en Hollywood," *Cinema*, December 22, 1940, 17.

42. "Charles B. Garrett Takes Bride," *FD*, July 17, 1934, 3; and "Down in Havana," *FD*, August 2, 1934, 11.

43. See Pierre de Ramos, "Charles B. Garrett," *Cinema*, October 10, 1948, 13; and Passenger list, *S.S. Havana*, Arriving New York, May 16, 1914, *New York Passenger Lists, 1820–1927* [database on-line], Provo, UT: Ancestry.com.

44. "Spanish Writer Joins Columbia," *FD*, April 16, 1931, 2; and "Along the Rialto," *FD*, May 31, 1935, 4.

45. "Along the Rialto," *FD*, September 29, 1929; December 8, 1931, 4; and April 11, 1932, 7; *Exhibidor*, January 6, 1940, 3; and Agramonte and Castillo, *Cronología*, 2:227, 234.

46. Her husband was Orlando de Cardenas; Kathy Glasgow, "Eyewitnesses to History," *Miami New Times*, December 19, 1996. Accessed September 4, 2015: http://www.miaminewtimes.com/news/eyewitnesses-to-history-6361193.

47. "Along the Rialto," *FD*, May 31, 1935, 4.

48. *Cinema*, January 14, 1940, 16.

49. "Cuba's General Report of May 1934" and "As of February, 1935," "Cuba-General" tab, in "Cuba Black Book," f. Cuba, b. 3, series 1F, UAC; see also Rene Carnizares, "Cuba," *Variety*, November 6, 1934, 68.

50. Agramonte and Castillo, *Cronología*, 1:351; "Cuba Rumbas vs. % B.O. Deals," *Variety*, November 27, 1934, 21.

51. Smith's surname derives from Irish ancestors who came to Cuba in the early nineteenth century; see Rodríguez, *Cine silente*, 126, fn 19. On the chains, see "Down Havana Way," *FD*, December 31, 1934, 5; and Weiner's General Report for June 1938, 2, f. 4, b. 6, series 5A, UAC.

52. "Cuban Film Business Up," *FD*, October 2, 1936, 1; "Attendance Up in Cuba," *FD*, October 9, 1936, 7; "Building Boom Will Give Havana 25 New Theaters," *FD*, October 5, 1937, 1, 9; Nathan D. Golden, Motion Picture Division, US Commerce Dept., "Review of Foreign Film Markets during 1938," 193–94, HBSBL. In 1936, UA reported annual grosses of $400,000 from Cuba; see Usabel, *High Noon*, 126.

53. Weiner's General Report for November 1936; and for July 1938, both f. 4, b. 6, series 5A, UAC; and Agramonte and Castillo, *Cronología*, 2:61.

54. Alonso et al., *Havana Deco*, 57.

55. *Mensajero Paramount*, August 1938, xxiii, no. 8, 14.

56. "Along the Rialto," *FD*, September 13, 1940, 6; and "Ballying Films in Big League Style in Havana," *Variety*, January 21, 1942, 12.

57. *ACRC 1941–42*, 142. On this construction boom, see "Cuban Business Gaining," *FD*, February 19, 1940, 6; "Cuban Imports at Record," *FD*, January 29, 1941, 3; "Warner Hits High in Cuba," *FD*, June 20, 1941, 6; and "Leg. Spurs Theater Building in Cuba," *FD*, July 3, 1941, 1.

58. "$400,000 Valcarce House to Be Ready in Winter," *FD*, September 18, 1940, 7; "New Havana Theatre Opens," *Variety*, April 15, 1941, 25; and *ACRC 1941–42*, 48. It opened with a premiere of *All This and Heaven, Too*, attended by an "audience of social and civic notables"; *Motion Picture Herald*, May 10, 1941, 46.

59. On United Artists' upgrade on Consulado, see Weiner, General Report of September 1937, f. 4, b. 6, series 5A, UAC. Columbia, MGM, and Universal were also on Consulado, while Fox, Paramount, Warner Bros., and RKO had offices on adjoining streets.

60. *ACRC 1941–42*, 78. On the "Film Club" organized by exhibitors and distributors, see Weiner, General Report for April 1937, f. 4, b. 6, series 5A, UAC.

61. See O'Brien, *Revolutionary Mission*, 213, 235–37.

62. *Cine-Mundial's* new Cuba correspondent said as much; see Luís Sánchez Amago, *CM*, June 1942, 299.

63. Pérez, *Cuba: Between Reform*, 201–5.

64. See "O'Connor and Lewis Swap," *Variety*, February 19, 1936, 22.

65. El Caballero King, "Honor a quien honor merece," *Cinema*, June 8, 1941, 5; and Ramón Peon, "Rellenos," *Cinema*, June 15, 1941, 4.

66. *Cinema*, October 7, 1945, 4; and *ACRC 1943–44*, 106. See also "Para. Makes Changes In Central America," *FD*, September 29, 1934, 2; and "Veinticinco años de exitos consecutivos en Cuba," *Cinema*, April 26, 1942, 13.

67. "Rapoport's Spot," *Variety*, March 7, 1933, 13; and *Cinema*, April 5, 1942, 16.

68. Rene Canizares, "Havana," *Variety*, January 26, 1932, 44; for a photo, see *CM*, September 1939, 406; and *ACRC 1942–43*, 20. For his birth in Italy, see Peter Rosario Colli's draft registration card, September 12, 1918, *U.S., World War I Draft Registration Cards, 1917–1918* [data-base online], Provo, UT: Ancestry.com, 2005. On his Cuban citizenship, see Peter Rosario Colli, Petition for Naturalization, October 26, 1971, *Florida Naturalization Records, 1847–1995* [data-base online], Provo, UT: Ancestry.com, 2011.

69. Joaquin Báez-Miró, "Henry Weiner toda una institución"; and Báez-Miró, "Honor, a Quien Honor Merece," *Cinema*, October 6, 1940, 17; and *ACRC 1943–44*, 106.

70. "Weiner, Co. M, 2 Ga. Inf.," in Carded Records Showing Military Service of Soldiers Who Fought in Volunteer Organizations during the Spanish-American War and the Philippine Insurrection, 1899–1927, RG94, U.S. National Archives & Records Administration.

71. Henry Weiner, Petition for Naturalization, May 22, 1900, *New York*, Index to Petitions for Naturalization Filed in New York City, 1792–1989 [database on-line], Provo, UT: Ancestry.com, 2007; and Henry Weiner, U.S. Passport Application, May 23, 1900, *U.S. Passport Applications, 1795–1925* [database on-line], Lehi, UT: Ancestry.com, 2007.

72. Báez-Miró, "Honor," 17.

73. Levine, *Tropical Diaspora*, 3–8; 19–20. See also Dana Evan Kaplan, "Fleeing the Revolution: The Exodus of Cuban Jewry in the Early 1960s," *Cuban Studies* 36 (2005): 129–54.

74. *Almanaque Hebrea Vida Habanara*, eds. S. M. Kaplan and A. J. Dubelman, 1944, 39-c.

75. "Anna Weiner," death date: 1927, *JewishGen Online Worldwide Burial Registry (JOWBR)* [database on-line], Provo, UT: Ancestry.com, 2008.

76. As quoted by Agramonte and Castillo, *Cronología*, 2:255; see also *ATW* 8, no. 3: 14.

77. Báez Miró, "Honor," 17; El Cabellero King, "Noticias del Momento," *Cinema*, August 17, 1941, 4; and Valdés-Rodríguez, "Un esplendido almuerzo-homenaje," 17.

78. *ATW* 6, no. 2: 3–4.

79. *ATW* 8, no. 5: 1.

80. *ATW* 13, no. 4: 2.

81. "Salute to Cuba," *ATW* 10, no. 3: 26; and "Welcome Home to Havana," *ATW* 7, no. 3.

82. *ATW* 13, no. 1: page not numbered.

83. *ATW* 10, no. 3: 5; and *ATW* 11, no. 2: 12.

84. ATW 2, no. 3: page not numbered.

85. Weiner, Reports for November 1936; May 1938; August 1938; and July 1938, f. 4, b. 6, series 5A, UAC.

86. To approach compliance to the "Law of 50 Percent," all new hires at UA Havana had to be Cuban. Letter from Weiner, November 23, 1937, "Employer's Liability" tab, in "Cuba Black Book."

87. Weiner to Arthur Kelly (UA VP), July 10, 1937, "Taxes" tab, in "Cuba Black Book."

88. "Cuba-Competitors" tab, "Cuba Black Book." For lists of employees at the various Hollywood offices, see *ACRC 1945–46*, 123–26. For average incomes in Cuba at this time, see Jorge I. Domínguez, *Cuba: Order and Revolution* (Cambridge, MA: Harvard University Press, 2009), 698.

89. Whitney, *State and Revolution*, 5, writes, "The best and most secure employers were often American businesses, since these tended to be less vulnerable to the vicissitudes of the export economy." For MGM, see *Cinema*, January 14, 1940, 16; for United Artists, see *ATW* 13, no. 4: 2.

90. Emphasis added. "Una Organización que Honra a Cuba: La Havana Business Academy," *Cinema*, August 16, 1942, 12. See also Pérez, *On Becoming Cuban*, 401.

91. This phrase is used to describe a visiting RKO executive, *Cinema*, September 7, 1941, 10.

92. On Selznick, see *Cinema*, May 12, 1940, 13. On Skouras, see *Cinema*, October 7, 1945, pages not numbered.

93. *ACRC 1943–44*, 101; *Cinema*, November 8, 1942, 17; *Cinema*, September 7, 1941, 10, respectively.

94. "Homenaje merecido," *Cinema*, July 9, 1944, 4.

95. For Saenz at RKO in 1932, see "Down Havana Way," *FD*, March 11, 1932, 3. For his resignation, see *ACRC 1954*, 72.

96. "La convencion del Caribe del RKO Radio in la Habana," *Cinema*, September 7, 1941, 10–12.

97. See Pérez, *On Becoming Cuban*; and Whitney, State and Revolution, 6.

98. *ACRC 1941–42*, 77; *ACRC 1940–41*, 75; and *ACRC 1945–46*, 89, 73.

99. For quote, see *Exhibidor*, January 1, 1941, 4; for names listed, see *ACRC 1940–41*, 154–55; see also *ACRC 1941–42*, 50–51; *ACRC 1943–44*, 111; *ACRC 1945–46*, 75. On Smith's start date, see "Col's Havana Exch.," *Variety*, March 25, 1931, 35.

100. ACRC *1943–44*, 113; and *ACRC 1940–41*, 55.

101. Fox ad: *Exhibidor*, January 10, 1940, 1; Paramount ad: *Cinema*, January 19, 1941, 10. By 1941, *Exhibidor* was also the official organ of the *Unión de Técnicos Cinematográficos Cubanos* and avidly advocated for a Cuban national film industry; see Agramonte and Castillo, *Cronología*, 2:59, 287.

102. "Los empresarios solo esperarán treinta días en el problema con la Fox," *Cinema*, June 11, 1939, 6; and Douglas, *La tienda*, 66, 69. On García's tenure at Universal, see Obit, *Variety*, May 15, 1963, 87.

103. Agramonte and Castillo, *Cronología*, 2:176.

104. Whitney, *State and Revolution*, 6.

105. Chávez, "Ambiente Cinematográfico Nacional," *Cinema*, June 18, 1944, 5; and July 19, 1942, 3; and Perdices, "SCN," *Cinema*, January 25, 1942, 3.

106. See Agramonte and Castillo, *Cronología*, 2:244; and "Pratchett, Block-Booking Emissary to Cuba," *FD*, June 19, 1940, 6.

107. "Yanks Clamp Down on Cubans in Decree Beef," *Variety*, November 27, 1940, 14.

108. Mary Louise Blanco, "Cuban Decree 'All a Mistake,'" *FD*, November 27, 1940, 8; and "Delay Cuban Decree Action," *FD*, September 18, 1940, 1.

109. "Translation of Cuban Decree No. 604, Modification of Decree 1396," US Commerce Dept., in f. 10, b. 67, series 2A, UAC; and "Havana Council Requests Fines for All Theatres Not Using Cuban Actors," *Variety*, May 26, 1954, 12; and Douglas, *La tienda*, 82, 103, 113, 115, 117.

110. Agramonte and Castillo, *Cronología*, 1:371; and "Story Woe Offs 'Garcia' til Armistice Day," *Variety*, October 31, 1935.

111. *A Message to Garcia*, dir. George Marshall (Twentieth-Century Fox, 1936).

112. Ibid.

113. Ibid.

114. For US promotion, see ads for *A Message to Garcia* in *Variety*, January 1, 1936, 50; and March 25, 1936, 26. The Cuban ad is from *Diario de la marina*, July 4, 1936.

115. *Diario de la marina*, July 2, 1936, 6.

116. Francisco Ichaso, review of *A Message to Garcia*, in *Diario de la marina*, July 7, 1936, 6.

117. Ibid.

118. Roosevelt, "The 'Forgotten Man' Speech," April 7, 1932, *The American Presidency Project*, http://www.presidency.ucsb.edu/ws/?pid=88408.

119. Michael Denning, *The Cultural Front: The Laboring of American Culture in the Twentieth Century* (London: Verso, 1997), 137.

120. For thoroughgoing analyses of this period of Hollywood history, see Ceplair and Englund, *Inquisition in Hollywood*; and Saverio Giovacchini, *Hollywood Modernism: Film and Politics in the Age of the New Deal* (Philadelphia: Temple University Press, 2001).

121. Chaplin, "*A Comedian Sees the World*," in *Woman's Home Companion*, October 1933, 15; 17, as quoted by Charles J. Maland, *Chaplin and American Culture: The Evolution of a Star Image* (Princeton, NJ: Princeton University Press, 1989), 130.

122. Karl Kitchen, *NYT*, March 17, 1935, 8, as quoted by Maland, *Chaplin*, 142.

123. *Modern Times*, dir. Charles Chaplin (United Artists, 1936).

124. Ibid.

125. Ibid.

126. For *Modern Times' Fausto* run, see listings in *El Mundo*, April 2–20, 6. For Weiner's assessment of Chaplin's appeal, see Cuba-Box Office Values, as of March 29, 1934, "Box Office Values" tab, "Cuba Black Book."

127. Whitney, *State and Revolution*, 122–48.

128. "Cronología," in Valdés-Rodríguez, *El cine*, 441.

129. I also suspect that Valdés-Rodríguez was one of many ex-PCC members who became disenchanted with Marxist orthodoxy generally (for reasons similar to those of artists who quit the CPUSA: i.e., top-down, doctrinaire rigidity) and, later, the PCC specifically (due to its 1938 alliance with Batista).

130. Valdés-Rodríguez, review of *Modern Times*, *El Mundo*, March 28, 1936.

131. Ibid. On Valdés-Rodríguez's biography, see "Cronología," in Valdés-Rodríguez, *El cine*, 441.

132. Ibid. In *Diario de la marina*, March 28, 1936, 6, Francisco Ichaso also loved *Modern Times* and asked explicitly: "Social content?" And then answered his own rhetorical questions:

it is "a satire against the babelism of recent times, against the incessant bustle in which Man is overwhelmed without purpose."

133. Valdés-Rodríguez, "El problema social en el cine," May 1, 1938, original source unknown, reprinted in Valdés-Rodríguez, *El cine en la Universidad de la Habana* (La Habana: Empresa de Publicaciones Mined, 1966), 328–31.

134. Ibid.

135. Ibid.

136. Whitney, *State and Revolution*, 123–74; and Argote-Freyre, *Fulgencio Batista*, 186–273.

137. Gellman, *Roosevelt and Batista*, 127, 153.

138. Ameringer, *Cuban Democratic Experience*, 13–14; and Gellman, *Roosevelt and Batista*, 181.

139. On *Mr. Deeds'* critical reception in Havana, see Agramonte and Castillo, *Cronología*, 1:377. On *Meet John Doe*, see chap. 4.

140. Valdés-Rodríguez reminds his reader that this was *Mr. Deeds'* moral in his review of *Mr. Smith Goes to Washington*, *El Mundo*, February 6, 1940, 6.

141. *Mr. Smith Goes to Washington*, dir. Capra.

142. Ad, *Diario de la marina* and *El Mundo*, both on February 4, 1940, both page 6. I am grateful to Consuelo Elba-Álvarez for identifying the photographs here; email correspondence with author, January 23, 2007.

143. By 1939, the ABC Party (Ichaso's) had aligned with Grau; see Whitney, *State and Revolution*, 173; and Argote-Freyre, *Fulgencio Batista*, 260–61. See also Ichaso, speech, given sometime in 1939, as quoted by Farber, *Revolution and Reaction*, 56.

144. Ichaso, review of *Mr. Smith Goes to Washington*, *Diario de la marina*, February 6, 1940, 6.

145. Ibid. The phrase "essay of national indignation" is from Santos, "Historia," in Valdés-Rodríguez, *El cine*, 8.

146. Ibid. Emphasis added.

147. Ibid.

148. Valdés-Rodríguez, review of *Mr. Smith Goes to Washington*.

149. Ibid. Emphasis added.

150. Ibid.

151. Gellman, *Roosevelt and Batista*, 179–83.

Chapter Four

1. "'Week-End in Havana' in Swank Cuban Debut," *FD*, January 12, 1942, 5; and *Exhibidor*, January 18, 1942, 3.

2. See the cover of *Cinema*, December 21, 1941; and *Cinema*, January 11, 1942, 5. For the lookalike contest, see *Exhibidor*, January 18, 1942, 3. Two months earlier, winners of Faye lookalike contests *in the United States* spent their prize vacations in Havana and met with Mayor Raúl Menocal; see "Distinguidas bellezas nos visitan," *Cinema*, November 2, 1941, 7, 12.

3. José Maria Santos, "Va Triunfando Hispanoamerica," *Bohemia*, January 4, 1942, 8–9, 81.

4. Elena de la Torre, "Romero, el invulnerable," *CM*, July 1941, 302; 336.

5. *Week-End in Havana*, dir. Walter Lang (Twentieth-Century Fox, 1941).

6. "Foreign Ad-Publicity Chiefs Set Campaigns," *Variety*, February 25, 1942, 14. "*America—Libre y Unida*" ran on the pages of *Cinema* and *Cine-dial*, a fanzine introduced in 1942. "*Unidos venceremos*" appeared on the title page of the *ACRC* and on the covers of *Cinemanía*, a fanzine introduced in October 1943.

7. Cosme de la Torriente, "Que es el Fondo Cubano-Americano de Socorro a los Aliados," May 6, 1943, printed in Mrs. Miniver handbill, author's collection, 6–7.

8. Fernández, as quoted by *Cinema*, June 14, 1942, 5. *The Navy Comes Through*, dir. A. Edward Sutherland (RKO Pictures, 1942).

9. Rosalie Schwartz, *Pleasure Island: Tourism and Temptation in Cuba* (Lincoln: University of Nebraska Press, 1997), 101; Pérez, *Cuba: Between Reform*, 282–83; and Gellman, *Roosevelt and Batista*, 190–94.

10. OIAA, "The Americas Cooperate for Victory" (Washington, 1942), 16, compiled in the Motion Picture Society for the Americas's (hereafter MPSA)) New Writers' Guide, f. 523–25, MPSA records, Margaret Herrick Library.

11. "Analysis of an All-American Policy," n.d., f. 1, b. 1, Series O-OIAA, Record Group 4: Nelson A. Rockefeller Personal Papers (hereafter RG4), Rockefeller Family Archives, Rockefeller Archive Center (hereafter RFA-RAC).

12. "Order Establishing the Office for the Coordinator of Commercial and Cultural Relations between the American Republics," August 16, 1940, Appendix, Donald W. Rowland, *History of the Office of Coordinator of Inter-American Affairs* (Washington, 1947), 280.

13. Bulletin, Report and Analysis Section, OIAA, December 4 & 6, 1941, Press & Radio Analysis, series O-OIAA, RG4, RFA-RAC.

14. See Fred Fejes, *The Office of the Coordinator of Inter-American Affairs and the Origins of United States Cultural Diplomacy* (New York: Columbia University-New York University Consortium, 1993).

15. Francis Jamieson, *Reminiscences of Francis Jamieson* (New York: Columbia University Oral History Collection, 1959), 96; and Rowland, *History of the Office of Coordinator*, 55.

16. Wendy L. Wall, *Inventing the "American Way": The Politics of Consensus from the New Deal to the Civil Rights Movement* (New York: Oxford University Press, 2008).

17. *En Guardia*, Year 1, n. 8 (Summer 1942), 24–25. All copies of *En Guardia* are from Series O-OIAA, RG4, RFA-RAC; finding aid number 789.

18. Coordination Committee Activities, #123, June 20–26, 1944, 4; and #144, November 14–20, 1944, 5; both in bound volumes, Series O-OIAA, RG4, RFA-RAC.

19. "Cagney on Salute to Cuba Airer," *Variety*, October 1, 1942, 6; MPSA Foreign Committee meeting minutes, October 15, 1942, in f. 4, b. 14, Walter Wanger Papers, Wisconsin Center for Film and Theater Research (WCFTR); and Memo, Hopper to Runyon, re: "Fiftieth Anniversary Broadcasts Saluting the Americas," February 8, 1945, 1, f. 13, b. 3, series 4F, UAC.

20. Rowland, *History of the Office of Coordinator*, 55; and Coordination Committee for Cuba operations as of 1944, f. 34, b. 4, Series O-OIAA, RG4, RFA-RAC.

21. "Garrett Heads Cuban Pix Section of OCIAA," *FD*, November 18, 1942, 8.

22. On the OIAA's nontheatrical program, see Rowland, *History of the Office of Coordinator*, 67–82. For Cuba specifics and film titles, see Coordination Committee Activities, as of February 28, 1943, 2; #136 (September 19–25, 1944), 1; and #158 (March 13–19, 1945), 6; in f. 34, b. 4; and "16mm Films Being Distributed in Latin America," p. 7, f. 56, b. 7, all from Series O-OIAA, RG4, RFA-RAC.

23. "Cuba," *En Guardia*, Year 2, no. 1, 18–21.

24. Ibid.

25. "Suggested Working Program for the Motion Picture Society for the Americas," 3–4, n.d., f. 4, b. 14, Walter Wanger Papers, WCFTR.

26. For Cuban trade press pride, see *Cinema*, May 11, 1941, 17; and *Exhibidor*, August 1, 1942, 4. For Durland at those screenings, see Valdés-Rodríguez, "En torno a los cine-clubes y su función

superadora," *Cinema*, December 2, 1956, 12–13. He also served as a film critic in Havana, according to "Production Code Administered by Nine Man Board," *Motion Picture Herald*, June 28, 1941, 62. For Durland at the PCA, see O'Neil, "The Demands of Authenticity."

27. The collaboration between the OIAA-MPD, the MPSA, and the Hollywood Left is laid out in hundreds of files held in the MPSA, MHL. For more details on the mechanisms of that collaboration, see my forthcoming article "The Strongest Bonds: Hollywood Diplomacy and the (Pan)American Way during World War II."

28. Perhaps most famously, the OIAA-MPD contracted Orson Welles to make a (never-produced) Pan-American feature; see Catherine L. Benamou, *It's All True: Orson Welles's Pan-American Odyssey* (Berkeley: University of California Press, 2007). For the OWI in Hollywood, see Clayton R. Koppes and Gregory Black, *Hollywood Goes to War: How Politics, Profits and Propaganda Shaped World War II Movies* (Berkeley: University of California, 1987).

29. Ceplair and Englund, *Inquisition in Hollywood*, 104–12.

30. *Blockade*, dir. Dieterle, written by John Howard Lawson (United Artists, 1938).

31. David Welky, *The Moguls and the Dictators: Hollywood and the Coming of World War II* (Baltimore: John Hopkins University Press, 2008), 71–77; 110–13.

32. "Garfield Planes to Mex, Cuba for 'Juarez,'" *Variety*, June 12, 1939, 6.

33. *The Great Dictator*, written and directed by Charles Chaplin (United Artists, 1941).

34. Michael E. Birdwell, *Celluloid Soldiers: The Warner Bros. Campaign against Nazism* (New York: New York University Press, 1999), 103–4, 108, 118.

35. "The Story of the Motion Picture Society for the Americas," 47–60, n.d., ca. 1944, 1–6, f. 567, MPSA records, MHL; and OIAA-MPD, "Statement of Activities, June 10, 1943," Lists #8-#10; #14, file 550, MPSA, MHL.

36. f. 4, b. 14, Walter Wanger Papers, WCFTR.

37. MPSA Weekly Report, period ending October 21, 1942, 1; Lists of "Features in Preparation," "Features Completed," and "CIAA Plus Value Feature Films," n.d.; all in f. 4, b. 14, Walter Wanger Papers, WCFTR. And Regional Division Reports, June 6–12, 1942, 1; and December 5–11, 1942, 2, in bound volumes, Series O-OIAA, RG4, RFA-RFA.

38. OIAA-MPD, "Statement of Activities," 6.

39. F. W. Ellis to Nelson Rockefeller, "Films for Mexico," February 2, 1942, 2, f. 488, MPSA, MHL.

40. Victor Borella to Rockefeller, "My Trip throughout the Country on the Spanish-Speaking Minorities Problem," April 2, 1943, f. 36, b. 5, Series O-OIAA, RG4, RFA-RAC.

41. "Suggested Working Program for the Motion Picture Society for the Americas," p. 7, n.d., f. 4, b. 14, Walter Wanger Papers, WCFTR.

42. "Story of the MPSA," 47.

43. "Features Completed," n.d., f. 4, b. 14, Walter Wanger Papers, WCFTR.

44. Durland to William Gordon (RKO), June 8, 1942, file for *The Navy Comes Through*, PCA, MHL.

45. *The Navy Comes Through*, dir. Sutherland.

46. Ibid.

47. Lewis A. Ehrenberg, *Swingin' the Dream: Big Band Jazz and the Rebirth of American Culture* (University of Chicago Press, 1998).

48. *Bataan*, dir. Tay Garnett (MGM, 1943).

49. Maurice Ries, "Evidence that U.S. 'Dollar Diplomacy' Wasn't an Organized Effort to Loot the Other Americas," July 27, 1943, f. 304, MPSA, MHL.

50. Maurice Ries, "Film to Offset 'Dollar Diplomacy Feeling,'" July 27, 1943, f. 583; Francis

Alstock, "Notes Prepared for MPD"; John C. Higgins, treatment, November 26, 1943, f. 264; and Breen to Ries, December 6, 1943, f. 228, all at MPSA, MHL.

51. "CIAA Plus Value Feature Films"; OIAA-MPD, "Statement of Activities," lists; "Story of the MPSA," 48; and Status of Projects, January 1-March 31, 1944, 139, Project Reports, bound volumes, Series O-OIAA, RG 4, RFA-RAC.

52. *Hemisphere Reel News*, June 1942, 3, Periodicals Collection, MHL; Report of Field Activities of the Coordination Committees, covering April 11–18, 1942, 2; and May 16–22, 1942, 1, Regional Division Reports, bound volumes, series O-OIAA, RG4, RFA-RAC; and "Story of the MPSA," 21.

53. Florence Horn, "U.S. Movies for Brazil," February 8, 1943, f. 264, MPSA, MHL.

54. Maurice Ries, memos, "Salving Old Inter-American Wounds," and "Use of the Dramatic Possibilities of the Building of the Panamá Canal," both July 27, 1943, f. 268, MPSA, MHL.

55. See Allen Rivkin, "Projects," November 23, 1942, f. 267; Rivkin, December 1, 1942, f. 263; and files 204–15; all at MPSA, MHL.

56. Foreign Committee meeting minutes, October 22, 1942, f. 4, b. 14, Walter Wanger Papers, WCFTR; and Foreign Committee meeting minutes, December 16, 1942, f. 263, MPSA, MHL.

57. "Emergency Program for Immediate Action," December 13, 1941, 4, f. 262, MPSA, MHL.

58. "Warners Planning Series of 'Good Neighbor' Pix," *FD*, May 10, 1939, 1; Welky, *Moguls and Dictators*, 175; "Quién Debe Hacer a Bolívar en el Cine?" *CM*, August 1940, 364; and *CM*, September 1940, 433.

59. "Story of the MPSA," 38.

60. Paul J. Vanderwood, "An American Cold Warrior: *Viva Zapata!*" in *American History/American Film*, ed. John E. O'Connor and Martin A. Jackson (New York: Frederick Ungar Publishing, 1979), 185–87; and "Story of the MPSA," 60.

61. "Feature Pictures Planned and under Consideration," n.d., f. 513, MPSA, MHL.

62. Halsey Raines and Gene Martel, treatment for "The Flame of Freedom (The Story of Jose Marti)," 1–26, f. 237, MPSA, MHL.

63. Ibid.

64. Minutes, meeting at (MGM producer) Jack Chertok's house, November 29, 1942; and memo, MPSA to Foreign Committee, August 19, 1941; both compiled in New Writers' Guide (f. 523–525), MPSA, MHL.

65. See "WB Does a Bit of Island Jumping," *Variety*, February 25, 1944, 18; "Story of the MPSA," 57; and Bruce F. Kawin, "Introduction," in *To Have and Have Not Screenplay* (Madison: University of Wisconsin Press, 1980), 27–32.

66. *To Have and Have Not*, dir. Howard Hawks, adapted by Jules Furthman (Warner Bros., 1944).

67. This trope was also shaped by *domestic* propaganda imperatives. See, for instance, Bernard F. Dick, *The Star-Spangled Screen: The American World War II Film* (Lexington: University Press of Kentucky, 1975), 165–71.

68. Coordination Committee Activities, covering September 12–18, 1944, Series O-OIAA, RG4, RFA-RAC.

69. "Content directive," undated, f. 74, b. 9, Series O-OIAA, RG4, RFA-RAC.

70. *Wake Island*, dir. John Farrow, written by W.R. Burnett and Frank Butler (Paramount Pictures, 1942).

71. See, for example, Koppes and Black, *Hollywood Goes to War*; and Jeanine Basinger, *The World War II Combat Film: Anatomy of a Genre* (Wesleyan University Press, 2003).

72. *The Story of Dr. Wassell*, dir. Cecil B. DeMille (Paramount Pictures, 1944); and *Bataan*, dir. Garnett.

73. The same photo of the Chaplin billboard that appeared in *ATW* (fig. 4.4) was used in *Cinema*, January 19, 1941, 15.

74. "El mayor acontecimiento del año," *Cinema*, January 19, 1941, 8–9; and Perdices, "SCN," *Cinema*, January 19, 1941, 3. On the press preview, see Cinemateca's file on *The Great Dictator*, at ICAIC. When it debuted in New York, *Bohemia* announced its "important place in the long *chaplinesa* history against tyranny"; Germinal Barral, "Charles Chaplin en 'El Dictador,'" *Bohemia*, October 27, 1940, 20–21, 54.

75. Carpentier, "Al margen del cable," *Tiempo*, January 24, 1941, compiled in *El cine, décima musa*, 126–27. Valdés-Rodríguez, review of *The Great Dictator*, *El Mundo*, 1941, reprinted in Valdés-Rodríguez, *El cine*, 62–69.

76. Agramonte and Castillo, *Cronología*, 2:317–18. See also, *ATW* 10, no. 2: 3, which published a photo of Weiner accepting the FRCT award.

77. The Great Dictator, dir. Chaplin.

78. "Palabras finales de Chaplin en 'El gran dictador,'" *Cinema*, January 5, 1941, 7; and "El mayor acontecimiento," *Cinema*, January 19.

79. For cine totals, see *ACRC 1943–44*, 20; and *ACRC 1945–46*, 39.

80. Chávez, "Ambiente Cinematográfico Nacional," *Cinema*, August 16, 1942, 3.

81. For ARTYC and FRCT membership, see *Cinema*, June 21, 1942, 3; and *ACRC 1940–41*, 182, respectively.

82. For these lists, see Agramonte and Castillo, *Cronología*, 2:317–18, 360, 408–9, 441; and *FD*: January 13, 1943, 15; January 18, 1944, 18; and January 15, 1945, 22. And, for both lists for years 1941–43, see *ACRC 1943–44*, 47.

83. *Meet John Doe*, dir. Frank Capra, written by Robert Riskin (Warner Bros., 1941).

84. "El Trofeo Presidente Batista Para El Año 1942," *CM*, March 1942, 137. Members of FRCT and Peter Colli attended the ceremony.

85. Chávez, "Ambiente Cinematográfico Nacional," *Cinema*, October 25, 1942, 3; *FDY* 1944, 821; and Regional Division reports, December 26-January 1, 1943, 4, Series O-OIAA, RG4, RFA-RAC. See also Usabel, *High Noon*, 182, on *Underground* (1941) as a top-grosser.

86. Sánchez Amago, "Lo Que Pasa en Cuba," *CM*, February 1942, 93.

87. On Stewart, see *Cinema*, April 27, 1941, 12; and April 16, 1944, 5. On Ford, Gable, Montgomery, and Taylor, see Lydia del Rio, "Los actors-soldados regresan," *Cinema*, October 7, 1945, 4. On Holden, see *Cinema*, June 28, 1942, 5. They also praised Capra and Huston for their enlistment in the Army Signal Corps; see *Exhibidor*, January 18, 1942, 2.

88. "Desi Arnaz, el simpatico artista cubano," *CM*, June 1943, 277. See also *Cinema*, October 22, 1945, 15.

89. See *Cinema*, July 12, 1942, 6; *Exhibidor*, July 12, 1942; and October 10, 1942, 1; Luís Sánchez Amago, "Lo que pasa en Cuba," *CM*, September 1942, 449.

90. "Cuban Film Employees Called to Colors," *FD*, October 13, 1942, 10.

91. *Cinema*, November 15, 1942, 13; *ACRC 1942–43*, 42. See also *Exhibidor*, November 1942, 1.

92. Carrerá (UNE president), as quoted by *Cinema*, May 24, 1942, 15.

93. "Warners Honored by Cuban Government," *Variety*, September 27, 1944, 1, 16; and photos, *CM*, November 1944, 565.

94. Colli to Warner, June 20, 1940, as quoted by Birdwell, *Celluloid Soldiers*, 83.

95. "Decree Blacks Out Havana's Theaters," *FD*, March 27, 1941, 1. For the decree's lifting, see *Exhibidor*, May 1, 1942, 3.

96. See *FD*: February 13, 1942, 1–2; August 27, 1942, 1; June 2, 1942, 1; July 20, 1942, 1; June 4, 1942, 1. On five-month lag time, see Nathan D. Golden, US Dept. of Commerce, *Motion Picture Markets of Latin America* (Washington: Government Printing Office, 1944), 97.

97. "Cuban Anthem to Open and Close," *FD*, January 20, 1942, 6.

98. Villazón Deus, *Exhibidor*, January 1, 1943, 3; and June 7, 1942, 1. Cuba's minister of war also advocated for these fundraisers, see Weiner to Schroeder, June 29 1942, f. Charities, b. 3, series 4f, UAC.

99. Villazón Deus, *Exhibidor*, July 5, 1942, 4; and *Cinema*, June 28, 1942, 5.

100. Weiner to Schroeder, June 29, 1942.

101. On *The Great Dictator*, see Weiner to Mulrooney, June 19, 1942; and on *Sergeant York*, Louise F. Smith to Alexander Korda, October 7, 1942, both in f. Charities, b. 3, series 4f, UAC. On *Mrs. Miniver*, see "Valcarce Circuit's Havana House Signs for Metro Pix," *FD*, May 11, 1943, 2. On *This Is the Army* at Teatro América, see Coordination Committee report, May 30-June 6, 1944, p. 3, Series O-OIAA, RG4, RFA-RAC.

102. Playbill, *Mrs. Miniver* at the Teatro América, May 24, 1943, p. 39, author's collection.

103. "Noticias de aqui y de alla," *Cinema*, July 12, 1942, 15. See also Pierre de la Chandee, "La Unificación de las Americas," *Cinema*, December 24, 1944, pages not numbered. *Cinema* covers also featured OIAA-counseled films *Going My Way*, *The Human Comedy*, *Thousands Cheer*, and *Tortilla Flat*.

104. "El cine y la guerra," *Cinema*, January 14, 1945, 2.

105. Perdices, "Son Cosas Nuestras" (hereafter "SCN"), *Cinema*, March 30, 1941, 3.

106. All Perdices, "SCN," *Cinema*, 3: review of *The Moon Is Down*, July 25, 1943; and review of *Watch on the Rhine*, April 30, 1944. See also review of *Man Hunt*, August 17, 1941; review of *Behind the Rising Sun*, February 13, 1944; and review of *Dragon Seed*, June 10, 1945.

107. All Perdices, "SCN," *Cinema*, 3: review of *Song of Russia*, November 19, 1944; and review of *Till We Meet Again*, March 11, 1945. See also review of *The Fighting Sullivans*, October 15, 1944, 3; and review of *Tender Comrade*, November 5, 1944.

108. OIAA-MPD, "Statement of Activities," List #8; "Story of the MPSA," 49. In MPSA Weekly Report ending October 21, 1942, 1, it was deemed good "Anti-Fascist" propaganda for the OIAA.

109. *Exhibidor*, October 31, 1944, 1; and November 7, 1944, 1.

110. On Cooper's casting, see *Exhibidor*, April 15, 1942, 1. On Flynn's experience in Spain, see Errol Flynn, *My Wicked, Wicked Ways*, reprint ed. (New York: Cooper Square Press, 2003), 227–38. On Hemingway, see Jeffrey Meyers, *Hemingway: A Biography* (New York: Harper & Row, 1985), 298–388.

111. "Los Próximos Estrenos," *Cinema*, May 14, 1944, 3; and "Por Quien Doblan las Campanas Preoccupe el Gobierno de Franco," *Exhibidor*, January 1, 1943, 11.

112. Weiner, general report for July, 1938, 2, f. 4, b. 6, series 5A, UAC. See also Ariel Mae Lambe, "Cuban Antifascism and the Spanish Civil War: Transnational Activism, Networks, and Solidarity in the 1930s" (PhD diss., Columbia University, 2014; ProQuest [Pub Num. 3617146]).

113. Koppes and Black, *Hollywood Goes to War*, 71.

114. *For Whom the Bell Tolls*, dir. Sam Wood, written by Dudley Nichols (Paramount Pictures, 1943).

115. María M. Garrett, "Sobre un Libro de Controversia Internacional," *Cinema*, July 25, 1943, 6.

116. For instance, "Los Próximos Estrenos," *Cinema*, November 5, 1944, 3, proclaimed it a "masterpiece of the Cinema," and a magnificent film about "the struggle for freedom of an oppressed people."

117. "Por quién doblan las campanas," *Cinema*, December 24, 1944, special edition, not numbered.

118. *Cinema*, cover, January 14, 1945.

119. "Story of the MPSA," 55; and *FDY* 1946, 690.

120. Perdices, "SCN," *Cinema*, May 6, 1945, 3. For Havana cines' closings and five minutes of silence, see *Exhibidor*, April 16, 1945, 3, 4.

121. Perdices, "SCN," *Cinema*, May 6, 1945, 3.

122. Ibid.

123. Valdés-Rodríguez, *El cine en la Universidad*, xiii-xiv. On Valdés-Rodríguez at the ARTYC, see Agramonte and Castillo, *Cronología*, 2:276.

124. *Exhibidor*, June 15, 1942, 1.

125. "Películas proyectadas en el curos de cine de la escuela de verano," in Valdés-Rodríguez, *El cine en la Universidad*, 381–82.

126. Valdés-Rodríguez, *El cine en la Universidad*, xiv-xv.

127. Len Daly (Publicity Dept.) to Walter Gould (Foreign Department Chief), July 27, 1943, pp. 2–3, f. Cuba 1/11/37–7/8/47, b. 39, Z Accessions, UAC.

128. Valdés-Rodríguez was admitted to the United States for one month beginning July 6, 1941, by State Department invitation; see NAI Number 2790468, RG85, Series Title: *Alien Passenger List of Vessels Arriving at Key West, Florida*, compiled in *Florida, Passenger Lists, 1898–1963* [database on-line], Lehi, UT: Ancestry.com, 2006. For more on his visit, see Agramonte and Castillo, 2:299–300. On the Museum of Modern Art's's role in promoting film studies in the United States and the world, see Haidee Wasson, *Museum Movies: The Museum of Modern Art and the Birth of Art Cinema* (Berkeley: University of California Press, 2005).

129. Valdés-Rodríguez, review of *The Great Dictator*, *El Mundo*, 1941, reprinted in Valdés-Rodríguez, *El cine*, 62–69.

130. Ibid.

131. On the OWI's contribution, see Koppes and Black, *Hollywood Goes to War*, 94.

132. *Keeper of the Flame*, dir. George Cukor, written by Donald Ogden Stewart (MGM, 1943).

133. Valdés-Rodríguez, review of *Keeper of the Flame*, *El Mundo*, 1943, reprinted in Valdés-Rodríguez, *El cine*, 79–80.

134. Ibid.

135. *Watch on the Rhine*, dir. Herman Shumlin, written by Dashiell Hammett and Lillian Hellman (Warner Bros., 1943).

136. Valdés-Rodríguez, review of *Watch on the Rhine*, 1944, reprinted in Valdés-Rodríguez, *El cine*, 131–36.

137. Ibid. Though Brau was Puerto-Rican born, he was raised in Cuba and Cubans claimed him as their own.

138. For instance, one leader of the 1957 attack on Batista's Presidential Palace was Carlos Gutiérrez Menoyo, who served during WWII as a sergeant of US forces in Europe; Jaime Suchlicki, *University Students and Revolution in Cuba, 1920–1968* (Coral Gables: University of Miami Press, 1969), 76.

139. Valdés-Rodríguez, review of *To Have and Have Not*, 1945, reprinted in Valdés-Rodríguez, *El cine*, 136–40. On its Teatro América debut, see Agramonte and Castillo, *Cronología del cine cubano*, vol. 3, *1945–1952* (La Habana: Ediciones ICAIC, 2013), 14.

140. For Aguirre's participation in the anti-Machado student movement, see Julio Velis, "Mirta Aguirre," *La Última Hora*, October 23, 1952, 5. For more biography, see also Leonardo Depestre Catony y Luis Úbeda Garrido, *Personalidades Cubanas Siglo XX* (La Habana: Editorial

de Ciencias Sociales, 2002), 8–10. *Hoy* began to be legally published in May 1938; see Farber, *Revolution and Reaction*, 85. See also Orlando Carrió, "Cronología de Mirta Aguirre," in Marcia Castillo Vega, ed., *Bibliografia de Mirta Aguirre* (La Habana: Editorial Letras Cubanas, 1988), 7–12.

141. Aguirre, reviews of *The Hour before the Dawn*, *Hoy*, September 6, 1944. See also review of *Days of Glory*, *Hoy*, December 22, 1944; and review of *The Story of Dr. Wassell*, *Hoy*, May 3, 1945, all reprinted in Mirta Aguirre, *Crónicas de cine*, vol. 1, eds. Olivia Miranda and Marcia Castilla (La Habana: Editorial Letras Cubanas, 1988), 48–50, 58–59, and 85–86, respectively.

142. Aguirre, reviews in *Hoy*: of *Destination Tokyo*, June 12, 1944; of *Counter-Attack*, July 5, 1945; of *None Shall Escape*, June 27, 1944; and of *Tomorrow, the World!* May 16, 1945, all reprinted in Aguirre, *Crónicas*, 1:32, 102–3, 27–28, and 92–94, respectively.

143. Emphasis added. Aguirre, review of *Watch on the Rhine*, *Hoy*, June 14, 1944, reprinted in Aguirre, *Crónicas*, 1:22–24.

144. Ameringer, *Cuban Democratic Experience*, 18, 21, 46; and Gellman, *Roosevelt and Batista*, 214.

145. Emphasis added. Aguirre, review of *Watch on the Rhine*.

146. Ibid.

147. OIAA, "The New Cuban Administration," pp. 3–9, f. 22, b. 3, Series O-OIAA, RG4, RFA-RAC.

148. "Towards the Organization of the World to Preserve the Peace," *En Guardia*, Year 4, no. 5 (March 1945): 33. On this postwar reorganization, see Rosenberg, *Spreading the American Dream*, 212.

149. May, *Big Tomorrow*, 140–41.

Chapter Five

1. Poster. Author's Collection. The poster's printer, José Oriol Ramos y Hermanos, was considered *the* printer of the film giro; see *Cinema*, October 19, 1958, 20.

2. Robert Sklar, "Havana Episode: The Revolutionary Situation of *We Were Strangers*," in *Reflections in a Male Eye: John Huston and the American Experience*, ed. Gaylyn Studlar and David Desser (Washington, DC: Smithsonian Institution Press, 1993): 63–77; and Tony Shaw, "Hollywood's Changing Takes on Terrorism: Re-viewing John Huston's *We Were Strangers*," *Journal of Contemporary History* (May 2016): 1–19.

3. *We Were Strangers*, written and directed by John Huston, co-written by Peter Viertel (Columbia Pictures, 1949).

4. Ibid.

5. Ibid. Mid-film, it is revealed that Fenner's character was actually Cuban-born, but his accentless English and the casting of John Garfield make it difficult to think of him as anything but American.

6. Ibid.

7. Cuban fan in *Estrellas Continentales*, forwarded from Ernesto P. Smith to Columbia's Foreign Dept., September 20, 1949; f. 594, b. 65, John Huston Papers, MHL. Cubans also appreciated that Huston visited Havana to get the details right; see J. Segovia, "El Realismo de John Huston," *Mañana*, August 21, 1949, 6.

8. Perdices, "SCN," August 14, 1949, 3.

9. "Just for Variety," *Variety*, July 5, 1948, 4.

10. Emphasis added. Aguirre, review of *We Were Strangers*, August 11, 1949, reprinted in *Crónicas*, 2:40–41.

11. For film noir as postwar sociopolitical critique, see Nicholas Christopher, *Somewhere in the Night: Film Noir and the American City* (New York: Free Press, 1997); Edward Dimendberg, *Film Noir and the Spaces of Modernity* (Cambridge, MA: Harvard University Press, 2004); Frank Krutnik, *In a Lonely Street: Film Noir, Genre, Masculinity* (New York: Routledge, 1991); and James Naremore, *More than Night: Film Noir in Its Contexts* (Berkeley: University of California Press, 1998).

12. Huston, *An Open Book* (New York: Da Capo Press, 1972), 42–47, 73, 130. The *Juarez* marginalia is from Mark Harris, *Five Came Back: A Story of Hollywood and the Second World War* (New York: Penguin, 2014), 34.

13. Henry Blanke to Geoffrey Sherlock, June 26, 1942; and Addison Durland to Jack Warner, July 2, 1942, both *Treasure of the Sierra Madre* file, PCA Records, MHL.

14. Gary Edgerton, "Revisiting the Recordings of Wars Past: Remembering the Documentary Trilogy of John Huston," in Studlar and Desser, *Reflections in a Male Eye*, 33–62.

15. Harris, *Five Came Back*, 409.

16. Joseph Breen to Jack Warner, August 23, 1946, and January 13, 1947, *Treasure of the Sierra Madre* file, PCA Records, MHL.

17. *The Treasure of the Sierra Madre*, written and directed by John Huston (Warner Bros., 1948); and May, *Big Tomorrow*, 244–47.

18. James Agee, *The Nation*, January 31, 1948, 136–37.

19. See Wall, *Inventing the "American Way,"* chaps. 6–8.

20. The nineteen included Howard Koch (Huston co-scenarist on *Sergeant York*), Lester Cole, Richard Collins, Edward Dmytryk, Ring Lardner, Jr., John Howard Lawson, Albert Maltz, Lewis Milestone, Irving Pichel, Robert Rossen, and Dalton Trumbo; see Ceplair and Englund, *Inquisition in Hollywood*, Appendix 4, 439–40. On the film titles, see Andrew J. Falk, *Upstaging the Cold War: American Dissent and Cultural Diplomacy, 1940–1960* (Amherst: University of Massachusetts Press, 2010), 107–8.

21. Ayn Rand, *Screen Guide for Americans*, 1947, as quoted by Ceplair and Englund, *Inquisition in Hollywood*, 213.

22. Ceplair and Englund, *Inquisition in Hollywood*, 275.

23. "Hollywood Proves—You Don't Have to Take It," *Variety*, October 28, 1947, 16.

24. Huston, *Open Book*, 134; and Jeffrey Meyers, *John Huston: Courage and Art* (New York: Crown Archetype, 2011), 130.

25. *Key Largo*, written and directed by John Huston, co-written by Richard Brooks (Warner Bros., 1948).

26. Huston to Margaret Chase, February 10, 1948, f. 218, b. 21, John Huston Papers, MHL.

27. Ibid.

28. *The Asphalt Jungle*, written and directed by John Huston, co-written by Ben Maddow (MGM, 1950).

29. Eric Johnston in 1946, as quoted by Thomas Schatz, *Boom and Bust: American Cinema in the 1940s*, vol. 6 of *History of the American Cinema* (Berkeley: University of California Press, 1997), 382.

30. Schatz, *Boom and Bust*, 4–5, 323.

31. "Poland's Charges," *Variety*, February 23, 1948, 15. The MPEA set out to help "the film industry exercise prudent selectivity of pictures going abroad" with "the best interest of our country" in mind; see Eric Johnston, "Film Knows No International Barriers," February 1947, 2, microfiche, reel 6, MPAA, MHL.

32. Wagnleitner, *Coca-colonization and the Cold War*, 270.

33. See Russell Holman (Paramount) to Francis S. Harmon, November 4, 1948; and Emmanuel Silverstein (Fox) to Harmon, November 10, 1948; microfiche, reel 14, MPAA, MHL

34. On *Key Largo*, see "Los Pistoleros del Cine," *Cinema*, October 24, 1948, 4. On *Treasure*, see ad, *Diario de la marina*, July 29, 1948, 8.

35. See "Just for Variety," *Variety*, April 9, 1948, 4.

36. Lawrence Grobel, *The Hustons* (New York: Scribner, 1989), 320. On Smith, see Peter Viertel, *Dangerous Friends: Hemingway, Huston and Others* (New York: Viking, 1991), 31, 45.

37. Viertel, *Dangerous Friends*, 34, 44; and John Leggett, *Ross and Tom: Two American Tragedies* (Boston: Da Capo Press, 1974), 381, 384. Huston also consulted with the president of the Cuban Academy of History and one-time ABC Society conspirator, Emetario Santovenia; see Dr. Baralt to Huston, undated, f. 594, b. 65, John Huston Papers, MHL.

38. Huston, interview, in Gerald Pratley, *The Cinema of John Huston* (New York: A. S. Barnes, 1977), 72.

39. Clipping, *NYT*, February 15, 1948; and Breen to Harry Cohn, September 3, 1948, both from *We Were Strangers* file, PCA Records, MHL.

40. Review of *We Were Strangers*, *Hollywood Reporter*, April 22, 1949, f. 592, b. 64, John Huston Papers, MHL.

41. Virginia E. Williams to Harry Cohn, May 9, 1949, *We Were Strangers* folder, PCA Records, MHL.

42. Lester W. Roth to Virginia E. Williams, May 16, 1949; and Arthur DeBra to Williams, May 19, 1949, *We Were Strangers* folder, PCA Records, MHL.

43. Bernard F. Dick, "The History of Columbia, 1920–1991," in *Columbia Pictures: Portrait of a Studio*, ed. Bernard F. Dick (Lexington: University Press of Kentucky, 1992), 16; and Axel Madsen, *John Huston: A Biography* (New York: Doubleday, 1978), 94.

44. Robert Nott, *He Ran All the Way: The Life of John Garfield* (New York: Limelight Editions, 2003), 238–311; Viertel, *Dangerous Friends*, 273–74; and Meyers, *John Huston*, 154.

45. MPAA memo, June 15, 1950, *We Were Strangers* folder, PCA Records, MHL.

46. See "Scramble to Get New U.S. Product on Arg. Screens," *Variety*, August 1, 1951, 10.

47. Columbia ad for *We Were Strangers*, *Mañana*, August 9, 1949, 6.

48. Ameringer, *Cuban Democratic Experience*, 122, 125–26; and Schwartz, *Pleasure Island*, 114.

49. Pérez, *Cuba: Between Reform*, 285.

50. Ameringer, *Cuban Democratic Experience*, 55–56; 135.

51. Ibid., 47–49; and Pérez, *Cuba: Between Reform*, 285–86. For a history of labor activism in Cuba, see Karl O. Magnusen and Leonardo Rodríguez, "Cuba, Labor, and Change," *Labor Studies Journal* 23, no. 2 (Summer 1998): 21–40; and Robert J. Alexander, *A History of Organized Labor in Cuba* (Westport, CT: Praeger, 2002).

52. Emphasis added. Chibás, as quoted by Ameringer, *Cuban Democratic Experience*, 80.

53. Ameringer, *Cuban Democratic Experience*, 50; for a full account of these plots, see Ameringer, *The Caribbean Legion: Patriots, Politicians, Soldiers of Fortune, 1946–1950* (University Park, PA: Pennsylvania State University Press, 1996).

54. *Bohemia*, August 14, 1949, 68, as quoted by Ameringer, *Caribbean Legion*, 116. Martin, *Early Fidel*, characterized the plotters as "an amalgam of idealists, delinquents and adventurers," including Castro, who had a romantic "idea of striking a blow for freedom with gun in hand" and a "*need* to express his heady passions in some heroic and preferably insurgent form" (31–32).

55. See *ACRC 1945–46*, 12, 98, 106, and 84.

56. Perdices, "SCN," *Cinema*, April 30, 1950, 3.

57. On "Yon" Wayne, see Patrick Symmes, *The Boys from Dolores: Fidel Castro's Classmates*

from Revolution to Exile (New York: Pantheon, 2007), 30. For the film dialogue, see *Flying Leathernecks*, dir. Nicholas Ray (RKO Radio Pictures, 1951). For fanzine coverage of Wayne's visit, see Cover, *Cinema*, May 20, 1951; and *Cinema*, May 13, 1951, 15.

58. Prío, as quoted by Ameringer, *Caribbean Legion*, 113.

59. For Lansky in Cuba in the earlier period, see Mark Galeotti, "Forward to the Past: Organized Crime and Cuba's History, Present and Future," *Trends in Organized Crime* 9, issue 3 (Spring 2006): 45–60. For the Aútentico era activities, see Ameringer, *Cuban Democratic Experience*, 39–40; and Eduardo Sáenz Rovner, *The Cuban Connection: Drug Trafficking, Smuggling and Gambling in Cuba from the 1920s to the Revolution* (Chapel Hill: University of North Carolina Press, 2008) 66–70.

60. Ameringer, *Cuban Democratic Experience*, 22, 29–30, 151, 177–79; Coltman, *Real Fidel Castro*, 22–28; and Suchlicki, *University Students and Revolution*, 47–57. For Ichaso's denunciation of these pistoleros as false revolutionaries, see "Eso que llaman revolución," *Diario de la marina*, June 26, 1948, 4.

61. Ameringer, *Cuban Democratic Experience*, 87, 12, 68, 150.

62. Franqui, *Diary*, 41.

63. See James Gilbert, *A Cycle of Outrage: America's Reaction to Juvenile Delinquency in the 1950s* (New York: Oxford University Press, 1986).

64. Douglas, *La tienda*, 111; "Cuba Censorship Hits Juvenile Attendance," *FD*, June 29, 1945, 1; and "Double Censorship Stirs Cuban Exhibs," *FD*, November 22, 1944, 1.

65. Berta Diaz Martinez, "La influencia del cine en la mente infantil," *Bohemia*, December 24, 1950, 29–32, 105–7.

66. Coltman, *Real Fidel Castro*, 16.

67. Fidel Castro, interview by Franqui, *Diary*, 6.

68. Angel Cubas Sánchez, interviewed by Pierre de Ramos, "Kaleidoscopio Cinematográfico," *Cinema*, July 18, 1948, 13. On Castro's peers, see Symmes, *Boys from Dolores*, 67–68.

69. Coltman, *Real Fidel Castro*, 27–33.

70. Castro, "The Dignity of Our Freedom Fighters," speech at the University of Havana, November 6, 1947, reprinted in Rolando E. Bonachea and Nelson P. Valdés, *Revolutionary Struggle, 1947–1958*, vol. 1 of the *Selected Works of Fidel Castro* (Cambridge: MIT Press, 1972), 132.

71. Ameringer, *Cuban Democratic Experience*, 44, 144; and Ilan Ehrlich, *Eduardo Chibás: The Incorrigible Man of Cuban Politics* (Lanham, MD: Rowman & Littlefield, 2015), 151.

72. Castro, "Yo acuso," *Alerta*, January 28, 1952, reprinted in Bonachea and Valdés, *Revolutionary Struggle*, 136–43. On *The Asphalt Jungle's* Havana premiere, see Ad, *Diario de la marina*, September 3, 1950, 14.

73. Perdices, "SCN," *Cinema*, April 15, 1951, 3.

74. *Sunset Boulevard*, written and directed by Billy Wilder, co-written by Charles Brackett (Paramount Pictures, 1950).

75. Clara Ronay, in Playbill, *Sunset Boulevard*, at the Teatro América, April 1951, author's collection, 14, 16.

76. Geza Polaty (Cuba manager) to John J. Glynn (International Dept. Chief), May 31, 1949, 1, f. Peter Colli, NY Visit, b. 16671B, Warner Bros. Archive, Cinematic Arts Library, University of South California, Los Angeles, California (hereafter WBA).

77. Pierre de Ramos, *Cinema*, July 2, 1950, 5; and Pedro Pablo Chávez, "Cinematices," *Cinema*, September 15, 1946, 3.

78. "Latins Hunger for Pix," *Variety*, May 23, 1946, 1, 14.

79. Emphasis original. Rafael de la Guardia, "La Verdadera Verdad," *Cinema*, July 29, 1945, 3.

80. For Warner Bros., see *ACRC 1945–46*, 104; and *Paramount International News*, March 20, 1947, 36.

81. Clift: *FD*, February 27, 1948, 2; and *Mañana*, September 13, 1950, 6. Cooper: Ameringer, *Cuban Democratic Experience*, 165. Flynn: *Variety*, December 15, 1948, 62; and *Variety*, August 24, 1951, 2. Johnson: *Variety*, February 15, 1946, 6; Mitchum: *Variety*, February 6, 1947, 4. Powell: *Cinema*, April 6, 1947, 15. Robinson: *Cinema*, February 18, 1945, 15 (including photo).

82. "Power and Romero Arrive in Havana," *Variety*, October 21, 1946, 1.

83. *ACRC 1946–47*, 108; and Pedro Pablo Chávez, "Cinematices," *Cinema*, July 21, 1946, 3.

84. "Skouras, Silverstone Host 600 at Havana Dinner," *FD*, April 29, 1947, 7; and "Con el amigo de ayer y el de hoy," *Cinema*, May 4, 1947, 15.

85. *Paramount International News*, September 28, 1951, 5; and *Cinema*, September 23, 1951, 5.

86. For example, see *Cinema*, June 15, 1947, 15.

87. *ACRC 1946–47*, 93; 95.

88. *ACRC 1945–46*, 81.

89. "Havana Making Pitch for Tourist Trade," *Variety*, December 7, 1949, 49, 51; and "UA's 6,750-Seat Cuban Showcase," *Variety*, June 21, 1950, 14.

90. "20th-Fox May Acquire Havana 'Show-Window,'" *FD*, November 6, 1942, 1, 2. The "show-window" in question was the Teatro Nacional; see *Exhibidor*, February 25, 1943, 4. On MGM, see "MGM to Build First-Run Theater in Cuba," *FD*, April 30, 1943, 1; and *FDY* 1946, 689. On UA's looks at the Teatros Prado, Nacional, and Campoamor, see Weiner to Walter Gould (UA Foreign Manager), October 5, 1944, and Gould to Weiner, October 11, 1944, f. 9, box 3, series 4F, UAC.

91. See "PAR, Cobian Form Cuban Circuit," *Variety*, October 31, 1944, 8.

92. See minutes of WB board of directors, June 21, 1945; Colli to Glynn, February 15, 1946; and Mestre to Harry M. Kalmine (VP, Warner Theatres), January 1, 1948, all f. 571, b. 16771A, WBA.

93. "Items belonging to Warner Bros.," Inventory, Warner Theatre Sale, #2, f. 581, b. 16771A, WBA. On the concessions trend, see Schatz, *Boom and Bust*, 293.

94. "Warner Execs Off for Havana House Debut," *Variety*, December 22, 1947, 10; "Cuba's Prexy Attends WB Theatre Opening," *Variety*, January 2, 1948, 4; and "Warners Gets Prado as Havana Showcase," *FD*, September 16, 1947, 1.

95. Wolfe Cohen (VP, International Department) to Mestre, July 8, 1946; Cohen to Colli, July 2, 1946; and Cohen to Colli, July 8, 1946; all f. 571, b. 16771A, WBA.

96. Mestre to Glynn, March 19, 1946; Mestre to Kalmine, January 21, 1948; and Kalmine to Mestre, February 2, 1948, all f. 571, b. 16671A, WBA.

97. "Havana Film B.O. Takes Sharp Dive," *Variety*, September 29, 1948, 25.

98. On the legalization of the UEECC, see Douglas, *La tienda*, 66. On the creation of the Unión de Empleados de Oficinas de Casas Aquiladores de Películas, see Agramonte and Castillo, *Cronología*, 2:174.

99. "Pay, Not Workers, 'Sit Down' in Cuba," *FD*, July 24, 1944, 1; Douglas, *La tienda*, 104–5.

100. See *Cinema*, December 17, 1944, 17, and July 7, 1946, 3; Agramonte and Castillo, *Cronología*, 2:440, and *Cronología*, 3:9; Douglas, *La tienda*, 109; and *ACRC 1945–46*, 64.

101. Pedro Pablo Chávez, "Cinematices," *Cinema*, July 21, 1946, 3; "Cuban President Mulls Minimum Wage Demand," *FD*, May 9, 1946, 7.

102. L. R. Milles and Carlos Orozco, "Patriotica Advertencia al Honorable Sr. Presidente de la Republica," reprinted in *Cinema*, July 7, 1946, 6. For the UNE's position, see "A la opinión pública," reprinted in *Cinema*, July 7, 1946, 3.

103. "All Havana Theaters Close," *FD*, July 3, 1946, 2; "Conference Averts Cuba Theater Strike," *FD*, July 23, 1946, 3; and "Cuban Pay Hikes May Bring B.O. Advances," *FD*, August 13, 1946, 1.

104. Glynn, report, "Miguel Esnard," April 25, 1951, 2, f: Esnard case; and "Weekly Business Report from Cuba," October 13, 1951, f: Union Demands; both Box 16671B, WBA.

105. Samuel Berger to Carl Milliken, January 14, 1947, microfiche, reel 11, MPAA, MHL; and Joaquin Rickard, "Re: Cuba—New Union Demands for Salary Increases and Other Benefits," February 7, 1952, 1, f: Union Demands, Box 16771B, WBA.

106. Colli to Glynn, "Re: Union Demands," December 14, 1951, f: Union Demands, box 16771B; and "Info compiled for the State Dept," 1951, f: Cuba Corporate Data, Box 16771A; both WBA.

107. Jones to Glynn, June 7, 1949, 4; f: Peter Colli, NY Visit; and 16771B; MPAA memo, "Re: Cuba—Checking Expenses," April 20, 1949, f: "CUBA"; all Box 16771B, WBA.

108. See "Dora Bacalchuck," "Esnard case," and "Juan Ponce case" folders, box 16671B, WBA.

109. Phone call transcript, March 14, 1951, 2, in "Esnard case," box 16671B, WBA.

110. "Hollywood Inside," *Variety*, August 16, 1950, 2; and "Uncertainties Abroad," *Variety*, August 23, 1950, 4. On Smith's brief reclamation and unloading, see *ACRC 1949–50*, 89–93; and *ACRC 1950–51*, 92–95.

111. On Teatro Warner, see f: Cuba #2, Box 16671 A, WBA; on Teatro Prado; see Colli to Cohen, February 11, 1954, f: Personnel, b. 16671B, WBA; and *ACRC 1955*, 100.

112. For Warner Bros.' "Economy Program," see Cohen to Colli, June 5, 1947, f: Peter Colli; and Cohen to Jones, f: Economy Program, November 5, 1947, both 16771B, WBA. For UA's, see Arthur Kelly (Executive VP) to All Foreign Exchanges," October 22, 1947, 1, f. 3, b. 6, series 4F; and Kelly to All Foreign Exchanges, November 29, 1948; and March 3, 1950, 2; both f. 15, b. 3, series 6B; all UAC. "Cut to the bone" is from Gould to Sam Berkeris, September 5, 1947, 2, f. 2, b. 6, series 4F, UAC.

113. "WB Maps Latin Overhaul," *Variety*, August 4, 1948, 13; "John Jones Made Warners Mexico Mgr," *Variety*, January 26, 1950, 4; "Reps WB in Cuba," *Variety*, May 18, 1950, 1; and "Geza Polata [sic] to Indonesia," *Variety*, January 20, 1954, 13.

114. "Havana," *Variety*, April 8, 1942, 53; and "Rosenberger to Cuba," *Variety*, April 25, 1944, 4. On Robert Pratchett, see *Cinema*, February 10, 1957, 40.

115. *Cinema*, April 28, 1946, 16, and July 6, 1947, 15; "Reps Metro in Cuba," *Variety*, May 5, 1954, 11; and "Four Loew's Int'l Shifts," January 26, 1956, 4. On O'Connor's return, see *ACRC 1957*, 74.

116. Walter Gould to Gradwell Sears, December 3, 1946, 2, f. 2, b. 6, series 4F, UAC.

117. On "broken heart," see Gould to Osmar Bromberg, April 3, 1947, 1; On "weak," see Gould to Sam Bekeris (Latin American regional manager), September 5, 1947, 2. On "his burden," see Gould to Jack Odell, April 29, 1948; all from f. 3, b. 6, series 4F, UAC.

118. H. W. Schroeder, December 19, 1949; and José Del Amo to Albeck (NY), July 8, 1952, both in f: Cuba, b. 47, Z Accessions, UAC.

119. For "intensified supervision," see Gould to Sears, January 13, 1947. For complaints about Weiner, see Picker to Katz, March 4, 1952, f. 7, b. 1, series 2f, UAC.

120. Albeck to Katz, May 16, 1952; f: Cuba, b. 47, Z Accessions, UAC.

121. Perdices, "SCN," *Cinema*, January 22, 1950, 3.

122. "20th-Fox Publicity Dept. in Havana Swept by Fire," *FD*, May 16, 1941, 2. On Universal's fire, see Casuso to MPAA, "Report on Conditions in Exchanges," February 6, 1948, f. 23, b. 6, series 6B, UAC. And Jones to Glynn, January 30, 1948; and Colli to Jules Levey, April 11, 1949; both in f: Havana, Cuba: Proposed Vaults Exchange, b. 16671A, WBA.

123. "Cuba," *Variety*, December 7, 1949, 12; Colli to Wolfe, May 11, 1950, f: Junking, box 16671A, WBA; and *Cinema*, May 14, 1950, 4.

124. "U.S. Distribs Move to Havana's 'Film City,'" *Variety*, November 29, 1950, 11.

125. See, for instance, Perdices, "SCN," *Cinema*, February 5, 1950, 3.

126. Agramonte and Castillo, *Cronología*, 3:337; and *ACRC 1950–51*, 12.

127. *Cinema*, February 20, 1949, 16. The quotation in the subhead comes from "Siguiendo el mundo," *Bohemia*, November 5, 1950, 15.

128. *A Foreign Affair*, written and directed by Billy Wilder, co-written by Charles Brackett (Paramount Pictures, 1948).

129. Gene D. Phillips, *Some Like It Wilder* (Lexington: University Press of Kentucky, 2010), 106.

130. *Paramount International News*, March 20, 1947, 35.

131. De Zarraga, review of *Edge of Doom*, *Bohemia*, October 8, 1950, 110. Polaty to Glynn, May 14, 1951, f: Ad & Publicity, box 16671B, WBA.

132. See Pierre de Ramos, "Kaleidoscopio Cinematografico," *Cinema*, July 11, 1948, 4; July 18, 1948, 13; July 25, 1948, 4; August 1, 1948, 15; and August 15, 1948.

133. *Cinema*, April 2, 1950, 12.

134. Garrett, "DICTADURA," *Cinema*, April 9, 1950, 13.

135. Armando Cejudo, "Reflejos Sintéticos," *Cinema*, August 26, 1945, 19.

136. Perdices, "SCN," *Cinema*, April 16, 1950, 3; August 17, 1947, 3; March 19, 1950, 3; and March 12, 1950, 3.

137. Perdices, review of *The Long Night*, "SCN," *Cinema*, February 15, 1948, 3.

138. *Till the End of Time*, dir. Edward Dmytryk, written by Allen Rivkin (RKO Pictures, 1946).

139. Emphasis added, Perdices, "SCN," *Cinema*, September 7, 1947, 3.

140. Emphasis added, Perdices, "SCN," *Cinema*, October 31, 1948, 3.

141. Emphasis added, Perdices, "SCN," *Cinema*, July 15, 1951, 3.

142. Ad for *Monsieur Verdoux*, *Diario de la marina*, April 27, 1948, 8.

143. Maland, *Chaplin and American Culture*, 260–86.

144. *Monsieur Verdoux*, written and directed by Charles Chaplin (United Artists, 1947).

145. John Beaufort, "An Assault from Mr. Chaplin," *Christian Science Monitor*, April 19, 1947, as quoted by Maland, *Chaplin and American Culture*, 241.

146. Agramonte and Castillo, *Cronología*, 3:172–73.

147. Ichaso, review of *Monsieur Verdoux*, *Diario de la marina*, April 30, 1948, 8, 10.

148. On their friendship, see Pierre de Ramos, "Francisco Ichaso," *Cinema*, November 7, 1948, 13.

149. Valdés-Rodríguez, review of *Monsieur Verdoux*, 1948, reprinted in *El cine*, 115–22.

150. Interviews by Pierre de Ramos with Valdés-Rodríguez, Don Galaor, Francois Baguer, Ichaso, and Leandro García, printed in *Cinema*, October 3, 1948, 14; October 17, 1948, 13, 16; October 24, 1948, 7, 8; November 7, 1948, 13; and December 5, 1948, 7, respectively.

151. Valdés-Rodríguez, as quoted by Díaz Martínez, "La influencia del cine en la mente infantil," 105–7.

152. Aguirre, "Hollywood se defiende," *Hoy*, November 12, 1947, and "La actividad policíacia de los congresistas norteamericanos," *Hoy*, November 26, 1947; both reprinted in *Crónicas*, 1:162–64, 166–68.

153. Aguirre, "Noticias norteamericanas," *Hoy*, June 1952; and Aguirre, review of *Payment on Demand*, *Vanguardia Cubana*, June 17, 1950, both reprinted in *Crónicas*, 2:65–70.

154. Agramonte and Castillo, *Cronología*, 3:86–87, 132–33, 172–73, 219–20, 286–87, 326.

155. Ibid., 3:219.

156. Valdés-Rodríguez, *El cine en la Universidad*, xv-xvi.

157. Valdés-Rodríguez's *El cine en la Universidad* reprints the Cine de Arte program notes

(for *The Asphalt Jungle*, see 42–44) and lists the movies shown in his summer class by year, 381–86. Also shown in Cine de Arte sessions were *Intruder in the Dust* and Clifford Odets's *None But the Lonely Heart*.

158. On Cabrera Infante, see Raymond D. Souza, *Guillermo Cabrera Infante: Two Islands, Many Worlds* (Austin: University of Texas Press, 1996), 25. On Pineda Barnet, see interview by author. On García Espinosa, see interview by author, Havana, Cuba, April 24, 2004; and García Espinosa *Conversaciones con un cineaste incomodo* (Lincoln, RI: Pukara-Fortitude Art and Cultural Org., 1997), 34. On Massip and Guevera (both attended the 1949 summer class), see José Massip, interview by author, Havana, Cuba, June 17, 2004; see also Valdés-Rodríguez, *El cine en la Universidad*, xvi. On Piñera, see interview by author; and Piñera, "Un homenaje merecido a José M. Valdés-Rodríguez," *Cinema*, August 29, 1954, 12. On Nelson Rodríguez, see interview by author.

159. For his attendance at Cine de Arte sessions, see Rodríguez Alemán, *La sala oscura* (La Habana: Unión de Escritores y Artistas de Cuba, 1982), 1:9–10; in fact, this collection of reviews is dedicated to Valdés-Rodríguez, "teacher, pioneer of film criticism in Cuba." See also Rodríguez Alemán, *Mañana*, June 11, 1953, 6. For further biographical information, see *Diccionario de la literature cubana* (La Habana: Editorial Letras Cubanas, 1984), 908–9.

160. See Rodríguez Alemán, *Mañana*, July 29, 1950, 6; July 13, 1949, 6; May 17, 1950, 6; and June 23, 1950, 6.

161. For US censorship, see Rodríguez Alemán, *Mañana*, review of *Caged*, September 16, 1960, 6. For reviews of *Act of Violence*, *Knock on Any Door*, and *Flamingo Road*, see Rodríguez Alemán, *Mañana*, September 25, 1949, 6, September 9, 1949, 6, and September 23, 1949, 6, respectively.

162. A number were avidly anticommunist, including Ichaso, Perdices, and Rodríguez Alemán. See Ichaso in *Cinema*, August 12, 1951, 7; Perdices, "SCN," *Cinema*, February 19, 1950, 3; and Rodríguez Alemán, *Mañana*, August 11, 1950, 6.

163. Aguirre, review of *His Kind of Woman*, *Hoy*, February 21, 1952, reprinted in *Crónicas*, 2:155–56.

164. On the ARTYC, see *Cinema*, December 47-January 48 special edition, pages not numbered. On Cuban anticommunism, see Ameringer, *Cuban Democratic Experience*, 21–22, 46, 48–49. 63–65, 162.

165. Aguirre, review of *Monsieur Verdoux*, *Hoy*, April 29, 1948, reprinted in *Crónicas*, 1: 224–26.

166. Aguirre, "Goldwyn defiende a Hollywood," *Hoy*, June 27, 1950, reprinted in *Crónicas*, 2:74–77.

167. *From This Day Forward*, dir. John Berry, written by Hugo Butler and Garson Kanin (RKO Pictures, 1946).

168. Aguirre, review of *From This Day Forward*, *Hoy*, August 16, 1946, reprinted in *Crónicas*, 1:140–42.

169. Aguirre, review of *Somewhere in the Night*, *Hoy*, December 3, 1946, reprinted in *Crónicas*, 1:157–58; and review of *Shadow in the Sky*, *Hoy*, August 1952, reprinted in *Crónicas*, 2:242–43.

170. *Mildred Pierce*, dir. Michael Curtiz, written by Ranald MacDougall (Warner Bros., 1945).

171. Emphases added. Aguirre, review of *Mildred Pierce*, *Hoy*, February 27, 1946, reprinted in *Crónicas*, 1:127–29.

172. On Goldman as blacklistee, see Dave Wagner and Paul Buhle, *Blacklisted: The Film Lover's Guide to the Hollywood Blacklist* (New York: Palgrave Macmillan, 2003), 20. *The Big Clock*, dir. John Farrow, written by Jonathan Latimer (Paramount Pictures, 1948).

173. Aguirre, review of *The Big Clock*, *Hoy*, November 9, 1948, reprinted in *Crónicas*, 1:292.

174. Aguirre, review of *A Foreign Affair*, *Hoy*, March 2, 1949, reprinted in *Crónicas*, 2:19–21.

175. Aguirre, review of *Intrigue*, *Hoy*, April 27, 1948, reprinted in *Crónicas*, 1:223–24.

176. Aguirre, review of *The Street with No Name*, *Hoy*, November 12, 1948, in *Crónicas*, 1: 293–94.

177. Emphasis added, Aguirre, review of *Flamingo Road*, *Hoy*, September 28, 1949, in *Crónicas*, 2:57–58.

178. Ameringer, *Cuban Democratic Experience*, 87–89; and Ehrlich, *Eduardo Chibás*, 80–140.

179. It was "prohibited for minors," see ad, *El Mundo*, July 15, 1950, 17.

180. Pérez, *Cuba: Between Reform*, 285; and Ameringer, *Cuban Democratic Experience*, 111.

181. As quoted by Ehrlich, *Eduardo Chibás*, 175; and Emilio Cancio Bello, "El Penúltimo Crimen del Gobierno," *Bohemia*, November 12, 1950, 51, 109–10.

182. Ichaso, "Caudillos y Programas," *Bohemia*, July 30, 1950, 43. On Ichaso's politics (disgusted with Auténtico corruption and supportive of Chibás), see Ehrlich, *Eduardo Chibás*, 167, 171; and Ameringer, *Cuban Democratic Experience*, 60.

183. *All the King's Men*, written and directed by Robert Rossen (Columbia Pictures, 1949). For the film's long run in Havana, see Ad, *El Mundo*, August 23, 1950, 17.

184. Valdés-Rodríguez, review of *All the King's Men*, *El Mundo*, July 18, 1950, 17.

185. Perdices, "SCN," *Cinema*, July 30, 1950, 3.

186. De Zarraga, review of *All the King's Men*, *Bohemia*, July 23, 1950, 108–9.

187. Aguirre, review of *All the King's Men*, *Hoy*, July 21, 1950, in *Crónicas*, 2:81–83.

188. On Chibás's "strong anticommunist stance," see Ameringer, *Cuban Democratic Experience*, 44; Ehrlich, *Eduardo Chibás*, 179.

189. Aguirre, review of *All the King's Men*.

190. Editors, "Una punta de lanza en la libertad de expression," *Bohemia*, August 13, 1950, 73. Ameringer, *Cuban Democratic Experience*, 48–49, 114; and Ehrlich, *Eduardo Chibás*, 178–80, 187–239.

191. *Bohemia*, September 30, 1951, 59.

192. Ameringer, *Cuban Democratic Experience*, 175.

Chapter Six

1. Jamieson, *Reminiscences*, 166.

2. For an example of early summer publicity, see *Cinema*, June 29, 1952, 12. For publicity as the debut neared, see *Diario de la marina*'s and *El Mundo*'s movie pages, starting July 20, 1952. *Viva Zapata!*'s debut was at the cines Trianon, Infanta, Metropolitan, Los Angeles, and Rialto.

3. Jonathan M. Schoenwald, "Rewriting Revolution: The Origins, Production and Reception of *Viva Zapata!*" *Film History* 8 (1996): 120.

4. *Viva Zapata!* dir. Elia Kazan, written by John Steinbeck (Twentieth-Century Fox, 1952).

5. See Vanderwood, "An American Cold Warrior: *Viva Zapata!*" 191, 195; and Richard Slotkin, *Gunfighter Nation: The Myth of the Frontier in Twentieth-Century America* (Norman: University of Oklahoma Press, 1998), 420–27.

6. Perdices, "SCN," *Cinema*, August 3, 1952, 3; and Valdés-Rodríguez, "Viva Zapata," *El Mundo*, July 29, 1952, 6.

7. Ichaso, review of Kazan's *East of Eden*, in *Cinema*, September 18, 1955, 38.

8. Cabrera Infante, review of *La rosa blanca*, *Carteles*, August 22, 1954, reprinted in *A Twentieth Century Job*, trans. Suzanne Jill Levine (New York: Harper & Row, 1984), 34.

9. Ad, *Cinema*, August 24, 1952, 2.

10. "Castro Biopic Via Jerry Wald," *Variety*, April 29, 1959, 1. Castro counted Hemingway's *For Whom the Bell Tolls* as a major influence; see Tad Szulc, *Fidel: A Critical Portrait* (New York: Post Road Press, 1986), 242.

11. Perdices, "SCN," *Cinema*, July 18, 1954, 3.

12. On the Havana press reaction against *Guys and Dolls*, see Pérez, *On Becoming Cuban*, 472.

13. Cabrera Infante, "Marlon Brando, un amigo," *Carteles*, March 4, 1956, 42–44, 48.

14. Walfredo Piñera, interview by author, Havana, Cuba, April 2004; and Nelson Rodríguez, interview.

15. Paterson, *Contesting Castro*, 17; and Gladys Marel García-Pérez, *Insurrection and Revolution: Armed Struggle in Cuba, 1952–1959* (Boulder: Lynne Rienner Publishers, 1998), 5, 8, 12.

16. Geza Polaty to Glynn, March 15, 1952, folder: Miscellaneous, box 16671B, WBA.

17. Szulc, *Fidel Castro*, 223–24; and Suchlicki, *University Students and Revolution*, 62.

18. Armando Hart, *Aldabonazo: Inside the Cuban Revolutionary Underground, 1952–58*, 3rd ed. (New York: Pathfinder Press, 2010), 79, 105; and Szulc, *Fidel Castro*, 228.

19. "Cuba's Fidel Castro Once Mex Film Extra," *Variety*, February 11, 1959, 4.

20. Renée Ramos Reyes, in *Four Women: Living the Revolution*, vol. 2 of *An Oral History of Contemporary Cuba*, ed. Oscar Lewis, Ruth Lewis, and Susan M. Rigdon (Urbana: University of Illinois Press, 1977), 26. 26; and Ramón L. Bonachea and Marta San Martín, *The Cuban Insurrection, 1952–1959* (New Brunswick, NJ: Transaction Press, 1995): 14–17.

21. Antonio Rafael de la Cova, *The Moncada Attack: Birth of the Cuban Revolution* (Columbia: University of South Carolina Press, 2007), 34, 37, 42.

22. García-Pérez, *Insurrection and Revolution*, 9.

23. Hart, *Aldabonazo*, 94; and Enrique Oltuski, *Vida Clandestina: My Life in the Cuban Revolution* (New York: John Wiley & Sons, 2002), 51.

24. "Fidel-as-hero" is from Moreno, *Before Fidel*, 167. Julia E. Sweig, *Inside the Cuban Revolution: Fidel Castro and the Urban Underground* (Cambridge, MA: Harvard University Press 2002), 1, calls this the "Cuban revolution's 'founding fathers' myth: that a handful of bearded rebels with a rural peasant base singlehandedly took on and defeated a standing army."

25. For a study of the M267's *llano*, see Sweig, *Inside the Cuban Revolution*.

26. Mario Llerena, *The Unsuspected Revolution: The Birth and Rise of Castroism* (Ithaca, NY: Cornell University Press, 1978), 38, 40, argues that Cubans' idea of revolution was "cloudy"; it was "associated in the public mind with heroic rebellion against illegitimate or excessively authoritarian power, nothing more." For examples, see Haydée Santamaría, *Moncada: Memories of the Attack that Launched the Cuban Revolution* (Secaucus, NJ: Lyle Stuart, 1980), 22–23, 82–83, 87–88; and Moreno, *Before Fidel*, 189.

27. Steve Cushion, *A Hidden History of the Cuban Revolution: How the Working Class Shaped the Guerrillas' Victory* (New York: Monthly Review Press, 2016), 129–73.

28. Moreno, *Before Fidel*, 28.

29. Franqui, *Diary*, 165; and Sweig, *Inside the Cuban Revolution*, 18.

30. Bonachea and San Martín, *Cuban Insurrection*, 341.

31. Sweig, *Inside the Cuban Revolution*, 114. On the tendency to leave Cuban popular sentiment unexamined, see Damian J. Fernández, "Politics and Romance in the Scholarship on Cuban Politics," *Latin American Research Review* 39, no. 2 (2004): 164–77.

32. Carrie Hamilton, *Sexual Revolutions: Passion, Politics, and Memory* (Chapel Hill: University of North Carolina Press, 2012), though mostly focused on post-1959 Cuba, surveys the scarce literature on gender norms during the republican period to assert the importance of *machismo* in

the anti-Batista insurrection. See also Michelle Chase, "Women's Organisations and the Politics of Gender in Cuba's Urban Insurrection (1952–1958)," in *Bulletin of Latin American Research* 29, no. 4 (2010): 440–58.

33. Pérez, *Structure*, 184, 190–93, 187, 189. See also Farber, *Origins*, 34–49.

34. Lewis et al., *Four Men*, 181, 189, 194, 225, 236–37; Moreno, *Before Fidel*, 21, 29; and Chase, "Women's Organisations," 454. Though he was too young to join the insurrection, Pablo Medina, *Exiled Memories*, 59, describes countless hours at Havana cines where he was deeply impressed by "the purposeful swagger of John Wayne" and "the grit of World War II soldiers."

35. Symmes, *Boys from Dolores*, 67–68; Lewis et al., *Four Men*, 516; Eire, *Waiting for Snow*, 39; Moreno, *Before Fidel*, 43–44; and Pérez, *On Becoming Cuban*, 365.

36. Moreno, *Before Fidel*, 172, 126.

37. Franqui, *Diary*, 162, 47, 64, 359.

38. Oltuski, *Vida Clandestina*, 73, 98; Moreno, *Before Fidel*, 138, 147; and Franqui, *Diary*, 162, 165.

39. Interviewee in 1972 Cuban film *Girón*, as quoted by Chanan, *Cuban Cinema*, 49; and Moreno, *Before Fidel*, 137.

40. Pineda Barnet, interview.

41. Symmes, *Boys from Dolores*, 143.

42. A number of historians have noted the growing anti-imperialism of the 1950s insurrection. As Pérez puts it, the insurrection "gradually transformed from a rebellion against the Batista government . . . to a war of national liberation." Pérez, *Structure*, 205. See also Paterson, *Contesting Castro*, 51.

43. Paterson, *Contesting Castro*, 51, 58–65.

44. Ibid., 35–39, 42–43.

45. For a fuller account of labor-M267 relations, see Cushion, *Hidden History*.

46. See Pérez, *Cuba: Between Reform*, 295–305.

47. Ibid., 307; see also Nelson Rodríguez, interview.

48. Paterson, *Contesting Castro*, 54–55; Sáenz Rovner, *Cuban Connection*, 90–91; and Schwartz, *Pleasure Island*, 137–38, 142–53. For the translation of these US mobsters' activities into a famous scene in Francis Ford Coppola's *The Godfather: Part II*, see *World Film Locations: Havana*, ed. Ann Marie Stock (Chicago: Intellect Books, University of Chicago Press, 2014), 38.

49. For a photo of Flynn in Havana with Pedro Armendáriz, Charles Garrett, and Enrique Perdices, see *Cinema*, July 1, 1956, 12.

50. Cuban critics writing in *Time* and *Bohemia*, as quoted by Pérez, *On Becoming Cuban*, 472.

51. Elia Kazan, *A Life* (New York: Anchor Books, 1988), 293, 297; and Richard Schickel, *Elia Kazan: A Biography* (New York: Harper Collins, 2005), 6–117.

52. Schickel, *Elia Kazan*, 140–211.

53. Ibid.

54. Eddie Mannix, as quoted by Vanderwood, "An American Cold Warrior: *Viva Zapata!*" 188; and Schickel, *Elia Kazan*, 198, 208, 236.

55. Brian Neve, *Elia Kazan: The Cinema of an American Outsider* (London: I. B. Tauris, 2009), 48, 51.

56. Schickel, *Elia Kazan*, 237; Schoenwald, "Rewriting Revolution," 114–15, 118, 120; Slotkin, *Gunfighter Nation*, 421; and Vanderwood, "An American Cold Warrior: *Viva Zapata!*" 191–92, 194.

57. Robert E. Morsberger, "Steinbeck's Zapata: Rebel versus Revolutionary," in *Viva Zapata!*

The Original Screenplay, ed. Robert E. Morsberger (New York: Viking Press, 1975), xxviii-xxx; and Schickel, *Elia Kazan*, 269–71.

58. *On the Waterfront*, dir. Elia Kazan, written by Budd Schulberg (Columbia Pictures, 1954); Schickel, *Elia Kazan*, 229–33, 274, 283–90; Kazan, *A Life*, 410–12, 500, 515; and Neve, *Cinema of an American Outsider*, 80.

59. Ad, *Cinema*, December 5, 1954, 5; and Cushion, *Hidden History*, 94–95.

60. Schickel, *Elia Kazan*, 305–6, 315–22.

61. *A Face in the Crowd*, dir. Eliza Kazan, written by Budd Schulberg (Warner Bros., 1957).

62. Peter Lev, ed. *Transforming the Screen, 1950–1959*, vol. 7, *History of the American Cinema* (New York: Charles Scribner's Sons, 2003), 107–25, 131.

63. "Anuncian la posibilidad," *Cinema*, November 29, 1953, 31; and Valdés-Rodríguez, "Es causa la TV de la crisis del negocio del cine?" *Cinema*, January 31, 1954, 26–27.

64. Mary Louise Blanco, "Cuba in 1954," *FDY* 1955, 901–2.

65. Pérez, *Cuba: Between Reform*, 296; and "Mestre's All-Film Cuban Station," *Variety*, October 3, 1956, 50. On the rise of television in Havana, see Yeidy M. Rivero, *Broadcasting Modernity: Cuban Commercial Television, 1950–1960* (Durham, NC: Duke University Press, 2015).

66. Mary Louise Blanco, "Cuba in 1955," *FDY* 1956, 638; "Cuba in 1956," *FDY* 1957, 912; "A Troubled Year," *FDY* 1958, 881; and Perdices, "SCN," *Cinema*, April 28, 1957, 3.

67. See *ACRC 1954*, 24; and *ACRC 1956*, 26, 38, 49.

68. "Quo Vadis," playbill, November 17, 1952, author's collection; and *Cinema*, August 10, 1952, 21.

69. Rodríguez Alemán, "Capri: Cine de arte," *Mañana*, October 24, 1953, 6; and Douglas, *La tienda*, 139.

70. *Cinema*, June 29, 1958, 30; and August 24, 1958, 14.

71. The number of cines in Havana peaked at 138 in 1955 (*ACRC 1955*, 99) before falling to 131 in 1958 (*ACRC 1958*, 99).

72. Perdices, "SCN," *Cinema*, February 13, 1955, 3; April 19, 1953, 3; and November 1, 1953, 3.

73. Ad, *Cinema*, June 28, 1953, 2.

74. See Perdices, "SCN," *Cinema*, April 5, 1953, 3. Even Valdés-Rodríguez was excited; see "The Trianón presents CinemaScope" and "El cine está en marcha hasta nuevos horizontes," *Cinema*, December 6, 1953, 14, and February 6, 1955, 36. The first cines to have Cinemascope were Carrerá's Payret and Trianon, where Fox claimed box office nearly doubled; see *Cinema*, July 25, 1954.

75. Douglas, *La tienda*, 140.

76. *Cinema*, July 19, 1953, 11; *Sangaree* (1953), Paramount Foreign Exchange Reports; and Massip, *Última Hora*, July 1953, 52, 59.

77. Polaty to Colli, February 16, 1953, f. Personnel, b. 16671B, WBA; and Moreno, *Before Fidel*, 100–101, 108, 131.

78. "Cuba Revolt Kills 70, Headlines Scream," *Variety*, August 12, 1953, 13. For the film's characterization of Farrago, see *Crisis*, written and directed by Richard Brooks (MGM, 1950).

79. Martin, *Early Fidel*, 228.

80. Perdices, "SCN," *Cinema*, August 9, 1953, 3, and March 20, 1955, 3.

81. Eire, *Waiting for Snow*, 242; and Cabrera Infante, *Infante's Inferno*, 89.

82. Moreno, *Before Fidel*, 41–42.

83. See entries for *The Leather Saint* (1956), *Little Boy Lost* (1953), *Run for Cover* (1955), *The Man Who Knew Too Much* (1956), and *The Lonely Man* (1957); all in Foreign Exchange Reports.

Piñera, interview, remembered Havana audiences laughing "hysterically" at *My Son John*'s anti-communist propaganda.

84. *Mambo* (1954), Foreign Exchange Reports.

85. *Santiago*, directed by Gordon Douglas (Warner Bros., 1956).

86. "Cuban Sensibility Touched," US Embassy, Dispatch 103, August 15, 1956, 5; and "Protests over Film Allegedly Derogatory to Cuba Increase," Dispatch 118, August 22, 1956, both from http://www.latinamericanstudies.org/embassy/R7-815-5-29-1957.pdf. Accessed March 2, 2017. "Charge WB's *Santiago* Distorts Cuban History," *Variety*, August 22, 1956; Pérez, "Incurring a Debt of Gratitude," 391; and Perdices, "SCN," September 9, 1956, 3.

87. Colli, "Weekly Business Report," April 21, 1956, f: Labor Demands 1956–59, box 16671B, WBA.

88. García-Pérez, *Insurrection and Revolution*, 24; Martin, *Early Fidel*, 164–65; "Batista, Bombs, and Betting," *Variety*, February 13, 1957, 85–86; and Ross Melnick, "Hollywood Embassies, Labour and Investment Laws and Global Cinema Exhibition," in *Hollywood and the Law*, ed. Paul McDonald et al. (London: BFI, 2015), 162.

89. Oltuski, *Vida Clandestina*, 98; Medina, *Exiled Memories*, 44; 97–98; and Pérez, *On Becoming Cuban*, 431.

90. Mary Louise Blanco, "A Troubled Year," *FDY* 1958, 882; Franqui, *Diary*, 186, 359; Paterson, *Contesting Castro*, 44; Oltuski, *Vida Clandestina*, 151; Colli to MacDonald, November 10, 1958; and Colli to Glynn, April 30, 1956, respectively, both in f. Personnel, box 16671B, WBA.

91. *Broadcast Transcripts of Radio Rebelde, July 1957-December 1958* (Princeton, NJ: Princeton University Library, 1989), microfiche, 227.

92. Colli to Polaty, February 26, 1953, f. Personnel, b. 16671B, WBA; and *FDY* 1957, 912.

93. "Comentarios editoriales," *ACRC 1958*, 16.

94. Rodríguez Alemán, "Crisis de ahora en el cine," *Cinema*, March 21, 1954, 34; and Polaty to Colli, March 2, 1953, f. Personnel, box 16671B, WBA.

95. "One big family" is John G. Glynn describing Peter Colli to James Bishop (auditor), September 27, 1955; see also Glynn to Colli, March 4, 1957; both from f. Personnel; and Glynn to Colli, February 23, 1955, f. Cuba Personnel-10/1/53; all b. 16671B, WBA.

96. Glynn to Polaty, "Economy," March 16, 1953, f: Economy Program; and Glynn to Bishop (auditor), January 24, 1956, f: Personnel, both box 16671B, WBA. On this general trend, see Cushion, *Hidden History*, 15, 28.

97. Perdices, "SCN," *Cinema*, July 1, 1956, 3.

98. In 1955, the Film Giro Syndicate represented some 5,200 members, divided into ten trade unions, including several for those in film *production*; see US Embassy, Havana, Dispatch 1309, June 29, 1955, enclosure, 2, latinamericanstudies.org, accessed March 12, 2017.

99. Polaty to Colli, February 16, 1953, February 19, 1953, and February 25, 1953; and Colli to Polaty, February 26, 1953; all f: Personnel, box 16671B, WBA.

100. P. J. Raff to Falcon, July 3, 1956, f: Personnel, box 16671B, WBA.

101. Colli, Weekly Business Report, April 21, 1956; Colli to Glynn, May 18, 1956; and Dr. Garcia Barreto to MPEA, March 12, 1957; and MPEA memo November 13, 1958. All from Labor Demands 1956–59, box 16671B, WBA. On the wave of labor militancy, see Cushion, *Hidden History*, 135. On employees winning back pay in 1959, see Colli to Raff, March 7, 1959; and O'Sullivan to Colli, March 27, 1959; both f. Personnel, box 16671B, WBA.

102. *ACRC 1954*, 141. MGM's new manager, Robert Schoham, also died suddenly; see "Obituaries," *Variety*, December 30, 1955, 15.

103. Valdés-Rodríguez, "Pepe Del Amo," *Cinema*, March 28, 1954, 18.

104. Valdés-Rodríguez, "En la muerte de Henry Weiner," *Cinema*, January 15, 1956, 4.

105. Fernando del Castillo, Jr., "De todo un poco," *Cinema*, March 16, 1958, 8–9.

106. Garrett, "'Corea' y los Coreanos," *Cinema*, March 2, 1958, 27. See also Perdices, "SCN," *Cinema*, March 9 and 16, 1958, 3.

107. Fernando del Castillo, Jr., "De todo un poco."

108. Angela Soto Cobián (recalling her father's exploits), interview by author, Havana, Cuba, June 10, 2004.

109. Rodríguez Alemán, "De la Moral, lo Moral y el Cine," *Cinema*, April 1, 1956, 15.

110. "*Cinema*, May 10, 1953, 6. Newsreel censorship was also reported in *FDY* 1958, 883. For their content, see *Cineperiódico* and *Noticuba* ads in *Cinema* throughout this period.

111. Perdices, "No aceptaremos jamás la Censura del Gobierno," *Cinema*, May 10, 1953, 3, 6.

112. Perdices, "SCN," *Cinema*, March 16, 1952, 3.

113. Perdices, "SCN," *Cinema*, May 19, 1957, 3.

114. Valdés-Rodríguez, "*El cine en la Universidad*," 384–86.

115. Mario Parajon, "Valdés-Rodríguez," *Cinema*, August 22, 1954, 14.

116. Valdés-Rodríguez, "En agosto será el estreno de 'La rosa blanca,'" *Cinema*, August 1, 1954, 22–23.

117. Valdés-Rodríguez, "Rebelión en la prisión," *Cinema*, January 9, 1955, 32.

118. *The Defiant Ones*, dir. Stanley Kramer, written by (blacklistee) Nedrick Young (United Artists, 1958).

119. Valdés-Rodríguez, review of *The Defiant Ones*, 1958, reprinted in *El cine*, 75–78.

120. Souza, *Guillermo Cabrera Infante*, 20, 23, 36; Tomás Gutiérrez Alea, *Poesía y revolución* (Filmoteca Canaria, 1994), 14; and Paul A. Schroeder, *Tomás Gutiérrez Alea: The Dialectics of a Filmmaker* (New York: Routledge, 2002), 1, 56.

121. Usabel, *High Noon*, 223; and Massip, "La nueva aparicion de Chaplin," *Última Hora*, February 12, 1953, 36.

122. See *ACRC 1955*, 12; and *Nuestro Tiempo*, May-June, 1957 edition, pages not numbered. For reviews, see Valdés-Rodríguez, "Rebelión en la pantalla," *Cinema*, February 7, 1954, 14; Rudolfo Santovenia, "Charles Chaplin nuevamente," *Cinema*, December 30, 1956, 13, and "En defensa de Chaplin," *Cinema*, April 13, 1958, 11; Cabrera Infante on Chaplin's oeuvre in *Carteles*, April 14, 1957, trans. in *A Twentieth Century Job*, 125–31; and Angel Lazaro, "Chaplin y la libertad de expresión," *Cinema*, July 28, 1957, 40.

123. Rodríguez Alemán, "Las 45 Películas de Chaplin," *Mañana*, October 18, 1953, 6; reprinted in *Cinema*, January 31, 1954, 35.

124. Castro, "History Will Absolve Me," October 16, 1953, reprinted in Bonachea and Valdés, *Revolutionary Struggle*, 164–221.

125. Rodríguez Alemán, "Las 45 Películas de Chaplin."

126. Rodríguez Alemán, review of *Rob Roy*, *Mañana*, September 10, 1954, 6.

127. See, for example, Rodríguez Alemán, "De la Moral, lo Moral y el Cine," *Cinema*, April 1, 1956, 15.

128. Rodríguez Alemán, review of *The Power and the Prize*, *Cinema*, March 24, 1957, 23; and of *The Camp on Blood Island*, *Mañana*, October 19, 1958, 4.

129. Rodríguez Alemán, review of *Towards the Unknown*, *Cinema*, April 7, 1957, 15.

130. Souza, *Guillermo Cabrera Infante*, 25–27; and Marie-Lise Gazarian-Gautier, "An Interview with Guillermo Cabrera Infante," in *Interviews with Latin American Writers* (Elmwood Park, IL: Dalkey Archive Press, 1989), 27, 40, 52–53. Cabrera Infante's autobiographical *Infante's Inferno* is filled with references to moviegoing and Havana's cines; he also writes about the scholarship

(125–26, 264), the Cine de Arte sessions (100), and the *Cine-Club de la Habana* (153). See also Ardis L. Nelson, "Chronology," in *Guillermo Cabrera Infante: Assays, Essays, and Other Arts*, ed. Ardis L. Nelson (New York: Twayne Publishers, 1999), xvi.

131. Cabrera Infante, review of *Anni facili* (1953), *Carteles*, June 2, 1957, trans. in *A Twentieth Century Job*, 136–38.

132. Cabrera Infante, *Carteles*, February 2, 1958, trans. in *A Twentieth Century Job*, 193–96.

133. Benamou, *It's All True*.

134. *Touch of Evil*, written and directed by Orson Welles (Universal Pictures, 1958); and Cabrera Infante, review of *Touch of Evil*, *Carteles*, April 17, 1958, trans. in *A Twentieth Century Job*, 242–45.

135. Cabrera Infante, review of *Something of Value*, *Carteles*, July 21, 1957, trans. in *A Twentieth Century Job*, 141–44.

136. Rodríguez Alemán, review of *Executive Suite*, *Mañana*, August 5, 1954, 6.

137. *The Bachelor Party*, dir. Delbert Mann, written by Paddy Chayefsky (United Artists, 1957).

138. Cover, *Cinema*, October 6, 1957, 18; *Cinema*, September 29, 1957, 8; and October 20, 1957, 26.

139. Reviews of *The Bachelor Party*: Piñera, "Testimonio de la crisis espiritual contemporánea," *Cinema*, September 29, 1957, 8; Cabrera Infante, *Carteles*, October 13, 1957, trans. in *A Twentieth Century Job*, 154–58; and Rodríguez Alemán, *Cinema*, October 6, 1957, 18.

140. Cabrera Infante, review of *Sweet Smell of Success*, *Carteles*, April 13, 1958, trans. in *A Twentieth Century Job*, 207–11.

141. Alfredo Guevara, review of *The Big Knife*, *Nuestro Tiempo*, May 1956, 16.

142. *The Big Knife*, dir. Robert Aldrich, adapted by James Poe (United Artists, 1955).

143. Cabrera Infante, review of *The Big Knife*, March 11, 1956, 52.

144. Valdés-Rodríguez, review of *A Face in the Crowd*, reprinted in *El cine*, 143–46.

145. Cabrera Infante, review of *A Face in the Crowd*, trans. in *A Twentieth Century Job*, 189–93.

146. Rodríguez Alemán, review of *A Face in the Crowd*, in *Cinema*, January 19, 1958, 2. On Batista's "electoral farce[s]," see Domínguez, *Cuba: Order and Revolution*, 124.

147. Aguirre, reviews of *Viva Zapata!*, *Hoy*, August 1, 2, and 26, reprinted in *Crónicas*, 2: 239–42, 252–53.

148. Aguirre, review of *I Want You*, *Hoy*, April 12, 1952; reprinted in *Crónicas*, 2:183.

149. Aguirre, review of *Phone Call from a Stranger*, *Hoy*, August 15, 1952; "Hollywood y los negros," *Hoy*, March 29, 1952; and "El policía del mundo," *Hoy*, April 18, 1952, all reprinted in *Crónicas*, 2:246–47, 172–74, and 187–88, respectively.

150. Aguirre, review of *The Unknown Man*, *Hoy*, March 15, 1952, reprinted in *Crónicas*, 2: 163–64.

151. Aguirre, review of *The Sellout*, *Hoy*, June 21, 1952, reprinted in *Crónicas*, 2:219–20.

152. Aguirre, "Dos cintas en colores," *Hoy*, June 15, 1952, reprinted in *Crónicas*, 2:233–34.

153. Massip's parents had participated actively in the 1933 revolution and the March 1935 general strike, for which his father was imprisoned and banished. In exile in the United States, Massip's parents taught anthropology courses at Smith College, where the young Massip attended some cine-club sessions, including a projection of *Battleship Potemkin*, which he remembered as formative. José Massip, interview by author, Havana, Cuba, June 17, 2004.

154. Massip, review of *Happy Time*, *Última Hora*, April 30, 1953, 36; and review of *The Clown*, *Última Hora*, April 9, 1953, 36.

155. Massip, review of *Don't Bother to Knock*, *Última Hora*, November 1952, 49; "Celuloide," *Última Hora*, August 1953, 48; and review of *Big Jim McLain*, *Última Hora*, February 26, 1953, 37.

156. Massip, "Celuloide," *Última Hora*, August 1953, 48; review of *Steel Town*, *Última Hora*, November 1952, 32.

157. *Thunder in the East*, dir. Charles Vidor (Paramount Pictures, 1951).

158. Massip, review *Thunder in the East*, *Última Hora*, March 19, 1953, 36.

159. Massip, review of *Come Back, Little Sheba*, *Última Hora*, June 1, 1953, 52.

160. Massip, *Última Hora*, November 20, 1952, 32.

161. Editors, *Nuestro Tiempo*, April 1954, 1.

162. For the history of the society, see Ricardo Luis Hernández Otero, *Sociedad Cultural Nuestro Tiempo: resistencia y acción* (La Habana: Editoriales Letras Cubanas, 2002).

163. Both Enrique Pineda Barnet and Massip told me this; interviews by author. Cabrera Infante and Franqui both dropped out of the society when they learned of its Communist affiliations; see Souza, *Guillermo Cabrera Infante*, 25.

164. Massip, interview by author; and Editors, *Nuestro Tiempo*, January-February 1959, 1.

165. See list of periodicals, including *El Mundo, Diario de la marina*, and *Carteles*, that supported *Nuestro Tiempo* against threats of censorship, in "Editorial," *Nuestro Tiempo*, July 1955, 3.

166. Massip, interview by author; Massip, *Última Hora*, November 27, 1952, 33; and Rodríguez Alemán, "Capri: Cine de arte," *Mañana*, October 24, 1953, 6.

167. *Give Us This Day*, dir. Edward Dmytryk, written by Pietro Di Donato (Eagle-Lion films, 1949).

168. Valdés-Rodríguez, *Cine en la Universidad*, 384; *Nuestro Tiempo*, December 1955, 7; and *Nuestro Tiempo*, January-February 1957, 7. On distributors' rentals, see Piñera, interview by author.

169. Massip, review of *Baby Doll*, *Nuestro Tiempo*, July-August 1957, pages not numbered. See also Valdés-Rodríguez, review of *Baby Doll*, *Cinema*, March 24, 1957, 15.

170. A.I., review of *The Catered Affair*, *Nuestro Tiempo*, December 1956, 16; García Espinosa, review of *The Defiant Ones*, *Nuestro Tiempo*, December 1958, 17; and Marta Santos Tomás, review of *The Harder They Fall*, *Nuestro Tiempo*, December 1956, 16.

171. Alfredo Guevara, review of *The Big Knife*.

172. Emphasis added. Massip, "Adios a Charlot y Llegada del Nuevo Chaplin," *Nuestro Tiempo*, July 1956, 15.

173. Emphasis added, García Espinosa, review of *A Face in the Crowd*, *Nuestro Tiempo*, January-February 1958, 20. For the top ten list, see *Nuestro Tiempo*, March-April 1959, 6.

174. Gutiérrez Alea, review of *On the Waterfront*, *Nuestro Tiempo*, January 1955, 8.

175. Massip, "Comentarios ante unas bofetadas," *Nuestro Tiempo*, December 1956, 18–19.

176. "Las mejores de '54," *Nuestro Tiempo*, March 1955, 8; Douglas, *La tienda*, 135; and Valdés-Rodríguez, "El cine en 1953," *Cinema*, December 31, 1953, 4.

177. Valdés-Rodríguez, "En torno a los cine-clubes y su función superadora," *Cinema*, December 2, 1956, 12–13.

178. Nelson Rodríguez, interview. Other founders included later filmmakers Gloria Argüelles, José del Campo, and Luis Costales.

179. Manuel Pérez, interview by author, Havana, Cuba, May 25, 2004.

180. List is derived from Nelson Rodríguez and Manuel Pérez, interviews by author. See also Cine-Club Visión's top ten listed reprinted in *Cinema*, January 20, 1957, 17.

181. Manuel Pérez, Nelson Rodríguez, and, Walfredo Piñera; all interviews.

182. "Just for Variety," *Variety*, January 13, 1959, 2.

183. "New York Sound Track," *Variety*, January 28, 1959, 4.

184. "Feldman Registers Titles of 4 Yarns," *Variety*, January 9, 1959, 2; and Mary Louise Blanco, "Freedom Comes to Cuba," *FDY* 1959, 845–46.

Epilogue

1. I am grateful to Consuelo Elba Álvarez, with help from Mario Naito and Miriam Learra, for identifying the date and location of *Por primera vez's* premiere in Havana; e-mail correspondence with author, November 14, 2017.

2. E.g., Welles's *Mr. Arkadin* (1955), and *The Goddess* (1958); see Valdés-Rodríguez, *Cine en la Universidad*, 51–64, 386.

3. Raúl Roa, "José Manuel Valdés Rodríguez," *Bohemia*, April 2, 1971, 56–57.

4. Law No. 169, as translated by the Havana Film Board and attached to Colli to Wolfe Cohen, April 3, 1959, f: Film Boards, box 16671B, WBA.

5. "Pictures Warner Banned by the ICAIC-November 16, 1960"; list attached to letter, Juan Falcon to Lester Cohen, December 8, 1960; and Agreement #16, attached to letter, Humberto Ramos (ICAIC) to Falcon, December 2, 1960; both in f. Misc., box 16671B, WBA.

6. MPEA memo no. 841, including reprinted letter, Film Giro Syndicate to Alfredo Guevara, November 19, 1959, f. Cuba New Gov't Decrees, box 16771, WBA.

7. Enrique López, interview by author, June 14, 2004. Massip, interview by author.

8. See files by film title held at ICAIC's Cinemateca in Havana; and (on *The Defiant Ones*) Lillian Guerra, *Visions of Power in Cuba: Revolution, Redemption, and Resistance, 1959–1971* (Chapel Hill: University of North Carolina Press, 2014), 100.

9. "Frank Scully, "Scully's Scrapbook," *Variety*, August 12, 1959, 76. In April 1959, David Selznick (who by then owned the rights to the film) sought to capitalize on *US* public interest in the Cuban Revolution by re-issuing *We Were Strangers*; see Shaw, *Hollywood's Changing Takes*, 17.

10. Pérez, *Cuba: Between Reform*, 315–26. On anti-Americanism, see also Mary Louise Blanco, "Crisis in Cuba," *FDY* 1960, 791. On embargo exemption, see MPEA memo no. 750, October 20, 1960, 2, f. Cuba New Gov't Decrees, box 16771, WBA.

11. Hilario González, program for *Viva Zapata!* October 20, 1960, files by film title, ICAIC.

12. Morsberger, "Steinbeck's Screenplay and Productions," 141.

13. Rivero, *Broadcasting Modernity*, 134–41.

14. Carlos Eire, conversation with author, April 25, 2007, St. Paul, MN.

15. MPEA memo no. 795, November 18, 1960, 2, f. Cuba New Gov't Decrees, box 16771, WBA.

16. R. Garcia Barreto (Havana Film Board lawyer) to Corkery (MPEA), January 16, 1959; Colli to Greenberg, April 27, 1959; and Colli to Cohen, May 7, 1959, all f. Labor Demands, box 16671B; WBA.

17. "Cuba Grabs U.S. Film Exchanges; Long under Castro 'Supervision,'" *Variety*, May 17, 1961, 3.

18. MPEA memo 795, November 18, 1960, 5.

19. "Ernest Smith Resigns," *Variety*, May 20, 1959, 8; "O'Connor Resigning as Metro's Cuba Manager," *Variety*, September 24, 1958, 10; On Colli, see *ACRC 1960*, 126.

20. By November 1960, the MPEA reported that only one US manager was left (O'Connor's replacement); see MPEA memo 795. Charles Garrett, then head of publicity at the Fox office, left in March 1961; "Cuba Confiscates," *Variety*, May 24, 1961, 5.

21. Hy Hollinger, "H'wood Pix 'Reeling' as Cuba Reels," *Variety*, January 5, 1961, 1.

22. For an image, taken from an ICAIC newsreel, of the removal of Warner Bros.' sign, see

Nicholas Balaisis, "Modernization and Ambivalence in Octavio Cortazár's *Por primera vez, Cinema Journal* 54, no. 1 (Fall 2014): 7.

23. "U.S. Winning Film Fight in Cuba," *Citizen News*, November 30, 1964, Cuba clippings file, MHL. For the start of these practices and "bait," see E. R. Rosenkrantz (MPEA) to Cohen, January 23, 1961; for *How to Marry a Millionaire*, see MPEA notice from G. Vietheer, March 22, 1961, both in f. Cuba New Gov't Decrees, box 16771, WBA.

24. Reynaldo Gonzalez, in interview with Enrique Fernandez, *South Florida Sun-Sentinel*, January 31, 1999. Enrique López Oliva, age eighty, interviewed by Victoria Burnett et al., in "With One Castro Gone, Questions About What the Other Castro Will Do," *NYT*, November 26, 2016, expressed the same sentiment: "When I was in Miami, people asked me why I didn't stay in Miami, and I said I wanted to see the end of the movie."

25. Yoani Sanchez, "When Life Imitates a Chaplin Movie . . . You Know You're in Cuba," reprinted by *Huffington Post*, September 29, 2010, http://www.huffingtonpost.com/yoani-sanchez/when-life-imitates-a-char_b_744410.html. Accessed September 2016.

Index of Films

Index of Subjects